POWER, POLITICS & PARLIAMENT

ESSAYS IN HONOUR OF JOHN R. NETHERCOTE

EDITED BY HENRY ERGAS & JONATHAN PINCUS

connorcourt

PUBLISHING

POWER, POLITICS AND PARLIAMENT

Essays in Honour of
John R. Nethercote

Edited by Henry Ergas
and Jonathan Pincus

Connor Court Publishing Pty Ltd

CONTENTS

Editors' Preface

A *Festschrift* is usually a book honouring an academic as scholar or researcher, with chapters by former students, colleagues, collaborators and those whose own work was strongly influenced by the honouree. Although John Nethercote held adjunct and visiting titles in universities, he was never a regular academic. It is for his editorial work done when his fulltime day job was as a public servant, and his subsequent editing and writing, that he is being honoured here.

We were conscious that the phrase 'public intellectual' is too narrow for John. Granted, he published on a wide range of matters, both contemporary and historical, contributing mightily to the shrinking public discourse on the public administration in its broadest sense, and on the governance of the polity in Australia and the Anglosphere; and this in various ways. However, many of his important contributions, including those during his work in the Public Service, were not made in the *agora*.

He himself has written that

> As an editor [of the *Canberra Bulletin of Public Administration*] my orientation was to what would interest readers; it was also about fostering debate on contemporary topics of government and public policy. The principal readership was government officials. Articles were not simply about government and administration but about matters, broadly defined, which were of interest, or ought to be of interest, to government officials. It was especially important to bring to their attention important books which they might [not] otherwise know about, and of which they should be aware even if not likely to read them.

In her essay, Meredith Edwards characterised John as a disciplinary 'boundary rider'; we prefer to say that he rode to the boundaries only to transgress them. His publishing embraced a range of disciplines and fields of research: government and public administration; public policy including international relations; political history and biography; federalism; constitutional, public and administrative law; economics; industrial relations.

Jill Adams recounts his heroic and productive entrepreneurial efforts at the *Canberra Bulletin of Public Administration* and its successors, the first decade of which was commemorated in a 27-page supplement to the October 1990 issue, with a Preface by Sir Frederick Wheeler. John's editing encompassed other periodicals, including the *Australasian Parliamentary Review* and the *Conference Proceedings* of the Samuel Griffith Society. In addition, John commissioned, edited or co-edited more than thirty fine collections of essays on topics of continuing importance, often contributing a chapter or two himself.

The *CBPA* and the books addressed the interests of several professional circles, the public service itself, and other government organisations; members of parliament and parliamentary staff; universities; journalists and others reporting on government and public policy; private organisations active in various fields of public policy including unions and staff associations.

On current or historical affairs, John's incisive opinions and book reviews, backed by meticulous scholarship, were more likely to be found in the *Canberra Times* and *The Mandarin* than in *The Australian*; occasionally, they appeared in the *Sydney Morning Herald*. Hardly a major political or Constitutional anniversary passed without John having contributed to its interpretation, either through an opinion piece, an interview or, frequently in earlier years, through a timely collection of essays.

There were, additionally and importantly, numerous less visible contributions. As many of the authors represented here attest, his generous, insightful but direct comments on drafts of their books invariably helped make good studies even better. His contributions in that respect focused on works dealing with government and politics; his favourites were the political biographies, which allowed him to put to full use his encyclopaedic store of knowledge.

It was to honour these many and varied contributions that we, the editors, embarked on this enterprise back in 2017. However, there was a serious barrier. Although we have been friends of John for decades, neither of us claims sufficient expertise in the intellectual fields that John has tilled. So, we sought help from the man himself to fill out a list of potential authors.

After the introduction by the Hon. John Howard, the contributions are arranged in four parts, with the first being an appreciation by Glyn Davis and a biography by Luke Malpas, as well as a recounting by Jill Adams of John's contributions to the breadth, importance and longevity of the *Canberra Bulletin of Public Administration*. Part 2 contains five essays on topics related to John's broader interests in political power, public policy and philosophy (from Gary Banks, Meredith Edwards, Loren Lomasky, Peter Kurti and Henry Ergas). Then follows essays on three matters central to John's own contributions: on parliament, the public service and public administration, by David Clune; Richard French; Don Hunn, John Martin and Elizabeth McLeay; William Coleman; and John Nethercote himself! In the fourth part, in addition to historical accounts and analysis (from Anthony Seldon, David Lee, John Edwards, Paul Kelly), authors Tom Frame, Patrick Mullins, Peter Edwards, Jeremy Hearder and Pam Burton reflect on their biographies and recount the nature of the assistance that John gave them when writing their books: it was substantial, including but going far beyond meticulous copy editing.

This brings us to a delicate matter. The present volume is to honour JRN, who has a deserved reputation of being the most diligent and accurate checker of all names and dates and citations, as well as spelling and punctuation. We could not produce a book that did not meet John's standards. Who better than John to do that job? This exacting process took some time: beside travelling, theatre going and attending test matches, John was working on many projects, with more being added to his list, as he responded to requests for assistance, or offered it. This meant that he read and worked on every contribution, except the Introduction by Mr Howard and this Preface.

When the text was almost finalised, on Tuesday, 3 May 2022, John suddenly and peacefully died. We as editors decided that references to John in the present tense would not be changed to past tense, exceptions again being the Introduction and Preface.

We wish to thank our authors for their contributions and their patience. Phillipa Baudert rendered invaluable assistance, for which we are most grateful, as we are to Michael Gilchrist at Connor Court. We hope this book will stand as a tribute to a dear friend, valued colleague and remarkable Australian.

Foreword

John Howard

Having a conversation with John Nethercote about Australian and related world politics was a case study in being diverted – a common phenomenon for most of us. It certainly was for me.

Commencing with his editing of a book on the Liberal Party in 2000, I had numerous conversations with John over the years that followed. A particular incident or project initiated the discussion. What followed, in a quite delightful fashion, were constant diversions into other equally absorbing issues.

John's knowledge of Australian politics, his anecdotes and insights, were truly prodigious. That he was invited to be fact checker for my book, *The Menzies Era*, was not only compelling but added to my enormous pleasure as an author. Our interactions were a tour de force through those momentous years.

He understood in full the Australian version of the Westminster system. He knew where Canberra resembled London and where it did not. Personalities were adroitly woven into his analyses of events. Whatever the issue, he always isolated a personal motive.

John Nethercote was the ultimate conversationalist. Not only was he well informed, but he was lively, humorous, and always keen to hear what you had to say.

Australia has lost a premier political commentator, historian, and cultural analyst. The rich and varied contributions in this festschrift are a fitting tribute to John Nethercote.

23 September 2022

PART 1

Introduction

Canberra Bulletin of Public Administration

A
Tribute
to
J R
Nethercote

A DECADE AS EDITOR

Editor — H F McKENNA   ISSN 0811-6318   Special Supplement to No 62   October 1990

Cover of special October 1990 Supplement, *Canberra Bulletin of Public Administration*, with cartoon by Geoff Pryor, reproduced with permission.

1

Aphorisms and Bow Ties

Glyn Davis

Which did we encounter first: the bow tie or the aphorisms, the sharp mind or the extraordinary knowledge of public service ways? Perhaps it was the sense of apparent contradiction bundled in one character, traditional values yet a love of stirring, a man who celebrates administrative thinking even as he gently mocks its practitioners.

Here is a person steeped in Australian political institutions – someone who worked for Nugget Coombs, advised Senate committees, wrote about the great and good of Australian public life, yet maintains an unruly streak. He probes and questions when others might just report.

These two threads of John Nethercote – purist and contrarian – are captured in the magnificent *Canberra Bulletin of Public Administration*. With this publication John Nethercote launched a memorable challenge to the existing, conventional, journals of record. His long and distinguished editorship produced issues with serious topics alongside cartoons from Patrick Cook and Geoff Pryor. He could survey current administrative trends yet, in one 1988 edition, find space to celebrate anniversaries of the Great Armada (1588) and the Glorious Revolution (1688-89). Chronicler and bowerbird, curating a journal never stuffy despite the weight of its subject matter.

And then there are the public appearances, those countless seminars and conferences. Audiences keen to hear the legendary John Nethercote reframe a debate with a striking metaphor, or retell the plot of a Wagner opera to illuminate a familiar figure from academia.

A wicked sense of when to drop the telling anecdote, to remind us what a previous generation thought of some old idea wrapped in new paper.

This contribution has been pursued through whichever institution or university plays host to John at that moment, usually centred around Canberra but with generous excursions to wherever scholars gather.

It has been a role often focused on encouraging others. The *Canberra Bulletin* listed numerous authorial names in large letters, but rarely his own. As editor, John Nethercote has a gift for drawing contributions from others, editing closely, soliciting their best work. These skills mark his many books, working with colleagues to produce something none might accomplish alone.

So this volume, capturing something of its subject and his wide interests, is welcome indeed. With fitting scholarly courtesy in the form of a *festschrift*, a book that draws on the writing of its subject to make further contributions to the field, editors Henry Ergas and Jonathan Pincus honour John Nethercote. The volume conveys something of the breadth of the man – the biographer and observer of politics, the engagement with policy processes, the understanding of parliament, government and public service, the sustained reflections on the evolution of the administrative state.

In John Nethercote's work resides history and philosophy, policy studies and a deep understanding of the people who together make up a governmental tradition. He views his subjects from many angles – as politicians and managers, as public intellectuals and privately flawed individuals. In this multiplicity of lenses we see something of the author, the lively conversationalist who turns suddenly to seriousness as the topic changes.

It says much about John that so many actors and scholars prove keen to contribute to this *festschrift*. Some are previous co-authors, others sparring partners or even raw material for his observations. All have been drawn at some point into John's world and invited to stay. My own experience is probably typical. As a very new academic, and with some trepidation, I sent an article on the writing of Aaron Wildavsky to the *Canberra Bulletin*, then new and just a little subversive, edited by a stranger with a reputation both warm and fierce. I expected, at best, a polite rejection. Instead there was enthusiasm, delivered amid some acute textual suggestions. The article was published, and many more prompted by the editor.[1]

Here is the John Nethercote we celebrate – liberal with his time, keen to encourage, inviting always greater courage in expressing opinions, boldness in presenting a case. It is why so many people, in this volume and beyond, have been moved by the boy from Blakehurst.

Inevitably, a *festschrift* only samples the larger life. This volume touches on, but does not expand, John Nethercote's journalism in the *Canberra Times* and elsewhere, his quiet advice to those in public life, his restless curiosity about the world. It cannot report fully the debates, serious and whimsical, nor perhaps the understated but fiercely held set of values. Yet that so much is conveyed through these pages is a tribute to the editors and contributors. For here is recognition of a proud Australian – someone who decided early to dedicate to his nation's politics and administration a lifetime of study, engagement and advocacy.

---

[1] Davis, Glyn, "Aaron Wildavsky, Public Policy, and the problem of state action", *Canberra Bulletin of Public Administration*, No. 52, October 1987, 90-96.

2

Nethers

Public servant–Editor–Storyteller–Luncher

Luke Malpass

John Nethercote, generally known behind his back as Nethers, is a man of many parts: public servant, Senate authority, editor, storyteller, Wagnerian, cricket aficiando, churchman, luncher. Other contributors to this volume will cover these aspects from personal experience. It is my particular honour – a dubious one perhaps – to write this chapter of this life.

The man that Paul Keating derisively called "the Clerk's clerk" is, like many accustomed to dealing with the written word, uncomfortable with using both personal pronouns and talking about himself. Far better – and vastly more interesting – to discuss ideas, news, events and keep to the practical business of editing words of others, than talking about oneself. This older Australian virtue of humility and letting others take the lead is something that, through his work, John has done for much of his professional life. At the same time, John also politely typifies that other great Australian virtue – gently calling bullshit (at least as often as possible) when the appropriate situation presents itself. For John this is often exercised in matters of public administration or of historical record, particularly with regards to Sir Robert Menzies or Australian political history. For much of his career, his vehicle was the *Canberra Bulletin of Public Administration*, which he steered as editor in two stints, 1974-75 and from 1980 to 2000.

Nethers has made a career of striking out against what he considers the intellectual fashions of the time, which are often political agendas that in turn hijack language and obscure the topic at hand.

A most obvious effort at this appeared in an essay in a book edited by economist William Coleman called *Only in Australia*, which I reviewed in 2016 for the *Australian Financial Review*'s Friday review section. Nethers contributed two chapters to this book which explored the distinctive character of Australian exceptionalism. In the first, he reflects on Australia's "talent for bureaucracy", giving an incisive analysis of the sort of federalism Australia has actually practised over the years, drenched in the favoured Australian language of equality. As each successive federal government tries to win votes by wresting responsibilities from the States, Nethercote is here worth quoting at length:

> The crucial point about federalism in Australia is the pervasiveness of doctrines of equality and equalisation, combined with a preference for the use of the word "national", often a cover for "central", and the decline of the word "federal". Although rarely recognised, realisation of equality in practice takes the form of standardisation, homogenisation, and even uniformity. It is the antithesis of diversity, variety, and choice. The quest for equality is at the expense of federalism.

In more recent times he has been increasingly scornful of the appropriation, even in news, of the word "progressive", for what are essentially soft left, vacuous governments, politicians or, worst of all, public policies. His prize illustration of lazy thinking is that which portrays "culture as the problem; leadership [i.e., the *fuehrer prinzip*] the answer."

Canberra Bulletin of Public Administration

A main reason for this festschrift marking Nethercote's life and contribution to the Australian intellectual landscape is his editorship of the *Canberra Bulletin of Public Administration*, with his key stint lasting for almost 20 years to 2000. It was his time at the helm of the *Canberra Bulletin* that, Nethercote says, "made me someone". There are several reviews of the *CPBA* and its importance as a journal for informing and broadening the intellectual life of the public service

– as well as fomenting mischief and attempting to strip out the bureaucratese from important issues around the management of the public service. To his great regret, bureaucratese, both in writing and thinking, continues to flourish, most lately evident in, of all things, a succession of what are called public service reviews.

The *CPBA* aimed at four issues a year. For most of its life, however, the *Canberra Bulletin* (as it was mostly known), running to 80,000 words an issue, struggled for money. Conferences were run to raise funds and (handily) provided author contributions. Sponsorships also helped in the quest for finance. As an editor, Nethercote generously spent time reshaping and restructuring the writings of authors little used to publication, but with something interesting to say. In this way he nurtured inexperienced writers, giving them confidence and a useful template on which to base future contributions. In *Public Service Today* (in an article which, revised, follows this essay), Jill Adams put it like this. Nethercote, she wrote,

> … encouraged younger or less experienced writers to publish in the *CBPA*, assisting them with his advice and careful editorial blue pencil. He was an editor who actively used his editorial pencil – not to rewrite material but to improve readability. As he noted in interviews … 98 per cent of his work as an editor was sitting in a quiet room at home going over text.

There was also an eye for detail and accuracy in this endeavour, something which he has brought to bear on editing and reviewing many books over more than 40 years – including, as fact-checker, John Howard's *The Menzies Era*, which Nethercote considers his most exhilarating assignment in publishing. Howard described John as a "fact-checker extraordinaire whose great political knowledge and attention to details have proved invaluable in the preparation of this book".

As a watcher and chronicler of Australian political history, he also has a keen eye for significant additions to the bookshelf. In my day job as an editorial leader writer and editor at the *Financial Review*, I was often on the receiving end of calls from John tipping me off about books or public service developments; they were invariably correct and worthwhile. In mid-2018, for example, a tip came in about a new book on William McMahon, a man many regarded as the worst prime minister of Australia. *Tiberius with a Telephone* by Patrick Mullins turned out, in my view, to be a major Australian political biography, covering the dying days of a long post-war conservative reign that is most often overshadowed in the literature by the coming of the Whitlam Government.

The great innovation that Nethercote brought to his editorship of the *CPBA* – along with the Council of the Institute of Public Administration Australia (ACT Division) – was to broaden the magazine into a more user-pays model of subscriptions and occasional book shop sales. Although always financially precarious, this meant the *CPBA* sang for its supper and was successfully rewarded as it did. For example, an issue on the "glass ceiling", published in 1994 (based on a 1993 conference), sold out and could not satisfy the consumer appetite. *CPBA* broadened to the point that at its peak almost half its subscriptions were from beyond Canberra. The "glass ceiling" was one of several "theme issues" under Nethercote's editorship that aimed to provide an up-to-date airing of views on actual trends in the public service.

In addition to these issues, it included a number of mainstay columns and columnists: important examples were the "Australian Thinker" columns by Mark Thomas from 1985 to 1990 – subsequently published as *Australia in Mind*, and the "From the Hansard" column that ran intermittently from 1986. John's travel and work undertaken in both London and Ottawa also meant he had a pool of international writers to draw upon, providing useful comparisons and contrasts from the four parliamentary democracies of the United Kingdom, Canada, Australia and New Zealand.

Reading through various issues of the *CPBA*, the breadth of content is wide-ranging and impressive, even if a bit patchy as one would expect for what was essentially an amateur publication produced in the spare time of an editor and offsiders who held senior roles in the public service and were trying to wrangle mostly unpaid contributions from similarly employed individuals. Measures of success for publications such as the *Bulletin* can be difficult: is success commercial or intellectual? If an ability to attract senior writers from the bureaucracy is a useful proxy, a study of contributions to *CBPA* shows a stark increase over the years of these contributions: the *Bulletin* was a place in which departmental heads and other senior officials wanted to be seen.

John himself reports that university librarians drew his attention to another performance indicator – vandalisation of issues. Few magazines compared with *CBPA* in extent to which articles were excised. Students themselves appreciated CBPA's A4 sized pages: they got full value from a photocopy.

It is perhaps also a testimony to John's energy that after his retirement from the *CPBA* in 2000, the publication only managed another four years. This may be a consequence of rapid growth of the internet, making much of the sort of material in the *Canberra Bulletin* easier and cheaper to access by other means.

Nethers the man

But who is the man behind the jovial bearded figure of J. R. Nethercote?

Nethers was born in the now-closed Crown Street Women's Hospital in Sydney on 1 March 1948. He grew up in the post-war St George district of Sydney in Bald Face, a newish precinct just west of Tom Ugly's Bridge leading into southern Sydney's Sutherland Shire. It was an area that, in many ways, was typical of the sort that advanced and thrived under the policies of Sir Robert Menzies and the then new Liberal Party. Although the area was in a Labor seat – at that time it was in the seat of Barton – today it is just inside the border of Prime Minister Scott Morrison's seat of Cook. The residents were, nonetheless, upwardly mobile. Barton curiously was held by the Labor leader, Dr Herbert Vere Evatt, QC, until he moved north to the safer seat of Hunter in 1958.

Nethers grew up in the same Australia as that of author Clive James, from nearby Kogarah, and former Prime Minister, John Howard, from Earlwood, only a few miles further away. All would gain Commonwealth Scholarships to university. All came from small business-owning backgrounds. St George was as middle Australia as it got and hearing John talk about it is to summon grainy images to mind of lean post-World War II fathers, washing the car at the weekend, or mowing lawns (before the Victa lawn mower) in front of brick houses in a growing and prosperous Sydney.

John was born to Arthur, a quantity surveyor who worked for himself from age 35, and was a choir master at St David's Presbyterian Church in Dalhousie Street, Haberfield – now part of the identity-challenged Uniting Church. His mother, Dorothy (née Steward) enlisted in Arthur's practice, working the calculator, and ran a drapery business for a decade. As a result, Nethers told me, unlike many men of his vintage, he always found it normal to live in a world where women worked, and continued to work after his brother, David, was born. (His partner of more than four decades has been Gail Radford who, in the late 1970s and 1980s, led introduction of Equal Employment Opportunity in the public service.)

In reflecting on parental influence, John has two particular recollections. From time to time, Arthur had him help with proof-reading "bills of quantities", the reports prepared by quantity surveyors. Not written in prose, they had to be meticulously accurate. John has wondered whether his formidable capacities in copy-editing had their origins in this unusual yet exacting experience.

Dorothy had two ambitions for John: that he should be well-educated, and that he should be presentable. He wryly comments: the first objective was accomplished; of the second, with his bow ties, extravagant pocket hankies, colourful jackets and panamas, Dorothy could be said to have been an over-achiever.

Nethers attended government schools at both primary and secondary level. He recalls that in the neighbourhood there was a fairly even distribution between attendance at government, Catholic and fee-paying schools. The orientation was business and commercial and an ambition to attend university was relatively unusual.

At Blakehurst High School, he first encountered the might of the

NSW teacher unions, then heavily influenced and run by Marxists (as they arguably are today). Some officials were prominent members of the Communist Party. As a member of the chess club he would play inter-school games against other government schools in the playground on wooden forms, in the dark, apparently because teachers were largely barred from working and supervising such after-school activities. This, it would seem, was a formative experience on a young lad about the excesses of organised labour.

His family hailed almost exclusively from England in the mid-19th century, the religion was protestant, non-conformist and evangelical, marked by what John calls "a lot of religious fluidity". This was typified by the protestant emphasis on choice and individual responsibility compared to Catholic emphasis on belonging. So, growing up in his teen years, he attended two Church of England churches, St Martin's in Blakehurst, and St Mark's South Hurstville, and he also frequently joined Arthur at St David's and attended a Methodist church. He remarks with a laugh that "which church you went to was heavily influenced by which girls you were trying to chat up". Irrespective of where he went, the most conspicuous biblical influence for him was the parable of the talents.

Over the years his evolution as a churchman – he thinks that being called a Christian is not strictly accurate as he has no doubt that he is not, and will never be, on even a very long list for the blessed company of all holy people – he has moved higher up the ceremonial ladder, now being a parishioner at the Anglo-Catholic parish of Christ Church St Laurence in Sydney ("the one true church"). This is probably because many of the cultural influences of the church important to him have been phased out in mainline protestant churches: the King James Bible and the Book of Common Prayer on which he was "quite hooked" – he is one of a small number of Anglicans who still occasionally attends BCP services. Apart from the beauty of both the KJV combined with the majesty of Cranmer's "matchless prose", "religiously speaking, the most important thing as long as I could imagine is that I could never work out in the protestant denominations, why the Holy Communion was not celebrated more often". These days he unashamedly talks about going to Mass. A love of good choral music and liturgy has also been a constant passion in John's life. His belief structure, he says, can be summed up by the golden rule: "Do unto others as you would have them do unto you" (he confesses to the occasional lapse when he has had to resist the temptation of doing unto others as they have done unto him!)

This was an upbringing of thrift, hard work and church activity. His mother became a frugal self-funded retiree who, by the time she died, had built a significant share portfolio. She would be precisely the sort of retiree targeted by the Labor Party's disastrous and election-losing 2019 pledge to hike taxes on franked dividends.

"Most of my parents' education came from the fact that they participated in churches that were cultural institutions of the era so they knew about music", Nethercote says. "It was also a household of books, on which a number of visitors commented."

Part of the evening routine was for young John to listen to the Argonauts Club, the children's session on the ABC – a cultural marker for boys and girls of the era: are you an Argonaut? Barry Humphries, for example, was an Argonaut. In the Nethercote household, the children's session was listened to at 5pm, and the radio stayed on for the 7pm news over dinner, followed by Parliament when it was sitting. Menzies often spoke at 8.00pm – so his speeches could be heard on broadcast nights in homes throughout Australia. This, John says, was a most telling experience, as the family did not get a daily paper except for Wednesday (building news) and Saturday.

John recalls:

> Listening to Menzies was an education. Perhaps first of all there was his delivery: clear, eloquent, arresting. Then there was the substance and the structure of his exposition. In the very best sense, Menzies was not simply a master of rhetoric, he was *the* master.

The prevailing tone of the area, Nethercote says, was sport, for which he had practically no aptitude. He boasts that as a cricketer his specialist position was twelfth man. But sport did not pass him by:

> The reason a St George person held his head high was we

were always formidable at cricket, and of course rugby league. Tennis players, including Ken Rosewall – and even the rugby union side – were very competitive.

"Sport was very much the big thing but I struggled. My extra-curricular activities mainly took the form of much reading, mainly historical, biographies in particular, but not much fiction with the important exception of Maigret thrillers, and a growing interest in film and theatre, strongly encouraged by Dorothy," he says.

After early difficulty he became increasingly absorbed by Shakespeare, playing the role of Shylock in the trial scene from *The Merchant of Venice* in a school production. He also endeavoured to master the arts of public speaking with the guidance of a noted elocutionist, Keith King, who, amongst other roles, himself made a mark as Shylock in the city of Sydney Eisteddfod and was something of a celebrity in the 1930s and 1940s. Debating, however, did not flourish at the school. He learnt (he thinks) the basics of a reasonable speech; more importantly, he never lacked confidence when called to a lectern or a microphone. He humorously recalls a speech at a Junior Red Cross function – a vote of thanks – at a very full Sydney Town Hall when he was 16. He has never had so large an audience since!

While not very impressed with the education on offer at the time, John has some clear recollections of teachers of quality, both for what they had to say and of their dedication. The big event of his school years was unquestionably the Ancient History class, particularly the honours group. It was led by Brian FitzGerald, later responsible for introducing sur-titles at Opera Australia productions. The education was grounded in the great texts of classical history – Herodotus, Thucydides, Aristotle, Tacitus and Plutarch among them. The group itself was intellectually able. One not surprisingly topped the State honours list in Ancient History; she, and another member of the class, later acquired doctorates in Roman History. This experience was the real start of his education.

Nethers managed to win a Commonwealth Scholarship at the University of Sydney which he attended from 1965 to 1968, graduating with an unquestionably workman-like Bachelor of Arts degree in Government.

Throughout his life, Nethers has remained in contact with the Department of Government. It was Professor Henry Mayer who made a major, early impact; Nethers attributes to him the big break from rote-learning which had characterised so much of his school years (with the main exception the Ancient History honours group). Mayer inculcated exacting analysis of any topic, reiterating that just because something was in a book did not make it true. He emphasised study of the meaning of words, and how meanings frequently shifted as authors developed their arguments.

According to Nethers, it would be wrong to say Mayer's classes were enjoyable but, those who survived, had formidable analytical skills as a consequence. Mayer's brash style of teaching has attracted criticism over the years. Nethercote understands this. He wonders, at least for those with his background, whether any gentler approach could have lifted the student from simply knowing a lot to understanding and thinking about what it all meant.

The head of the department, the enormously erudite and infinitely courteous Professor Dick Spann, also had a great and growing influence on him. No-one could rival Spann for wisdom and insight. He had an instinctive and often infectious feel for nuance, irony and hypocrisy. Widely read, his learning was immense. His classes in political philosophy and thought remain memorable. At the Coombs Royal Commission, Nethercote worked closely with Spann on his wide-ranging study of public service heads of department, recently quoted by the High Court of Australia in its decision on ?

Subsequently, when they were both in London for a time, Spann gave Nethers a new education as they frequented the theatres and concert halls and, of a different kind, as they travelled the countryside. No matter where they were, Spann was able – impromptu – to explain meaning and significance, whether about a village in the Cotswolds, a bookshop in Hay-on-Wye, a performance of *Antony and Cleopatra* or *Coriolanus*, Mahler's *Das Lied von der Erde* (conducted by Pierre Boulez), or Wagner's *Das Ring Der Nielbulungen* at Covent Garden.

Others on the Faculty made their mark – Ken Turner on Australian politics; John Power on political thought; Roger Scott on politics of new states; Trevor Matthews on British political philosophy.

In consecutive years, Hugo Wolfsohn, professor of political science at Latrobe, gave penetrating lectures on the politics of Nazi Germany and, subsequently, the political culture of India. John also recalls very lively contributions to seminars by fellow students. They included Murray Goot, later a professor at Macquarie University; Frank Frost, an alumnus of the Parliamentary Research Service; and Martin Krygier, a professor emeritus in the Law School of the University of New South Wales.

John, fortuitously, also attended decidedly high-grade seminars on Australian foreign policy in the History Department. These were led by Neville Meaney. They subsequently became friends and typically went to the theatre together, being among other things fortunate enough to see all three of Shakespeare's *Henry VI* plays with Alan Howard as the King and Helen Mirren in the role of Margaret of Anjou. To John, Meaney's two volumes on Australian foreign relations in the early decades of the Federation are very significant contributions to the early history and government of the Commonwealth.

Another member of the history department, Edwin Judge, later Professor of Ancient History at Macquarie University, delivered a masterly series of lectures on the late Roman republic (that the regime was approaching its end was probably not appreciated at the time). The lectures were object lessons in how much is to be learnt about politics from ancient writers, in this case Cicero and Plutarch in particular. Moreover, it was a point not lost on such masters of the field as Machiavelli and Montesquieu.

Fortunate in his time in Sydney, he had similar good fortune in later university studies. He took a course in Australian government at the Australian National University under Professor L. F. Crisp, author of *Australian National Government* and biographer of Ben Chifley, and Professor Gordon Reid, premier authority on Australia's parliament. His knowledge of bureaucracy was greatly enhanced by superb lectures on Jeremy Bentham by Dr Len Hume whose book, *Bentham and Bureaucracy* (Cambridge, 1981), is a splendid example of scholarship at the highest and most refined level. His good fortune continued when he undertook research on Whitehall and the Canadian public service at the London School of Economics under Professor Peter Self, a major figure in enhancing the intellectual foundations of public administration beyond the abstractions derived from scientific management. By good fortune, at the LSE, John was able to attend illuminating seminars on federalism, first by Rufus Davis of Monash University, based on his upcoming book, *The Federal Principle*; and another led by Professor William Letwin.

Three other scholars played formative roles in shaping John's approach to the study of government generally and Australian government in particular. Soon after arriving in Canberra, he met Dr Roger Wettenhall, head of the School of Administrative Studies at the newly opened Canberra College of Advanced Education, now the University of Canberra. Wettenhall was active across a very broad front which included machinery of government, the government of Tasmania and education of administrators. It was his unrivalled expertise about public corporations and statutory authorities which was of greatest significance to John and complemented what he was learning about departmental administration in his work at the Public Service Board. In the mid-1980s they combined in launching the series of books covering Australian Commonwealth administration which still endures.

Establishment of the *Newsletter of the RIPA (ACT Group)*, forerunner of the *CBPA*, led to John's appointment to the ACT Council of the Institute of Public Administration and an immediate friendship with Robert Parker, Professor of Political Science in the ANU Research School of Social Sciences. Parker was author of one of the most influential books on public administration, *Public Service Recruitment in Australia* (1942), which advocated graduate recruitment to the general administrative ranks of Australia's public services. Fifteen years later Parker was appointed to the Prime Minister's Committee on Public Service Recruitment headed by Sir

Richard Boyer; the Boyer report laid the foundations for programs of graduate recruitment during the 1960s and early 1970s.

While on the staff of the Coombs Royal Commission John encountered Gerald Caiden of the University of Southern California. Caiden had spent five years at the ANU early in the 1960s. Astonishingly energetic, he eventually wrote four books about the Australian public service and published upwards of 20 academic papers. For the royal commission he wrote a fiery paper on efficiency in government. It was not only with his exceptional expertise on the APS that Caiden made his impact; though a doctoral graduate of the London School of Economics, and author of a major study of the Canadian public service, Caiden essentially brought the fervour of scientific management of the American variety to research on administrative practice in Australia. His work was also an antidote to mainstream public administration in that it was not dominated by the concepts, framework and doctrines of the Northcote-Trevelyan report on the *Organisation of the Civil Service*. Unlike the local approach to study of a public service, Caiden knew that a full knowledge had to include analysis of employer-employee relations and the role of unions in shaping the practice of a career service.

In his final years at Sydney John also served in the Naval Reserve. Outside of class he was Treasurer of the Sydney University Association of Cultural Freedom – a strong anti-Marxist club on campus: "We didn't have anybody who didn't support Australia's participation in the Vietnam war and we supported conscription." It had other interests and one priority was supporting amendments to the Constitution concerning Aboriginals in 1967, on which it sponsored three lunch-time lectures.

In 1969 he spent a year as a high school teacher at Martyrs Memorial School in Papua New Guinea, "doing work for which I was totally unsuited". To him it remains "a memorable time but I floundered". The pupils were very forgiving, however. The fun included climbing Mt Lamington at Easter. Mt Lamington, a volcano, had erupted in 1951, wiping out the original Martyrs School, killing the totally admirable headmistress, Margaret de Bibra, most of the teaching staff of the New Guinea Mission, and 4,000 Orakiva.

Another highlight was a production of *Macbeth and the Witches* in Papuan dress for the school's play night.

In 1970, John was recruited as an Administrative Trainee in the public service in Canberra. It was a scheme designed for young graduates and had been running for a number of years. It was a key initiative of Sir Frederick Wheeler, Chairman of the Public Service Board since 31 December 1960, and continuing personal overseer of the program.

Trainees were sent around to a number of departments during their first year, interspersed with courses on economics, industrial relations, constitutional and public law. One cannot help but feel that the public service would be better served today if new recruits had the same experience.

It was during this early period that Nethers reached what he calls the highlight of his career when on assignment to the Cabinet Office: fixing drinks for Sir Robert Menzies. This was an important job which involved keeping the keys to a very modestly stocked liquor cabinet and aportioning the libations carefully to ensure there would be sufficient to freshen up Sir Robert's glass as the function progressed.

Following the trainee year John went to the Public Service Board and shortly after joined what was known as the Secretariat, whose key function was organising and minuting formal meetings of the Public Service Board. The Secretariat was a "top group" of people, highly intelligent, with deep and stimulating knowledge of both public service and Australian Government. He attributes his own expertise in these fields to the enlightenment of these exceptionally able colleagues.

Perhaps the most significant piece of public sector reform John was involved in was the Coombs Royal Commission on Australian Government Administration, travelling around the country from 1974 to 1976, holding public hearings as a basis for its large report and its four volumes of research papers.

There was much to admire about RCAGA, he reflects, and both the Commission and the public service response had a depth, expertise and insight which modern day, quick and essentially superficial reviews do not even seem to seek to emulate. Even so, and with the benefit of subsequent work in Ottawa and intensive research in Whitehall, he sees little evidence that this is an effective instrument of fostering and maintaining quality in government and administration. In the Australian public service, historically, he views the Boyer report of 1957-58 on recruitment, which opened the door for graduate staffing of general administrative ranks, and greatly expanded roles for women, starting with, eventually, removal of the marriage bar, as of greater significance.

The Boyer report and subsequent overhaul of key parts of the public service legislation laid important foundations for the public service of the second half of the 20th century. Of comparable significance was Australia's most formidable experience in administrative governance under the leadership in the 1960s of Sir Frederick Wheeler. The hallmarks of this accomplishment were a firm grasp of underlying philosophies of government and administration; clarity and rigour in structure and organisation; high professional and ethical standards; fostering and development of able staff; and competitive pay and conditions of employment.

John contends that it shows the superficiality of much work on government that the Boyer report – with an implementation record that almost any public service review would envy – and the Wheeler achievement, have been practically lost to history. Meanwhile, the RCAGA is oft seen as the start of the modern era of public administration, if rarely so by informed observers. Ironically, in a great many respects, the RCAGA marked the end of the post-war reconstruction period so far as administration was concerned. Moreover, perhaps the greatest force for change, computers and information technology, find practically no place in academic or even popular versions of the narrative, and there is certainly not much in the RCAGA report.

It was to the Fraser Government to whom the RCAGA report was presented. Times were moving on, not least as a consequence of its immediate predecessor, the Whitlam Government. The ascendancy of the public sector, commencing with the Great Depression and gaining great momentum during the Second World War, was faltering; no longer was it automatically assumed that there was nothing that government could not do better than business. And the power of unions was being contained.

There are two other experiences in government which marked evolutions in John's thinking. During the mid-1970s Australian students of government started to look less at Westminister/Whitehall for guidance and illumination, and more to Ottawa, then in the thrall of Trudeaumania, as the enthusiasm for the political milieu of the present Canadian prime minister's father was known.

John had thought Australian government should be studied on its own terms. While he was interested in British politics and administration, it was a field of its own, not a handbook for Australia. For similar reasons he held reservations about the Canadian government as exemplar, most of which he still holds. At the same time, he became increasingly absorbed in Canadian government itself and he continues to be. He especially found in the many differences between Canberra and Ottawa – notwithstanding formal similarities – the source of critical questions which helped to enlighten more general questions of government.

He, for example, found Canada's much greater preoccupation with "merit" a puzzle. As in Australia, it was about competence for the job, and also partisan neutrality politically, but in Canada it was much more about a level-playing field in staff selection, ensuring candidates for appointment were treated equally. In Australia, merit was more elitist, about ranking candidates for promotion and finding the best person. In Australia, merit was an instrument of management; in Canada, during the period he was studying its public service closely, management regarded merit (or, at least, the merit system) as a restraint on its prerogatives.

Likewise, he found the contrast between Australia's then arbitration-based public service industrial relations and Canada's collective bargaining structure – strongly influenced by American practice – instructive.

A consequence of his early research on Canada, the leading theme of which was the tensions between management and merit, he was invited to provide comprehensive analysis for the Public Service Commission of Canada of two major reports: the Royal Commission on Financial Management and Accountability; and the Special Committee on Personnel Management and the Merit Principle. The combination of the two reports amounted to further bureaucratisation of management and additional power for unions in the staffing system. Nethers doubted that this amounted to "reform", certainly not desirable reform anyway.

His six months in Ottawa in 1979 were a major highlight for Nethers, particularly professionally; his only regret is that the assignment was so brief; nevertheless he learnt a great deal. Not least they alerted him to the fact that the academic activity called "comparative government" was potentially highly misleading. As much, possibly more, was to be learnt from contrasts, and this applies to Britain as well as to Canada. Since this period he has expanded his interests in Canada beyond the public service to include the Parliament and the workings of federalism which he considers much more robust than Australia's.

In mid-1984 John was appointed Secretary to the National Inquiry into Local Government Finance, chaired by Professor Peter Self of the London School of Economics. This was a fascinating post, revealing to him many aspects of Australian government, State and local, which up to that point had largely been under his radar. During its inquiries he met a great many people active at community level in Australia's public affairs. There was much diversity; more importantly, there was much to admire.

On cricket

A great love of John's life – in addition to concerts, movies and theatre – is Test match cricket, which he dates back to watching the third test match at the Sydney Cricket Ground in 1959 – the only draw in an Ashes series which Australia won 4-0. He is now closing in on watching 100 test matches at the ground.

The best series he nominates were against the West Indies in 1960-61 under captains Richie Benaud and Sir Frank Worrell and the 2003-04 series against the great Indian side that included the prodigious run-scoring abilities of Sachin Tendulkar, Saurav Ganguly, V. V. S. Laxman and Rahul Dravid. Richie Benaud and Ian Chappell were two great test captains. Dennis Lillee the best fast bowler, Neil Harvey and Ian Chappell among the best batsmen playing for Australia; he had the good fortune to be present as Harvey produced his highest innings, 231 not out at Sydney in January 1963; he still treasures a lively memory of Arthur Morris, in the St George colours, scoring a half-century against a Fijian XI at Hurstville Oval in 1960. Shane Warne was unsurpassed as a bowler of spin. Lance Gibbs's match-winning performance at the SCG in 1961 remains a vivid memory. Among wicket-keepers, Wally Grout remains strongly in his mind.

Of the non-Australians, Martin Crowe and David Gower – both Duncan Fearnley-wielding strokeplayers make the list. Anyone who has had the pleasure of sitting in the SCG members' pavillion and watching cricket with Nethers can attest to his encyclopaedic knowledge of and appreciation for the game. It is a past-time, not a sport. It has spectators, not fans. And the best places to watch it are the Adelaide Oval (before reconstruction) and the Basin Reserve in Wellington. Cricket should be observed mostly in silence, broken by occasional applause for a well-executed stroke or an especially fine piece of fielding. On the predilection of Australian cricketers to be baseball-style "batters" who play shots as opposed to "batsmen" playing strokes: "I deplore anything that robs English of its natural elegance and eloquence, especially in relation to cricket!"

Travels

No account of Nethers' life would be complete without mention of his travels. As often as possible he heads off for extended periods, mainly for the United Kingdom, Western Europe, North America and the Pacific islands; a favourite trip was to India for a meeting of the Inter-Parliamentary Union. He enjoys the life and society of these places, concerts and theatre, Test cricket when available, cultural institutions, and the architecture and ambience of old cities where the traveller is awakened in the morning to the ringing of church bells. He has travelled the great rivers of Europe from the Black Sea to the North Sea, the Elbe and the Neckar, as well as the Amazon and the Mississippi. He has seen performances of half Shakespeare's plays at Stratford-upon-Avon, several at Stratford, Ontario, and the Folger Theatre in Washington, DC; he has heard the Vienna Philharmonic in the Musikvereinsal; the Berlin Philharmonic in the Philharmonie (but, sadly, not the Royal Concertgebuow in the Concertgebuow in Amsterdam). He has attended sittings of the House of Commons and the House of Lords at Westminster; the House of Commons and the Senate in Ottawa; the Assemblée Nationale at the Palais Bourbon, and the Senat in the Palais Luxembourg; the Bundestag and the Budesrat in Berlin; and the Senate of Spain.

And he has worshipped in innumerable churches and cathedrals including a midnight mass for Christmas Eve in Notre-Dame de Paris, presided over by the Cardinal Archbishop; Lincoln Cathedral; a Boy Bishop evensong at Salisbury Cathedral; a St Stephen's Day mass in St Stephen's Cathedral, Vienna, again with the Cardinal Archbishop presiding; and Pilgrim masses at Santiago de Compostella (but not after walking the Comino). His favourite church is Notre-Dame de Chartres about which he has written an essay, "Henry Adams and the Cathedral Church of Notre-Dame de Chartres."

Beliefs

Despite editing mostly books revolving around figures and events on the conservative side of politics, John Nethercote has never been a member of the Liberal Party although he always had many friends in the party. He also has quite a number on the Labor side – he especially values his friendship with the late Victorian Senator Barney Cooney – and he is actively conscious that partisan disposition and character are by no means the same thing. He describes his political views as always inclined towards liberty, constitutional government, economic freedom and personal responsibility.

Even in the big days of Keynesianism in the 1970s, he always held the view that government should be a last resort, not the first. In this sense, he muses, he was perhaps counter-cultural, something that emerges particularly in the earlier days of his editorship of the *Canberra Bulletin*.

A core belief he holds is that if government is going to dole out money for some project or other, it should be matched with what people can raise in the private economy. While in charge of the *Bulletin*, he was keen on subscriptions, not grants, and regarded diversity of funding essential to its independence.

His preferred political authors are Aristotle, Machiavelli, Edmund Burke, Alexis de Tocqueville, Michael Oakeshott and J. S. Mill (especially *On Liberty* and *Considerations on Representative Government*) and, more generally, Dr Johnson. And he thinks that all Australians should have a working familiarity with Menzies' *The Forgotten People* in addition to *The Federalist Papers*.

These helped to drive his interest in, and a fondness for, constitutions and federalism, and to resist concentrations of power and uniformity – a particular *bete noire*. But there are always ambiguities within these, he explains. He is also implacably against plebiscites in any circumstances, which he describes as Bonapartist. With much reticence he acquiesces in referendums, provided they are based on specific questions.

After leaving the public service in 1999, John has had a string of academic associations. For nearly a decade he has been an Adjunct Professor at the Canberra campus of the Australian Catholic University, and always seems to be editing or reviewing several books at a time. Over lunches in Double Bay and elsewhere, his enthusiasm for the ideas in them is infectious: his eye for detail is intimidating. It is a mark of his influence that anyone writing a book in an area on which he is expert is advised to have him read the text well before publication to catch unnecessary misconceptions as well as mistakes, and thereby avoid embarrassments afterwards. That, after all, is what an editor does: improve copy, fact-check, give suggestions for clarity and, often times, save writers from themselves.

3

Canberra Bulletin of Public Administration

1973-2004

For professionals and teachers of public administration, but
... open to others.

L. F. Crisp, 1, 1 1973

Jill Adams

How did the *Newsletter* of the (then) Royal Institute of Public Administration (ACT Group) grow to become the lively and respected *Canberra Bulletin of Public Administration (CBPA)*? And what was the nature of *CBPA*'s impact?

This essay goes some way towards telling that story. Numerous difficulties notwithstanding, *CBPA* came to play an important role as a source of information about, and forum for discussion of, public administration and its management in Australia for more than thirty years. In 2004 it was replaced by a new Institute of Public Administration Australia (IPAA) publication, *Public Administration Today (PAT)*. It covered State and territory developments as well as the Commonwealth. For readers not privy to discussions of the ACT Council of IPAA, the passing of *CBPA* came as a surprise and shock. The *Bulletin*'s demise deserves to be marked. This essay examines *CBPA* between 1973 and 2004, the period when it was an ACT publication.

The author of the first article in the ACT *Newsletter* that grew to become the *CBPA* exemplifies its character. He was L.F. Crisp, then Professor of Political Science in the Faculties at the Australian National University. He had previously been Director-General of the Commonwealth Department of Post-War Reconstruction. He spanned two worlds – professional public administration and universities – as the Institute and *Newsletter* would for the next three decades.

In 1953 the founders of the ACT Group of the Institute had debated whether to extend membership beyond public administrators and academics. As it happened, their decision to affiliate with the Royal Institute of Public Administration (RIPA) in the United Kingdom automatically opened their doors to a wider membership. As B. W. Hartnell, the founding Secretary of the ACT Group, said on the 20th anniversary of the first meeting of ACT members:

> . . . The Institute provides a vehicle for talking together regularly, by those who are practising public servants, and by those who observe the activities of such people . . . The Institute thus gives the professional public servant an opportunity for self-criticism. (1, 2 1973, 5).

With the passage of time administrators and academics have been joined by other groups of observers, always present, but less numerous in the early years – those in the community sector with an interest in government, and people in business and commerce. They included lobbyists; journalists; information technology and communication companies; consultants of all types; other professionals, lawyers and economists especially; and former public servants who, for various reasons, wish to keep in contact with former colleagues and maintain their knowledge about government and public service. Many, like Crisp, have been practitioner (public servant or politician) one day and observer – and often critic – the next.

Why, after 20 years of regular monthly meetings and study groups, and the Autumn seminars at Thredbo, established in 1970, did the 449 members of the ACT Group decide in 1973 that they needed a newsletter? Members already received two journals as part of their subscription, one, *Public Administration* (UK), from RIPA in the United Kingdom (until the formal link with RIPA was severed in 1979) and another, *Public Administration* (Sydney), begun in 1939, published by the NSW Group. The subsequent change in name of the Sydney journal to the *Australian Journal of Public Administration* (*AJPA*), brought some clarity.

The ACT Group's Annual Report noted that the *Newsletter* was intended "to provide a means of communicating general items including short articles or abstracts that may be of interest to members" (1972-73 *Annual Report*, 2). It would also provide a forum for discussion within the Group and publish addresses and reviews of parliamentary papers, journal articles, book reviews and the like (3, 1, 1975). ACT membership had risen from an initial 64 in 1953 to more than 400 for the first time in 1972. Crisp noted that "the ACT Group, one way or another, has been the most considerable single source for the journal [*Public Administration* (Sydney)] since 1955" (1, 1, 1973, 5). It was anticipated, therefore, that the activities of the ACT Group and the local academics would provide sufficient copy for a newsletter.

Two years after the *Newsletter*'s launch ACT membership had risen by 159, totalling 568 individual members (the highest number of individual members ever to be recorded by the ACT Group). There were 40 corporate members, mainly government departments and agencies.

How did a mimeographed newsletter of around 20 pages, with humble origins and expectations, turn into a respected journal like the *CBPA*? How did the ACT Institute, with its honorary office-holders, manage it, not least financially? What was the role of its editors, all of whom, until 1996, received only a very modest honorarium? Who wrote for it and who were its readers? How did it change to meet changing circumstances and demands?

Timing and location

The Institute was lucky with its timing and benefited from its members being close to the Commonwealth government. The election in 1972 of the Whitlam Government brought with it tremendous changes in government and the public service, including establishment of the first comprehensive review of the public service in fifty years, the Royal Commission on Australian Government Administration, headed by Dr. H. C. Coombs, retired Governor of the Reserve Bank. A few years later, dismissal of the Whitlam Government and its replacement by a ministry of different hue, was also a major event for government in Australia. These events could not help but draw attention to national government, politics and public administration in Canberra. Many saw the Commonwealth as more important and exciting than State government. It was no wonder membership grew.

And the debates were not only internal to the public service, as they had tended to be in the past. Members of the Commonwealth government and its public servants were beginning to participate conspicuously in seminars and conferences. The culture was opening government administration to public debate in a way that was not yet obvious in London, Ottawa, Wellington, nor in Australia's state governments. The *Newsletter* was able both to benefit from and reflect the lively debates and dramas of the times.

Two decades later, those surveyed as part of the Institute's review of *CBPA* in 1996 recognised this was still important:

> The national focus and its geographical propinquity with the centre of government were complementary, and the practice of devoting a large proportion of the content to topical conference proceedings was almost unanimously welcomed. The ability to present in one issue a range of views on an important topic and current theme from senior players was seen as a great advantage, provided it came out quickly.... Everyone agreed that *CBPA* was complementary to the *AJPA*, not in competition with it (P. O'Neil, "Review of *CBPA*", 1996, 5).

Despite proximity to government, membership fluctuated. There were hard times to come for the Institute and new strategies and members had to be found to help to pay the bills.

Relations with the Institute

The *Newsletter* was created as part of the Institute's expansion of services to its ACT members. By 1977, under the guidance of the then editor, Sue Hamilton, the *Newsletter* had undergone its first upgrade:

> The *Newsletter* is now typeset, resulting in a more attractive and easily readable publication, as well as enabling us to achieve significant economies in postage because of the reduced bulk and weight of each issue. The Council envisages that the *Newsletter* should continue its present role of complementing the *AJPA* by publishing items of topical interest, as well as keeping members informed of local ACT Group matters. Council has re-constituted its Editorial Committee to assist and advise the Editor of the *Newsletter* accordingly (1977 Annual Report, 5).

A year later the ACT Group published, in association with ANU Press, its first commercial monograph, *Reforming Australian Government: The Coombs Report and Beyond*, edited by Cameron Hazlehurst of the ANU Research School of Social Sciences and J. R. Nethercote, then on the staff of the Public Service Board. It was based on papers presented at a one-day conference. Since then the Group (now called Division) has issued many other publications (often in association with the Sydney publishing house, Hale & Iremonger).

While an average of 40 members attended the monthly meetings, 700 copies of the *Newsletter* were being distributed every quarter. After a survey of members, the editor concluded that "while there is evidence that some members read the *Newsletter*, few are prepared to contribute articles" (5, 4 1978). Nevertheless, it had "engendered a significant degree of interest and support from members of other groups and non-members" and became available on subscription to non-members outside the ACT (1978 Annual Report, 4). By 1979 there were 45 non-member subscribers paying $6 a year. By 1985 subscriptions from elsewhere in Australia amounted to about a quarter of all copies published; by 1996 they had risen to one-third, and by 2000 48 percent of copies were distributed outside the ACT. Readership of *CBPA* was spreading well beyond the local area.

The Institute's finances were tight and the first advertisement to appear in the *Newsletter* (on the back cover, 8, 3 1981) was for Qantas, part of sponsorship of the 1981 National Conference held in Canberra and organised by the ACT Division. But advertisements did not necessarily mean more money for *CBPA*; some, like that of Qantas, were linked to goods and services (international conference speakers were flown out at the cost of an economy class fare but were seated in First or Business class, for example) provided to the Institute nationally and did not directly benefit the ACT Group. IBM Australia quickly replaced Qantas on the back cover, a position it continued to occupy for the next 10 years as part of its long-term support for the Institute (9, 3 1982).

The change of name in 1982 from *Newsletter of the AIPA (ACT Division)* to *Canberra Bulletin of Public Administration (CBPA)* was considered to reflect more accurately "its contents and its now expanded form covering AIPA news and the texts of addresses to the Group, but also short articles on topical issues, longer scholarly papers and a developing book review section" (1982 Annual Report, 2). *CBPA* sought additional advertisers in 1985 and by the late 1980s I P Sharp, Westpac, Qantas, Telecom and AMEX all had regular adverts in each issue. According to the Group's financial statements,

> *CBPA* advertising revenue and sponsorships amounted to between $500 and $3 000 a year for most of the 1980s and 1990s, but in 1996 it reached a peak of $16 500, partly as a result of a three-year sponsorship commitment of the Public Service & Merit Protection Commission.

The 1980s were a time of expansion of Institute activities; an office was set up, and the *CBPA* grew in size, consistently reaching more than 300 A4 pages each year. The office was initially located at University of Canberra, "a very congenial base from which to move the Institute from being a voluntary body to a more business-oriented body" (Annual Report 1992, 17). The ACT Council had decided that the Group, its publications and *Newsletter* should be self-reliant (apart from a continuing Commonwealth government grant) and not dependant, as *AJPA* was, on the benevolence of any government department or academic institution. In 1992 the office moved to premises in Belconnen, paying a commercial rent, representing "a further step in the process of placing the Division on fully business lines" (Annual Report 1992, 17).

Early in the 1980s there was an exchange of letters between the President of the ACT Council and the editor pointing out that the size of *CBPA* was putting financial pressure on the Institute, but acknowledging that its conference income was linked to the printing in *CBPA* of the proceedings. As the 1986 Annual Report stated:

> . . . a major and growing part of the Division's activities has been its programme of conferences, seminars, workshops and luncheon meetings . . . an important source of material for the Division's publications.

This allowed:

> . . . the *CBPA* to provide members with access to a considerable spectrum of material which might not otherwise come to their notice and might easily become inaccessible.

There was so much going on that a monthly news-sheet, *AdminNews*, was begun in 1984 to keep members abreast of ACT activities and government initiatives affecting the public service. Even so, there were difficulties on two fronts. This was a particularly busy time for *CBPA*'s editor, John Nethercote, then serving as Secretary of the National Inquiry into Local Government Finance chaired by Professor Peter Self. The 1985 Annual Report commented that:

> . . . the expansion of the *CBPA* has brought with it some difficulties in organising its timely publication. These difficulties have been especially apparent in 1985 . . . Measures are in hand to restore a regular pattern of production and circulation of copies to members and subscribers (3).

Things did not improve quickly:

> The difficulties experienced in 1985 in achieving regular and timely publication have been addressed but not yet fully overcome. The need for expert assistance in the marketing and distribution of CBPA was being pursued (1986 Annual Report, 11).

The second difficulty was that the Institute's financial problems at this time were so severe that it had to seek a bank loan (the editor was a signatory to the loan) in order to pay staff and sustain its core activities. After the 50th issue in 1987 the numbering of *CBPA* changed from volume and numbers to continuous numbering beginning at number 51, allowing for greater flexibility in publication.

Theme issues, incorporating papers on one subject drawn from several conferences, and sometimes ancillary papers, began in 1984 and became common. Examples around this time included: Public service reform (11, 1 1984); affirmative action and equal opportunity (12, 1 1985); the Ombudsman (12, 4 1985); and deregulation and privatisation (13, 3 1986). The advantage of this practice for the Institute was clear: "Individual issues on specific themes are frequently purchased in bulk for use in training courses by government departments and organisations." (1985 Annual Report, 3)

This reflected one of the main aims of the editor – to publish material useful for public service professionals. Since 1987 all issues of *CBPA* have had a retail price listed on the cover so they could be sold separately on a one-off basis. Sale of theme issues contributed significantly to the Institute's finances and spread knowledge of its activities to new markets. A special number, "Women, Organisations and Economic Policies", for example, combined material from three conferences providing a broad coverage of the issues from a diverse range of perspectives.

> Distributed to two thousand subscribers the number had a readership much exceeding that available to any other method. It was an important example of the benefits of incorporating publication of conference proceedings in an established magazine rather than other ad hoc forms. (1994 Annual Report, 18-19)

Celebrating its 50th number, the Institute reported that the *CBPA* "confirmed its growing reputation as 'Australia's leading periodical in the fields of government, public administration and public affairs'. " (1987 Annual Report, 8; author's emphasis). Who said there was no competition with *AJPA*? But pride comes before a fall. 1986 was to be the apogee of ACT membership. There was a total of 659 members, made up of 561 individual members and 98 corporate members. Another 270 non-members subscribed to *CBPA*.

By the late 1980s all was not well. Only two issues of *CBPA* appeared in 1989:

> The back-log in material for publication in the Bulletin stems from the suspension of publication on several occasions in the late 1980s owing to lack of finance to fund production. As the Institute's financial position improves and stabilises it is hoped that publication will progressively become more timely and more regular (1990 Annual Report, 18).

After all, the report noted, *CBPA* "is a major revenue earner for the Division and will hold its place as a major activity" (1990 Annual Report, 20). A year later the Institute's new National President, Richard Humphry, proposed "a new national periodical based on *CBPA*", discussions "fully supported by the ACT Division". There were "major financial matters to be resolved before the proposal can be realised" (1991 Annual Report, 15, 16). The proposal to make both journals – *AJPA* and *CBPA* – available to all members nationally as a benefit of membership" ... generated a level of anxiety amongst some members of the Institute of a perception that the 'nationalisation' of *CBPA* inevitably entailed the abandonment of *AJPA*. It is important that this perception be eradicated." (Richard Humphry, "Message from the National President', *AJPA* 50, 3 1991, 232).

It took another 13 years for the financial questions to be resolved.

From fairly early in *CBPA*'s history members in other divisions of the IPAA had been offered subscriptions, either as part of their State or territory membership or as a personal subscription in addition to their local membership. Clearly, the more copies printed the cheaper the cost per copy, allowing the ACT Group to keep prices down for its members and/or generate more income to support IPAA programs generally. For some time Western Australia and the Northern Territory had included *CBPA* in their local membership and, at the end of 1991, the NSW Division, the Division with the largest membership, decided to do likewise.

It was nevertheless a difficult time for the ACT Group:

> The past year has been a difficult period. ... The conference market, upon which the Division depends heavily for its viability, has been very depressed, with attendances markedly lower than in recent years, and profit margins significantly reduced (1992 Annual Report, 5).

Only the funds coming in through "contracts from government departments to assist them in promotion of their programs" were keeping the Institute afloat (1992 Annual Report, 5)[1].

Financial difficulties notwithstanding, the size of some of *CBPA*'s issues around this time was very substantial – 191 pages (no. 58, 1989), 179 pages (no. 61, 1990) and 172 pages (no. 69, 1992) – further stretching the strained finances.

Difficulties were exacerbated by non-appearance of issue no. 71 of the *CBPA*, due out late in 1992. According to the editor at the time, John Nethercote, planned articles were never completed or were completed so late as not to warrant publication. Several articles submitted in 1992 and presumably intended for issue no. 71 saw the light of day in no. 73 in September 1993 with the following apology "Submitted in 1992. *CBPA* regrets the delay in publication". The remainder of no. 73 included seminar papers from 1991, published nearly two years after they were given.

(This was not the first time that issues of CBPA had failed to appear. The third and fourth issue of volume 7, due for publication in the second part of 1980, never appeared, and the next volume began with a change of editor and no mention of the gap[2].)

The financial position of the ACT Group remained "fragile" for several years (1993 and 1994 Annual Reports) and the frequency and timeliness of *CBPA* again began to deteriorate and the cover date to bear little relation to the date of distribution. Only two issues were published in 1994, the second one, a massive 224 pages, was not distributed until July 1995, and only one issue appeared in 1995, finally distributed in December.

In 1994 the Motor Trades Association of Australia (MTAA) agreed to fund appointment of a Book Review Editor, leading to an immediate increase in book reviews. During 1995, as part of a series of cooperative ventures with several Commonwealth agencies, the ACT Council sought their views on its direction and activities: "Most frequently mentioned was the timeliness of the Institute's publication, the *CBPA*", both in terms of the number of issues published per year, but also that material published was often dated by the time of distribution (1995 Annual Report, 6). As a result, the ACT Council made funding available late in 1995 to expedite publishing and it commissioned a review of *CBPA* which reported in early in February 1996.

The Review, chaired by a former President of the ACT Division, Pamela O'Neil, acknowledged that the ACT Group "faces a quandary in accepting subscriptions for 1996 when its obligations for 1995 remain unmet" (O'Neil, "Review", 1996). It considered "ceasing the publication of *CBPA*" but found "overwhelming support" from senior public servants and academics for *CBPA* provided it was produced regularly and punctually. Respondents reported that "*CBPA* was of a very good quality, useful for academics in their teaching . . . but even more valuable for practitioners and students" ("Review", 1996, 5). At this stage *CBPA* attracted some 1 500 subscriptions per annum. With additional counter sales it made a modest profit of just under $14 000 for the Division, mainly because the editor's services were largely voluntary. The Review decided "to aim for more frequent and regular publication than had been achieved in recent years. The pursuit of this goal was greatly assisted by significant grants from the Public Service & Merit Protection Commission and the Department of Finance" (1996 Annual Report, 18).

The Review pointed out the potential to expand readership to all IPAA members. At this stage, only members from Western Australia and Northern Territory received it as part of their membership, with members from Queensland and Tasmania offered it as an optional extra. New South Wales had dropped previous support for it. Expanding readership to all IPAA members would increase circulation to around 5 000 – significantly reducing unit production costs and increasing the attractiveness of *CBPA* to advertisers ("Review", 1996, 9). It recommended that the Institute should:

- Continue regular production of the *CBPA*, at around 400 editorial pages per year over four issues
- Maintain the focus on contemporary practice of public administration
- Establish an Editorial Management Board
- Create two part-time positions, General Editor and Managing Editor, to replace existing editorial arrangements
- Pay these positions at an appropriate rate ("Review" 1996, 3).

The modest honorarium previously provided to the editor was abolished and two editorial positions, paid on a more commercial scale, were created. John Nethercote was appointed general editor and Virginia Wilton managing editor. An editorial management board was established under the chairmanship of Maureen Allan (later Ian Primrose, then Trevor Rowe) with Pat Barrett, Michael Delaney and Peter Hamburger. Those board members continued to the final issue of *CBPA*.

The result was a slimmer but more regular *CBPA*. The general editor was John Nethercote, until he resigned in April 2000, then Jenny Stewart, for a year, and Russell Ayres for the next four and, finally, Danette Fenton-Menzies. They worked with the Editorial Board to bring out the smaller journal four times a year. In 1997 the Institute concluded that the management of *CBPA* by the Editorial Board had ensured that the Institute receives "a full return on the additional funding now available to *CBPA* as well as a beneficial broadening of editorial direction" (1997 Annual Report, 17).

Nonetheless, finances continued to be a major problem. The 1997 Annual Report referred to "these straitened times" and commented that "notwithstanding that the distribution of each number exceeds 1 000, *CBPA* continues to be a heavy burden on Institute finances". During 1999 the Institute "actively sought to establish closer links with the private sector, tertiary institutions and other professional associations in presenting a variety of information on issues relevant to the public and private sectors" with several successful cooperative efforts. It also set up direct links with the National Institute of Governance at University of Canberra.

> *CBPA* continues to survive under austere financial conditions. It thus continues to be especially grateful to PricewaterhouseCoopers for their strong and continuing support which also, by diversifying our sources of funding, reinforces the independence of the magazine in providing IPAA members and other readers with informed analytical coverage of developments in government and administration (1999 Annual Report, 23).

There was also a decline in membership. A new level of corporate membership was created especially for companies with 10 or less staff (2000 Annual Report, 3).

By 2001 attempts to gain additional sponsors bore fruit with six "Gold sponsors" – all private sector corporations. By 2004, 22 percent (16 of 73) of the Institute's corporate members were private sector companies.

Russell Ayres, celebrating IPAA's 50th anniversary, put it nicely in a *CBPA* editorial in 2003:

> Over this time the character of the Institute has changed a good deal. Particularly notable has been the increasing involvement of the private sector. At the time of writing (and with elections pending) the current Divisional Council has 14 members, with eight from the private sector. At the same time there has been a clear shift in the membership patterns. Whereas there are now 308 individual members (compared to a peak of 561 in the mid-to-late 1980s), the financial base of the organisation and much of its vitality comes from the significant support of 73 corporate members, including an increasing number of companies.

This trend was clearly driven by the need the private sector has to "get to know" government and how it operates. There is, however, also a further motivation in many cases: many IPAA members from the private sector are former public servants who continue to have close ties with their former profession, both commercially and socially. IPAA provides a venue for such people to maintain their contacts with public administration and a means for them to continue making a contribution to its health and development (109 2003, 4).

CBPA underwent a further overhaul in 2001. It gained a new running subtitle: "Australia's journal of public sector management practice" and its aims underwent a change. Prior to 2001 *CBPA's* statement of purpose read:

> The purpose of *CBPA* is to publish articles and commentaries of professional merit on government administration, public policy and public affairs.

In 2001 this was changed to:

> *CBPA* aims to generate debate and disseminate information about major trends and developments in public sector management in Australia, with a particular focus on the national level.

The layout changed to three column pages and the paper turned yellow. The yellow paper lasted only until the end of 2002 when, to the relief of many, it was replaced by an off-white paper. Nevertheless, in my view, but others may disagree, the layout was improved with clear headers to guide readers and introduction of photos of authors where available. Not surprisingly, one reader (Paddy Gourley) expressed his view that the subtitle claimed too much, "carrying as it does the implication that the nation has adopted the *CBPA* as its one and own" and pointing out that "*CBPA* should be concerned with more than mere 'public sector management'. It should cover public administration generously defined" including the role and workings of Parliament and the judiciary (100, 2001). The subtitle nevertheless remained.

By this time the monthly news-sheet *AdminNews* had ceased and an electronic newsletter was attempted; it lasted for only one issue, perhaps because it required more of the office staff than was reasonable.

Timely distribution remained something of a problem, as the editor, perhaps cheekily, noted in the February 2003 number: "PS: This issue of *CBPA* has been delayed due to a series of problems. I trust our readers have missed us!" (106, 2003, ii).

But, in general, the Institute had achieved a more regular and slender journal than that produced during the extravagant but financially straitened 1980s and 1990s. The final issue of *CBPA* provides a justification for the change to a national journal:

> It was felt that there was a need for a journal where conversations could be had between the different levels of government... *PAT* [*Public Administration Today*] will have editors in each State and territory who will be providing articles, interviews, seminar papers, etc to promote discussions across the jurisdictions (112, 2004, iii).

Readers

Who read *CBPA* and its predecessor? In 1973, Hartnell, the founding secretary 20 years earlier, recalled that the focus of the Institute was to provide "a vehicle for talking together regularly, by those who are practising public servants, and those who observe the activities of such people" (Hartnell 1, 2 1973, 5). By 1978 readers outside the ACT had begun to subscribe to the *Newsletter* and, by the end of the period, almost half the readership lived outside the local region.

A survey of the ACT mailing list in 2000 showed that most recipients were Commonwealth government employees; and by far the majority of corporate members were Commonwealth government agencies or their libraries. One quarter of members (including many who were retired) received their copies at their private addresses so any institutional affiliation is unknowable. Nevertheless, only eight percent of the mailing list was sent to university addresses and, of those, half were at the ANU or the University of Canberra. There were only 250 subscribers to *CBPA* who did not belong to IPAA and nearly 200 IPAA members in the Northern Territory and South Australia who received it as part of their membership. Of those who were employed outside government or academia and had addresses that indicated their place of employment, five percent were companies, two percent non-government organisations or associations and two percent were located overseas.

A concurrent survey of readers closely reflected the mailing list and showed that 35 percent of respondents were employed in the APS and 67 percent were male. Forty-nine percent had read *CBPA* for 10 years or more and 75 percent for more than five years. There were few women or readers younger than 35. This was a narrow, loyal but declining demographic base.

Commenting on the survey, Peter Hamburger, an Editorial Board member, suggested that the readers were people with a "serious interest in public administration and proficient in reading books without pictures".

Why read *CBPA*? The overwhelming reason – given by 90 percent of respondents – was "information on public sector issues" with other reasons cited including a "study resource", "to consult back issues" and as a supplement to other news media on public sector issues. Ninety-five percent said they referred to back issues at least occasionally (making an irrefutable case for the consolidated Index eventually compiled). Views on *CBPA* were largely positive with 92 percent rating it credible, 89 percent informative, 84 percent relevant, 76 percent unique and 73 percent easy to read. More than half also read *AJPA* (84 percent academics compared to 48 percent from the APS) and 20 percent also read the *Bulletin* or *Business Review Weekly*. Compared to other journals 32 percent thought *CBPA* better than *AJPA*, 11 percent worse, 30 percent better than *Business Review Weekly*, 20 percent worse, and 28 percent better than *In Government* or *Directions in Government*. *AJPA* was seen more as complementary than as a competitor.

Most supported the current balance of content but there was some support for more articles and more highlights of parliamentary committees and fewer personal profiles, interviews and obituaries. There was no support for more than four issues a year, running counter to John Nethercote's long held view that the information and intellectual needs of the public service profession would best be met by a monthly publication.

Authors – writers and speech givers

The perennial call of all editors was made: "Contributions and ideas welcomed". Who answered the call?

The number of people who wrote specifically *for CBPA* was a very small fraction of those published *in* it. If editors, columnists and the book reviewers (of whom more later) are excluded the proportion of authors writing material specifically for *CBPA* was frequently less than 20 percent.

Many, if not most, of the articles, were based on addresses to conferences, seminars or panels, or talks already given on radio. Others may have appeared as articles in the press. This reflects the Institute's early agreed intent: to provide a record of papers given at ACT IPAA events, but very soon broadened to include co-hosted seminars or events of interest in which IPAA had no role and that may or may not have been held in Canberra. Nethercote pointed out that many – especially officials – could not be persuaded to write an article for the *CBPA* but, if invited to deliver a speech and given a specific deadline, they would almost invariably draw on a text which could then become an article. Providing a platform was, he stressed, often the only route for getting people into print.

At times, particularly in the late 1980s and mid-1990s, this approach appeared to squeeze out articles written specifically for *CBPA*, but perhaps the editors found these too difficult to obtain. A count of two periods, chosen fairly randomly from the middle years of *CBPA*'s existence, shows that during the four years from 1985 to 1988, 72 percent of all articles (excluding editorials, columns and book reviews) were previously delivered (though often significantly revised and edited) speeches, conference papers, essays, newspaper articles or broadcasts. Ten years later, in the four-year period from 1995 to 1998, this had risen to 82 percent of all articles.

Many of these papers were from seminars and events that IPAA co-hosted, such as the Australian Institute of Administrative Law forum, or where IPAA had not been involved, such as the Economic Society of Australia and the National Press Club – significantly broadening the scope of material brought to the attention of IPAA members.

Academics authored many if not most of the articles written specifically for *CBPA*. In the later period they also gave a fair share of the speeches.

Going back to *CBPA's* beginnings as a newsletter in 1973, three of the first five articles written (excepting a four page extract from Walter Bagehot's writings inserted by the editor) were by academics: Geoffrey Sawer on Post-Double Dissolution meetings of the Australian Parliament; Peter Jones on the Australian Assistance Plan; and Professor R.N. Spann of the University of Sydney on the Coster and Jeffrey reviews of public service staffing. The other two were by Germanus Pause, a public servant who had previously been a research scholar at ANU, on policy coordination, and someone writing as "Anon", of whom we shall hear more in the next section.

For some academics the span of *CBPA's* years paralleled their career. Professor John Warhurst, for instance, wrote his first article, on tariff policy administration in 1979 as a postdoctoral fellow at ANU (6, 1). Ten years later Associate Professor Jenny Stewart, just before she, too, became a post-doctoral fellow at ANU, wrote on industry policy (59, 1989) in the first of her nine articles. Professor John Uhr, while a Harkness Fellow, wrote on "leadership and the chance of change" in 1986 (13, 4), the first of 11 articles. Professor Pat Weller began writing in 1975, a commentary on the Corbett Report on the South Australian Public Service (3, 1) when he was a Research Fellow at ANU and, following his move to Queensland, contributed more than a dozen articles to *CBPA*.

Other careers, like those of Professors Roger Wettenhall, John Halligan, and Richard Mulgan were either well-established or underway by the time *CBPA* began. As President of the ACT Group, 1973-75, and editor of *AJPA* for many years, Roger Wettenhall has written for both *AJPA* and *CBPA*. His first article in *AJPA*, on administrative boards in 19th century Australia, was in 1963; his first of eighteen articles for *CBPA* was in 1979 (6, 2), on statutory authorities. From that time it has been rare for a year to go by without a contribution from him. Similarly, John Halligan made his first contribution in 1987, on reconstruction of departmental machinery of government, and Richard Mulgan joined in, on managerialism, in 1995. Each contributed frequently to both journals, taking into consideration the topicality of the subject and the readership they were seeking[3].

Many academic authors, interested in but located outside Canberra, frequently chose to publish in the *CBPA*. Some had been in Canberra, often with the Coombs Royal Commission on Australian Government Administration (1974-76), during the 1970s and retained their interest in the workings of the Commonwealth government and their Canberra friendships. Scott Prasser, for instance, a researcher at the RCAGA, went to the Royal Melbourne Institute of Technology and then the University of Southern Queensland, and not only wrote several articles and book reviews early in the 1980s but was also on the Editorial Board in 1995 and a joint editor in 1996. Other ex-Canberra or non-Canberra academics who wrote several articles included: David Corbett (South Australia), Peter Coaldrake (Queensland), Glyn Davis (Queensland, then Victoria), Geoff Hawker (Canberra, then Sydney), Julian Disney (Sydney), Andrew Hede (Queensland), Colin Hughes (Canberra and Queensland), Dean Jaensch (South Australia) and Anna Yeatman (New South Wales). Academic contributions were not limited to those in Australia. Visitors to Australia were quickly involved, with Peter Self, for example, then Professor of Public Administration at the London School of Economics, writing his first article in 1976 on administrative reform and the machinery of government.

People working in the private sector featured as authors from the early years and continued to provide a steady flow of material. Peter Cullen, a prominent lobbyist, wrote on lobbying in the very first volume (1 , 4 1974), Andrew Hay, Director of Chapman Hay Ltd wrote on "Public servants and politicians: attitudes, accountability and power" (6, 4 1979) and John Reid, Chairman of James Hardie Industries, provided a businessman's view of public administration in the next issue (7, 1 1980). A Thredbo Seminar on pressure groups and the public service generated two papers from the private sector, one by W. J. Henderson, Director-General of the Associated Chamber of Manufacturers and another by Eric Walsh, a former journalist and well-known government lobbyist (2, 4 1975).

The seven contributions by Jack Waterford of the *Canberra Times* between 1986 and 2001 reflect his wide-ranging interests in community access to information and in judicial and political affairs. Other private sector authors, like Athol Yates, author of six articles in the 2000s, have taken a broad interest in relations between the sectors and have contributed to both *CBPA* and the administration of the Institute. As already discussed, the private sector has played a strong role in supporting *CBPA* as sponsors, in co-hosting seminars and conferences with the Institute and, more recently, being involved in its direction as members of the ACT Council.

Union officials have been a rarer breed in *CBPA*. The first article by a union official was by Paul Munro, a member of the Coombs royal commission, 1974-76, on arbitration in 1979 (6, 4), with a second one, on affirmative action, in 1985 (12, 1). A few others appear but they, and discussions of industrial issues, are few and far between, perhaps reflecting the strength of the *Australian Journal of Industrial Relations* as a location for airing these issues. Some that did appear include: Domenica Whelan on "Industrial democracy, a union view" in 1984 (11, 3); Bill Mansfield's "Privatisation: a trade union viewpoint", in 1986 (13, 3); Peter Moylan on making the new machinery of government work in 1988 (54); Peter Colley on sustainable development in 1992 (69); Sue Powell on women's work and the union, and Anna Booth on the glass ceiling, the latter two both in the same issue in 1994 (76).

Top public servants have been at the centre of the Institute in the ACT since its foundation. The first meeting of the ACT Group was hosted by W. E. (later Sir William) Dunk, Chairman of the Public Service Board (1947-60) and the Group's inaugural President; it is not surprising that speeches by departmental heads feature strongly. The first two speeches by serving departmental heads were in the second volume of *CBPA*. The first, a talk given to the ACT Group by Alan Renouf, Secretary of the Department of Foreign Affairs, on new challenges in foreign policy administration in 1974 (2, 1), was followed the next year by a paper to the ACT Thredbo Seminar on "The Public Service and the Parliament, Press and Pressure groups" by John Menadue, the recently appointed Secretary of the Department of the Prime Minister & Cabinet, and published in the *Newsletter* in 1975 (2, 4). These were joined by a submission to the Coombs Inquiry on policy formulation and administration by Sir Arthur Tange, Secretary of the Department of Defence, also published in the same year (2, 3 1975). Subsequent talks to the ACT Group by agency heads D. R. Steele Craik, Auditor-General in 1975 (3, 1); K. C. O. (later Sir Keith) Shann, Chairman of the PSB (5, 2 1978); Sir Geoffrey Yeend, Secretary of the Department of Prime Minister and Cabinet (6, 2 1979); and R. W. (later Sir William) Cole, Chairman of the Public Service Board in (6, 3 1979) were published in the early years of the *Newsletter*.[4]

Several top public servants appear in the *CBPA* many times, but almost all their articles are reproduced speeches. For example, eleven of Peter Shergold's speeches are printed. Ian Castles, with seven contributions, is one of a very few actually to have written an article specifically for *CBPA* while a serving agency head (on the facts and fancies of bureaucracy (53 1987)).

It is also possible to track the careers of sonic public servants through the journal. Stuart Hamilton, for example, became Secretary of Community Services and Health in 1988, wrote his first article, a case study of government policy implementation, while still an administrative trainee with the Public Service Board (3, 2, 1976). He also produced the *Newsletter*'s first flow chart, one that flowed over four pages! There are a number who moved from the public service to the private sector: Gary Sturgess, for example, wrote his first article as Director-General of the NSW Cabinet Office and his later ones as a consultant policy adviser to government. Others, like Michael Keating and Meredith Edwards, moved from the senior public service to academia and continued to contribute throughout.

Members of Parliament were frequently invited to speak at the Institute's seminars and meetings and these papers have been consistently included in *CBPA*. John Kerin, MP, (and subsequently a minister in the Hawke and Keating governments), and Senator Alan Missen, for example, spoke at the Thredbo seminar on Parliament and the public service in 1975 (2, 4) and R.V. (later Sir Victor) Garland, MP, and Minister, at a Bateman's Bay seminar a year later on relations between Ministers and Departments (3, 3 1976). Ministers were slower to join the pages and it was not until the early 1980s that ministers featured in any number.

While the focus of *CBPA* was primarily on national (and very occasionally on ACT) government, interest in State, territory and international developments in administration was reflected in a smattering of articles by both Australian and international authors (again, often as a republished article or speech given in their home country, or a talk when they visited Australia). By the time the ACT *Newsletter* started, *AJPA* had established a reputation for coverage of Australia's State and territory developments so the emphasis in Canberra was to stick with what it was closest to, the Commonwealth government and the ACT. Papers about State developments appear occasionally, mainly from seminars and workshops, with a few articles on specific State reform inquiries or initiatives. On the whole, *AJPA* is the journal to read to learn about Australia's State governments.

Interest in international developments tended to be more widespread. The editor for many years, John Nethercote, frequently made space for an array of quotes from notables overseas and, while some tended to be historical in nature, others were taken from recent reports or speeches from the United Kingdom or Canada (his favourite sources of inspiration). Summaries of recent developments and reports in times of change became part of the editor's input. The first authored articles to focus on international practice were by two public servants, Germanus Pause, of the Department of Urban and Regional Development, on policy coordination in France and Germany (2, 2 1974), and E. M. W. Visbord, at Prime Minister and Cabinet, on economic policy formulation in the United States and Australia (3, 2 1976). One of the very few articles on the Pacific island states to appear in *CBPA* was by John Langmore, then in the PNG National Planning Office, in 1978 (5,1).

The first internationally-sourced articles by international writers – apart from that by Peter Self already referred to – were a speech by a British MP, Tony Benn, on Mandarins in modern Britain, given in

February 1979 and reprinted in the Autumn issue (7, 1 1980), and a Canadian paper by Jack Manion, Secretary of the Treasury Board of Canada, on the Canadian public service, and a reprint of a Canadian article on Freedom of Information, both in 1981 (8, 1).

Anonymity and pseudonyms

It was not long before some authors asked for the cloak of anonymity or a pseudonym. The first article to be signed "Anon" is a review of the 1974 report of the Commission of the Inquiry into the Australian Post Office (2, 3 1975) which debated the benefits of departmental structures against statutory corporations. The second assumed a pseudonym, "Narcissus", to write an occasional column called *Bureau shuffler's corner* on changes in departmental administrative arrangements. It was both descriptive and analytical "where appropriate". The then editor, Sue Hamilton, noted that she "would prefer to receive contributions under pseudonyms, if public servants wish to use them, than not to receive contributions at all" (3, 4 1976, 20).

In 1981, one public servant used a pseudonym, Mark Thomas, that he brought with him from writing for the *National Times* and the *Canberra Times*, with no indication to readers that it was a pseudonym. During the next decades the pseudonymous author wrote 14 articles and dozens of book reviews for *CBPA*. He claims that it provides separation between his work life and his more literary life. His articles included an occasional series on Australian thinkers, such as Donald Horne, B. A. Santamaria, Geoffrey Blainey), and Hugh Stretton, later published as a book (*Australia in Mind*, Hale & Iremonger/IPAA (ACT Division), 1989). One of his book reviews led the book's author, James Walter, to respond to the review of his *The Ministers' Minders* and call it "facile and wilfully misleading" (no. 53 1987,109).

Another author, S. R. Kelleher, is believed by most to be a pseudonym, The *CBPA* indicted it was a pseudonym by footnoting the author as "S. R. Kelleher is a longstanding observer of government and administration". Her/his article contained a strong criticism of the Efficiency Scrutiny Unit's report on the Public Service Board in 1987 (52 1987). Its final paragraph concluded that the report "has all the appearance of a predetermined solution in search of a justification . . . The plain intellectual slackness of the document makes it a disappointing and unsatisfying read."

The name/pseudonym was used again in 1988 to reflect further on the changes and the enhanced role of the Department of the Prime Minister and Cabinet (54). Another article signed by S. R. Kelleher, but for the first time without a footnote indicating that it was a pseudonym, appeared in 1989 on departmental secretary appointments (58). Nearly ten years later S. R. Kelleher (this time footnoted as "a policy analyst based in Canberra", 89 1998, 4) appeared again with a zesty critique of three articles written by and about the Department of Finance in conference papers reproduced in the previous issue. This clearly caused some rumbles and, it is whispered, a resignation of one or two from membership. The Annual Report for 1998 noted (17):

> During the year discussion arose about an article analysing views contained in a number of speeches by some senior officials. One aspect raised was the apparently pseudonymous authorship of the article. The Editorial Management Board reviewed its policy and decided that, while as a general rule the authorship of articles should be transparent, anonymous contributions, providing they meet the necessary standards in every other respect, are acceptable on the basis that there may be valid reasons why an author might prefer to publish without disclosing their identity. The *CBPA*, in agreeing to publish such contributions, is following well-established literary practice.
>
> In future, the editor of the *CBPA* will inform the convenor of the Editorial Management Board of the impending publication of any article likely to attract controversy.[5]

Columnists

Much of the distinctive character of *CBPA* was created by its columnists. Many columns were authored (or compiled) by the editors. Some columns came and went with great speed, sometimes but rarely to reappear; others appeared sporadically or lapsed when the editor had too many other commitments, or the columnist moved on or changed their work priorities. Few, rather surprisingly and unfortunately for the readers, outlasted the individual who began them. Columns included:

- *Bureau Shuffler's corner*—an editor's column explaining and reviewing departmental changes (intermittently from 1976 until 1978).

- *Coombswatch*, monitoring administrative change in the light of the RCAGA report (from 1977 to 1979).

- *From the journals*, article summaries (from 1974 to 1982 with several hiccups).

- *Recent government publications* (from 1974. to 1980 on an occasional basis. Reappeared in 2004 as "Summary of major reports released by the Government").

- Fictional stories with an administrative theme by S. M. Westrop – another pseudonym based on the maiden name of a public servant – (seven from 1976 to 1979).

- IPAA Annual Awards for Annual Reports, and for Excellence in Public Sector Management. The awards were reported from 1983-1986, then disappeared until 1995 when they resumed.

- Radio broadcast transcripts from 1981.

- *Australian Thinkers* by Mark Thomas (11 articles from 1985 to 1990).

- *From the Hansard*, five columns from 1986 to 1993. The column returned in 1997 to cover the new Public Service Bill, and again in 2000, then morphs into "From the Parliament", a series of seven thematic articles by Ken Randall, parliamentary editor, from 2001 to 2003.

- *From the Papers, the Media,* or *the Newspapers*, six sporadic columns between 1986 and 2000.

- Cartoons by Geoff Pryor for a year or so from 1986.

- *International trends* by the Public Service and Merit Protection

Commission as part of its four year sponsorship (10 articles from 1996 to 2000).

Many of these columns fulfilled the role of *CBPA* to inform and keep its readers up to date. Most of the compilations and analysis columns – the *Bureau Shuffler's corner*, *From the Press* and *From the Hansards*, and, in the early days, some of the book reviews—were compiled by the editor of the time. When editors found it impossible to find authors who would address some of the controversial issues of Australian government and administration these were addressed through these columns. *From the Hansards* and *From the Papers* allowed coverage of difficult issues without them being raised by individual authors.

Book reviews and letters to the editor

While, from the very beginning, editors sought to engage readers by inviting letters to the editor, they were rare. It was not until 2000, when Jenny Stewart took over the editorship, that they became a regular part of *CBPA;* thereafter it was unusual for there not to be a letter or two.

Book reviews were part of the journal from the very start. The first was in the second issue, a review of Hal Missingham's book on the bureaucratic hurdles he faced as Director of the Art Gallery of NSW (1 2, 1973). An early survey of ACT members provided limited information except that the few who did respond wanted more book reviews, more papers by prominent people, more often (6 2, 1979). As the *From the Journals* column ended, the number of book reviews increased to around four or five each issue and then more, until, in Spring 1982, ten book reviews took up 38 pages.

Thereafter it was rare, except when seminar papers on a theme topic constituted the whole issue, for there to be none. At times, the book reviews were almost the only articles written expressly for *CBPA*. In the late 1980s the number of book reviews rose: in No. 57 of December 1988 there are 22 reviews spread over 30 pages; April 1989 had 15 reviews; and others around that time had 12 or so. A significant drop off followed early in the 1990s and it was not until

1994, when the Motor Trades Association of Australia came to the rescue and funded appointment of a Book Review Editor, that the number of reviews rose again. The December number of that year had 13 reviews and the next issue a massive 33 reviews over 43 pages. Subsequently the number of reviews fluctuated issue by issue but, excepting those issues dominated by conference papers, continued to be around five to 10 until the early 2000s when the numbers dropped yet again. A letter to the editor bemoaning the dearth of reviews in the last issue but one (111, 2004) led to a resurgence of nine reviews in the final issue.

For many readers the book reviews became a favourite part of *CBPA*, and John Wanna, a later editor of *AJPA* , has noted that *CBPA* had a consistently better book review section than *AJPA* (Chalmers, Jim & Davis, Glyn "*CBPA* at 25: Speaking truth to power" *CBPA* 95, 2000, 3).

Spats, rejoinders and referees

Many of the tiffs in *CBPA* were between authors and reviewers of their books. One difference of opinion involved two Members of Parliament but not the author. Both agreed that the book was "awful" but Leo McLeay, the Deputy Speaker of the House of Representatives, claimed that Senator Chris Puplick's review was "inaccurate, superficial and misleading" (54, 1988). Chris Puplick's response began like this: "I am genuinely surprised poor Leo is quite so incapable of either reading or understanding . . . " (54, 1988). Enough said. Other examples:

- Allan Peachment wrote to the editor to say that he found the review of his book, *The Business of Government*, by Dr Bruce Stone to contain "sloppy analysis" and to be "trivial, misleading and factually incorrect" (75, 1993).
- Professor Sam Ball criticised the review article by Geoff Edwards on India's economy, finding it "unfair and unbalanced" (105, 2002).
- Roger Wettenhall found that Richard Broinowski's review of Sam Richardson's book, *No Weariness*, "ignores the main

thrust of the book" and considered his "snide remarks" to be "much more an attack on the person of the author than a review of the book" (105, 2002).

Other spats relate to articles or reprinted speeches.

Paddy Gourley (in 101, 2001) penned a four-page response to a speech by Peter Shergold (in 99, 2001) arguing that Shergold's "contribution is unfortunately marred by errors, distortions, a range of curious opinions and a neglect of major issues affecting current workplace relations in the Service". As always, the author was invited to respond and Shergold did so, claiming that he found Gourley's "catabolic fireworks . . . tremendous fun" and admitting that "I am properly corrected on a couple of points" (101, 2001). He further noted that "such responses to important issues of public administration are to be encouraged" and the editor did so in his opening editorial, inviting readers to send in letters to provide a wider range of views (but without success).

Paddy Gourley (perhaps encouraged by this debate) again wrote in to criticise Graeme Dobell's article, "Ministers, Media and the Military: Tampa to Children Overboard" (104, 2002), saying that Dobell "kicks off his article with a bout of slurs, untruths and stereotypes" (105, 2002). Dobell did not respond.

An article by W. B. Pritchett, Secretary, Department of Defence, 1979-84, on the management of Australia's defence, in no. 57, 1988, drew a response from two parliamentary committee staffers claiming that "so divorced from reality are the perceptions he presents . . . perceptions which appear not to have progressed past the early 1970s" (59, 1989, 75-8). Pritchett responded in the same issue.

In 1990, John Nieuwenhuysen, Director of the Bureau of Immigration Research, criticised Scott Prasser's article on the Bureau in the previous issue, noting that the article "is very silly" and expressing concern that the paper was not refereed (60, 1990). The editor, John Nethercote, confirmed that the paper was not refereed and added:

> *CBPA* practice is to seek comments of referees in the regular academic manner where this is warranted by the content and format of the article. This is however a time-con-

suming process which is not always productive. On other occasions, *CBPA* practice is to take informal soundings from appropriate people before accepting a contribution for publication. As readers well know, it is also *CBPA* practice, as has occurred in this instance, readily to publish rejoinders which take issue with the substance of published contributions (60, 1990, 41).

A short repost by Prasser followed the Nieuwenhuysen article (43).

CBPA was never a refereed journal. Intended to be topical and focused on government professionals, it was not something that suited its aim or readership. Nevertheless, the first refereed articles appeared in the next year. An article on Sallyanne Atkinson, former Lord Mayor of Brisbane, by Mark Neylan, and another by Andrew Hede on "Next Steps" in Britain, were marked as such in the Contents and footnoted, "This is a refereed article" (65, 1991).

The question of refereeing became increasingly important for academics in the late 1980s. The Dawkins reforms of higher education began to take into account the referee status of journals for which academics wrote in evaluating the "educational profiles" of their institutions. As noted in *AJPA* in 1989, "since funding decisions will bear some relationship to these profiles, academics must necessarily always be conscious of the referee issue, and editors must ensure that proper procedures are in place" (*AJPA* 48 (1), 1989, 2). By the early 1990s articles by academics began to be counted for university research funding. To be counted they had to be refereed. Journals like *AJPA* and the *Australian Journal of Political Science*, both more scholarly than *CBPA*, made explicit statements that they were refereed journals (see *AJPA* 55 1, 1996, 3 and its Notes for Contributors). The *CBPA* did not follow, but offered to referee specific articles by academics so that they could gain academic points. This was an option only rarely taken up. Nevertheless, many considered publishing in refereed journals necessary and, perhaps, more prestigious, and subsequent editors of *CBPA* found this a barrier to attracting more articles from academics.

Editors[6]

There have been just six editors since the *Newsletter* began in 1973.

- John Nethercote, 1973-1974 (1, 1 to 2, 2) and 1980-2000 (8, 1 to 95)
- Helen Dent, 1975-1976 (2, 3 to 3, 3)
- Sue Hamilton, 1976-1980 (3, 4 to 7, 2) [7, 3 and 7, 4 were never published]
- Jenny Stewart, 2000 (96 to 98)
- Russell Ayres, 2001-2003 (99 to 110)
- Danette Fenton-Menzies, 2004 (111 and 112).

Until 1996 editors were honorary, receiving at most small honoraria to cover their costs. The first three editors were public servants, though John Nethercote moved to the parliamentary departments then left the public service during his long second editorship. Jenny Stewart was the first academic, followed by Russell Ayres, then a consultant at the National Institute of Governance, but also a former long-term public servant.

It did not take long for the editors to seek assistance from other Institute of Public Administration members. In 1979 Sue Hamilton convened an editorial committee of two academics, Geoff Hawker, CCAE, and John Warhurst, ANU, and two public servants, Chandler Khera, CSIRO, and Ruth Campbell, Public Service Board. John Nethercote began his second period of editorship supported by Sue Hamilton, John Warhurst, Ian Thynne and Bridget Ballard, but appeared to take main, if not sole, responsibility. It was not until 1985, when theme issues began to appear and *CBPA* began to publish seminar proceedings from other associations, that the first guest editor appeared to help edit these substantial issues. Thereafter it became common for one or more to appear on the cover in some editorial role. Helen McKenna, a public servant, became an associate editor for five years from 1987 to 1992. She was followed by Scott Prasser for the next four years.

From 1994 a Book Review Editor (in order: Kate Krinks, Amelia Simpson, Elissa Keen, Trish Payne, and Russell Ayres), funded by the Motor Trades Association of Australia, has taken responsibility for that part of *CBPA*. About this time the Institute's ACT office staff began to assist in the publishing process.

A parliamentary editor, Ken Randall, was brought in by Russell Ayres to add to the depth of *CBPA*; but otherwise few changes were made. Virginia Wilton remained managing editor until 2004 when that function was rolled into the editorial role of Danette Fenton-Menzies.

It is difficult to identify the impact different editors have made. *CBPA* developed over time and what aspects of this relate to the editor or other factors is hard to discern. It is clear that the role was time-consuming.

So what did the role entail? Like all editorial positions it required planning and overseeing production of *CBPA*, quality control, and the seeking of contributions. Because of the nature of the enterprise it required an editor who could draw on a network of friends, colleagues and ex-colleagues, and other contacts and sources to keep in touch with emerging administrative trends in Australia and abroad. The editor also needed to consult with the Institute's program committee to coordinate conference and seminar proceedings and, in the latter years, with the Editorial Management Board.

The first five editors brought considerable knowledge of, and interest in, federal public administration to the job. The first three were staff members of the Royal Commission on Australian Administration, an experience which developed and enhanced their interest in public administration. The fourth, Jenny Stewart, had studied and written on the behaviour of government for many years while the fifth, Russell Ayres, was both a student of public administration and a former senior public servant.

Asked why he chose to continue as editor for over more than twenty years, John Nethercote said the main reasons were his interest in the subject matter, the friendships he made, and the opportunity it gave him to raise for public debate questions he thought important.

Russell Ayres concurred, noting that the "core interest of the Editor's role is that you can observe and to some degree influence the flow and direction of ideas, experience and debates in public sector management and administration in this country" (110, 2003, iii).

In the early years few issues were without substantial contributions from the editor. The diary and notes, the digest of journal articles and government documents, the collections of quotes, the extracts of texts, speeches and papers, and columns like *Coombswatch* and later the collections of Hansard quotes or press comment, were all unnamed and were largely the work of the editors. From the first volume, with its collection of quotes from Walter Bagehot and other historical sources, John Nethercote made clear his strongly held belief that ideas and practices from the past remained relevant to current administration, and he continued to provide illustrations of this throughout his editorship, often in an unsympathetic environment.

In so many ways Nethercote set the tone of the *Newsletter* in his first editorship. It was intended to be topical and to inform professionals, but Nethercote would create a *Newsletter* that would do this in a lively way, encouraging interest and resisting bureaucratese and high theory. It aimed to be read with enjoyment. It would not be as earnest as most scholarly journals.

The *Newsletter* quickly adopted a less formal tone than *AJPA*, including a wider range of material, such as obituaries, cartoons, speeches, short opinion pieces, and the occasional flurry of quotes or extracts from historical or current sources to accompany articles or seminar papers. To gain the attention of skimming readers, especially of senior public servants, Nethercote began selecting "grabs" of pithy quotes highlighting key, or controversial, points from each article and inserting them in larger print. This contributed to making *CBPA* easy to read and readily accessible to busy professionals in public service and elsewhere.

Nethercote also had a pedagogic purpose – to improve the quality of public administration. By being lively and attracting and holding readers' interest the *CBPA* would keep public servants informed and enhance their understanding so that they would be better administrators. He believed that it was important for public servants to understand the broader context of the various public service agendas and reforms. Because *CBPA* could often provide an inside view of public service activities, it would also inform students and academics about the "real" world of public administration. When possible *CBPA* would also analyse (the "icing on the cake"), but informing was its priority.

Another aspect of this attempt to be lively was that *CBPA*, particularly after Nethercote resumed the editorship early in the 1980s, was always trying to expand. Unlike *AJPA*, which had a captured readership because it was distributed to all IPAA members, *CBPA* had an incentive to increase its readership beyond ACT members. Being topical and lively increased its readership and the ACT Division's revenue. By the time Russell Ayres began his editorship in 2001, 48 percent of *CBPA* subscribers lived outside the ACT.

Nethercote developed a vast array of friends and contacts through his work, interests and travels, and gained ideas for conferences such as that on the "glass ceiling", all the rage while he was visiting Canada in 1992. He persuaded many of his friends abroad to write articles for *CBPA* or to have their papers published in it, extending the scope of administrative comparisons beyond Australia. He also encouraged younger or less experienced writers to publish in the *CBPA*, assisting them with his advice and careful editorial blue pencil.

He was an editor who used the editorial pencil very actively— not to rewrite material but to improve readability. As he noted in interviews in 2006 and 2007, 98 percent of his work as editor was sitting in a quiet room at home going over text. Few others were keen to volunteer for this work – there was a clear separation of function between the Council and *CBPA*, though once the Institute office was established its staff provided significant administrative and proof-reading support. Nethercote, unlike editors of many other publications, was willing to redraft and edit interesting material which he considered not written well enough for publication, in order to bring it into *CBPA*. He is of the view that two-thirds of the material provided to him was not publishable in the form it was provided and most conference papers and articles required "shaping up" and polishing ("sand papering" as he called it). This, together with compilation of several columns, totalled around ten hours a week, and left the largely honorary editor little time to write editorials which, under his reign, were rare. The downside of this approach was that it impinged, sometimes very noticeably, on the timeliness (or lack thereof) of publication.

Thus, during the 1980s and 1990s, the editor faded from the reader's direct view except when writing an introduction to a theme issue. Most of the work of the editor was behind the scenes.

Creation of the news-sheet, *AdminNews*, in the mid 1980s removed from the editor of *CBPA* the need to discuss the forthcoming program and activities of the Institute. In fact, there was little sign in *CBPA* of its owners. Reference to IPAA was scant. Many public servants and students reading *CBPA* in libraries would have had no idea that it was published by the ACT Division of IPAA. It was not until September 1996 that a calendar of local Institute events reappeared.

As already noted, the Institute's financial difficulties were an ever-present shadow throughout Nethercote's years as editor and there were times when it was necessary to run a conference in order to obtain enough money to pay for printing an issue of *CBPA*. Unfortunately, seminars were rarely priced to take into account the cost of publishing proceedings and papers in *CBPA*, perhaps reflecting a time when public servants were unused to realistic event-costing and managing business activities. It took many years for the Institute to recognise that it was a small business and not just a voluntary organisation. The 1996 Review of *CBPA* noted:

> John Nethercote has edited almost all the issues, individu-
> ally or jointly with guest editors. Production of the Bulle-
> tin has made heavy demands of his time (which has mostly
> been provided without charge. (Review, 1996, 4).

The decision by the Council to change to commercially paid editors after the Review brought to an end this last piece of voluntarism.

When Nethercote resigned the editorship in 2000 a short tribute was penned by the incoming editor, Jenny Stewart, noting:

> John's flair for editing showed in every issue – in his
> identification of issues; and his meticulous attention to

detail. *CBPA*'s many contributors over the years owe much to his encouragement and advice . . . While *CBPA* will develop in new directions, I hope it will always retain the integrity and warmth which characterised the Nethercote style at its best (*CBPA* 96, 2000, ii).[7]

With the editorship of Jenny Stewart in 2000 a "From the editor" column reappeared after almost twenty years. For the first time for years the editor was communicating in print to the readers. Perhaps that is why there was an unprecedented flurry of letters to the editor which continued apart from a few gaps to its conclusion.

Russell Ayres managed the redesign of *CBPA*. The redesign resulted in a somewhat shorter publication, with briefer articles.

Impact of ownership

CBPA is distinctive in that it is not a government publication but in both editorial direction and management it was in the hands of serving administrators. (1997 Annual Report, 17).

As L. F. Crisp noted back in 1973, "Academics are useful handmaidens for the Institute but the active leadership of the ACT Group should come overwhelmingly from the top leaders of the Service" (1 1, 1973, 7). And, on the whole, it has. Has the nature of its leadership and ownership limited *CBPA*'s critical ability?

According to John Nethercote, editor for more than twenty years, most of the Council wanted the Institute to be a prestigious centre for lively debate and saw the *CBPA* as central to that prestige. Throughout his years of editorship he says he never received pressure from any member of Council to write or accept material critical, or not critical, of the government-of-the-day or of the public service leadership. There was only one intervention and that was from Richard Humphry, then National President of IPAA, who complained regarding an article written by Nethercote in the *Canberra Times* about the Metherell affair in NSW (in which Humphry was involved). Nethercote was identified as editor of *CBPA*.

While many of the Presidents of the ACT Group were public

service departmental or agency heads, often of the central agencies promoting the change agenda, they supported *CBPA*'s debates about the change program, even when critical, because they gave the "reforms" publicity. Nethercote argues that he was always keen to include controversial articles – after all, controversy increased sales and the profile of *CBPA* – but often found it hard to do so. With around 75 percent of the content drawn from speeches, conferences and seminars, it is less the choice of the editor than the choice of those designing the IPAA seminars and conferences (often including the editor) as to who and what gets published. If they were organised by those at the top of the public service, and often in association with a government agency, as they often were, the speakers were unlikely to be highly critical of current administrative policies or practices. Ownership, sponsorship and commercial interest may, therefore, have a more subtle influence.

Nethercote says that he found it difficult to get academics to criticise the government when Labor was in power, but it was easier to get critical articles after 1996 (following election of the Howard Government). When he was unable to get writers to address topics he thought should be covered, he often resorted to compiling an *In the Press* or *In the Hansards* column to cover the topic.

There are several examples of this. Two will illustrate. The first one, the Pay-TV case, was about the level of detail ministers could be held to be responsible for in relation to their department's activities. This was covered by 12 pages of extracts from Hansards in number 75 (December 1993) but there were never any articles. A second example was resignation of the Secretary of the Immigration Department, reported from the press and Hansards in number 61 (1990) and again, *From the Hansards*, in 64 (1991). Again there were no articles on the subject. The intervening issues, primarily of conference papers and transcripts, appear to have squeezed out discussion of the resignation and the changing nature of the tenure of department Secretaries.

When one scans the contents there are topics that *CBPA* might have been expected to cover which it did not. Some early examples that receive selective, limited or no coverage are: the calling of top public servants to the bar of the Senate over the "loans affair" in 1975; the "meat substitution racket" of 1981 which raised questions about the role of the minister in relation to administration of his department; the "Midford Paramount shirt case" of 1987-1993 which centred on how devolved authority had facilitated administrative bungling; and the fracas in 1992 between a Senator (Bronwyn Bishop) and the Tax Commissioner (Trevor Boucher) which raised questions about open accountability to Parliament and its treatment of official witnesses.

In general, there appear to be few articles about maladministration, administrative failures or scandals. Part of this is due to the fact that *CBPA* was published quarterly and many of these issues are covered by other, more immediate, sources. Secondly, finding authors prepared to write about these topics was very difficult. Nevertheless, one might expect that the "administrative learnings" of these events and failures would be appropriate material for *CBPA*. In 1973 Hartnell hoped that the Institute would provide a vehicle for "talking together regularly, by those who are practising public servants, and by those who observe the activities of such people. ... The Institute thus gives the professional public servant an opportunity for self-criticism" (1, 2 1973, 5).

There is little in *CBPA* that suggests that public servants were keen to grasp the "opportunity for self-criticism" in terms of putting words on paper. There are few pieces reflecting on past policies or administrative practices and reassessing their success. Academics have been critical of New Public Management, and of policies like corporatism, managerialism, privatisation and outsourcing, and a few retired public servants, like Paddy Gourley, or those using pseudonyms, have had their say, but almost no working public servants have been willing to reassess administrative practices critically in *CBPA*.

In later issues, it appears that if articles did appear it was only after the dust had settled, not while debate about the issue was raging. The Government's policy of IT outsourcing, begun in 1997, for example, was covered only after the government had reversed its previous policy. An academic and a private sector researcher wrote articles on the implications of the Humphry report of the matter in number 99 in 2001, well after continuing criticisms in the late 1990s, Audit report findings, and the Humphry report in 2000.

Discussion of children overboard/certain maritime incident was also slow to appear, with the editor, Russell Ayres, noting in issue 103 (March 2002) that there were no articles on the topic and "there has been copious coverage of this issue in so many forums that *CBPA* – at least in this issue of *CBPA* – does not need to add to the material already around" but anticipates that there might be "considered coverage" in future issues. And there was – in the next three issues and concluding in number 106 with an analytical *From the Parliament* article on the incident from Ken Randall.

A contrary example is removal of Paul Barratt as Secretary of the Department of Defence in 1999 because of a loss of trust and confidence on the part of the Minister for Defence. The matter went as far as the Federal Court and raised significant issues about the power of ministers in relation to their top public servants. It was addressed by Patrick Weller of Griffith University in "In Hot Pursuit of a Departmental Secretary" (*CBPA*, 93, October 1999).

This is unfortunate, both for readers of the day keen to understand the changing dynamics of public administration, and for students and practitioners looking back and seeking informed debate about the issues involved. *CBPA* could not always compete with other parts of the media that paid their authors for their articles and who offered faster publication. Much of *CBPA*'s content was interesting, relevant, informative and useful. It was often lively but, in my opinion, became less so in its later years. The theme issues, often purchased by government departments for training, cover their topics well but tend not to be analytical or critical of current government policies, nor of public service implementation or management methods.

It may be too much to ask—when the Institute is headed by top public servants and co-hosts seminars with the central government departments who are usually those leading the reform agenda—to expect much critical analysis as its long-term editor, John Nethercote, regarded keeping readers informed and interested as his key task, and analysis as a bonus.

As is clear from its Annual Reports, the Institute was heavily reliant upon agencies as sponsors, partners and as Council members. More recently, it is possible that the Institute's increasing reliance on private sector sponsorship could make it difficult to write critically about the sector in terms of contracting, IT outsourcing, etc. Many of the Gold sponsors are companies with extensive contracts with government.

Concluding thoughts

One of the Institute's aims has been to be the professional focus of public servants and *CBPA* has been one arm of that. In the early days there were few other relevant professional organisations in Canberra for those involved in or keen observers of public administration and the Institute's membership, for which *CBPA* was a significant drawcard, burgeoned. More recently, other, more specialised organisations and associations have developed, and new linkages between the public sector and academia, such as the Australia and New Zealand School of Government and the National Institute of Governance, have stolen the headlines. Council members have equally demanding commitments with other associations and, from outside IPAA, the Institute seems to have a less commanding position than previously.

But throughout the years, 1970-2000, *CBPA*, along with its more scholarly sister journal, the *AJPA*, has held a central position in debating public administration in Australia. *CBPA* has met its aim— to chronicle and examine, sometimes to analyse and criticise—in an easy to read, lively, topical journal that has been consistently relevant to the working life of its large public service readership, and enlightening for students and teachers of public administration.

The editors, public administration enthusiasts all, found much grist for their mill in the reshaping of the public service in the '70s, '80s and '90s and *CBPA* has become a repository of knowledge about public sector management and what makes the public sector different from the private sector. Its mix of authors and opinions has been a major strength, as has been the variety of material it has published, from academic articles to radio transcripts, obituaries and extracts from the press and Hansard. Readers have been able to open each issue with a sense of anticipation, never knowing what gems might be inside, but certain that most issues will provide insights, stimulation and great book reviews.

While to John Nethercote every issue that came out was a miracle, and it was amazing that the *Newsletter* continued so long, what has amazed *CBPA*'s readers has been the consistent strength and variety of the material published, its readability and its pertinence for both professionals and observers.

Note

I would like to thank Professor Roger Wettenhall and Dr Russell Ayres who persuaded me to undertake this research and lent their copies of *CBPA* to me. Thank you also to Jenny Kelly, from IPAA's ACT Office, for making available their Annual Reports and other documents. Russell Ayres also provided encouragement, guidance and suggestions and edited the final text. John Nethercote subjected himself to two lengthy lunchtime interviews and read and commented on a draft.

This essay was written with the support of the University of Canberra/IPAA Public Administration Research Trust Fund.

The Research Fund is also supporting compilation for publication of a consolidated Index covering all 31 years of the *Newsletter* and *CBPA*.

Endnotes

[1] It may be worth noting here that the exemplar of the Australian institute, the Royal Institute of Public Administration in Britain, after seventy years entered into receivership in 1992. It sold its journal to the publishers, Blackwell. Richard Chapman, writing about RIPA's demise, considered that "the introduction of corporate membership arrangements [in the early 1950s] undermined the attractions of individual membership" ("The Demise of the RIPA: An Idea Shattered", *AJPA*, 52, 1993, 471).

[2] None of the local libraries with sets of the journal (the National Library, the Australian Public Service Commission or the University of Canberra) have

copies of vol. 7 nos. 3 or 4. John Nethercote has confirmed that these issues were never published.

[3] Those interested in who writes for public administration journals might find an article by Roger Wettenhall in which he analyses who submitted articles to *AJPA* during his editorship from 1989-1996 ("Reflections on *AJPA* and other public administration journals", *AJPA*, 56(1), 1997) of interest.

[4] One aspect of the Yeend paper is very unusual in *CBPA*. It was one of only two papers to appear in both the ACT journal and *AJPA*. The ACT *Newsletter* published a three-page extract while the full text was subsequently reproduced in *WA*. Only Roger Wettenhall has had the same article published in both journals, though the article had a different title in each: "Statutory Authorities and Government Business Enterprises: Some Observations on Recent Policy Papers", *CBPA*, 13(2), 1986, 83-9; and "Guidelines for Statutory Authorities", *AJPA*, 45(4), 1986, 299-309.

[5] This could not be taken for granted. The article was published deep in the issue in question without any prominence on the cover or in the contents pages. There appeared to be "some rumbles". These were especially regrettable in terms of the APS's admirable intellectual broadmindedness, but it was heartening to note how thoroughly *CBPA*'s contents were scrutinised by people in high places. John Nethercote, editor of *CBPA* at the time of publication, has provided the following information: "I recognised that the article would ruffle feathers and that the most senior officials in the APS had hitherto shown remarkable forebearance with *CBPA*'s free-wheeling approaches by people in high places."

[6] Mr Garland was unusual in that he took up his ministerial office physically within his department.

[7] A special issue of *CBPA* was devoted entirely to the editorship of John Nethercote. The material in the Special Supplement to No. 62, October 1990, is not repeated here.

PART 2

Power, Public Policy and Philosophy

4

Ethics and the Statutory Officer

Gary Banks

The astute statutory officer will consider her or his
responsibilities in the context of responsible parliamentary
government and ... an informed familiarity with its history,
trends and practices.[1]

– J. R. Nethercote

The integrity of the public service, and of public institutions generally, has traditionally been taken for granted in Australia. University courses in public administration generally uphold the conception of public servants being motivated purely by public interest goals. Programs of the Australia and New Zealand School of Government (ANZSOG) for senior public servants, for example, have their foundation in Harvard Kennedy School's "public value" framework, in which the main issues for "public managers" have to do with the practicalities of getting desired outcomes for society within the constraints of available resources and the "authorising environment".[2] The more pragmatic "public choice" paradigm of the Chicago and Virginia schools of economics, in which public servants respond to personal and organisational incentives as well as public duty, has gained little foothold.

The "white knight" conception of public servants has been shaken in recent years, however, by revelations of unethical and even corrupt behaviour at both Federal and State/Territory levels.

Among various documented examples, Victoria's Independent Broad-based Commission Against Corruption (IBAC) found in "Operation Ord" that millions of dollars had been siphoned from school programs over several years for the personal benefit of the Director of School Resources and senior colleagues in the Department of Education. In a separate case, "Operation Dunham", public servants were found to have corrupted the procurement process for a major IT project for Victoria's schools, with financial losses totalling some $240 million. The watchdog body found – unsurprisingly, given the number of officials and extended time periods involved – that the Department exhibited entrenched cultural problems of self-entitlement and non-compliance, in addition to more straightforward administrative incompetence.[3]

More recently, Health Department officials in South Australia were found to have been receiving sizeable "kickbacks" from public works contractors, again over an extended period. The Independent Commissioner Against Corruption stated his view that the State's "public administration is plagued by maladministration and very poor conduct, both of which foster environments that make individual corruption possible and ... extremely difficult to detect...".[4]

Apart from such outright corruption, and personal misdemeanours like bullying or sexual harassment, there are multiple documented instances of behaviour by public servants at variance with the norms of the Westminster system as practised in Australia. These include complicity in political manoeuvres (such as critiquing the policy platforms of non-governmental parties, use of taxpayers' funds to finance electioneering, tailoring "evidence" to support a government's agenda, the unwarranted withholding of information from public scrutiny and providing Opposition parties with ammunition against an incumbent government) as well as such lapses from basic administrative craft as failing to provide complete advice, or even to document the basis for significant decisions.[5]

There are as well multiple instances of senior public servants taking on private-sector roles on "retirement" that seek to leverage their public sector connections in matters such as government procurement (for example, naval defence) or regulation (for example, casinos).

An apparent rise in such behaviours, or at least in their exposure, has resulted in increased attention being given to "ethics and integrity" by training institutions, public service commissions and public sector leaders. For example, in 2014 the NSW Public Service Commission produced a comprehensive manual, *Behaving Ethically*, which outlines core values to be upheld – integrity, trust, service and accountability – and principles that guide their implementation. The principles, such as acting with honesty, placing public over private interest, providing non-partisan advice and taking responsibility for actions, are equally relevant to other jurisdictions and might have been expected to be widely understood.[6]

ANZSOG itself has created a post of Associate Dean with a focus on public service integrity, the inaugural appointee being the former head of the Victorian Education Department brought in to remedy the systemic failures identified by IBAC.

The "unique place" of statutory bodies

The increased attention to ethics in public administration usually focuses on departments of state. With respect to statutory authorities, the NSW manual only briefly notes their "… unique place in the Westminster System", observing that "their functions and powers are set out in legislation" and that "they cannot be directed in the exercise of these unless there is a specific provision in legislation".[7]

This class of public sector entity nevertheless plays a key role in Australia's system of government, Federal and State. It comprises several functional categories:

- *regulatory authorities* designed to protect citizens and their environs and/or to promote more efficient markets (like Australian Securities and Investments Commission; Australian Prudential Regulation Authority; Australian Competition and Consumer Commission; Environment Protection Authority, etc);

- *advisory and advocacy bodies* (like the Australian Human Rights Commission; Productivity Commission; Administrative Review Council; Australian Law Reform Commission, etc);

- essentially *informational bodies* (like the Australian Bureau of Statistics, Bureau of Meteorology, etc);
- *government corporations* that provide key services to the community, such as public utilities (Australia Post, NSW Electricity, etc) or bodies such as the Australian Broadcasting Corporation or Commonwealth Scientific and Industrial Research Organisation);
- bodies that serve as **overseers** or "watchdogs" safeguarding the operational integrity of public administrations, like the Public Service Commissions; Auditors General; Information and Privacy Commission; Ombudsman; ICAC and IBAC; Immigration Appeals Tribunal, etc.

While accounting for a relatively small share of public sector employment, independent statutory bodies can have a disproportionate impact. Indeed, almost by definition, the protections in legislation they enjoy are reflective of the importance attached to integrity of decision-making in their operations.

Differing in roles and focus, such bodies are characterised by significant independence from executive ministerial control and, in some measure, from Parliament. This is generally not absolute, but framed such as to enable them to exercise their duties without interference or undue influence. As Nethercote has observed, "these bodies are not independent in any general sense. They have on particular matters, in accordance with the constituent legislation, freedom from ministerial direction".[8]

In economists' language, those provisions are designed to create a "neutral incentive environment" for the making of findings, recommendations or rulings.

The human factor

This distinctive feature of statutory bodies may be seen as providing greater assurance about their conduct. But, no matter how well conceived or structured, legislation cannot guarantee that an institution will conduct itself appropriately in all circumstances.

Holders of statutory office and their staffs are *human* after all.

And, notwithstanding the guidance and protections afforded by their legislation, when exercising the discretions available to them such personal traits as judgment, values and temperament can be expected to come into play, conditioned by the wider incentives of the operating environment.

Statutory protections can, indeed, give these subjective factors wider rein. Among other things, they can incubate a "we know best" culture; or foster "group think", or what the regulatory literature refers to as "mission creep". Such behaviour can have major impacts on societal outcomes. For example, the Independent Audit of NBN Public Policy Processes, conducted by Bill Scales, AO, (a former statutory officer and departmental secretary) found "The ACCC overstepped its authority by advising the Panel of Experts that Fibre to the Node was not a stepping stone to Fibre to the Premises," noting that this unsolicited advice "became influential in relation to the decision by the Government to proceed with NBN Mark II".[9]

Subjects of occasional controversy

It should not come as any surprise, therefore, that statutory bodies have had their share of controversy, including about the ethics of their conduct. In each of the institutional categories outlined above, in recent years there have been findings of improper political dealings, decisions at variance with evidence, provision of misleading information, leaks of privileged material, abuse of power, neglect of due process, denial of natural justice – the list goes on.

In a key difference with departments of state, there have also been some public conflicts between statutory officers and government ministers, with the Triggs/Brandis clash over the postponed timing of the Children in Detention Inquiry being perhaps the most publicised instance. Another relatively recent example at State level was the clash between Premier Dan Andrews and the Victorian Ombudsman, Deborah Glass, over her report exposing unlawful use of parliamentary allowances by Labor MPs at the 2014 election.

Such phenomena are not new, with a contest of wills between Trade Minister John McEwen and Tariff Board Chairman G. A. (Alf)

Rattigan, being a famous example.[10] Such exchanges have tended to attract more media attention in recent decades.

Episodes of this kind can leave scar tissue on an institution as well as on its leader. And, depending on the issues and how they are dealt with, they can result in a loss of credibility and authority, weakening effectiveness.

That a statutory officer or agency comes under fire – whether from political or other quarters – should not of itself be cause for concern. Independent statutory bodies are often so constituted precisely because their fields of operation are inherently subject to conflict and contention. Their decisions can upset ministers or create losers, who may be inclined to "shoot the messenger", even (perhaps especially) when those decisions are well founded.

Agency heads may therefore console themselves (as I sometimes did myself at the Productivity Commission) with the thought that "if we were not being criticised by someone, we would not be doing our job". Nevertheless, no statutory officer can afford to ignore or dismiss criticism, particularly from the government. At the very least, it is important to be clear about the basis for it. In particular, criticisms about how an agency goes about its work deserve more attention than the inevitable disagreements from time to time about its findings or recommendations.

This essay explores some of the ambiguous ethical territory surrounding statutory officers and their offices. It was initially prompted by the highly publicised cases involving the AHRC and ICAC in the lead up to a conference at which I was an invited speaker (discussed below). My point of reference, however, remains the institution I know best, the Productivity Commission, and its predecessors, the Tariff Board (1921-74): the Industries Assistance Commission (1974-90); and the Industry Commission (1990-96).

I must declare to having worked for all four of these bodies at different times and (uniquely) at nearly all levels of the hierarchy. Inevitably, it was the decade and a half spent as Chairman of the Productivity Commission that most impressed on me the challenges inherent in the statutory officer's lot.

Origins and purpose of "the Commission"

The Productivity Commission is the lineal descendant of the Tariff Board, created in 1921. The Board had strong statutory provisions relating to independence and operational transparency, given the distributional implications of its recommendations. Policy guidelines and decision criteria were, however, somewhat ambiguous. These were interpreted for much of its life, no doubt bolstered by the prevailing protectionist orthodoxy, as requiring it to recommend tariffs at levels necessary for local industries to compete with foreign imports. This essentially lasted for 40 years until Rattigan's appointment as Chairman, after which emphasis began to be placed on the impacts of import protection on the wider economy and society.

This change of orientation, significant as it was, occurred without any change to the Board's enabling legislation and in the teeth of considerable opposition from the government of the day. It illustrates that the leadership of a statutory body can matter a great deal to how it functions and behaves, regardless of the content of its enabling legislation.

The consequences of the new Chairman's approach, supported by an astute senior officer, W. B. Carmichael (eventually to become Chairman himself), were more far-reaching than might have been imagined at the time.

Gough Whitlam, Leader of the Labor Opposition, 1967 to 1972, understanding that the new approach to manufacturing protection would promote economic growth and therefore the wherewithal for an ambitious social policy agenda, publicly declared himself a "Rattigan Man" and lent his party's support to the embattled institution. On being elected in December 1972, he brought the Tariff Board into the Prime Minister's portfolio and commissioned a review by Sir John Crawford that led to creation of a successor body, the Industries Assistance Commission (IAC), with a remit to examine all areas of government assistance to industry.[11]

Subsequently the IAC's remit was further expanded, and its name changed, under the *Industry Commission Act 1990 (Cth)* and the

Productivity Commission Act 1998 (Cth), such that the contemporary agency can potentially address any policy-related impediments to industry performance and higher living standards throughout the economy.

It is clear from the Crawford Report that the Commission was intended to serve as a "counterweight" to the undue influence on public policy of special interests. This meant that the body and those who led it were frequently at odds with sections of industry and the labour movement. On occasion this extended to frictions with government itself.

The obligation of the Commission to expose its work to public scrutiny proved an effective discipline on it to be rigorous in its analysis and to follow due process. It was understood that any opportunity to undermine the credibility of the Commission's findings would be exploited by special interests.

In such an environment, potential pitfalls could be present in seemingly small matters. The Commission's relations with ministers, Opposition politicians and "Interested Parties" all provided fertile territory for ethical dilemmas and, as I hope to show, have some relevance to the recent experience of other statutory bodies.

"Not *necessarily*, Minister"

As noted, statutory bodies are normally created in areas of public administration where actions and decisions need to be taken free from ministerial (and other) interference. The bodies nevertheless remain creatures of executive government and operate under a minister with whom it is desirable to have an effective working relationship.

For the minister and government, there can be much at stake in how the body does its job, and this can at times make the relationship a challenging one to manage. Ministerial support for agency funding, programs of work, etc, needs to be fostered, and this without courting infringement of independence.

Proper "arm's length" advice

In three terms as Chairman of the Commission, I reported to two Liberal and five Labor Treasurers or Assistant Treasurers, most of whom needed some assistance in coming to terms with what "independence" meant in relation to the Commission.

In particular, it was not always fully appreciated that the Commission's statutory obligation was to provide the advice needed to enhance economic welfare as interpreted by the Commission, based on its statutory guidelines, as opposed to what may have been seen as most suitable or expedient by the government of the day.

Any differences of interpretation with a minister in this area tended to be flushed out by the very first report produced.

Sometimes the source of concern was a broader interpretation by the Commission of its terms of reference than the government had intended: for example, that our inquiry into *First Home Ownership* chose to look at relevant Commonwealth tax provisions (like negative gearing and capital gains) as well as State stamp duties, or that the inquiry into *Impediments to Regional Industry Adjustment* chose to look at impediments that stemmed from restrictive workplace regulation.

But the main issues generally revolved around the Commission's findings and recommendations. This is natural, given the political challenges which they could present. These traditionally loomed largest for inquiries involving the more successful rent-seeking industries, notably producers of cars and clothing, which tended to have support within the public service as well as within the Parliament. While there was recognition that protection rates needed to be (further) reduced, there was always some anxiety as to what degree of reduction the Commission would end up recommending. Even though a government was not obliged to accept its recommendations, a Commission report could make its preferred way forward more difficult. Indeed, on a few occasions, the government chose to announce its position pre-emptively (for example, Tasmanian Freight Subsidisation under the Coalition in 2006; Default Superannuation provisions under Labor in 2012).

It follows that an important, indeed crucial, part of Commission "etiquette" was to avoid divulging or discussing recommendations with the government ahead of a report being formally submitted to it. This obligation is nowhere specified in legislation, but was traditionally regarded as a matter of common sense – in keeping with the requirement in the Act that any written communications between the Minister and the Commission be made publicly available.

It is an example of the "right thing" procedurally and ethically also being the right thing politically and institutionally. If the existence of any private discussions were to come to light, the Minister would lose the benefit of being able to cite a report as objective and independent, and thus to advance a policy course more successfully. And the Commission would soon lose the trust of its stakeholders and the wider public.

During the Commission's 2010 inquiry into Executive Remuneration, for example, Senator Barnaby Joyce accused the Commission of having discussed a contentious recommendation with the Assistant Treasurer, Chris Bowen, in advance of the draft report being released. That it could be reported that, at least to my knowledge and that of my staff, no such conversation had taken place was not only good for the credibility of the Commission and its report, but also for the capacity of the then government to advance that particular recommendation.

This is a subset of the general proposition that it is best for a statutory officer to avoid any circumstance where people may have cause to doubt his or her distance from the government when it comes to deliberations, recommendations and decisions.

For example, a press conference to announce that same Executive Remuneration Inquiry took place while I was on leave overseas, and had the Treasurer and the Government's chosen external Associate Commissioner, Alan Fels, standing shoulder to shoulder before the cameras. I found on return that this had put the inquiry somewhat on the back foot in terms of gaining the trust and participation of the business community. More recently, the release of the Commission's agenda-setting report, *Shifting the Dial,* was conducted in similar fashion. Given that most of the recommendations in that report would need to be implemented by the States rather than the Commonwealth, this may again have been unhelpful.

Key stakeholders need to understand and believe that a report by an independent statutory body is a report *to* Government, not "co-produced" *with* it. Any blurring of this fundamental distinction could be expected to reduce the influence of a report and, if repeated, of the institution itself.

Independence within bounds

By the same token, statutory independence does not constitute a licence to roam at will. Most statutory bodies have their fields of operation demarcated in their legislation. Nevertheless, "mission creep" is a well-documented phenomenon, particularly among regulatory bodies, and can lead to actions and outcomes never envisaged when the agencies were established. This was placed in relief by the NSW Supreme Court's finding that ICAC had exceeded its remit in prosecuting a case which, although involving a public official, did not involve any corruption of a public official in the exercise of duties. The Commissioner's response was to argue that the legislation should therefore be amended to validate its actions retrospectively. The declared "architect" of the legislation was moved by this to observe: "ICAC is proposing a fundamental change to its terms of reference. If that is to happen, then it should be the subject of extensive public debate".[12]

Being independent from government in relation to its primary functions does not mean that an organisation must remain cloistered. Most statutory agencies need political support to be effective and it is desirable that their leaders develop a respectful and (ideally) trusting relationship with the government. Effective, continuing communication with ministers is important to this, as is the tone of any public pronouncements by either party.

Few statutory bodies could be said to have the right to a permanent existence, notwithstanding their statutory foundations. They all need to be seen to be adding value in terms of their rationale for being, especially by the government of the day and desirably by the Parliament as well. If not, governments have options available to them. They may amend the legislation or, at an extreme, repeal it and abolish the body. The Commission experienced more than one round of the former and would have suffered the latter had Labor won the 1998 Election.

In the Commission's case, the government controls the quantum of its resourcing and, just as importantly, the number and "quality" of its inquiries. Both have been squeezed at various times in the institution's history. In the case of the Industries Assistance Commission, the Government created another body, the Temporary Assistance Authority, to advise on assistance needed by industry to adjust to tariff reductions. More recently, the Productivity Commission has seen reviews suited to it, including on core industry assistance matters, directed elsewhere under both Labor and Coalition governments.

Dealings with "the Opposition"

The work of many statutory agencies is politically sensitive and thus of great interest not only to the Government but also to Opposition parties. While statutory officers face challenges in dealing with the government, it can be even trickier dealing with the Opposition. Mis-steps can undermine not only the relationship with the government, but also affect community perceptions about agency independence and non-partisanship. In some cases, they can be fatal, as illustrated by the forced resignation of the Commonwealth Ombudsman, Allan Asher, in 2011, for furnishing Senator Sarah Hanson-Young, a member of the Australian Greens, with questions to use in Senate Estimates hearings.[13]

Any government body with the power not only to provide policy advice to government but to criticise its policies publicly will tend to attract particular interest from Opposition parliamentarians. Over the years, Commission reports have been enlisted politically, as well as being a source of policy ideas. As noted, a notable early instance was Whitlam's conversion in Opposition to free trade "Rattigan" thinking.

This is as it should be. The role and purpose of most statutory bodies, including the Productivity Commission, transcends the interests of the government of the day. Also, as in the Commission's case, helping the Opposition gain a greater understanding of policy problems and options can help build political support for legislative actions, or at least lessen resistance.

That said, issues have often arisen with how the relationship is handled in practice, both in formal and informal settings.

As the Commonwealth Ombudsman case illustrates, Senate Estimates in particular is fraught territory for an independent statutory officer. All sides of politics commonly use it as an opportunity to score points off each other. It can be challenging to respond to such questioning without being seen by one side or the other to be transgressing political neutrality. More than one senior official has seen a successful career come to an end following an ill-judged performance at Senate Estimates.

My own rules for survival were to come armed with the facts (or bring a colleague who was), to play a "straight bat" and avoid the temptation to elaborate or, worse, sermonise. Forbearance under attack is also desirable. However, not all statutory officers have chosen to approach things that way; and some appear to have consciously chosen the opposite approach.

One of the key benefits of Senate Estimates is not the inquisitorial sessions themselves, which too often descend into farce, but how these condition the behaviour of officials when on the job. "Would this pass the Senate Estimates test?" was commonly a question to self when considering how to respond to an issue. In the end, the best preparation for Senate Estimates is having nothing to hide.

Dealing with politicians can be even trickier *outside* such formal settings. For example, a member of the Opposition would occasionally phone my office wanting to "have a chat". Any conversation in such circumstances is risky as one never knows how it will be reported. But refusing to speak could offend and potentially store up trouble for later. My approach was to take the call and see where things went. If amber lights began to flash, say because a policy issue under review was brought up, my fall back was to say I was happy to continue but convention required that a member of the Treasurer's staff attend as well, which normally had a chilling effect. On occasion such a meeting would proceed.

Such an approach not only helps to maintain trust with the minister, it has the longer-term benefit that, while the Opposition members concerned might initially feel dissatisfied, once in government again they could rest assured that those newly in Opposition would be treated the same way.

Engagement with "interested parties"

Most statutory bodies need to deal with a range of "interested parties" external to politics in the course of their deliberations. Such public engagement, at arm's length from government, is often a key part of the rationale for the body itself. How these consultations are conducted can matter a great deal not only to the substantive outcomes, but also to how a statutory body is perceived. Appropriate access, fair hearings and balanced use of the information provided are all to be expected, but not always delivered.

For example, issues of contention in relation to ICAC have been the inquisitorial nature of its hearings, reportedly likened by its previous head, Megan Latham, to "pulling the wings off insects" and the withholding of "exculpatory evidence" from those affected by an investigation, which in one well-publicised instance could have seen a senior NSW Government official – a statutory officer himself – wrongly sent to prison.[14]

The Productivity Commission's principal stakeholders can be thought of as those *seeking* policy changes (whether budgetary or regulatory in nature) and those who would be directly or indirectly *affected* by them. Unlike some other bodies, the Commission's *raison d'être* as a counterweight to vested interests has seen it pay at least as much attention to the latter as the former.

The Commission's own approach to engaging with stakeholders has evolved significantly over time. In the early days, the main forms of consultation were written submissions and public hearings based on them. The conduct of hearings tended to be courtroom-like: they could be intimidating to individuals and tended to favour representative bodies or specialists. As the Commission's remit moved into areas of social and environmental policy it became apparent that more accessible and "inclusive" approaches were required. In time, hearings became more a forum for discussion than cross-examination, and advances in information technology made it easier to appear.

This not only enfranchised many who had previously not had a voice in policy debate, it enabled access to information and insights not otherwise available. Where draft reports were issued and discussed in these ways, final reports invariably differed in significant respects for the better.

That said, not all engagement with interested parties could be fully transparent. Sometimes the most useful insights were gleaned in private conversations, particularly those held as part of an initial round of "industry visits" used to scope an inquiry. Since the information so derived would ultimately be exposed and tested in a public report, it is hard to see this posing ethical concerns. On occasion, the records of such meetings were protected from Freedom of Information requests on that basis.

More difficult considerations arose, however, where an interested party wished to speak in private after the formal consultation process had closed, but prior to the reporting deadline. Other stakeholders could be justifiably concerned about the potential for any such meeting to influence the Commission's final thinking on a matter, and could use this to raise doubts about the report. Another rule was therefore introduced that no further private consultations would be held in the few weeks prior to completion of a report unless instigated by the Commission itself for specific reasons and noted publicly.

A more commonplace ethical issue is the "freebie". While gifts to public officials now generally have (low) dollar limits attached to them, including when received for speaking at an event, there is ambiguity in other areas. An invitation to attend a major sporting event in the relative comfort of a corporate box, for example, appears to be looked upon more favourably than receiving an expensive bottle of (real) champagne. My wife used to ask why I never got invitations to events like other senior officers in the public service. Part of the answer was that I refused most of those I did receive, as did my fellow Commissioners (sometimes reluctantly), particularly where there was a potential link to a Commission activity. But also I probably received fewer offers, as the Commission's *modus operandi* should suggest relatively low expected returns to a donor. Statutory bodies with determinative powers might have faced stronger temptations.

Exercising discretion

The legislation governing statutory bodies establishes their powers and processes, and broad decision criteria. But it cannot be too prescriptive about how these are exercised. Independent bodies are often created for the very reason that decisions involving significant discretion in certain areas of government need to be exercised on their merits.

Apart from the usual disagreements about findings and recommendations, areas of contention have related to *what* these organisations chose to do (as in the ICAC's *Cunneen* case) and *when* they chose to do it (AHRC's review of children in detention). Such issues have also arisen for the Commission throughout its history

Deciding what to investigate

The Productivity Commission can only undertake formal public inquiries at the request of government. So while the Commission can influence topics, it cannot determine them, let alone proceed to inquire into them.

Like the AHRC, the Industries Assistance Commission initially had the power to initiate its own public inquiries. The logic for this was that areas of high protection should not be able to escape public review, and this should not depend on government agreeing. The power was never formally exercised and, on this basis, was removed following a major review of the IAC by John Uhrig in 1983. Some well-placed observers considered that the reviewer had failed to understand the power of that provision to leverage formal inquiry requests from the government.

Subsequently, when the Productivity Commission was created, it was granted the power to undertake and publish its own research studies. It soon became apparent that such self-initiated studies had the capacity to become *de facto* public inquiries. This had potential to cause grief to the government of the day, and thus to the relationship between it and the Commission. So the choice of what to do assumed considerable importance. It was resolved by a combination of seeking suggestions and testing ideas with government departments, while retaining the freedom to make an independent call. This stream of work was also seen as more appropriate for informational reports, containing findings rather than recommendations, including to lay the groundwork for formal public inquiries at a later stage.

When to do it

The controversy around the deferred timing of the AHRC's inquiry into children in detention raised a number of ethical and other issues, some of which the Productivity Commission has confronted in its own work, if in a different context.

As noted, unlike the AHRC, the initiation of Commission inquiries and specification of reporting dates are matters for the government. And, within limits specified in statute, the government also decides when to release a final report presented to it. The only discretion available to the Commission in relation to timing is release of a *draft* report. However, draft reports tend to be significant events, when much of the public debate takes place.

Experience suggests that the announcement of a Commission inquiry before an election can be good politics for a government, signalling its willingness to "do something" (but without actually having to do it). For example, a number of inquiries into assistance to the pork industry, which traverses several marginal electorates up the east coast, started this way. But for the Commission to release a draft report before an election was to court political mayhem and policy failure. This prospect was not always appreciated by a government when first launching an inquiry.

Thus, on more than one occasion, the Commission found good reason to defer release of a draft report until an election was called and the caretaker conventions came into force. In a sense, holding off might be seen as helping an incumbent government politically, to the extent that a report is critical of its policies. But, in my view, any ethical concerns in that respect are overtaken by the reality that a policy report released in the lead-up to an election would become a political football, with the risk that recommendations in the public interest would be pre-emptively rejected out of hand.

It was therefore of some interest to me that similar reasoning was used by Gillian Triggs in defending the AHRC's decision to defer its high profile inquiry until after the 2013 election. Two differences are that (a) her decision related to the *commencement* of an inquiry, and (b) occurred early in the electoral cycle (and at a time when numbers in detention had risen steeply). Nevertheless, these could perhaps be seen as matters of degree. More significant considerations relate to the Chair conferring with ministers about deferring the inquiry and later denying that discussions had taken place.

Ethical use of the media?

A number of statutory bodies, as an important part of their functions, have a role in informing the public about the activities for which they are responsible. This can be to promote compliance, or reassure the public that issues are being addressed, or simply to show how the agency goes about its work.

If anything, this need has been increasing in line with public expectations and a more obtrusive media. The greater transparency around Reserve Bank board meetings and increased public utterances by the Governor (particularly the current one) provide an illustration of this.

Contemporary media can present some challenges and ethical dilemmas for statutory bodies and those leading them that do not arise for department heads, given their different roles. These have not always been surmounted well.

For example, there have long been complaints from business about one-sided "trial by media" tactics by the Australian Competition and Consumer Commission. A notorious instance was a coordinated raid on Caltex's offices in Australia in 2006, with the staged removal for the benefit of news cameras of a large number of filing boxes, none of which were found to contain incriminating evidence and some of which reportedly were empty.

This and other incidents contributed to the commissioning of the Dawson Review in 2003, which found a need for a code of conduct in relation to the media.[15] A decade later similar issues came to the fore in the Harper Review of Competition Policy, which again recommended such a code. It was finally implemented by the ACCC in October 2016.

There have also been reports of leaks of privileged information by regulatory and other agencies, some of which have been known to favour certain journalists.

The Commission has not been immune to such pressures and opportunities, going back to the latter days of the Tariff Board. The media has been important to the Commission's influence on key topics over the years, not least on industry assistance, and an important ally when it came under pressure from vested interests or government. That some of this interaction occurred covertly may not have been entirely appropriate, but on occasion it proved highly effective.

Capture and culture

The enabling legislation for statutory bodies is designed to provide formal protections against ministerial direction and other sources of influence, but this does not mean that influence cannot occur. There is a large literature on the "capture" of regulators by regulated entities. This has been associated more with overseas experience than here, although Victoria's former Building Commission is one documented exception[16] and the regulated "gold plating" of electricity transmission infrastructure identified in a PC review in 2012 may be another.

There have also been suggestions coming out of the recent Financial Services Royal Commission that the Australian Prudential Regulation Authority and the Australian Securities and Investment Commission had been captured by large financial institutions, based in part on a perceived reluctance to litigate, in contrast to the Australian Competition and Consumer Commission (ACCC). These accusations lack foundation. The preference for approaches such as "Enforceable Undertakings" over fines or litigation is consonant with the "responsive regulation" literature promoted by the OECD and ANZSOG. In my experience, it is likely to be more effective in remedying identified problem areas than the litigious and prescriptive approaches which those agencies were encouraged to adopt. (As an aside, the ACCC has lost many of its legal battles, at considerable cost to the taxpayer.)

That said, there are other forms of capture to which statutory bodies are prone.

A key one is capture by an agency's own staff and the culture that can develop within an organisation. Those joining a statutory authority are more likely to have self-selected through personal alignment with its mission than would be the case for the public service as a whole. Human rights, workers rights, environmental protection, consumer protection, privacy protection, administrative justice, anti-corruption and other areas inhabited by statutory authorities are likely to attract people with a special interest in advancing such causes. And those people are also more likely to stay longer and rise to more senior levels.

This can have the consequence that the officials on whom a statutory officer often must rely may have developed their own collective view of the agency's mission and how it is best prosecuted. This might include, for example, an adversarial and punitive attitude towards regulated entities, such as has been variously remarked on in relation to the Australian Taxation Office and the ACCC; or a view that certain parties must be supported almost regardless, as observed about certain decisions of the Administrative Appeals Tribunal and the Immigration Appeals Tribunal; or that the body's role and powers should go further than its legislation provides, as ICAC maintained following the High Court decision in the *Cunneen* case.

"Bottom-up" cultures and associated groupthink can prove resilient and very difficult for an agency's leadership to overcome. This is commonly observed about the Australian Broadcasting Corporation (ABC), where board appointments by Coalition governments that were clearly intended to help bring about change have seemingly had little impact. A former Deputy Chairman of the ABC has described the organisation as "ungovernable";[17] another board member called it "unreformable".[18]

This phenomenon may help to explain the comparative rarity of regulatory capture of the standard form in Australia, noted previously. On the other hand, it can be conducive to capture by *non*-regulated groups or individuals, such as social or environmental activists whose particular interests and beliefs are more closely aligned with agency staff than with the wider community. The ABC's consistently one-dimensional coverage of such issues as "asylum seekers" and "global warming" seems illustrative of minority group symbiosis.

The Productivity Commission and its predecessors have not been immune to "cultural reinforcement". The institution was conceived as a counter force to vested interests, with a mission directed at promoting economic efficiency and growth. It naturally attracted to its staff many young economists who saw an opportunity to advance trade liberalisation and other market-oriented reforms, most of whom developed an antipathy to government "preferment" of uncompetitive industries. Many of these people stayed and rose through the ranks, and developed strong links with like-minded reformists in academia and other places.

With the passage of time, the Commission's advocacy of market forces in the pursuit of economic efficiency and growth began to be seen as antipathy to government intervention *per se*. As a result, its influence on policy decisions began to wane and its inquiry load diminished. This emboldened those threatened by its work and their political supporters to ask why the organisation should continue to exist.

Partly in response to this existential threat, a more balanced approach was gradually forged, including in the language of its reports. Public perceptions of the Commission were also transformed by the opportunity to conduct inquiries into areas of social and environmental policy, such as gambling and "greenhouse". Its position is now considerably more secure than could have been said two decades ago.

Some implications

In summary, how statutory bodies conduct themselves is influenced not only by their mission, but also by the incentives they face and the motivations, judgment and ethics of their staff and leadership.

This suggests that governance and accountability arrangements are as important for statutory authorities as for other parts of public administration. Given the special status of statutory bodies, there is a limit to which ministerial oversight can or should perform this role. Being creations of the legislature, Parliament itself has a duty that should be discharged, not only as guardian of their independence,[19] but also as an accountability mechanism. Parliamentary committees are central to this and have proven an effective, if sometimes brutal, means of exposing a range of ethical and other performance issues.

Decision-making processes for the appointment of statutory officers are arguably even more important than for department heads, not least because of the extended security of tenure. It is particularly important that appointments not be made primarily on political grounds if they are to command public respect and bipartisan support (and be discharged competently). This received recognition at the Commonwealth level some time ago with introduction of procedural requirements that included advertising of vacancies and vetting of candidates by senior officials prior to ministerial consideration.

It is not clear how well this system has been working in practice. It has not prevented a number of appointments being seen as "captain's picks" or from becoming politically contentious. (The appointment processes for the previous two chairs of ASIC and the current chair of the Productivity Commission have been cases in point.) The fact that agency heads themselves are generally regarded as being more "political" these days is likely to have reduced confidence in their vetting role. Alternatives include giving Public Service Commissioners greater powers in relation to statutory appointments (as in New Zealand) or forming an independent standing body expressly for such appointments. But how such a panel itself is chosen then becomes the issue.

The integrity and ethics of statutory officers are important not only in their own right, but also for the longer term effectiveness of the institutions they lead. Recent history confirms that ethical failures often result in wider performance failures and can erode the respect needed for statutory officers to discharge their duties "responsibly".

References

Albrechtsen, Janet, "It's too late to reform the ABC", *The Australian*, 19 October 2018.

ANZSOG, *What is Public Value? Public admin explainer*, Melbourne, 2017

Asher, Allan, Opening Statement for Additional Estimates, Commonwealth Ombudsman, 17 October 2011.

Healey, Deborah, "The ACCC and the media: improving the ratings", *UNSW Law Journal*, 2003, 305.

IBAC (Independent Broad-based Anti-corruption Commission), 2017 *Exposing and preventing corruption in Victoria – Special Report on IBAC's first five years*, Victorian Government Printer, December.

ICAC SA (South Australian Independent Commission Against Corruption), *Looking Back*, SA Government Printer, October 2019.

Moore, Mark, *Creating Public Value: Strategic Management in Government*, Harvard University Press, Cambridge, MA, 1995.

Nethercote, John, "Who is a 'good' Ombudsman?", *Canberra Times*, 31 October 2011.

Nethercote, John, "Independent Statutory Authorities – A veritable chestnut of Australian Government", *Canberra Times*, 6 July 2015, *Public Sector Informant*.

Nethercote, John, "Human rights limits", *Canberra Times*, 29 June 2015.

Ombudsman, Victoria, *Own motion investigation into the governance and administration of the Victorian Building Commission*, Victorian Government Printer, December 2012.

PSC (Public Sector Commission) NSW, Behaving Ethically: A guide for NSW government sector employees, 2014.

Rattigan, G. A., *Industry Assistance: The Inside Story*, Melbourne University Press, Melbourne, 1986.

Scales, Bill, *Independent Audit of NBN Public Policy Processes*, Department of Communications, Canberra, July 2014.

Shergold, Peter, *Learning from Failure*, APSC, Canberra, 2015.

Sloan, Judith, "Their ABC is just ungovernable", *The Australian*, 18 August 2011.

Sturgess, Gary, "ICAC's history shows there was no drafting mistake", *The Australian*, 25 April 2015.

VAGO (Victorian Auditor General's Office), *Compliance with Building Permits*, Victorian Government Printer, December 2011.

VAGO, *East West Link Project*, Victorian Government Printer, December 2015.

Wettenhall, Roger, "Parliamentary Oversight of Statutory Agencies: A Post-Uhrig Perspective", *Australasian Parliamentary Review*, 20(2) 2015.

Endnotes

[1] John Nethercote, "Independent Statutory Authorities – A veritable chestnut of Australian Government", *Public Sector Informant*, July 2015.

[2] Mark Moore, *Creating Public Value: Strategic Management in Government*, Harvard University Press, Cambridge, MA, 1995; ANZSOG, *What is Public Value? Public admin explainer*, ANZSOG, Melbourne, 2017.

[3] IBAC (Independent Broad-based Anti-corruption Commission), *Exposing and preventing corruption in Victoria – Special Report on IBAC's first five years*, Victorian Government Printer, December, 2017.

[4] ICAC SA (South Australian Independent Commission Against Corruption), *Looking Back*, SA Government Printer, October, 2019.

[5] Peter Shergold, *Learning from Failure*, APSC, Canberra, 2015; Scales, Bill, *Independent Audit of NBN Public Policy Processes*, Department of Communications, Canberra, July 2014; VAGO, *East West Link Project*, Victorian Government Printer, December 2015.

[6] PSC (Public Sector Commission) NSW, *Behaving Ethically: A guide for NSW government sector employees*, 2014.

[7] Ibid., 15.

[8] John Nethercote, "Human rights limits", *The Canberra Times*, 29 June 2015.

[9] Bill Scales, *Independent Audit of NBN Public Policy Processes*, Department of Communications, Canberra, July, 2014.

[10] G. A Rattigan, *Industry Assistance: The Inside Story*, Melbourne University Press, Melbourne, 1986.

[11] Ibid.

[12] Gary Sturgess, "ICAC's history shows there is no drafting mistake", *The Australian*, 25 April 2015.

[13] Allan Asher, Opening Statement for Additional Estimates, Commonwealth Ombudsman, 17 October 2011; John Nethercote, "Who is a 'good' Ombudsman?" *The Canberra Times*, 31 October 2011.

[14] Chris Merritt, "ICAC leaps ahead but stumbles at a vital hurdle", *The Australian*, 6 April 2018.

[15] Deborah Healey, "The ACCC and the media: improving the ratings", *UNSW Law Journal*, 2003, 305.

[16] VAGO (Victorian Auditor General's Office), *Compliance with Building Permits*, Victorian Government Printer, December, 2011.

[17] Judith Sloan, "Their ABC is just ungovernable", *The Australian*, 18 August 2011.

[18] Janet Albrechtsen, "It's too late to reform the ABC", *The Australian*, 19 October 2018.

[19] Wettenall, Roger, "Parliamentary Oversight of Statutory Agencies: A Post-Uhrig Perspective", *Australasian Parliamentary Review*, 20(2), 2005.

5

The Public Policy Process in Australia
Reflections from Experience*

Meredith Edwards

This essay is written from the perspective of a policy adviser in the Hawke-Keating years (1983 to 1996). It deals with reflections on the process of developing policy in terms of the three main but related roles of a policy adviser: the analytical, the administrative and the relational. It puts the policy cycle framework in a practical context, across a career as a policy adviser within government and as a "boundary rider" between the public sector and academia. It also compares the policy context of the 1980s and 1990s to that which policy advisers face in the first quarter of the 21st century. Specifically, reflections covered include: considering the political, economic and social context; covering all stages in the policy process, although not necessarily in any order; the importance of attention to organisational structures and processes; dealing with ministers and their staff; the power of networks, dialogue and relationships; managing the researcher-policy practitioner interface; and being pragmatic as well as managing ambiguity.

Of the many roles John Nethercote plays in public life, there are two with which I can particularly identify. Nethercote has been a boundary rider – across disciplines and between the public service and academia. He also has been a catalyst for change in his role as networker and especially a facilitator of dialogue.

I spent fourteen years (1983-97) as a senior Australian public servant, mostly as a policy adviser. This is a narrow public service perspective in that it does not include implementing policies and programs or undertaking corporate roles. Yet my experience was broad in other ways. As a public servant, I was twice employed as a ministerial consultant: I was responsible to the secretary of the department while also working to a minister and, unusually, worked from within bureaucracy rather than on the minister's personal staff.[1] Contributing to a broader view, I came to the public service from academia as a researcher with radical policy ideas, having also built up strong links with non-government organisations. I was therefore more comfortable as a "boundary player" and being a catalyst for change than were many of my public service colleagues.

I was most fortunate to work in the Hawke-Keating era of activist reform and, in that context, able to provide policy advice on a number of major (mainly social) policy changes – which I would call reforms in the true sense of the word[2] – notably: simplifying youth allowances; developing a child support scheme; introducing the Higher Education Contribution Scheme (HECS); developing a national housing strategy; and assisting long-term unemployed people back into work.

Since the period in which I was most active as a policy adviser, there have been many significant changes in the policy environment that tend to render policy outcomes more uncertain, including: global forces more influential on domestic issues; technology advancing in unanticipated directions; a 24/7 media cycle has become entrenched; tight budgets, not helped by an ageing population; society is more networked; power is more dispersed (including to ministerial advisers and non-government players); a blurring of boundaries across sectors; growing citizen distrust in governments; and minority governments more common.

In addition, within public services it is now commonly argued that the capability to develop policy and to coordinate responses across government(s) has declined alongside a loss of institutional memory.[3] Not unrelated is an apparent lack of courageous political leadership.[4]

Despite rhetoric to the contrary, there is much evidence of a risk-averse public service environment with middle management becoming less, and not more, empowered, so holding back innovative policy initiatives.[5] Recently the (then) head of PM&C, Martin Parkinson, called on public servants to "Think big. Aim high. Experiment. Be ruthless. Ask the simple questions if something is not working". [6] But there remains a big gap between the talk and the action.

These factors indicate a very different and more challenging policy-making environment from the 1980s and 1990s. Most of the fundamentals of good policy process remain, however, and it is still true that "good process makes not only for good policy, but ultimately for good politics too".[7] As such, the "fundamental principles of good policy processes should be timeless, even if the manner of their execution must adapt to the times".[8] Effective policy development still requires good analysis combined with an artful mix of process, people and politics.

The fundamentals remain constant for the three main but related roles of a policy adviser: the analytical, administrative and relational roles. Brian Head describes these roles well: the analytical role includes examining and comparing policy options, as well as evaluating current policies and programs; the administrative role is about how to proceed with developing policy including coordinating relevant agencies and paying attention to organisational processes and structures; and the relational role involves testing how acceptable might be policy choices, consulting, negotiating and ultimately taking into account political and financial constraints.[9]

What follows are my reflections as a policy adviser playing the analytical, administrative and relational roles in developing policy in the 1980s and 1990s; reflections that should resonate with policy advisers of today. It may also inform researchers interested in the practicalities of the policy process.

Reflections

Any good policy development process will follow some form of organising framework. Many have appeared in the relevant literature of the past 50 years or so. My observation is that, the complexities of the real world notwithstanding, an attempt at a systematic approach to policy development can yield significant benefits in addressing policy problems. Indeed, when chairing an inter-departmental committee (IDC) I would refer to different policy cycle stages we might be in or going into to give a context to our work.

In my practice, I used a policy cycle framework that is a variant of the Bridgman and Davis so-called "policy cycle model". This framework is reflected in my book on the policy process.[10] It is outlined below. But there are several possible levels and modes of analysis of the policy process. What follows, therefore, goes beyond the policy cycle approach to encompass other factors important in successfully achieving policy outcomes: placing the problem in a broader economic, social and political context; carefully choosing appropriate organisational processes and structures; the role of participants and the value of their networks; the role of values and, of course, politics as the paramount factor in affecting policy outcomes.

Considering the context

A policy proposal tied to the government's current priorities is likely to get a better hearing than if it is not. A good starting point is the party policy platform and party ideologies which set the boundaries as to what may and may not be possible in both the short and longer term. As a former federal Labor minister, Nicola Roxon, remarked: "Neglecting to provide advice that reflects the government's platform is one of the biggest ministerial pet peeves".[11] This does not require public servants to compromise on providing impartial advice, but they do need to be attuned to the government's agenda.

The economic, social and political context was highly relevant in the policy development processes around introduction of Australia's Child Support Scheme in the 1980s. This scheme was introduced at a time of a large budget deficit and hence the need for new revenue sources. But it was also a time of concern about poverty amongst those on low incomes, particularly sole parent families. The ministers for Social Security and Finance at the time both had a stake, therefore, in a scheme that would reduce pressure on the budget as well as assist in alleviating child poverty. It was the right policy at the right time. Contrast this with the environment that faced development of a National Housing Strategy in the late 1980s and early 1990s, when policies advanced to assist low income households in housing stress into rental accommodation failed, notwithstanding a comprehensive research process, because the focus of government and the public at that time was on high interest rates that inhibited people from gaining a foothold in home ownership.

Other factors may be relevant in a policy context, such as: issues relating to timing (for example, when an election is likely to occur); institutional arrangements (for example, "how" different agencies or levels of government relate to each other); and who are the key actors to influence within relevant organisations. Political leadership is crucial: Hawke and Keating were leaders who demonstrated political courage by making tough decisions alongside being good communicators and, above all, great persuaders. (How different the scene has been during the last decade and a half!)

Covering all policy stages

The policy environment can be likened to a stormy sea, with the policy adviser trying to guide a small boat across choppy waters.[12] The effort required is great, and there can be considerable risk, but there can be successful ways to navigate a course.

In the 1980s and 1990s, complex policy questions required involvement of a diverse range of players across sectors. It was a messy policy environment, and at times politically chaotic. In spite of this, my experience was that identifying stages in policy development as a guiding framework, if used flexibly, can assist considerably in policy advising. In other words, a systematic approach to policy development, such as the policy cycle approach, can yield significant benefits of order and process in addressing policy problems.[13]

Using a policy cycle framework, my book on policy development explained how four major policies developed through each policy stage:

- identifying the issues (defining and articulating the problem);
- understanding key values and other questions before advising on options and proposals;
- policy analysis (collecting relevant data and information and clarifying objectives);
- undertaking consultation;
- moving toward decisions;
- implementation; and
- evaluation.[14]

Because these policy initiatives were significant, complex, cross-departmental, and involved politically sensitive issues, it was important to cover each of the policy stages. Far from being a linear process, it was more like an improvised dance.[15] Stages were often visited in a different order, or revisited, and there was backward as well as forward movement across stages, or even overlapping stages. In this sense the process can be seen as iterative. In some cases, it would have been inefficient to backtrack; in other cases, backtracking seemed to be the only way to move towards a solution.

Backtracking on original intent occurred when, for political reasons, the child support proposal needed to be introduced in two phases instead of all in one go. Problem identification can overlap with a policy idea where the policy idea gives a momentum to the reform agenda. Similarly, overlaps can occur between policy analysis and consultation or policy analysis and clarifying the problem. It was clear to me, however, that unless each stage is covered, major policy proposals will have less chance of emerging into reality. A good policy process is necessary, if not sufficient, in most instances, to ensure policy objectives are achieved.[16]

Some political scientists have been skeptical of the policy cycle approach. Hal Colebatch has suggested that the policy cycle approach fails to consider the full range of policy actors involved and their relative importance in policy-making.[17] But consultation – tailored to the sensitivity of the issue and who is to be consulted as well as when – is, in fact, taken into account in both the Bridgman and Davis version as well as my own (see below).

It has also been argued, for example, by Everett, that the policy cycle is a form of "rationalism".[18] Given that policy environments are full of complexities, it is not likely that anything approaching classical rationality in the decision-making process will be observed. As the two original authors of *The Australian Policy Cycle*, Bridgman and Davis (both with public service policy experience) have remarked, "The policy cycle is logical … but does not embody formal rationality". And they would also agree with another policy practitioner, Gary Banks, that, far from a rigid sequential approach, there will be "loops and iterations" and that models of "good process" are about "what *should* be rather than what is".[19]

While controversial among political scientists, in my experience, the policy cycle framework can serve as a bridge between the ideal of the process and the practice; as a valuable, if rough, guide to action in pursuing success for a policy position. It certainly was a concept familiar to fellow public servants, and sharing the same language helped us to work out together where we were at and what might be the next steps.

Clarifying the problem: the policy problem needs to be identified and well-articulated for it to be owned by the public. Once the problem is clarified people tend to ask, "what can we do about it?"

In the radical Child Support reforms of the 1980s, it was relatively easy to articulate the problem – why should children suffer and taxpayers foot the bill just because parents decide not to live together? By way of contrast, as already mentioned, while there was general agreement that housing affordability was important as an issue, there was no agreement on which aspect needed to be addressed.

Sometimes the power of a simple idea assisted articulation of the problem and gets it on the policy agenda. For example, in developing policies to assist the long-term unemployed in the first half of the 1990s, the idea of a "job compact" provided the necessary underpinnings for policy; imposing some obligation on the part of the long-term unemployed helped to make the policy acceptable to the public. [20]

The notion of a "policy window" is relevant here: that window occurs when acknowledgement of the problem is combined with ideas on a solution that respond to political interest[21] – the problem, policy proposal and politics all come together. In addition, the language used to communicate with and influence a broad audience about these issues matters.

Agenda-setting matters as well. Policy issues can emerge from inside as well as outside of government. Ministers are generally better able to place policy problems on a crowded agenda. This might be at their own initiative, but often they respond to external pressures.

Understanding values before putting options: too often policy development stalls because policy advisers put policy options to ministers without taking account of the values that will govern their decisions.[22] This is particularly where the problem is complex and where there is electoral sensitivity. The trade-off between efficiency in spending and more equity in outcomes is often framed by values.[23] In cases where decision-makers have deeply held beliefs (for example, on euthanasia or same-sex marriage), then no number of policy options or amount of evidence to support them is likely to make a difference.

Politics ultimately determines whether a policy progresses from stage to stage and at what pace; values link policy and politics.[24] It may be a frustrating realisation that politicians might be motivated more by values and emotion than "rational" analysis of the evidence before them.[25] As Bromell has remarked:

> Relying on evidence and empirical analysis alone is like trying to sit on a one-legged stool – it is neither stable nor comfortable for any length of time. Effective policy advisors therefore have to engage not only with relevant data and empirical analysis, but also with emotions and social psychology, and with values and moral argument.[26]

Public servants are not well-placed to weigh value-based criteria. This means that the policy process is assisted when ministers give some direction, for example, through a set of principles to guide policy development. A statement of principles from ministers can also inform the criteria by which options are assessed.

My experience was that, where it was possible, confronting ministers early with key issues before presenting them with policy options assisted them to clarify their objectives and to speed up the policy process. The issues stage could be made easier if the process started with possible matters on which they could agree and then moved to harder decisions from which principles were derived and which took into account political values. This is often a point in the process missed in traditional textbooks on the policy process. In the case of child support, it was necessary to argue and decide whether to use an administrative or a court-based system before dealing with the issue of whether to use a formula. In turn, that issue was desirably decided before the critical issue of which government agency to use to assess, collect and enforce payments.

The *policy analysis* phase is where policy advisers can really show their expertise: relevant data and research are analysed and options are assessed for likely consequence based on an understanding of the decision-maker's value framework but also based on key criteria, such as efficiency, equity and administrative feasibility amongst others.[27] This is also the stage where key players – especially those internal to government – can be expected to interact extensively and where their departmental or other differences emerge.

It is unrealistic to expect "evidence-based policy" when policy and politics mix. A purist approach is flawed when it does not take into account people and their values or beliefs, or the politics, including where power lies. However, evidence-*influenced* policy can lead to both good policy and good politics.[28] When the environment is receptive, evidence can be powerful both in clarifying a problem and in moving towards a solution.

Once ministers have decided what they want to do – as a consequence of their values and/or pressure from electors or party supporters – they will seek evidence to support their decision so they can justify the policy in public.[29] Often what is sought, therefore, is more "policy-influenced evidence" or "values-influenced evidence" than evidence-influenced policy. This challenges public servants who want to stay clear of values and politics in presenting evidence.

Apart from the need to tailor evidence to the nature of the policy issue, I found different forms of evidence were needed at different stages of the policy cycle.[30] Evidence about better practice, especially international comparisons, can be a great benefit in developing policy options. Policy transfer from elsewhere can be useful if adapted appropriately to local circumstances.

It is also important to curate the evidence: to decide who should get the evidence and why, from whom it should come and why, as well as deciding what the policy-makers need and when, and the best ways to communicate it. This is particularly challenging now as the public appears more selective about what evidence to trust in the "post-truth" world.

In the **consultation** phase, participation by stakeholders and, more broadly, citizens who are potentially affected by a possible decision, will vary according to the nature of the issue, its complexity and sensitivity. Processes could be formal or informal, continuous or episodic. Who to consult, why, when in the policy process, and how, are critical process questions.[31] Good judgment is therefore needed. Today, engaging stakeholders, if not co-designing with them, is recognised as more important; but, at the same time, there does appear to be a disjuncture between that recognition and the reality.[32]

Moving to policy decisions: ultimately, following refinement of original proposals, the pivotal stage of decision-making occurs in what can be a highly political context. This is where the political, policy and administrative impacts of a proposal are weighed up and cabinet consideration brings all perspectives together and "arguments translate to a decision".[33]

In my major policy experience, *implementation of cabinet decisions* was the most neglected and poorly performed policy stage. Too often, ministers announced decisions but then lost interest as they refocused on new issues on the agenda. There are many factors that can derail policy intent, including lack of clarity around interpretation of the decision, or respective responsibilities in the implementation process; insufficient resources allocated; insufficient attention to coordination and collaboration between agencies; or a shortage of time.[34] Despite recent focus on policy implementation, there often appears to be a disconnection between the aims of policy and the reality of delivery.

Evaluation is the final stage in policy development, where questions of effectiveness, efficiency, and continued appropriateness of objectives are assessed. Ideally it is also a stage of policy learning. A good evaluation process, as occurred in the early 1990s on long-term unemployment issues, is incorporated into the policy process before the decision stage. Evaluation needs to be timely, involve a range of people who hold a stake in the policy or program, and ensure a wide dissemination of results.[35]

Evaluation can be highly political. For example, evaluation documents can be changed as they proceed from technical experts and ultimately to the minister. In addition, those best able to assess the impact of a change, such as front-line workers, are not necessarily involved.

A welcome recent sign is greater acknowledgement of the need to experiment with new approaches and "learning from failure" alongside the monitoring of outcomes.[36]

Attending to organisational structures and processes

A framework of stages in developing policy is only part of the story if desired policy outcomes are to have a chance to succeed. A common thread in good policy processes (often not given due attention in the theory of policy-making) is careful consideration of organisational structures and processes within which policy work occurs.

A successful policy adviser will give attention to both strategy and tactics: not just addressing the important or high level ends as well as means, but also tactics to deal with more immediate matters and to manage daily processes.[37] In fact, the single most important lesson I learnt from my time as a public servant, as keen and impatient as I was to get desired outcomes, was the critical role of policy processes and structures if desired outcomes were to have any chance of success.

Ministers can tactically by-pass inter-departmental committees (IDCs) and use other less conventional or more innovative mechanisms such as carefully selected task forces which might include not only public servants, but also ministerial advisers and/or external experts; and/or taskforces of relevant ministers.[38]

Some of the key questions I found that a policy adviser might need to assess include:

(a) What structures best fit the task? Are structures needed for a whole-of-government approach or something less cross-cutting? Is there to be an IDC or a taskforce or some other arrangement?

(b) What policy stages are to be followed and in what order? Is there to be formal consultation or informal consultations; continuing or episodic? If a formal process, are meetings to be made public or kept confidential? Is the evaluation to be internal or external?

(c) If the policy issue has a longer-term objective, can it be achieved in one budget measure or should the policy objective be phased in over time?

(d) Should the policy issue from a line agency be shared with central agencies and/or go before a minister or ministers for guidance? If so, when?

(e) Who should be involved: which agencies, public servants, ministerial advisers, non-government players; when in the process; and with what accountabilities?

These are examples of how a policy official can exercise agency. Another factor is how policy advisers interact with ministerial staff as described below.

Dealing with ministers and their staff

Because a minister (or group of ministers) is pivotal in the policy process, "managing up" effectively to a minister can take considerable skill, including, critically, learning on the job about their relevant characteristics. Are they extrovert, or introvert; do they think in pictures and need oral briefing or do they prefer reading words on a page; are they highly intuitive or more analytical? Nicola Roxon, a minister in the first Rudd and the Gillard governments, provided some advice to public servants, including to be "strategically smart and adapt advice" by framing it in the light of to whom you are talking, and "Ascertain at the beginning if your minister is a talker or a reader when it comes to processing advice".[39]

The relationship of ministers and their staff with the public service has evolved over time.[40] In the 1980s, the attitude of some senior public servants with whom I worked was that "ministers come and go, but we remain". At that time ministers answered for the actions of officials (as well as their advisers). By the early 1990s, as a consequence of a series of deliberate changes to public service tenure, departmental structures and reward systems, the balance of power had switched to the political executive. This put public servants in the front-line defending ministers and their staff.[41] Today, there are more ministerial advisers than ever before (although not necessarily with the same level of policy expertise as in the past).

A learning experience for me arose from a newspaper article in 1996 that claimed that senior officials in PM&C regarded the advisers in the Prime Minister's Office (PMO) as "amateurish". This claim sparked fury from the PMO and also from the Prime Minister himself. The article came some months after an intensive effort by senior PM&C officials to build up good relationships with the newly elected Prime Minister, John Howard, and his staff.[42] Such a setback can quickly destroy trust that might have taken months to build up. This illustrates how important it is to take care in building up and maintaining a respectful and trusting relationship with a minister's office, however time-consuming that may be. This is a precondition for being able to offer frank and fearless advice.

Placing value on networks and relationships

The role of relationships and policy networks of players, at whatever stage of the policy process, should never be underrated in assisting policy development and affecting its outcomes.[43] Aside from a minister or ministers, key players on just one policy project could include elected officials, public servants, interest groups, non-government organisations from the community, business and elsewhere, researchers, consultants and think tanks, and also the media. People who you know or have known in various capacities both inside and outside of government can often turn out to be valuable later on in assisting a policy agenda move on.

Informal networks of key players were especially important in putting long-term unemployment on the agenda early in the 1990s, where key ministerial advisers, bureaucrats and academics were in constant if informal contact.[44] But it also occurred in other cases, being particularly beneficial in the case of child support where informal contacts with the legal profession, social welfare and women's groups assisted in minimising adverse comments on the proposed reform.

Collaborating or "managing across" with people from other agencies inside of government to the outside, and vice versa, is needed if any complex policy issue is to move toward a resolution. But it needs to be a strategic process about: why collaboration is needed; when should this occur; with whom; and how. It may mean upfront informal bilateral discussions followed by broader collaborations depending on the sensitivity and complexity of the issue.

Policy advisers' networks have widened as the sources of policy advice to ministers have broadened. Although policy advising remains a major function of public servants, increasingly they compete with private and other non-government advisers.

Managing the researcher-policy practitioner interface

Not all research is or should be attempting to inform policy. And there currently exists a real conflict for those academics who, while wanting to have policy influence, face incentive structures in universities that emphasise publications in what are rated as quality journals.

There is considerable evidence that, if research is to inform policy, it is not the written word as much as dialogue, interaction (for example, in round tables) and continuing related mechanisms (and relationships) between policy practitioners and researchers that work best.[45] Moreover, that dialogue is helped if the matters discussed are of concern to the government of the day. Busy policy people will use trusted experts, but otherwise are not in the habit of reading what are often dense research papers.

None of the major social policy exercises in which I was involved would likely have seen the light of day without involvement of academic researchers at key stages in policy development. The success stories were of researchers going beyond their written words to interact and engage with policy-makers, and to convince them of the worth of their ideas. Hence the importance of dialogue and of building relationships and trust across the sectors, if not also being "boundary-riders".

In 2007 an ANZSOG project interviewed senior officials on both sides of the Tasman to find out what research processes they would most value. In the process the fragility of the academic-public servant relationship came to the fore, best illustrated by one humorous, if it were not so pointed, rhetorical question from a senior official: "What is the difference between an academic and a terrorist? You can negotiate with a terrorist". More positively, what they did identify as most needed were round tables with experts on matters of concern to them and also the use of knowledge brokers to assist in bridging the researcher-policy practitioner gap.[46]

If policy influence is the goal, then, as unpalatable as it may seem to some, research cannot be a stand-alone activity; it should, instead, be viewed, as policy-making is, more as a process. For research to affect policy, it needs to be part of the policy process and vice versa.

Nethercote has ruminated on this issue and queries whether academics should be involved in offering solutions to public policy problems other than in some incidental role:

> Where a university is better placed to make a contribution is less in prescription than in diagnosis, in responding to the question, what is the "mischief"?, leaving the question of what is the remedy to those with experience in the field.[47]

My case studies on developing policy indicate that policy ideas from academics can assist in advancing a policy. For example, the idea of using the tax system to assess and collect child support came from an American researcher. But that is not to deny that the greatest value of academic policy research usually comes in assisting in identification of the problem and in analysis, if not also evaluation.[48]

Being pragmatic and managing ambiguity

A policy idea can at times assist ministers get out of a bind with a particular problem that has so far not been resolved, but it rarely translates into practice without significant modification. Second best or even third best solutions may need to be accepted. Hence, anyone involved in the policy process needs to be pragmatic about what can be achieved, including dealing with trade-offs and ambiguity – from policy objectives to policy decisions. French, a former Minister in the Canadian government, refers to "fast and frugal forms of rationality that sacrifice any pretence to optimisation".[49]

Trade-offs are the name of the game for policy and political players. They come in many forms, for example, between exercising strong leadership and dealing collaboratively within networks; facing political demands, including short time-spans while also facing a shortage of resources; being responsive to a minister's agenda while the public support for it might be lacking; managing risk or fearing failure while also being innovative.

Relationships get tested when there is more than one person to whom you "manage up" – as a ministerial consultant working out of a department, I was answerable both to the public service head of the department as well as the minister. Similarly, I faced the same uncertainty when working from PM&C on youth allowance policy but reporting to a line minister who was assisting the Prime Minister on youth affairs.

A highly valued quality of a person who provides policy advice is good judgment. This is hard to define and is partly based on experience, but also in some ways it is innate. Good judgment relates to having clarity about the longer-term desired outcomes and being able to use both a strategic and tactical approach to get there, accepting trade-offs and being adaptable so as to take political sensitivities into account. An example would be involving those who are to be responsible for implementing a policy in the early stages of policy development, knowing when to listen and to take notice, and when to challenge them on possible implementation hurdles.[50]

There is a related need to be able to deal with ambiguity. A senior policy adviser will often leave a meeting with a minister or ministers without clarity around what was meant by what was said. How a policy adviser responds to that circumstance is obviously going to be critical. Good judgment is required on how to gain the needed clarification, including assessing whether the minister actually understood what was said at the briefing session, or simply judged it best politically not to have that clarification.

Concluding observations

Coming toward the end of my working life, most of which has been spent either assisting in development of policy or commenting on policy related processes and issues, I remain of the view that a policy development framework can be invaluable in contributing to good policy processes being followed. On its own, even as a normative framework, it can be rather sterile, if not simplistic to follow. As indicated above, organisational structures and processes within which policy analysis occurs is important; as also, is the combination of players for any policy exercise – ministers, their advisers, public servants, academics and other non-government players. An important reflection relevant to both academics wanting to be boundary players with the public sector and public servants wanting to be outward focused, is not to neglect the critical role that can be played by engaging in dialogue and interaction. Above all of this is the paramount importance of that least in control factor for policy advisers – the politics – which will determine whether policy progresses from stage to stage and, if it does, at what pace.

Let me end on a most salutary reflection: however hard you might try, any good policy outcome you may have had some input into can be eroded, if not reversed, sometime in the future. But, as this contribution has attempted to show, the more effort put into the process of developing policy, the more durable it is likely to be.

References

Althaus C., Bridgman P. and Davis G., (6TH edition), *The Australian Policy Handbook*, Allen and Unwin, Crows Nest, NSW, 2017.

ANZSOG, Research Reference Group, *Enhancing ANZSOG's Contribution to Better Government: future research directions*, October 2007.

Banks, Gary, *Successful Reform: Past Lessons, Future Challenges*, Keynote address to the Annual Forecasting Conference of the Australian Business Economists, Sydney, 8 December 2010.

Banks, Gary, *The Governance of Public Policy: Lectures in Honour of Eminent Australians*, ANZSOG, 2014.

Banks, Gary, "Whatever happened to 'Evidence based Policy making'"? Rattigan Lecture, 2018.

Beauchamp, Glenys, "The Role of Government in Innovation", in IPAA, *Twelve Speeches 2016: A Year of Speeches from Public Service Leaders*, IPAA, 2016.

Behm, Allan, *No, Minister: So You Want to Be a Chief of Staff?*, Melbourne University Press, Melbourne, 2015.

Bridgman, Peter and Davis Glyn, "What use is a policy cycle? Plenty: if the aim is clear", *Australian Journal of Public Administration*, 2003.

Bromwell David, *The Art and Craft of Policy Advising: A Practical Guide*, Springer International Publishing, New York, 2017.

Cairney Paul and Kwiatkowski Richard, "The politics of evidence-based policymaking: how can we maximize the use of evidence in policymaking?", *Palgrave Communications Special Issue*, Palgrave, 2017.

Colebatch, Hal (ed.), *Beyond the Policy Cycle: The Policy Process in Australia*, Allen and Unwin, Sydney, 2006.

Edwards, Meredith, with Howard Cosmo, Miller Robin, *Social policy, Public Policy: From Problem to Practice*, Allen and Unwin, Sydney, 2001.

Edwards, Meredith, "Ministerial Advisers and the Search for Accountability", *Canberra Bulletin of Public Administration*, 105, September 2002.

Edwards, Meredith, *Research Social Science and Public Policy: Narrowing the Divide*, Occasional Paper, Policy paper #2, Academy of the Social Sciences, 2004.

Edwards, "The Policy-Making Process" in Woodward, Dennis, Parkin Andrew and Summers, John, *Government, Politics, Power and Policy in Australia,*9th edition, Pearson Australia, Melbourne, 2010.

Edwards, Meredith, "Making Research more relevant to Policy: evidence and suggestions," in Bammer et al, *Bridging the "Know-do" Gap: Knowledge Brokering to Improve Child Well-being'*, ANU e-press, 2010.

Edwards, Meredith and Evans, Mark, *Getting Evidence into Policy Making,* ANZSIG Insights, Parliamentary Triangle Seminar Project, Canberra, March 2011.

Edwards M., Halligan J., Horrigan, B. and Nicoll G., *Public Sector Governance in Australia,* ANU e-press, 2012.

Edwards, Meredith and Stewart, Miranda, "Pathways and Processes toward a Gender Equality Policy', in Stewart, Miranda (ed.) *Tax, Social Policy and Gender,* ANU e-press, 2017.

Edwards, M, Head, B, Tiernan, A and Walter, J, "Policy Capacity Decline: trends, causes and remedies", Paper presented to the Australian Political Studies Association (APSA) Conference, Monash University, 25-27 September 2017.

Everett, S., "The Policy Cycle: democratic process or rational paradigm revisited", *Australian Journal of Public Administration,* 62(2), 2003.

French, Richard, "The Professors on Public life", *The Political Quarterly,* 83(3), 2012.

Head, Brian, "From Knowledge Transfer to Knowledge Sharing? Towards better links between policy and practice", in Bammer, Gabriele et al, *Bridging the "Know-do" Gap: Knowledge Brokering to Improve Child Well-being'*, ANU e-press, 2010.

Head, Brian, "Toward more 'Evidence-Informed' Policy Making?" *Public Administration Review,* 76(3), 2015.

Head, Brian and Crowley, Kate (eds.) *Policy Analysis in Australia,* Policy Press, Bristol, 2015.

Holland, Ian, "Parliamentary committees as an arena for policy work" in Colebatch H. (ed.), *Beyond the Policy Cycle: The Policy Process in Australia,* Allen and Unwin, Sydney, 2006.

Howard, Cosmo, "The Policy Cycle: a model of post-machiavellian policy making?', *Australian Journal of Public Administration,* 64(3), 2005.

Keating, Michael, "Defining the Policy Advising Function" in Uhr, John, and Keith McKay (eds), *Evaluating Policy Advice,* Federalism Research Centre, ANU, Commonwealth Department of Finance, 1996.

Kingdon, John, "Agenda", *Alternatives and Public Policies,* HarperCollins Australia, Sydney, 1995.

Mackie, Kathleen, "Success and Failure in Environment Policy: the role of policy officials", *Australian Journal of Public Administration,* 75(3), September 2016.

Maley, Maria, "Conceptualising Advisers' Policy Work: the distinctive policy roles of ministerial advisers in the Keating Government, 1991-96", *Australian Journal of Political Science,* 35(3), 2000.

McClelland Alison and Edwards Meredith, "The Policy Cycle in Theory and Practice", *Public Administration Today,* Issue 20, October-December 2009.

Nethercote, J. R, "What Servants are for", *Sydney Morning Herald Web Diary,* 27 June, 2002.

Newman, J., Cherney A, and Head B. W., "Do Policy Makers Use Academic Research? Reexamining the 'Two Communities Theory of Research Utilization'", *Public Administration Review,* October 2015.

Nutley, S. Walter, I and Davies, H., *Using Evidence: How Research Can Inform Public Services,* Policy Press, Bristol, UK, 2007.

Parkinson, Martin, IPAA Annual Address to the Public Service, in *Twelve Speeches 2016: A Year of Speeches from Public Service Leaders,* IPAA ACT Division, 2016.

Powell Alison, Davies Huw, Nutley, Sandra, "Missing in action? The role of the knowledge mobilisation literature in developing knowledge mobilisation practices", *Evidence and Policy,* 13(2), 2017.

Productivity Commission, *Shifting the Dial: 5 Year Productivity Review,* August 2017.

Shergold, Peter, *Learning from Failure: Why Large Government Policy Initiatives Have Gone So Badly Wrong in the Past and How the Chances of Success in the Future Can be Improved,* APSC, 2015.

Strangio, Paul, 'tHart, Paul, Walter, James, *The Pivot of Power,* The Miegunyah Press, Melbourne, 2017.

Varghese, Peter, "Parting Reflections', in *Twelve Speeches 2016: a year of speeches from public service leaders*, IPAA/ACT Division, 2016.

Weller, Patrick, "Policy professionals in context: advisors and ministers" in Crowley K and Head B (ed.), *Policy Analysis in Australia*, Policy Press, Bristol, UK, 2015.

Wilenski, Peter, *Public Power and Public Administration*, Hale and Iremonger, Sydney, 1986.

Wiltshire, Ken, *Public Policy Drift*, Public Policy Discussion Paper, IPAA, 4 April 2012.

Endnotes

1* An earlier version of this chapter was published by ANU Press in Trish Mercer et al., *Learning Policy, Doing Policy*, ANU Press, Canberra, 2021. I am grateful for insightful comments I received on an earlier draft of this chapter from Russell Ayres, Alison Smith, Trish Mercer, Jonathan Pincus and Pamela Burton. I remain responsible for any errors and all views expressed.

From 1984, ministers were able to appoint consultants who were not under the Public Service Act. In addition, "Consultants can, with the agreement of the department head, work within the department itself as additions to the public service staff numbers." See Peter Wilenski, *Public Power and Public Administration*, Hale and Iremonger, Sydney, 1986, 194.

2 John Nethercote is scathing when people use "reform" when they really mean "change". I use "reform" in the way that Gary Banks does: he suggests "reform" be used only to refer to policies which lead to change that is likely to bring a net benefit to the community over time. See *Successful Reform: Past Lessons, Future Challenges*, Keynote address to the Annual Forecasting Conference of the Australian Business Economists, Sydney, 8 December 2010, 4-5.

3 See, for example, Gary Banks, "Public Inquiries, Public Policy and the Public Interest," Inaugural Peter Karmel Lecture, Academy of Social Sciences in Australia, July, 2013,14; *The Governance of Public Policy: Lectures in Honour of Eminent Australians*, ANZSOG, 2014; David Donaldson, "'Urgent': former secretaries assess public service capability", *The Mandarin*, 12 February 2018, provides views from a range of ex-departmental secretaries, as well as Martin Parkinson, current Secretary, Department of Prime Minister and Cabinet.

4 Meredith Edwards, *et al.*, "Policy Capacity Decline: trends, causes and remedies", Paper presented to the Australian Political Studies Association Conference, Monash University, 25-27 September 2017.

5 Allan Behm, *No, Minister: So You Want to Be a Chief of Staff?* Melbourne University Press, Melbourne, 2015, 135-36; Productivity Commission, *Shifting the Dial: 5 year productivity review'*, August 2017, 198-200.

[6] Cited in Harley Dennett, "Get Ready for More Disruption: Parkinson floats national citizen survey", *The Mandarin,* 12 December 2017.

[7] Gary Banks, "Good processes underpin strong, innovative policy", *Australian Financial Review,* 22 March 2013, 2.

[8] Gary Banks, "Return of the Rent-Seeking Society", The Stan Kelly Lecture, The Economic Society of Australia, Melbourne, August 2013 in Banks, *The Governance of Public Policy,* 43.

[9] Brian Head, "Policy Analysis and Public Sector Capacity", in Brian Head and Kate Croley (eds.), *Policy Analysis in Australia,* Policy Press, Bristol, 2015, 53.

[10] See Catherine Althaus, Peter Bridgman, Glyn Davis, 2018, *The Australian Policy Handbook,* Allen and Unwin, 6th edition, 2018; Meredith Edwards, *Social Policy, Public Policy,* 2001.

[11] Cited in David Donaldson, "Be Responsive and don't be Rude: Nicola Roxon – advice to public servants", *The Mandarin,* 14 August 2017.

[12] Edwards 2010a, "The Policy Making Process" in Dennis Woodward et al, *Government, Politics, Power and Policy in Australia, 9th edition,* Pearson Australia, 425.

[13] See for example, Catherine Althaus, Peter Bridgman, Glyn Davis, *The Australian Policy Handbook,* 2018; Edwards, *Social Policy*; Meredith Edwards, *Social Science Research and Public Policy: Narrowing the Divide,* Occasional Paper, Policy paper #2, Academy of the Social Sciences, Canberra, 2004; Banks, *Successful Reform, 2010.* See also Ken Wiltshire, *Public Policy Drift,* Public Policy Discussion Paper, IPAA, 4 April 2012 and basis of Per Capita and Institute of Public Affairs Report, *Evidence Based Policy Research Project,* 2018.

[14] Edwards, *Social Policy,* 4.

[15] Althaus, Bridgman and Davis, *The Australian Policy Handbook,* 31.

[16] Michael Keating, "Defining the Policy Advising Function" in John Uhr and Keith McKay (eds.), *Evaluating Policy Advice,* Federalism Research Centre, ANU and Commonwealth Department of Finance, Canberra, 1996, 63; Banks, *Successful Reform,* 9; Althaus., *The Australian Policy Handbook,* 6th edition, 2017, 52.

[17] Colebatch, Hal, *Beyond the Policy Cycle: The Policy Process in Australia,* Allen and Unwin, Sydney, 2006.

[18] S. Everett, "The Policy Cycle: Democratic Process or Rational Paradigm Revisited?", *Australian Journal of Public Administration,* 6(2), 2003.

[19] See P. Bridgman and G. Davis, "What use is a policy cycle? Plenty: if the aim is clear", *Australian Journal of Public Administration,* 2003, 62, 3.101. Also, a similar point is made by Banks, Gary, "Whatever happened to "Evidence based Policy making""? Rattigan Lecture, 2018.

[20] See Edwards, *Social Policy,* 178

[21] John Kingdon, *"Agendas", Alternatives and Public Policies,* Harper and Collins, Sydney, 1995.

22 For example, in the case of the reform of youth allowances in the 1980's, in the absence of such ministerial guidance, at one stage, the relevant IDC put before ministers sixteen options also referring to numerous other options that could be considered. See Edwards, *Social Policy,* 2001, 29.

23 See examples in Edwards, *Social Policy,* 181.

24 See, for example, Behm, *No Minister,* 20.

25 Paul Cairney and Richard Kwiatkowski, "The politics of evidence-based policymaking: how can we maximize the use of evidence in policymaking?", *Palgrave Communications Special Issue,* Palgrave, 2017; Richard French, "The Professors on Public life", *The Political Quarterly,* 83(3), July-September 2012.

26 David Bromwell, *The Art and Craft of Policy Advising: A Practical Guide,* Springer International Publishing, New York, 2017, 95-6.

27 For example, see criteria used for Child Support and HECS in Edwards, *Social Policy,* 75-6; 115-6; 118.

28 Brian Head, "Toward More 'Evidence-Informed' Policy Making?", *Public Administration Review,* 2015, 76(3).

29 See, for example, Paul Strangio *et al., The Pivot of Power,* The Miegunyah Press, Melbourne, 2017, 227- 8.

30 See Working Nation example in Meredith Edwards, "Making Research more relevant to Policy: evidence and suggestions," in Bammer et al., "Bridging the 'know-do' gap: knowledge brokering to improve child well-being", ANU e-press, 2010, 59.

31 See Meredith Edwards., *Public Sector Governance in Australia,* ANU e-press, 2012, 53-172.

32 See, for example, Glenys Beauchamp, "The Role of Government in Innovation", November, in IPAA *Twelve Speeches 2016: a year of speeches from public service leaders,* IPAA, 2016, 90; Verona Burgess, "It has home-grown hindsight, but can the public change?" *The Mandarin,* 4 October 2017.

33 See Althaus et al., *The Australian Policy Handbook,* 169; Peter Shergold, *Learning from Failure: Why Large Government Policy Initiatives Have Gone So Badly Wrong in the Past and How the Chances of Success in the Future Can be Improved,* APSC, 2015, 26-30.

34 See Edwards., *Public Sector Governance,* 2012, 223; 230.

35 Edwards, "The Policy-Making Process" in Woodward *et al., Government, Politics, Power and Policy in Austral*ia, 421; Michael Keating, "The Productivity Commission on more Effective Government" Part 2 of 2, in *John Menadue – Pearls and Irritations,* 14 December 2017, 2.

36 See Althaus, et al, *The Australian Policy Handbook,* 14; Peter Shergold, *Learning from Failure,* 2015, 63-82; Productivity Commission, *Shifting the Dial,* 203.

37 See Behm, *No Minister,* 197-8.

[38] See, for example, Edwards, *Social Policy*, 185.

[39] Cited in Donaldson, "Be Responsive and Don't be Rude", 14 August 2017.

[40] See Maria Maley, "Conceptualising Advisers' Policy Work: the distinctive policy roles of ministerial advisers in the Keating Government, 1991-96", *Australian Journal of Political Science*, 35(3), 2000; J. R. Nethercote, "What Servants are for", *Sydney Morning Herald Web Diary*, 27 June, 2002; Meredith Edwards, "Ministerial Advisers and the Search for Accountability", *Canberra Bulletin of Public Administration*, 105, September, 2002; Ian Holland, "Parliamentary committees as an arena for policy work" in Hal Colebatch (ed.), *Beyond the Policy Cycle: The Policy Process in Australia*, Allen and Unwin, Sydney, 2006.

[41] Nethercote, "What Servants are for".

[42] Edwards, "Ministerial Advisers", 18.

[43] See Edwards, *Research Social Science and Public Policy*, 6; Behm, *No Minister*, 215-6; Althaus et al, *The Australian Policy Handbook*, 229-30.

[44] See examples in Edwards, *Social Policy*, 145-6, 188. Also, Meredith Edwards and Miranda Stewart, "Pathways and Processes toward a Gender Equality Policy", in Stewart, (ed.), *Tax, Social Policy and Gender*, ANU e-press, 2017, 341.

[45] For evidence, see: Sandra Nutley et al, *Using Evidence: how research can inform public services*, Policy Press, 2007; ANZSOG, *Enhancing ANZSOG's Contribution*, 2007; Brian Head, "From Knowledge Transfer to Knowledge Sharing?, Towards better links between policy and practice", in Bammer, *Bridging the "Know-do" Gap*; Head and Crowley (eds.), *Policy Analysis in Australia*. For discussion of the "spectrum" of interaction, see Gary Banks, "Could Academic Research be more Policy Influential? Commentary", in *Public Administration Review*, January/February 2016 and Joshua Newman et al, "Do Policy Makers use Academic Research", *Public Administration Review*, October 2015.

[46] ANZSOG, Enhancing ANZSOG's Contribution.

[47] J. R. Nethercote, "Academics are quite rightly kept away from policy meddling", *The Canberra Times*, 22 July 2011, Media Monitors,1.

[48] Edwards, "Making Research more Relevant to Policy", 59-61.

[49] French, "The Professors on Public life", 538.

[50] See, for example, child support case study in Edwards, *Social Policy*, 84; 95.

6

The Eclipse of Laissez Faire Utilitarianism

Loren E. Lomasky

Utilitarian transitions

Philosophers share with economic historians the puzzle of trying to make sense of Great Britain's post-1750 century-long efflorescence of robust free market liberalism which then, seemingly at its pinnacle of authority, rapidly crumbled under the assault of doctrines favourable toward state interventions into market arrangements. The reason that the puzzle is partly the property of philosophers is because both rise and decline occur under the predominant influence of utilitarianism. What features of utilitarianism render it, first, hospitable to *laissez-faire* but, then, to regimes of economic planning and redistribution? This essay represents a preliminary foray in exploration.

Because the realm of ideas is not autonomous, it is conceded at the outset that modifications in the views espoused by thinkers may have less to do with changes in the theory than with what is going on in the world. Certainly, during the long century in which, first, the waxing and, then, the waning of *laissez-faire* utilitarianism plays itself out, transmutation of the economic environment is profound. David Hume and Adam Smith write prior to the advent of the Industrial Revolution and the consequent transition to corporate capitalism. Their conclusions on economic matters assume a coincidence between ownership and management that weakens as managers replace entrepreneurs in executive seats. Control of impersonal corporate entities moves to the top of policy agendas.

Similarly, growth of labour unions increasingly supplants individual labour contracts. New realities rendered solutions to old problems moot.

No less profound in its implications is the maturation of the modern nation state. Hobbes's so-called leviathan was a functional pygmy by comparison with the bureaucratic managerial state that emerges during the 19th century. This was an age of technology, and technological spread was evident not only in mines and mills but also in the halls of government. Simply because state machinery had become so much more potent than was previously the case, putting it in gear to address situations that formerly had been beyond the domain of feasible political control became appealing if not, indeed, irresistible. Almost simultaneously we observe Bismarck's founding of a nascent welfare state, new parliamentary manufacturing and labour regulations for Britain, and the post-Civil War Slaughterhouse cases in the United States affirming the power of local governments to regulate trade and production. Governance of the advanced industrial powers of the West became increasingly democratic, and so pressures to serve the perceived interests of a broadened electorate multiplied. Alexis de Tocqueville observed that equality, even more than liberty, is the regnant ideal of democracies. It may, then, have been inevitable that stratagems for enhancing social and economic equality would move to the fore of political debate. In particular, socialism emerges as the idea of the age (or, rather, along with nationalism, one half of the pair of great ideas), initially in the scribbled musings of visionaries such as Claude-Henri de Saint-Simon and Karl Marx and, then, as the program of political parties seriously contending for governmental ascendancy.

That utilitarian prescriptions were influenced by these and other exogenous factors is hardly to be wondered at; what would have been remarkable is if theory had proven itself impervious to such seismic environmental tremors. This essay hereby acknowledges but will not further investigate their impact on utilitarian economic analysts. Instead, the focus will be on threads endogenous to utilitarian theory which, taken together, help to explain the journey away from what Adam Smith called a "system of natural liberty".

Who are the utilitarians?

If anyone is a utilitarian, then Jeremy Bentham, James Mill and John Stuart Mill are. Although they differ amongst themselves, their work defines the classical utilitarian paradigm. Nor is it controversial to include, within the next generation, Henry Sidgwick, William Stanley Jevons and Francis Edgeworth. Some may question, however, reading the tradition back to Hume and Smith. Contemporary taxonomists of the history of moral philosophy would be more comfortable classifying them as moral sentimentalists insofar as for each the foundation of judgments of approbation and disapprobation resides in innate human propensities either to share in or to spurn the affective responses of other individuals. Yet when Hume and Smith do institutional analysis, their assessments, almost without exception, are based on efficacy with regard to satisfying human preferences. Smith's classic work in economics is, from title page onward, concerned to investigate the conditions under which a nation's wealth is advanced or retarded. Wealth is not an ultimate value, but because it affords the means through which the needs and pleasures of the populace are served, studies undertaken in *The Wealth of Nations* merit a place within the moral sciences as much as do the chapters of *The Theory of Moral Sentiments*.

> Like Smith, Hume writes in opposition to mercantilist policies that place fetters on trade across borders.[1] His status as a proto-utilitarian is, however, most evident in his classification in A Treatise of Human Nature of justice as an "artificial virtue."[2]

Hume goes on to explain that justice and injustice predominantly concern title to property, and that rules governing ownership arise in response to impulses to conserve and increase wealth. These rules may bear little connection to our natural sentiments of approbation, thus the classification of justice as artificial. Regard for principles of justice is nurtured by moral education that might well go against the grain of people's instinctive responses. Hume gives the example of returning lost property to its rightful owner, a heedless wastrel, who will surely squander it. The virtue of justice requires us to rise above our immediate inclination to place the property in worthier hands and instead observe the rules governing ownership. These in turn are justified by the fact that security of possession under a law that is no respecter of persons generally conduces to human well-being. Here, as with Smith's endorsement of wealth-creating policies, we observe a moral stance that can, without distortion, be dubbed utilitarian.

It would be unprofitable to use this occasion to wrangle about fine points in the definition of utilitarianism. Nor is it necessary to limn a bright line separating utilitarian theories from those to be filed away in some other ideological pigeonhole. For present purposes, a theory is said to be (more or less) utilitarian to the extent that it satisfies the following eight conditions, ordered roughly in descending importance:

1. *Consequentialism.* The rightness or wrongness of actions, desirability or undesirability of rules, admirability or unattractiveness of dispositions of character, and similar appraisals are ultimately a function of the nature of the consequences they actually, probably, or for the most part generate. It may be more perspicuous to phrase the condition negatively: nothing other than the quality of consequences is an ultimate determinant of moral value.

2. *Comparativeness.* Evaluations are comparative. The recommended action, rule, disposition, etc., is that which achieves a consequential pay-off higher than that of feasible alternatives. So, for example, an action that generates considerable misery will be the right action should it be the case that all other actions open to the agent would produce yet greater misery; one that yields joy for thousands is wrong if another course yields joy for millions.

3. *Individualism.* The units of utility are reckoned in the coin of the well-being of distinct individuals. In classical versions of utilitarianism these units are pleasure/absence of pain; subsequent formulations fasten on preference-satisfaction as basic.

4. ***Universalism.*** Everyone's well-being matters. This is laudably simple. Not so simple, however, is nailing down the scope of "everyone." Does "everyone" include/exclude non-human animals, potential but non-actual persons, and so on? Different thinkers advance different scope judgments.

5. ***Aggregationism.*** Overall social assessments (also known as "social welfare functions") are an additive function of the well-being of all affected parties. Each is to count equally with every other. However, because the capacity of some to experience pleasure/satisfy important preferences may be greater than that of others, it does not follow that these "equal" parties will enjoy similar influence within the calculus.

6. ***Determinacy.*** There exists, at least in principle, a decision-procedure for determining between any actions, rules, etc., which is to be preferred. That is, there cannot exist a situation in which there does not exist among an agent's/legislator's alternatives a right one.

7. ***Interpersonal comparability.*** There exists some rationally ascertainable metric, not necessarily fine-grained, in terms of which benefits/harms to the affected parties can be weighed against each other pursuant to aggregation.

8. ***Cardinality.*** Well-being measures of individuals and across individuals can be arrayed not merely on a greater/less than scale (ordinal comparison) but on an absolute scale (compare to height and weight).

The classical utilitarians satisfy all eight of the conditions, although it needs to be said Mill's addition to the hedonic mix of a qualitative dimension of higher/lower pleasures may render cardinality problematic. A. G. E. Moore-style utilitarianism[3] that recognises valuable items other than subjective conscious states deviates modestly from the utilitarian paradigm; yet further toward the periphery but still recognisably utilitarian in impulse are Kaldor-Hicks welfare economics and cost-benefit analysis. Paretianism is situated a further hop from the centre.

Reversing chronology, Hume and Smith are, if not utilitarians, then proto-utilitarians, especially insofar as their theories appraise economic institutions.[4] It is, then, not unduly strained to give them early position on a line that extends through Bentham, the Mills, and beyond.

Utilitarian transformations

The analysis that follows identifies six attributes of classical utilitarianism and its offshoots that help to explain its transformation into a handmaiden for the managerial and redistributive state. It is not claimed that any one of these by itself, or even all six taken together, are sufficient to effect that transformation. Rather, they are better understood as conditions promoting susceptibility to new currents. Thus, as fashions in politics and economics change, utilitarianism does not exert a conservative drag but rather is readily hitched to the wagon of a "progressive" agenda.

Utilitarian flexibility

Of all moral theories, utilitarianism is the most protean. It can be put to the service of any cause for which relevant consequentialist calculations yield the requisite sums. In this respect it is unlike theories which, in Nozick's words, feature "side-constraints" on permissible action.[5] A side-constraint is a rule or protection that rules out otherwise feasible courses. In Nozick's own libertarian theory, side-constraints are the reflection of individuals' Lockean rights to life, liberty and property. No matter how attractive it is to perform action A, should it be in violation of someone's rights, then one must refrain from A.

Rights theory is not the only conception of ethics in which side-constraints feature prominently. Kant's Categorical Imperative stands athwart all intended programs that cannot be consistently universalised. So, for example, Kant himself took this to imply that, regardless of consequentialist pay-offs, one may never lie to promote someone's happiness or commit suicide in order to escape the pain of further life.

Natural law ethics maintains that reason is privy to moral norms that obtain at all places and times. Natural law is superior even to positive law as a regulator of personal conduct. Its dictates are overriding. Virtue ethics insists that one ought in all circumstances to act as the virtuous agent would, and its usual formulations go on to argue that dispositions of loyalty, temperance, justice and so on decline to bend to temptations to adopt unworthy means to secure undisputed goods.

It should be noted that for all of these theories, consequentialist assessment is acknowledged to play an important role in the lives of individuals and polities. It is reasonable, all else equal, to aim for the result that promises the greatest balance of good over bad. Only for the utilitarian, though, for whom the greatest happiness of the greatest number stands as supreme law, is the *ceteris paribus* clause dispensable.

Critics frequently attack utilitarianism's willingness to bend strictures of permissibility. Utilitarians will, it is alleged, intentionally frame an innocent man for a capital crime if the resultant gain in civic peace is positive. Similarly, it will countenance slavery, dispossession, torture and the like whenever the sums work out.

Against this sort of stylised critique utilitarians adopt one of two defensive strategies. The first is to observe that if *all* the effects are given due consideration (for example, chance of being detected, establishing damaging precedents, corruption of character, etc.) it is almost never the case that framing the innocent will optimise utility. If, however, the situation is known to be truly exceptional, then one must bite the bullet and undertake what ordinarily must not be done.

The second defensive strategy is to maintain that ethics proceeds not case-by-isolated-case but rather as a matter of affirming and respecting rules governing interactions. Because regularities are fundamental to moral assessment, the proper target of utilitarian calculation should, therefore, be the rules promulgated by societies and also those to which individuals subscribe in governing their personal conduct. Thus, if "Punish only the guilty" is a rule the utility benefits of which are manifest, then utilitarian assessment itself prohibits framing the innocent.

These two strategies are adopted, respectively, by *act utilitarianism* and *rule utilitarianism*, each of which is represented in the literature by innumerable variants. Although the rule variant is more conservative in its implications for conformity to standard moral practice, it is important to note that even rule utilitarianism is potentially revolutionary. As conditions and capabilities change, rules that formerly served utility may no longer continue to do so. The utilitarian will, therefore, be willing to support fundamental transformations of the norms that regulate societies.

The fundamental question for the utilitarian as with the engineer is: What works? This cannot be effectively answered merely by inspecting venerable precedent but instead requires constant exploration and experiment. Hume and Smith themselves are radical innovators in calling for relaxation of restraints on the flow of specie as well as general expansion of the liberties of labour and capital. A century later the reigning orthodoxy is more Manchester than mercantilism, and it is not surprising that the philosophically radical J. S. Mill calls into question several of its settled precepts. Against other Ricardians, he rejects in *Principles of Political Economy* the fixed-by-nature status of laws of distribution:

> The laws and conditions of the production of wealth, partake of the character of physical truths. There is nothing optional or arbitrary in them. Whatever mankind produce, must be produced in the modes and under the conditions imposed by the constitution of external things, and by the inherent properties of their own bodily and mental structure . . .

> But it is not so with the Distribution of Wealth. That is a matter of human institution solely. The things once there, mankind, individually or collectively can do with them as they like.

Matters of human institution are just the sort of thing one would expect to be capable of continuous improvement as scientific knowledge expands and the civilising effects of mass education are felt. Accordingly, Mill does not feel bound by the practice of prior generations. He explores with no little sympathy alternatives to private property regimes. Although he declares himself a "socialist,"

Mill is in no sense doctrinaire; about the only structure he rejects out of hand is generalised state ownership of the means of production.[6] In these gentle pre-Leninist days, "socialism" seems to have meant for Mill some device for furthering the formation of moderate-sized workers' cooperatives.[7] It excludes neither individual ownership stakes nor competition among firms. Moreover, there exists a presumption in favour of maintaining the existing scheme of property rights because, according to classical utilitarian theorists, the pleasure of experiencing an increase in one's condition is less intense than the pain of an equal-magnitude worsening. Still, the presumption is defeasible. Where adjustments can be achieved with minimal disruption to the pursuits of affected parties, social experimentation is not only acceptable but welcomed. So, for example, Mill advocates progressive death duties to go along with industrial reform, both in the service of enhanced self-directedness on the part of the working class. Consequentialist calculation is multiply speculative. It not only incorporates contestable causal predictions but additionally rests on uncertain judgments about how to measure individual utilities. It is not, I hope, unfair to say that utilitarians more than most theorists are in a position to make it up as they go. No prodigies of imaginative dexterity are needed to justify an appealing action or policy by contriving a plausible story that makes it the winner in the utility sweepstakes. Whether the desired result be war against the hated foe, peace in our time, eugenic selection, socialism or, for that matter, free market capitalism, there exists a utilitarian-endorsed causal avenue which arguably takes one just there and nowhere else.

It is not necessary to embrace the cynicism of the Stalinist recipe for making omelettes by breaking a few eggs to be willing to countenance incursions on some for the sake of others. Nor need one suspect that utilitarians are invested with less integrity or more gullibility than their theoretical opponents.

The point is that when outcomes and outcomes alone rule, then there is no independent check on means alleged to take one there. This is the other respect in which utilitarianism and other strains of consequentialism are uniquely protean. When a nostrum widely heralded as the wave of the future sweeps into public view, utilitarian evaluators will, understandably, be disposed to view it as validated by impersonal ethical criteria. This will especially be the case when alterations to the external environment or technologies of social melioration render the proposal one concerning which history does not speak in an unequivocal voice.

It is easy for 21st century analysts to condescend to socialist enthusiasts of the 19th. They, unlike us, did not have the example of central planning in Cuba, North Korea and, especially, the Soviet Union, to offer a salutary caution. Utilitarianism unlike, say, rights theory, is entirely prospective,[8] and therefore it is prone to all the errors – but also the insights – of the social science of the day.

Utilitarian privilege

Many ethical theories, Kant's most conspicuously, feature prescriptions that hold for all human beings (indeed, in Kant's case, all rational beings whatsoever). Utilitarianism, at least in its more sophisticated versions, is not among these. Rather, according to utilitarianism, it may prove to be the case that procedures which are off-limits to most people may be acceptable when undertaken by a moral elite.[9]

For example, it may be optimific that most people regard property holdings as something close to sacrosanct, not subject to infringement without the owner's consent. However, an agent possessed of an exceptional degree of discernment – whether Robin Hood or bureaucrat – may be in a position expeditiously to juggle property holdings for the sake of the greater good. All people need to be guided by rules of some kind or other, but those of keen mind are capable of grasping the import of subtle conditionals that would mystify the ordinary run of human beings. The mid-20th century utilitarian, R. M. Hare, renders the difference in acuity as between "archangels" and "proles,"[10] with the former entitled to employ a degree of discretion barred to the latter. The upshot of utilitarian privilege is that precepts may permissibly be publicly endorsed by the cognoscenti as incumbent on all even if they hold themselves immune from its dictates. (Compare to Plato's philosopher-kings who, in *The Republic*, spin "Noble Lies" in service to the polity.) This is not to be understood as hypocrisy – a vice to which theorists of all persuasions are vulnerable – but as a strict implication of utilitarian optimisation.[11]

To the extent that adherence to norms is a necessary condition of moral behaviour, there exists a conservative tendency in all theories of ethics. That is because the only norms to which people are in a position to adhere are those that precede their activities. The experience of an earlier age always conditions demands on the present; the future is mute. Because of time's directionality, this asymmetry cannot be evaded. Theorists who understand the nature of the bias can act to compensate for it by exempting themselves or a chosen elite from its strictures, however. A "vanguard" of acknowledged "best and brightest" will be granted privileges withheld from the masses.[12]

There exists, of course, the considerable technical problem of identifying the members of the elite and ascertaining that their motives are, indeed, congruent with concern for the general happiness. What bears emphasis is that this is, indeed, a technical problem and not a contradiction within the underlying theory. Just as classical economists acknowledge a division of labour within the economy, sophisticated utilitarianism recognises a division of moral labour within the populace. Those who are capable of navigating independently of homely moral precepts are afforded liberty to do so. What matters is progress, not adherence to the dead hand of the past.

Emergence of the bureaucratic state managed by a technocratic elite conduces to privilege. Public servants occupy their positions not in virtue of some antiquated, corrupt spoils system but on the basis of merit. If any are to be judged capable of exercising discretion on behalf of the general good, who has better entitlement to that status? Especially insofar as their positions do not allow them easily to enrich themselves but do give them considerable latitude to utilise their expertise so as to act on behalf of the public, it may seem pathologically hidebound, not to mention counterproductive, to confine within narrowly defined pathways limits on the ability of public servants to serve the general weal.

Whatever else utilitarians might be, they are not hidebound. If they spot an opportunity to accrue additional quanta of utility, they are disposed to pounce. Accordingly, they are apt to identify themselves as proponents of expertise-based privilege. The central privilege is to rearrange social structures, at least on an experimental basis, in quest of superior outcomes impersonally considered. Utilitarians, while recognising the importance to prosperity and stability of the rule of law, are also inclined to combine that with tolerance for technocratic discretion. That there may be a severe tension between these two strands was not clearly spelled out prior to Hayek's *The Road to Serfdom*.

Human (in)equality

A lively topic of debate throughout the modern period is the sources of human inequality: inherent or a function of environmental factors? The early utilitarians by and large plumped for the latter. Smith opines:

> The difference of natural talents in different men is, in reality, much less than we are aware of; and the very different genius which appears to distinguish men of different professions, when grown up to maturity, is not upon many occasions so much the cause as the effect of the division of labour. The difference between the most dissimilar characters, between a philosopher and a common street porter, for example, seems to arise not so much from nature, as from habit, custom, and education.[13]

If human beings are inherently equal along most relevant dimensions, then several conclusions hospitable to a free order suggest themselves. First, as Locke had previously observed, no one possesses an inherent authority to rule over others. Their natural political condition is one of equality.[14]

Second, it follows that each possesses a fundamental right to the exercise of his own labour and to dispose as he may see fit of its product. Decisions about consumption and investment properly reside in the hands of each individual and those with whom they contract. Whether or not based on Locke's model of human beings in a state of nature, this is the essence of Smith's "system of natural liberty."

Utilitarianism meshes uneasily with theories of natural rights (one thinks of Bentham's dismissal of "nonsense on stilts"), and so it would be an error to extrapolate directly from Lockean to Smithian equality. The latter is not a metaphysical precept grounded in God's universal patrimony but rather is set forth as an empirical datum. Moral dicta do not follow directly therefrom (recall Hume's strictures about deriving an "ought" from an "is"), but when placed within a utilitarian normative framework, human equality is, arguably, supportive of economic freedom.

The classical utilitarians are not of one mind concerning whether man is uniformly egoistic in motivation, but all concur that self-love is a powerful spur to activity. People can be relied on to act in their own self-interest. They will not always be prudent, nor will they always accurately appraise the factors necessary for them to achieve success in their chosen endeavours, but always they will be assiduous in desiring to advance their condition. Not even the most well-meaning of onlookers will wish their good with equal intensity. Accordingly, all else equal, each individual should be left at liberty to pursue her own good (Jefferson's "pursuit of happiness") howsoever she sees fit.[15]

The point of the premise of empirical equality is that, at bottom, all else *is in fact* equal. Developed talents distinguish and set human beings apart one from another, but these differences are wider than they are deep. The street porter may never become a philosopher, but he can come to learn to use various of the philosopher's techniques of practical logic in his own pursuits. The best teacher is his own experience. Because individuals have a settled interest in their own advancement, they are continually impelled to develop their capacities – in contemporary parlance, their "human capital" – so as more effectively to avail themselves of whatever opportunities present themselves. For this an order of freedom, economic and otherwise, is requisite. Paternalism exercised by one's supposed betters is apt to be counterproductive insofar as it works against the lessons that would otherwise be provided by the sting of failed experiments. No one has put this more powerfully than Mill:

He who lets the world, or his own portion of it, choose his plan of life for him, has no need of any other faculty than the ape-like one of imitation. He who chooses his plan for himself, employs all his faculties. He must use observation to see, reasoning and judgment to foresee, activity to gather materials for decision, discrimination to decide, and when he has decided, firmness and self-control to hold to his deliberative decision … It is possible that he might be guided in some good path, and kept out of harm's way, without any of these things. But what will be his comparative worth as a human being? It really is of importance, not only what men do, but also what manner of men they are that do it.[16]

Conversely, with one important exception, when the task of tending to people's well-being is exported to the state, it will be pursued with less knowledge, energy, and steadiness. That one exception is education of the young. Because people are mostly similar in their raw state, the appropriate way to add value is to invest in their nurture when the rate of return on that investment is greatest. Mill maintains that parents have a strict duty to educate their children so as to enable them to be self-directed choosers of their own path within the greater society. The state's role is to enforce that duty, as it enforces all other justified claims, and to subsidise families that lack the means to purchase competent instruction. It is not to supplant the parental role by itself supplying educational services which, Mill fears, would then be a further source of imposed conformity.

Mill was the last of the classical utilitarian theorists most of whose most important works were produced prior to the appearance of Darwin's *The Origin of Species* (1859). Darwin's most enthusiastic receptors became persuaded of the overriding importance of inheritance. Natural selection is the mechanism through which species set themselves apart but also, claimed the Darwinists, through which individual species members are set apart. It was evident to the crudest empiricism – and, with the benefit of hindsight, we might say *only* to the crudest empiricism – that human beings are arrayed into distinct races, that these races differ appreciably with regard both to somatic and mental qualities, and that within each race there exists a similar range of abilities fixed by nature and relatively impervious to meliorative environmental engineering. Ironically, in the country that two centuries previously pioneered resistance to natural hierarchy, the fresh idea that enlivened the intellectual classes was the inexorability of human inequality.

The theory of evolution applied to human affairs yielded doctrines of racialism, eugenics and Social Darwinism. These substantially penetrated classical economic thinking[17] but, even less overtly, Darwinist thinkers took to heart the message of inequality. If people are arrayed on an impermeable continuum of ability, then a social policy predicated on the fiction of human equality is certain to be less effective at securing human happiness than one more realistically grounded.

Exacerbating the problem of producing a desirable product from a mixed bag of raw material is the ideology of a democratic age. In Britain and the United States, representative institutions were too deeply entrenched to be altogether circumvented by reformers, but enlightened thinkers endorsed correctives to a crude majoritarianism in which the votes of congenital dunces carry equal weight with those perched at the apex of evolution, that is, themselves. The utilitarian predilection for direction by technocratic elites is, then, reinforced by the onrush of Darwinian enthusiasms. Not only is the elite currently capable of guiding affairs better than can ordinary citizens, but their status as the highest product of evolution ensures that it will always be so. Street porters, the children of street porters, and their children's children, will never be capable of fulfilling the functions of philosophers. Indeed, imposition of egalitarianism can only be frustrating to them. Better to centralise social planning and to, to the greatest extent feasible, remove from untutored hands decisions more skilfully made by experts.

To avert possible confusion, I note that the advent of Darwinism does not strictly entail a program of restricted economic freedom. On the contrary, some important utilitarian evolutionists, most conspicuously Herbert Spencer, remain true to a doctrine of robust *laissez-faire*.[18] Insofar, however, as there exists a predisposition within utilitarianism to engineer from above (e.g., Bentham's proposals for penal reforms, Mill's partiality toward socialist experimentation), Darwinism provides a "scientific" rationale for that practice.

Marginalism

The marginalist revolution that gives birth to neo-classical economics occurs in the same decade as Mill's death. The entrance of the one and exit of the other is, if nothing more, symbolic of a sea change in thinking about the role of the state in effecting economic progress. The old Ricardian school taught the world about limits. Its predominant message was the futility if not the perverse consequences of state intrusion into production and exchange. The new economics offers expansion of limits. Because parties adjust their behaviour at the margin, no revolutionary upset is needed to bring about significant improvements in outcomes. Slight alterations in the parameters confronting decision-makers can in fact lead them to adopt policies substantially more conducive to public good. The models developed by Menger, Jevons, Walras, and their neo-classical successors set out the conditions under which markets efficiently allocate goods with a heretofore unachieved precision and rigour. Under conditions of perfect competition in which property rights are well-defined, buyers and sellers are numerous and thus unable to affect prices, all parties possess full and equal knowledge, transaction costs are zero, and change is instantaneous, free markets operate without blemish. The converse is that where one or more of these conditions fail to obtain – that is, to a greater or lesser extent in all actual markets – then decentralised exchange relationships operate imperfectly: thus the (unfortunately named) theory of "market failure."

It is not as if the classical utilitarian economists were oblivious to ways in which the invisible hand of the market can be steadied by timely assistance from the visible hand of government. Smith, for example, writes about the necessary role of the state in providing what later came to be known as public goods and in superintending the supply of money, qualifications albeit peripheral to the theory of free markets.

The new economics repositioned them at the core. Virtually no branch of exchange was without imperfections that could not, in theory, be smoothed by intervention. The "in theory" qualifier is important because among the theorist's deviation are some that are strictly ineliminable: knowledge is never fully and equally possessed by all transactors nor can adjustments to change be made to occur instantaneously. But flaws not altogether eliminable can be reduced via active governmental intervention. Informational deficits, for example, can be addressed through requirements of mandatory information provision and product standardisation. Even where the state does not intervene, either out of technical or political constraints, there exists a presumption of the acceptability of intervention should the political or technological landscape shift. *Laissez-faire* was at best a handy rule of thumb, at worst an outmoded dogma that hindered human improvement.

Transformation of capitalist production over the course of the 19th century enhanced apprehensions of market failure. The gospel of economic freedom had drawn power in its infancy from campaigns against the inefficiencies and injustices of crown-conferred monopoly. But the new railroads, utilities and other mega-corporations that gave the appearance of being natural monopolies spoke against the adequacy of unregulated markets. Similarly, increasing velocity of information and transportation flows enabled individual companies to capture greater market share and thus to enjoy power to set terms of trade with which others must comply willy-nilly. Industrial labour unions also rendered the old models irrelevant through their capacity to monopolise the supply of workers and thus block free exchange of labour for wages. It was not that advanced economic theorists had given up on the salutary effects of competition where it existed, but they came to believe that governmental regulation was necessary to avert collusion and protect consumers from exploitation. The state had become the guardian, not the scourge, of economic competition.

Calculation at the margin is especially relevant to considerations of wealth effects on individual happiness. It was already a commonplace for the classical economists that an increment of income to the poor generates more utility than does the same amount coming to the rich, and so an equal society tends to be a happier society. The new economics was, however, able to develop mathematically sophisticated distributive models displaying the utility consequences of wealth transfers. Innovations such as individual income tax and social insurance rendered it possible to put these abstract models into effect. To be sure, these theorems of welfare economics presupposed equal capacity to generate utility among human beings, and the Darwinian anti-egalitarian hypotheses mentioned in the previous section called that into question. Rearguard actions in defence of old-fashioned *laissez-faire* could, then, be fought in opposition to siphoning off resources to lower orders too insensate to turn them into high-quality pleasures.

That is not the whole story, however, about the relationship between Darwinism and redistribution. Activist policies endorsing in-kind transfers of various merit goods to the poor (education, arts, uplift programs) rather than purchasing power which they would predictably squander express the spirit of inherited inequality. The upshot is, again, pursuit of an ethical ideal via greater governmental involvement in people's lives.

The elusive self

"[W]ith respect to his own feelings and circumstances, the most ordinary man or woman has means of knowledge immeasurably surpassing those that can be possessed by anyone else," avers Mill in defence of his core claim that interference with self-regarding behaviour is liable to be utility-diminishing.[19] The conception of the self in play here is of an entity transparent, except perhaps in unusual circumstances, to introspection. Hume's empiricism of impressions and ideas that exhaust the components of the self supports transparency as does the associationist psychology of James Mill.

During the course of the 19th century, however, this strand of empiricism falls increasingly under suspicion. Ironically, Wilhelm von Humboldt, along with Harriet Taylor, the cited inspiration of *On Liberty*, shares much of the blame. Humboldt advances an organic conception of the unfolding self in which achieving one's highest good requires full and free flowering of the unique potential that makes one the precise individual who one is. Toward this end liberty from outsiders' artificial constraints and shackles is absolutely necessary for personal flourishing.[20] It is, of course, this theme that Mill orchestrates so skilfully in *On Liberty*. What neither he nor Humboldt grasps, however, is that the implications of the organic model are not unambiguously friendly to individual liberty.[21]

The individual complete in her flourishing may be fully aware of the goods that constitute the excellences of her life, but immature beings are precisely those that have not adequately developed the attributes that will mark their mode of achievement. Therefore, they may be entirely acquainted with the pleasures that now appeal, but they do not enjoy any privileged access to those in which their fully formed selves will revel – provided, that is, that the fully formed self is not derailed by the immature self's refusal to put away the trinkets of childhood so as to move on to a higher condition of being. It could be argued, moreover, that the individual is the one *least able* to grasp what constitutes her fulfillment because future possibilities invariably are veiled and distorted by current satisfactions. For the organic self, then, there exists no presumption of superior first-person insight.

As Hegelian Idealism made its way across the Channel to influence and merge with British utilitarianism in the works of thinkers such as T. H. Green and Bernard Bosanquet, first-person prerogative receded yet further. The self that appears to introspective consciousness, the empirical self, is distinct from and of lesser normative authority than the ideal self (latent in the manner that the adult is present but unactualised in the infant).[22] If the person that appears to me is not the one that in the truest sense is me, then the choices of the former do not carry determinative weight over the condition of the latter. "I know my own good" is ambiguous because the "I" that claims to know is not the being to whom the good redounds – at least prior to the person's emergence from epistemic immaturity. It is, then, the task of well-meaning others to provide direction and sustenance to those who are emerging from the chrysalis of their own dependency. Just as the flower will not bloom unless the seed falls on fertile ground and is sustained by life-giving waters, so, too, will human beings wither if they are not provided with an environment in which their potentialities might come to fruition. Even the metaphor of plant and the soil in which it grows understates the dependency, because it misrepresents as two distinct entities a unitary continuum. Man is not distinct from the society in which he is embedded and so, when the social order prescribes a direction to be followed, this is not to be thought of as one party exercising compulsion over another. It is the whole seeing to the part, and the part contributing to the ac- tualisation of the whole. We have come rather a long way from Mill's one simple principle of liberty.

The romanticist/Hegelian self is less prominent as a player in the market than in other areas of social policy. Insofar, however, as it undercuts the authority of consent, it calls into question the ethical underpinnings of freedom of contract. Mill himself denied that the doctrine of freedom went so far as to allow a man to sell himself into slavery; why, then, should it be thought to justify wage slavery? In the interests of people's true selves, they may permissibly be blocked from entering into economic arrangements inimical to their self- actualisation. And since they themselves are denied the perspective from which they can see the rationale for such protections, the more finely honed moral sense of elites must be harnessed on their behalf.

Coupled with themes adduced in the preceding two sections, the doctrine of the elusive self provided a further step toward the legitimacy of a managerial elite.

Fabian socialism

Ultimately, the *coup de grace* to classical liberalism was dealt by socialism's capture of the British utilitarian tradition, especially in the form of the Fabian Society. Spearheaded by Sidney and Bea- trice Webb, and drawing in luminaries such as George Bernard Shaw and H. G. Wells, the Fabians exemplified a distinctively British socialism. Short on the prolix theory that renders Marx's *Kapital* and the byzantine musings of his disciples almost unread- able, the Fabians specialised in straightforward consequentialist reasoning concerning how the ills of the capitalist system could be mended. Non-revolutionary in tone and non-threatening in manner, Fabians presented themselves as can-do thinkers able and willing to meet the demand for reform measures. Their socialism was not so much a rejection of liberalism as it was a further twist to the new liberalism that came to prominence in the years after J. S. Mill's death. What Bentham was to the beginning of the century, they were to its close.

What made Fabian socialism flourish? Not mass membership; the Fabians were always a select group of upper middle-class intellectuals who proselytised predominantly among their social peers. This was not a liability but an asset. Unlike Marxians promoting revolution from below, Fabians were tinkerers from above. It was almost impossible to be alarmed by those of the mild mien of the Webbs – at least not until, in old age, they became credulous devotees of the shining new society to the east being engineered by Stalin. Hardly threats to the establishment, they were unmistakably of it.

Second, their energy was prodigious. For almost half a century the Webbs and their associates produced tract after tract addressing the questions of the day. They never lacked of an abundance of views. Their social contacts were impeccable, extending not only throughout the intelligentsia but also to leading political figures among the Tories and Liberals as well as Labour. Even where their voice was not decisive, it was heard. Moreover, they tended prudently to their institutional base, founding the London School of Economics in 1895 and providing publication outlets for succeeding generations of gifted aspiring social reformers. The upshot was that they were at the intellectual centre of a transforming Britain. Even those who broke with the Fabians did not reach back to what seemed the hopelessly antiquated principles of classical liberalism but, instead, turned to alternative paths of social reconstruction. The long march from Hume and Smith to the cusp of the 20th century was complete.[23]

Postscript: utilitarianism and *laissez-faire* today

Remarkably, the classical liberalism that, a century ago, seemed as dead as Herbert Spencer, is once again a vigorous contender in the

ideological and philosophical wars. After a long and lingering ill-
ness, socialism expired in 1989, mourned by coteries of academics
in American and European humanities departments but few others.
Even the expansive welfare state is under duress from theorists and
political activists and commentators brimming with confidence that
they can redirect a social vehicle that went off course when Victoria was Queen. The recrudescence of classical liberalism is a tale
well worth the telling, but not here and now. Instead, I close with the
question: Is utilitarianism apt to be of significant support to the new
libertarianism of the 21st century?

Prominent contemporary classical liberals, including Richard
Epstein, David Friedman and, especially, F. A. Hayek, are self-
described "utilitarians." Without denying their entitlement to attach
to themselves whichever labels suit their fancy, this is a utilitarianism
of the "Free-markets-yield-terrific-results!" sort, not studied attention
to theoretical underpinnings. I believe that they call themselves
utilitarians mostly by way of distinction from Randian or natural
law absolutisms, not because of a commitment to the enterprise
of measuring and then aggregating welfare totals and advancing
normative judgments accordingly. There is no doubt that in some
sense their respective stances are consequentialist, but I believe them
too unspecified to admit of any finer categorisation.

But even if contemporary libertarianism has not yet been
recreated on sophisticated utilitarian foundation, the question
remains whether the project is feasible. My answer is, in a word,
no. The feature of utilitarianism most inimical to liberalism is
aggregationism. The utilitarian is prepared to countenance the
imposition of sacrifices on some whenever compensating benefits
will accrue to others. In Rawls's words, utilitarianism does not take
with sufficient seriousness the separateness of persons.[24]

Although Rawls's liberal theory of justice aims to distinguish
from utilitarianism is on the opposite end of the liberal spectrum
from libertarianism, his critique applies with equal force to so-
called classical liberal utilitarians (who might less misleadingly
be classified as rule Paretians). What the renaissance of classical
liberalism does indicate, however, is that the swing away from *laissez*

faire by post-Millian utilitarianism was based on questionable judgments about what can be achieved through market orders and what by governmental managerialism. Utilitarianism may never again be the closest philosophical ally of classical liberalism, but neither is it likely to become its most formidable foe.

Endnotes

[1] A valuable collection of Hume's occasional pieces is *Essays: Moral, Political, and Literary*, ed. Eugene Miller, Liberty Press, Indianapolis, 1987. See, especially, "Of Commerce," 253-67; "Of Money," 281-94; "Of the Balance of Trade," 308-326; "Of the Jealousy of Trade," 327-31.

[2] See *Treatise* Bk II, Part II, Section 1, "Justice, whether a natural or artificial virtue," Selby-Bigge, ed., 477-84.

[3] See *Principia Ethica*, 1903.

[4] So, too, is the moral sense theorist and teacher of Adam Smith, Francis Hutcheson, who declares in *An Inquiry into the Original of our Ideas of Beauty and Virtue*, "That Action is best which accomplishes the greatest Happiness for the greatest Numbers; and that worst, which in like manner, occasions misery."

[5] Robert Nozick, *Anarchy, State, & Utopia*, Basic Books, New York, 1974.

[6] In Ch. 5 of *On Liberty* he writes, "If the roads, the railways, the banks, the insurance offices, the great joint-stock companies, the universities, and the public charities, were all of them branches of the government . . . not all the freedom of the press and popular constitution of the legislature would make this or any other country free otherwise than in name." John Stuart Mill, *Utilitarianism, Liberty, Representative Government*, Everyman's Library, London, 1910, 165

[7] This is the interpretation of Nicholas Capaldi in *John Stuart Mill: A Biography*, Cambridge University Press, New York, 2004.

[8] Nozick dubs his entitlement theory of property rights as "historical" because it looks backwards to the circumstances in which holdings were generated. There can be no historical theory of utilitarian entitlements because causality does not run backwards.

[9] The working out of this theorem of utilitarianism in layer upon layer of subtlety is to be credited to Henry Sidgwick. See *The Methods of Ethics*, Dover Publications, New York, 1966, Bk. IV, Chap. V, 485-495. Bernard Williams sardonically characterised this view as "Government House utilitarianism" in virtue of its appeal to colonial administrators and other would-be shepherds of the hoi polloi. Such status-differentiation, however, is anticipated by Mill's authorisation in Utilitarianism of people experienced in a variety of pleasures to pronounce on which are higher and which lower.

[10] See *Moral Thinking: Its Levels, Method, and Point*, Oxford University Press, New York, 1981.

[11] It is one of the grounds on which Rawls in *A Theory of Justice* takes exception to utilitarianism. Against discretion to dissemble he endorses among the precepts of justice a "principle of publicity."

[12] The younger Mill, following Coleridge, refers to this elite as a "clerisy."

[13] *Wealth of Nations*, Book. 1, chapter 2.

[14] "[T]here being nothing more evident, than that creatures of the same species and rank, promiscuously born to all the same advantages of nature, and the use of the same faculties, should also be equal one amongst another without subordination or subjection." *Second Treatise of Government* §4.

[15] The feminine pronoun is employed not simply in fidelity to dogmas of political correctness, of sanctified merit though they be, but to underscore the insistence by J. S. Mill in particular but also the other classical utilitarians of explicitly including women in their doctrine of liberty.

[16] *On Liberty*, Ch. 3, "Of Individuality, as One of the Elements of Well-being", op. cit., 117.

[17] See David M. Levy, *How the Dismal Science Got Its Name: Classical Economics and the Ur-Text of Racial Politics*, University of Michigan Press, Ann Arbor, 2001.

[18] Spencer's theory of evolutionary fitness is independent of and precedes Darwin's. It is worth investigating whether that chronology has some bearing on Spencer's continuing commitment to classical liberal ideals – and whether the eclipse of his evolutionary theory by that of Darwin is a factor in his marginalisation as the 19th century draws to a close.

[19] *On Liberty*, Ch. 4.

[20] *The Limits of State Action*, Liberty Fund, Indianapolis, 1993.

[21] Humboldt penned *Limits of State Action* during his early twenties. In later life he was renowned especially for the educational reforms he carried out as a Prussian bureaucrat. It does not seem unfair to suspect that the young man's libertarian enthusiasms were tempered if not extinguished by his later years in state service.

[22] See John Plamenatz, *Consent, Freedom, and Political Obligation*, Oxford University Press, Oxford, 1938.

[23] It could be argued that the efflorescence of Fabian socialism was not an independent causal factor in the decline of classical liberalism but one of its symptoms. While not rejecting that appraisal, I believe it worth noting that the remarkable assemblage of personalities and talents that assembled around the Fabian banner certainly catalyzed forces that otherwise would have percolated more slowly through English intellectual culture.

[24] See John Rawls, *A Theory of Justice*, Harvard University Press, Cambridge, MA, 22-3. I have advanced similar arguments against utilitarianism in *Persons, Rights, & the Moral Community*, Oxford University Press, New York, 1987.

7

Religion and the Ethics of Citizenship in a Secular Society

Peter Kurti

Secularism and religious freedom in Australia[1]

Religion has become front page news in Australia. Findings handed down at the end of 2017 by a Royal Commissioner investigating allegations of sexual abuse committed by clergy are only part of the story; but they, alone, have done much both to catch the attention of the wider public and to diminish the social standing of religious institutions in Australia.[2] There are, however, other factors explaining renewed contemporary interest in religion.

One is Islam's increasing influence in Western countries, including Australia, along with conflict generated by radicalised fundamentalist forms of Islam. Another is the mounting challenge to religious freedom posed by attempts, often made with disconcerting vigour, to exclude religion as a protected category in anti-discrimination legislation.

A broader culture war against religion is being waged in Australia. A notable feature of this war is inflamed arguments about the appropriate place, if any, that religion should occupy in the formation of public policy in Australia's secular liberal democracy.

While contemporary discussions about diversity in Australia focus, for the most part, on race, gender, and sexual orientation, they need also to embrace the religious diversity of our multicultural population.

Respect for diversity, however, must not give way to the strictures of identity politics that elevate the notional rights of a group above those of the individual. The danger posed by identity politics is that diversity can become a factor for social division and the diminution of liberty. As such, diversity needs always to be tempered by the rule of law.

At the outset, a brief survey of two recent key issues that have provoked this renewed debate – same-sex marriage and the charitable status of religious not-for-profit bodies – will help put some loose folds of flesh on the argument to be developed.

Fuelled by distaste for religion in any form, social progressives have thereby helped to keep it in the news by their determination to eliminate any public expression of religion, or any influence that it might have, in society. The problem, as identified by these progressives, can be stated succinctly: in a diverse society such as Australia, it is highly likely there is always going to be a substantial proportion of the population that finds any religious argument or reason for a policy unacceptable.

Is it not, therefore, reasonable to argue that the only acceptable grounds for public policy in a secular liberal democracy should be secular ones, and that religious grounds cannot ever be relied upon to advance public policy. It is a contention that defenders of religious liberty need to answer.

This debate is the product of a rising tide of secularism, something different from the increasing secularisation of society. *Secularisation* is the process a society goes through as its attachment to religion diminishes and it becomes more secular.

Secularism, however, refers less to a diminishing concern for the religious than to a conscious process of actively promoting the secular. Hence, the *Oxford English Dictionary* defines "secularism" as: "the view that religion and religious considerations should be deliberately omitted from temporal affairs."[3]

However, since a policy of deliberate omission can take different forms, the term, "secular", can be used in elliptical ways. In terms of the formulation of public policy, a more precise definition of a policy

ground or reason as "secular" has been offered by Robert Audi, a
political scientist:

> [A] secular reason [is] one whose normative force, that is,
> its status as a prima facie justificatory element, does not
> depend on the existence of God (or on denying it) or on
> theological considerations, or on the pronouncement of a
> person or institution *qua* religious authority.[4]

In the hands of secularism's more aggressive proponents, however, an absence of justificatory dependence on God is often elevated
to a concerted effort to banish altogether any element of religious
influence, in any circumstance, from the public sphere.

This chapter will examine the relationship between the religious
and the secular by focusing on the underlying principles at stake in a
plural society. The forcible exclusion of religion amounts to a betrayal
of the underlying principle of neutrality which ought to inform a
properly secular society in which faith and public life are reconciled.

Far from excluding and marginalising religious citizens, the
secular liberal state should aspire to embrace the principles of
individuality and diversity, and to protect those principles by the
imposition of procedural and legal limits on what the state can do.
The liberal order, in other words, stands for peace through toleration,
and for liberty protected by the rule of law.

Threats: No place for "meddling" believers?

Same-sex marriage

Urgency to pass legislation amending the *Marriage Act 1961*
mounted swiftly following declaration of the results of the Australian same-sex marriage survey on 15 November 2017.[5] The result of
the postal survey had been decisive, and amendments to the Act
were finally passed by the Commonwealth Parliament on 7 December 2017.

Concerns were expressed, however, about the haste with which
the amendments were passed. The editorial writer of *The Australian*
considered the government's "poor preparation and lukewarm com-

mitment to freedom of religion, conscience, and belief" had led to a legislative outcome that appeared to brush aside concerns held by many Australians about the strength of religious protections.[6]

A sizable minority of respondents to the postal survey – 40 per cent – were opposed, in some cases, on religious grounds, to any change in the law. Commentators, such as Richard Ackland, a columnist, argued that this losing minority is simply not entitled to demand legal provisions to protect their freedoms of speech, conscience, or religion:

> There are strong grounds for a campaign to counter the expansion of religious freedoms and to reduce the ones that already exist. When you consider the hateful, cruel, bitter, and downright false contribution of religious voices during the recent survey, why would anyone want to give these institutions more open-ended "freedoms'? There is a long and sorry history of churches meddling in society's freedoms and undermining citizens" human rights and private lives.[7]

Arguments such as these, which focus exclusively on the perceived – and acknowledged – failings of the Christian church, hardly do justice to the cultural and religious diversity which is so characteristic of Australia's thriving multicultural society. This is a diversity that is reflected in successive returns for the Census conducted by the Australian Bureau of Statistics.[8]

Charitable purpose

Religion continues to contribute to Australian society in ways beyond the practices of individual believers. Many charities, or not-for-profits (NFPs), functioning in Australia today, for example, either remain, or were in their early days, Christian organisations, such as the St Vincent de Paul Society and the Benevolent Society.[9]

The charitable purpose of advancing religion has been part of the English Common Law tradition for over 400 years. The preamble to the *Charitable Uses Act 1601*, also known as the *Statute of Elizabeth*, influenced the judgment in a late 19th century case, *Commissioners for Special Purposes of Income Tax v Pemsel* [1891], which established four heads of charitable purposes including "the advancement of religion".

Even though the definition of charity and the heads of charitable purposes have been amended by the Commonwealth Parliament, charity law in Australia still follows English Common Law closely. The *Statute of Elizabeth* and *Pemsel* continue to influence Australian courts.[10]

This legal tradition, together with the well-established presence of faith-based NFPs in Australia, has not deterred a recent move by a Victorian Upper House MP, Fiona Patten, to attempt to amend that state's *Charities Act 1978* to exclude the advancement of religion as a charitable purpose. According to Ms Patten (who formed the Australian Sex Party in 2009):

> The notion that the advancement of religion is a charitable purpose would be questioned by most people in our community these days. I don't believe that the community thinks that advancement of religion is a charitable purpose.[11]

Ms Patten does not substantiate her belief with any evidence as to the precise views of people in the community. Underlying her rhetoric, one might reasonably suppose, is a determination to check the capacity of religious not-for-profits – including healthcare, welfare, and aged-care agencies – to influence the formation of law and public policy.

Responses: Religion assumes the discourse of politics

Nearly forty years ago, in BBC Reith Lectures delivered in 1978 and speaking specifically about Christianity, Edward Norman, an English ecclesiastical historian, warned of the dangers of what he called "the politicisation of Christianity". He feared that this process was, in part, a symptom of spiritual decay.

This decay, Norman argued, was not the consequence of an assault by the enemies of religion; rather, it was due to the surrender by Christian leaders of Christianity's claims to an understanding of the nature of humankind:

> Christians have adopted the moralities of secular political ideologies and promote them for what they think of as

authentically Christian social ends. They are redefining their own moral identity and their own claim to significance in society in terms of an external context dominated by ideologies which have no other end for man [sic] in prospect except as part of the material process.[12]

When conflicts do arise between religious people and organisations, they are now as likely to be about sharply defined political beliefs as they are to be about points of theology. Some religious people and organisations, clearly, now hold that politics does not so much involve a choice between reasonable alternatives but is rather the assertion of self-evident moral truths.

Anxious about the marginalisation of religion in public life, some religious organisations in Australia have responded over time by adapting their stance on key political issues of the day and altering the ideological basis of their contributions. In other words, they seek to influence formation of public policy by substituting the more acceptable modes of secular discourse for the discourse of theology.

Religious bodies such as the National Council of Churches in Australia (NCCA), for example, frequently take positions on social and economic issues by attempting to recast the propositions of theology as unvarying secular, moral principles.

In November 2016, the NCCA endorsed the international COP22 Interfaith Climate Statement.[13] According to an accompanying media release, this statement, signed by 304 religious leaders from 58 countries, declared, among other things, that the continued use of fossil fuels is ethically untenable and called for "shifting public finances away from fossil fuels, increasing financing to end energy poverty with renewable energy, and ensuring a just transition that protects human rights and vulnerable communities."[14]

The Statement, itself, was cast wholly in secular, humanist terms which appealed to general principles of justice, moral obligation, and the duties of "trustees to Mother Earth."[15] Mention of God, if made at all, was scarce. When even religious organisations abandon the language of theology, the process of secularisation may be said to be well advanced.

Secularisation has marginalised religion. One consequence is that some religious people stake their ground in secular social discourse, expressing their endorsement or rebuttal of political policies by means of the language of justice and rights. This ideological switch is one development characteristic of the settlement developed in most liberal democracies between the religious and the secular.

The secular settlement and the primacy of individual autonomy

Arguments that religion can never, in any circumstances, inform the development of public policy in a secular liberal democracy reflect significant changes that have occurred in the attitude of Western culture to religious belief.

One change often cited to account for this displacement of religion, and the diminution of the prestige and power of religious institutions, is the complex process of the modernisation of society, together with progress made in science and technology.

According to this view, empirical methodologies and their accounts of causal explanation have rendered metaphysical worldviews redundant. Religion, in turn, has become restricted to overseeing the means of salvation and, as a result, far more individualised.

Steve Bruce, a sociologist, traces these changes to the Protestant Reformation of the 16th century which also played a major part in laying the foundations of liberal democracy:

> What were initially religious arguments inadvertently encouraged individualism, egalitarianism, and diversity, which in turn combined with growing and structural differentiation to shift governments in the direction of secular liberal democracy.[16]

Yet just as the status of Christianity in modernising liberal democracies has changed, so, too, sizeable non-Christian religions have emerged in the West since the 1960s, in large part due to changing patterns of migration. Many migrants came from countries more religious than their new homes in the West; the immediate impact of this has been to increase the public visibility – if not the acceptance – of religion in the West.

This has not, however, stemmed the tide of secularisation, a process widely regarded as irreversible – unless a reversal of the increasing cultural autonomy of the individual is conceivable. "Unless we can imagine some social forces that will lead us to give up that freedom, we cannot imagine the creation of a detailed ideological consensus."[17]

The primacy of individual autonomy is a key component of the classical tradition of the "secular settlement" developed by liberal democracies. There are two principal elements of this settlement. The first is that the private and public spheres of life are to be clearly demarcated. The religious beliefs and practices of the individual are tolerated in the private sphere, but not in the wider public sphere where all religion is excluded.

The second element of the settlement is that religious bodies such as schools, hospitals, and welfare agencies, are permitted to retain certain privileges – such as exemption from some anti-discrimination laws, and certain tax advantages – on condition that they do not rock the social, political, and cultural boat.

Indeed, the Victorian threat to deny religion as a charitable purpose, and withdraw from it certain long-standing privileges, referred to earlier, suggests that religion, at least in the minds of some, is doing too much rocking of society's boat already.

Threats to the secular settlement

This secular settlement works as long as those seeking accommodation are tolerant of all others. In some circumstances, however, the settlement comes under threat. Thus, if a minority – whether a religious one or an anti-religious one – rejects the principle of a demarcation between the private and public spheres, and seeks to impose law or policy on the tolerant majority, such action will threaten the liberties of those with whom the dissident minority does not agree.

For example, when same-sex marriage activists urge the removal of anti-discrimination exemptions from religious groups committed to a traditional form of marriage, they effectively seek to impose their views and beliefs on those with whom they disagree.

The settlement will also be destabilised when a minority seeks to do something in private that offends against a principle shared by the wider society. For example, the desire by some Muslim women in Australia to wear the *niqab*, or some other form of Islamic veil, in public places, is frequently resisted by non-Muslims because it is said to offend tenets fundamental to a secular liberal society, such as the equal status of women.

Demands, such as these, for the public privileging of religion have, in the opinion of scholars such as Steve Bruce, helped to provoke antagonism towards religion. This has been driven, in part by the increased presence in secular societies of non-Christians, such as Muslims, who have not been party to the gradual evolution of the demarcation of private and public spheres.

Indeed, this troublesome public presence of religion might serve to confirm, rather than reverse, the privatisation of religion and so strengthen liberal commitments to the secular settlement.[18] In addition, Bruce is sceptical that concerns about the marginalisation of religion are shared by members of wider secular society:

> To the extent that some Christians now behave like a disadvantaged minority and make a fuss about their rights, they simply confirm the view of the secular, or only nominally Christian majority, that religion is more trouble than it is worth.[19]

Secular protagonists certainly often depict religious argument in very blunt terms. Their caricatures of religion present it as it were little more than "a crude prescription from God, backed up with threat of hellfire, derived from general or particular revelation [contrasted] with elegant simplicity of a philosophical argument."[20]

No wonder that calls in Australia for any form of religious argument or opinion to be banished from the public square of this country's secular liberal democracy are becoming increasingly strident. Yet this is a travesty of the neutrality to which a liberal polity ought to aspire.

Liberalism and the Recovery of Reasonableness

The secular liberal state must aspire to be a neutral state. It must establish, and enforce, principles for regulating disagreements between citizens who adhere to widely diverging conceptions about, for example, what constitutes the good life. Whereas these conceptions, themselves, are hardly neutral, the secular state must remain committed to a neutrality that stands, at the very minimum, for respect for the diversity of those conceptions.

This is an understanding of the modern secular state that has been elegantly expressed by Stephen Macedo, a political scientist, who has described the state as, "associations of more or less reasonable people who agree on some things and disagree on others, whose reasonableness we wish to respect and whose allegiance we hope thereby to engage."[21]

As religious reasons advanced for backing a public policy will always be unacceptable to some portion of the wider population, secular liberals often urge restraint upon citizens with religious convictions who wish to contribute to policy discussions. Such restraint entails that religious grounds for reforming policy must be recast in secular terms.

In the view of many secular, liberal critics of religion, this is the only acceptable form in which religious reasons can ever be presented and propounded in discussions of public policy. It is, the argument goes, a mark of responsibility on the part of the religious citizen to exercise a "doctrine of religious restraint" by not relying solely on religious reasons to advocate for favoured policies.

On justifying the "doctrine of religious restraint"

One factor behind the call to exercise restraint is a belief that by invoking religious grounds in support of public policy positions, such citizens somehow fail to show respect to their secular peers and thereby threaten to polarise a pluralistic society. Religion, it is feared, "is surely divisive, and, as such, should be avoided by people of good faith and thus by citizens committed to living in harmony with their compatriots."[22]

The doctrine is a moral, rather than a legal restraint, of course, and can be understood, broadly, in two ways. First, it can be understood as covering only public discussion of policies; and, second, it can be understood as extending to include any kind of religious motivation that might influence a religious believer's decisions about policies.

The doctrine of religious restraint does not call for a thoroughgoing privatisation of religious belief which excludes it from any engagement. Kraig Beyerlein, a sociologist, and Christopher Eberle, a philosopher, have noted that the doctrine advocated by secular liberals is fundamentally *inclusive* rather than *exclusive*:

> [The position of secular liberals] is not that citizens should refrain from supporting coercive laws for religious reasons, but that citizens should also include secular reasons in their rationale for this support. Citizens are free to have religious reasons, and even to care about them, but they must also have secular reasons for their favoured public policies.[23]

Proponents of the doctrine accept that religious convictions can form part of the reason a citizen may advocate a coercive law; they simply cannot be the *only* component. Where religious convictions cannot be complemented by secular ones, they must be privatised.

But as Beyerlein and Eberle note, if a citizen has a compelling religious rationale for supporting a public policy, why should those convictions be excluded? "Surely the strong presumption should be that citizens may make political decisions in accord with the dictates of conscience, *irrespective* of whether the dictates of conscience arise from religious or secular considerations." [Italics in original][24]

If religious citizens *are* committed to living in harmony and to engaging critically in discussions of public policy, it is hard to understand why sincerely expressed views based on religious grounds should be considered disrespectful. As Beyerlein and Eberle have remarked:

> Religious reasons are no more and no less controversial than secular reasons and so it is arbitrary to appeal to di-

visiveness as a basis for advocating restraint regarding religious reasons but *not* secular ones.[25] [Italics in original]

Appeals to the doctrine of restraint represent an attempt to limit the contribution that religion can make to public policy discussion. They are made on the assumption, first, that whatever contribution religion might make to such discussion, it will be an unhelpful one; and, second, that secular reasons are, therefore, always to be preferred to religious ones.

Yet, as noted earlier, religion continues to make a distinctive and important contribution to Australia's liberal, secular society. This contribution might well serve to undermine secularist certainty about the inevitable demise of religion. But other factors are also in play that account for resurgence of interest in religion.

Religion in a post-secular society

The re-emergence of religion is unlikely to reverse the process of secularisation. At the very least, however, it may challenge the pace of its progress and change public awareness of religion. If that is so, the very nature of a secularised society may have to reconsidered.

One thinker who has considered the impact of religion's resurgence on secular society in some detail is the philosopher and political scientist, Jürgen Habermas. He has queried the progress of secularisation and used the term "post-secular society" to describe a secularised environment which needs to adjust itself to the continuing existence of religious communities and the influence they exert.[26]

One factor that Habermas argues helps to explain this shift in public consciousness is that religious groups are increasingly functioning in the public sphere as what he calls, "communities of interpretation."

> They can attain influence on public opinion and will formation by making relevant contributions to key issues, irrespective of whether their arguments are convincing or objectionable. Our pluralist societies constitute a responsive sounding board for such interventions because they are increasingly split on value conflicts requiring political regulation.[27]

Whereas proponents of the secularisation thesis insist that religion is disappearing from public life in the course of modernisation, Habermas argues that, on the contrary, the influence and relevance of religion continues to grow. On the basis of Habermas's analysis, it seems appropriate to describe Australia not simply as a secular society, but as a *post-secular* one where religion, if not resurgent, is certainly re-emergent.

However, one challenge confronting a post-secular society, such as Australia, is to ensure that a plurality of cultural and religious worldviews does not undermine the civic cohesion of the secular liberal state. How, then, should citizens live in a post-secular society?

Citizenship and the reciprocity of expectations

All citizens share membership of an inclusive community – the democratic state. Life in the post-secular democratic state is, therefore, marked by the need to strike a balance between the experience of shared citizenship and this increasing plurality of religious beliefs and worldviews. The principle that allows this post-secular balance to be struck is tolerance.

Frequently confused with "respect", tolerance is better understood as the civic arrangement, secured by the rule of law and the democratic will of the people. Tolerance disarms quarrelling parties and secures peaceful coexistence. Nor is tolerance to be confused with indifference: rather, it involves the agreement by some citizens to concede the beliefs and practices of other citizens that they, themselves, reject.

Furthermore, and more importantly, the practice of tolerance demands of all citizens an expectation of what Habermas describes as "an ethics of citizenship" that extends beyond mere obedience to the law. It requires citizens to practice a reciprocity of civic expectation:

> Religious citizens and communities must not only superficially adjust to the constitutional order. They are expected to appropriate the secular legitimation of constitutional principles under the premises of their own faith.[28]

He acknowledges that the process of learning this ethics of citizenship can be painful. It requires that the norms of citizenship are framed in language that all citizens can understand. In effect, this means that if the religious citizen wishes to support a policy for *religious* reasons, those reasons must be translated into secular terms so that consensus may be reached.

However, this seems to assume that if religiously based claims are to be translated into accessible, secular terms and still retain their meaning, religious and secular claims are bear a high degree of semantic similarity. Alternatively, it could simply mean, as James Boettcher, a philosopher, has argued that:

> Politically relevant religious judgments are sufficiently supported by secular reasons which bear some meaningful resemblance to underlying religious premises, perhaps by addressing the same themes and values.[29]

Boettcher argues that Habermas favours *resemblance* between religious and secular reasons rather than *close similarity*. He cites Habermas's example of a religious response to the issue of genetic testing and suggests that the notions of inherent dignity and individual autonomy might serve as partial, secular translations of a religious conception of persons as sacred and created by God.[30]

Lines that separate?

Developing an ethics of citizenship along the lines that Habermas suggests supposes that there is an identifiable boundary between the private sphere of religious utterances and the broader public sphere in which the decision-making processes of the state are conducted. It is the observance of such a boundary that makes possible the cultivation of reciprocity in civic relationships.

Habermas is emphatic that the liberal virtue of tolerance must be cultivated and practiced to ensure that neither the private sphere nor the public is unhealthily predominant. Mutual recognition is constitutive of shared citizenship:

> The democratic state must not pre-emptively reduce the polyphonic complexity of the diverse public voices because

it cannot know whether it is not otherwise cutting society off from scarce resources for the generation of meanings and the shaping of identities.[31]

Indeed, as Boettcher argues, the ethics of citizenship in a plural society will be strained if non-religious citizens view religion as irrational and incompatible with modern society. Boettcher also holds that, "non-religious citizens must remain open to the possibility that religious doctrines are a source of important moral intuitions and judgments, some of which have not yet received an adequate secular translation."[32]

But are plural perspectives, even when translated into secular terms, genuinely reconcilable? If they are not, Habermas's attempt to permit religious citizens to participate in public discussions about policy must fail.

His prescription remains heavily dependent on being able to define a line of demarcation – Habermas describes the line as a "threshold" – on one side of which religious reasons are inappropriate and on the other side of which unrestricted religious argument is permissible. As Patrick Neal, a political scientist and critic of Habermas's argument, has remarked:

> If the citizen's claims in the name of a "pious life" are serious enough to outweigh any claims of restriction on reasons outside the threshold, it is not obvious why they are not serious enough to outweigh claims of restriction within it.[33]

The discreet claims of religious and political authority are bound to be intractable. Therefore, it seems that Habermas is striving for consensus where none is likely to be found. If a citizen believes she has a fundamental duty to obey God, and that that duty takes priority over all others, she will be unable to rest assured "that martyrdom at the hands of the political authority will not be expected of her."[34]

This leaves unresolved the outstanding problem of how effectively to describe and defend an appropriate place for religion in a contemporary, post-secular society. One step in the right direction to resolving this difficulty might be to ask whether it is even possible to describe such a demarcation in the first place. For as long as secularism is considered to be about the relation between two realms – that of the state and that of religion – keeping them distinct will be difficult.

Fixing on religious diversity in a secular society

A better approach might be to stop thinking of secularism as a political arrangement for attempting to keep religion separate from the state. Instead, a more fruitful approach to the ethics of citizenship in the post-secular state might be to begin with the needs and wellbeing of the individual citizen.

One thinker who eschews the idea that the focus of secularism needs to be on the relation of the state to religion is Charles Taylor, a philosopher. He warns of a preoccupation with what he calls "the fetishisation of institutional arrangements". This reflects the notion of "the people" as the single entity serving as the source of the sovereignty legitimising the state.

It is certainly true that "the people" expresses the sense of common purpose underlying the democratic state; but Taylor wonders what, and for whom, this state is actually for. The problem is that this notion of collective identity – founded on principles such as the rule of law, and key cultural and social tradition – can assume an untouchable status threats to which, of any kind, must be thwarted.

Taylor argues that secularism ought, instead, to be concerned with how the democratic state responds to the diversity of all citizens in protecting all citizens whatever their outlook. Once a key political ethic basic to the state has been established – such as the rule of law and the protection of human rights – it can be shared by all citizens regardless of their outlook or belief:

> The point of state neutrality is precisely to avoid favouring or not disfavouring not just religious positions, but any basic position, religious or non-religious. We cannot favour Christianity over Islam, but also religion over against nonbelief in religion, or vice versa. [Citizens] can concur on the principles, but differ on the deeper reasons for holding to this [political] ethic. The state must uphold the ethic, but must refrain from favouring any of the deeper reasons.[35]

Australia is a country that is growing progressively more diverse in terms of its cultural, ethnic, social, and religious profile. As it does so, the need to balance freedoms enjoyed by a diverse population against historical identities that might obscure those freedoms becomes increasingly important. In Taylor's view, "fixation on religion" is symptomatic of this tendency to avoid responding to diversity.

Why is religion considered such a threat, attracting the ire of critics such as Richard Ackland, as noted earlier?[36] Ackland's preoccupation with "religious voices", it will be recalled, hints at a concern that religion is not merely an irritant but actually poses a deeper threat to the integrity of secular society.

Taylor traces this fixation with religious discourse to the very epistemic distinction between secular and religious language employed by thinkers such as Habermas in their efforts to devise a compact between the two realms. It is also fixation with this distinction that drives efforts to limit the use of religious language. The idea, Taylor says:

> Seems to be something like this. Secular reason is a language that everyone speaks, and can argue and be convinced in. Religious language operates outside this discourse by introducing extraneous premises which only believers can accept. So let's all talk the common language.[37]

The result is that when religious language comes to the same conclusion as secular reason, it is superfluous; when it comes to a contrary conclusion, it is dangerous. Religion and religious language can, accordingly, be sidelined. It is a view widely held, and assiduously promoted by critics of religion who point to any number of past conflicts between religion and the state to support their view.

Conclusion

If the process of secularisation is, indeed, irreversible, efforts to introduce religious reasons to the formation of public policy are likely to be regarded as either superfluous or dangerous for some time to come. Proponents of aggressive secularism, in the pursuit of their own peculiar conception of "neutrality", may well succeed in banishing religion altogether from the public sphere.

However, this chapter has sought to argue that the exclusion of religion in the name of secularism amounts to a betrayal of the neutrality to which a secular society ought properly to be committed. Rather than attempting to segregate the religious from the secular, an appropriate ethics of citizenship needs to affirm a commitment to respecting and upholding the diversity of all citizens.

An Australian secular society denuded of religion will be an impoverished society because religion continues to shape the outlook and aspirations of many. Attempts to deny the contribution that religion and its institutions make in Australia is both intolerant and contrary to the principles of a democratic society.

All this matters, as Ian Harper has noted, "because the interplay of competing views and sentiments within the public arena is the stuff of robust democracy. Without it, as Hayek pointed out, the open society is threatened and liberty itself is compromised." [38]

Religion shapes the lives of many Australians and exerts in important influence on the way they participate in families, communities, and wider society. It thereby makes an essential contribution to our shared public life. Continuing antagonism to religion in the name of secularism can only diminish that public life, and, with it, the lives of all Australians.

Peter Kurti is a Senior Research Fellow with the Religion & Civil Society program at the Centre for Independent Studies

Endnotes

[1] I am grateful to Dr Jeremy Sammut for comments he made on an earlier draft of this chapter.

[2] The final report of the Royal Commission into Institutional Responses to Child Sexual Abuse was handed down on 15 December 2017. https://www.childabuseroyalcommission.gov.au/recommendations

[3] *The New Shorter Oxford English Dictionary*, 5th Edition, Oxford University Press, Oxford, 2002.

[4] Robert Audi, *Religious Commitment and Secular Reason*, Cambridge University Press, New York, 2000, 89.

[5] On 15 November 2017, the Australian Bureau of Statistics announced the results of the Australian Marriage Law Postal Survey. A total of 12.7 million (79.5%) of eligible Australians expressed their view, with the majority (61.6%) indicating that the law should be changed to allow same-sex couples to marry. All states and territories recorded a majority "Yes" response. (Source: https://www.ag.gov.au/marriageequality).

[6] "Marriage legislation puts religious freedom in doubt", *The Australian*, 8 December 2017, http://www.theaustralian.com.au/opinion/editorials/marriage-legislation-puts-religious-freedom-in-doubt/news-story/ce9ec86ca4a6f93aadafab5ba283fee1

[7] Richard Ackland, "Why extend the church's "freedom" when it's abused what it already has?" *The Guardian*, 14 December 2017, https://www.theguardian.com/australia-news/2017/dec/14/dont-extend-churches-freedom-when-theyve-abused-those-they-already-have

[8] In the 2016 Census, Australians were asked to identify their religion in response to the question, "What is your religion?" with the option of "No Religion" placed at the top of the list of available answers. Whereas the 2011 Census showed that 22 per cent of Australians identified as having no religion, by 2016 the figure had risen to 30 per cent, indicating that more than two thirds of Australians continue to retain some degree of religious allegiance and affiliation.

[9] Peter Kurti, *Hallowed Institutions: Religion and the Roots of Liberty and Prosperity*, Occasional Paper 144, Centre for Independent Studies, Sydney, 2016, 21.

[10] See further, Peter Kurti, *In the Pay of the Piper: Governments, Not-for-Profits, and the Burden of Regulation*, Issue Analysis 139, Centre for Independent Studies, Sydney, 2013, 6.

[11] Wendy Williams, "Advancement of Religion as a Charitable Purpose in Question", *Pro Bono Australia*, 15 December 2017, https://probonoaustralia.com.au/news/2017/12/advancement-religion-charitable-purpose-question

[12] Edward Norman, *Christianity and the World Order*, Oxford University Press, Oxford, 1979, 58.

[13] COP22 Interfaith Statement on Climate Change, http://www.interfaithstatement2016.org/read_the_statement

[14] Media release COP22 Interfaith, http://www.ncca.org.au/images/stories/News__Media_Releases/General_News/FOR_IMMEDIATE_RELEASE-COP22Interfaith-16Nov2016.pdf

[15] COP22 Interfaith Statement on Climate Change, as above.

[16] Steve Bruce, *Secularization: In Defence of an Unfashionable Theory*, Oxford University Press, Oxford, 2013, 39.

[17] Ibid., 55.

[18] Ibid., 220.

[19] Ibid., 223.

[20] Jeremy Waldron, *God, Locke, and Equality: Christian Foundations in Locke's Political Thought*, Cambridge University Press, Cambridge, 2002, 20. See also, Peter Kurti, *The Tyranny of Tolerance: Threats to Religious Liberty in Australia*, Connor Court, Brisbane, 2017, 165 et seq.

[21] Stephen Macedo, *Liberal Virtues: Citizenship, Virtue, and Community in Liberal Constitutionalism*, Clarendon Press, Oxford, 1990, 38.

[22] Kraig Beyerlein and Christopher Eberle, "Who Violates The Principles of Political Liberalism?: Religion, Restraint, and the Decision to Reject Same-Sex Marriage", *Politics and Religion*, 7, 2014, 240-264, 244.

[23] Kraig Beyerlein and Christopher Eberle, as above, 243.

[24] Ibid.

[25] Ibid., 244.

[26] Jürgen Habermas, "Notes on a Post-Secular Society", *New Perspectives Quarterly*, September 2008, 17-29.

[27] Ibid., 20.

[28] Ibid., 27.

[29] James W. Boettcher, "Habermas, religion, and the ethics of citizenship", *Philosophy & Social Criticism*, 2009, 35(1-2), 215-238, 228.

[30] James W. Boettcher, as above, 228.

[31] Jürgen Habermas, op. cit., 29.

[32] James W. Boettcher, op. cit., 232.

[33] Patrick Neal, "Habermas, Religion, and Citizenship", *Politics and Religion*, 7, 2014, 318-338, 336.

[34] Ibid,, 337.

[35] Charles Taylor, "The Polysemy of the Secular", *Social Research,* 76(4), "The Religious-Secular Divide: The US Case", Winter 2009, 1143-66, 1153.

[36] See reference 6, above.

[37] Taylor, op. cit., 1162.

[38] Ian Harper, "Religion Matters for Faith, Hope and Love" in Gary Johns (ed.), *Really Dangerous Ideas: What Does and Does not Matter*, Connor Court, Ballarat, 2013, 38.

8

Can Columnists be Civilised?

Henry Ergas

I

Early in the winter of 1950, as the Cold War threatened to turn hot, Joseph and Stewart Alsop sat down to do something they had never done before. Although still young, the Alsop brothers had already cemented their position among the leading columnists in the United States. Consummate Washington insiders, related by marriage to the Roosevelts, hosts of the city's most important dinner parties at a time when America's power and prestige were at their peak, they seemed to have little to fear. Yet, what they were proposing, Stewart wrote to a close friend, "had my palms visibly sweating." They were planning to accuse Louis Johnson, President Harry Truman's Secretary of Defense, of lying.

The reaction was thunderous. No matter how compelling the brothers' case against Johnson may have been, *The New York Herald Tribune*, their main employer, would not use the word "lie". Papers to which the column was syndicated refused to run it, with some reminding the brothers of the press's responsibility to uphold the country's institutions, respect its most senior officials, and be measured in tone and outlook. It was a lesson the Alsop brothers, whom their biographer rightly calls "the guardians of the American century," would never forget.[1]

All that seems light years away. Even before Donald Trump had entered the White House, *The Washington Post* had begun to refer to his claims as lies; *The New York Times* followed suit a few months later. The election, *New York Times* executive editor Dean Basquet said in October 2016, "forced us … to get comfortable with saying something is false;" in doing so, he added, it "changed journalism," burying – to the acclamation of some and the condemnation of others – what little remained of the ethic of self-effacement which had characterised the Alsop era.[2]

That change comes on top of many others. Already weakened by the rise of broadcasting, newspapers have been hammered by the Internet, which has fragmented the media environment into millions of pieces while forcing newspapers to compete with every other form of content for consumers' scarce, and often fickle, attention. At the same time, the advertising revenues on which newspapers relied for a high and until then rising share of their income have shrunk as new, more effective advertising channels emerge, both in the form of competing content providers and of platforms such as Google, Facebook and Twitter. Forced by intensified competition for advertising to ramp up their subscriber numbers if they are to survive, many newspapers are being driven to be more partisan and strident, reaching out – above the din of the Internet – to those readers who have strong views and are willing to pay to see their view confirmed.

As for the columnists, their position is even worse: time-starved consumers, their opinions already largely fixed, have little tolerance for subtleties; they may eat salad at lunch but for commentary they demand red meat, delivered quickly, preferably with the blood dripping. Adding to the pressures, consumers are no longer merely passive readers; instead, whatever columnists write is promptly put through the grinder by on-line mobs whose default mode is frequently the insult and whose default style is frequently the tirade. And with editors desperate for snippets that could go viral, everything is pushing commentary to be even more polarised than the paper as a whole, unleashing a race in which columnists and commentators try to be heard by turning up the volume.

That picture, a vast simplification of a reality that is complex, nuanced and affected by counter-tendencies, nevertheless captures the essence of our predicament. Can intelligent commentary, which is willing to stake its ground clearly, but does so by appealing to reason rather than to instinct, survive in an age of anger? And, even if it can, is it destined to play any useful role?

There are no sure or simple answers to those questions. But what may be helpful is to place the issues into the perspective of how we got to where we are. In his *Outlines of the Philosophy of Right*, Georg Hegel wrote, I believe rightly, that philosophy is our time apprehended in concepts. What he meant is that when they think historically, people are giving and asking for reasons, in more bloodless and dispassionate terms than is the case in historical reality. We try, in looking at the past, to understand our own subjectivity: why things present themselves to us as they do. Human history is littered with setbacks and even horrors; but there always remains the need for self-comprehension which picks up the pieces and sets out anew.

II

In setting off on that journey, it seems reasonable to adopt the narrative pattern so aptly recommended to the White Rabbit in *Alice in Wonderland*: " 'Begin at the beginning', the King said gravely, 'and go on till you come to the end: then stop.' "

As far as beginnings are concerned, suffice it to say that while printing spread enormously rapidly in Europe after Gutenberg introduced his movable-type printing press in 1450, the first periodic English news sheets did not appear until the early 1620s; it took another fifty years for the term, "newspaper", to enter the English language, and it was only in the first two decades of the 18th century that the terms, "journalist", and "editor", were coined.[3] Nonetheless, by the time those terms had become part of the vocabulary it was clear that the rise of the print media was both a major contributor to, and an integral part of, a broader reshaping of Western society.

The word, "newspaper", itself hints at the change. After all, the essence of modernity is the conviction that the present is unlike the past and that the future will differ from the present. The very idea that there is always news – something novel and important in the universe – was new: yes, it was obvious to the medieval mind that things happened, but those events were disturbances – such as wars, plagues, or natural disasters – against the backdrop of a fixed reality. The notion that reality itself was constantly changing as a result of purposive human action marked the rise of a radically different world view.

Every bit as important was the evolving context in which this world view took hold. It is well-known that, during the seventeenth and eighteenth centuries, European societies underwent a process of functional specialisation. Under feudalism, political, economic and social life were essentially merged; in the transition to the modern world, each of these became a separate domain. Political functions – the task of ruling – became the duty of specialised structures, which today we would call the state; economic activity moved out of the home into markets, which were rapidly growing and evolving, albeit still wrapped in the embrace of guilds and other forms of regulation; and a secular social sphere emerged, taking shapes that went from formal structures – such as lodges and fraternities – to informal meeting places such as coffee houses, reading rooms and salons.

A crucial interaction occurred between this social sphere and the political domain. The idea that rulership rests on some type of consent had a long history: for example, in *Behemoth*, written in 1668, Thomas Hobbes articulated the principle that "the power of the mighty hath no foundation but in the opinion and belief of the people." And although *Behemoth* remained unpublished during Hobbes's lifetime, the relation of rule to consent was clearly expressed by John Locke and given a foundation in human reason by Montesquieu, only gathering strength after that.

The process by which that strength became overwhelming was complex and protracted; what matters here is that the development of a social sphere, distinct from both church and state, implied that there was now an actor, a social subject, which was the source of the consent whose foundational role those writers and others asserted. That actor was "the public" which expressed itself through what came to be known as "opinion," a term which, like the Greek word, *Doxa*, referred to beliefs that, rather than having the certainty which characterises statements of fact or logical inferences, involve an element of human judgment. Moreover, deliberation – the process of arriving at and testing opinion in the light of reason – gave judgments some type of legitimacy or of validation as truth. Finally, and crucially for our purpose, deliberation was inherently public, with the print media both underpinning the process and reflecting its outcome.[4]

It is therefore in this period that Rousseau, in the *Discourse on the Arts and Sciences* (1750), coined the term, "public opinion"; in England, a similar term – "general opinion" – had developed, but "public opinion" replaced it in the 1780s. The Physiocrats had used the term, "enlightened opinion," to mean "an opinion purified through critical discussion in the public sphere to constitute a true opinion;" thus, a clear link was established between the formation of opinion, critical public commentary, and truth, with the whole presupposing and resting upon some underlying communicative process.

As that link was being forged, another important notion was gaining ground: that of civility. One can, somewhat unusually, identify a time and a place for the arrival of this term in its modern meaning: the publication of Erasmus's *De Civilitate Morum Puerilium* – On Civility in Children – which appeared in 1530 and which, by the standards of its age, became an extraordinary bestseller, going through some 130 editions during the next two centuries.[5] Erasmus's text is almost entirely concerned with outward behaviour: how to present in public (a term which itself came to mean something along the lines of "in the presence of others") and, more broadly, how to relate to other people. Those were vital questions as the rise of cities and the growth of commerce meant entering into relations with strangers, in dealings which were governed neither by hierarchical nor by familial codes of conduct. The answer as to how those relations should operate lay partly in new standards of etiquette; but it mainly involved cultivating, from childhood, an incessant form of self-control that, instead of the warrior ethic of honour and fealty, took stability, predictability, and the taming of passions as its core virtues.

Civility was, in that sense, an indispensable ingredient in rational deliberation; without the calm, informed and considered exchange of views, arguments degenerated into quarrels and quarrels into violence. And it also became the expected standard for discussions in print, which, although it was often honoured in the breach (as even the most casual examination of the debates between Diderot, Rousseau and d'Alembert would show), ensured that those who deviated from that standard were roundly criticised.

All this ascribed, indeed, a lofty role indeed to the ancestors of today's mastheads, who were to be the bearers and recorders of the process of rational will formation; and no one expressed that role in loftier terms than Immanuel Kant. The Kantian conception is as complex as it is brilliant. Reduced to a handful of propositions, it stated that, ultimately, the legitimacy of state action can rest only on morality; morality, in turn, can only be known through reason; reason's proper exercise presupposes communication, for – as Kant put it in *The Critique of Pure Reason* – "The touchstone whereby we decide whether our holding a thing to be true is conviction or mere persuasion is ... the possibility of communicating it and of finding it to be valid for all human reason"[6]; as a result, "The public use of one's reason must always be free, and it alone can bring about enlightenment among men."[7]

To be legitimate, the sovereign's decisions therefore had to be public and open to scrutiny – this was Kant's "Principle of Publicity"; but for that public scrutiny to confirm those decisions' legitimacy, "the public" needed the ability, underpinned by the freedom to speak and write, to debate their merits in the light of reason. Informing that debate was the task of the print media.

In many respects, our ideal of the press's role has not changed since that formulation – seen in terms of public purpose, newspapers should seek to enlighten: they should help citizens understand the world they live in, grasp its ever-changing realities, scrutinise public action, explain and clarify competing points of view and, in all those ways, support civil but critical discussion and the formation of a rational public will.

III

Our conception of what the print media should do thus dates back to the 1700s; but our notion of how papers should actually do it only emerged in the closing years of the 19th century and at the beginning of the 20th century. The driving force was dramatic change in the newspaper industry's economics.

Until the late 1800s, there were few economies of scale in production of newspapers: the costs involved in setting up a newspaper were relatively low, as were the fixed costs of continuing supply relative to the variable costs of paper, printing and distribution. As a result, larger circulation papers could co-exist with a multitude of smaller papers, generating intense competitive pressures and low newspaper prices in those countries which permitted open entry. With commercial advertising still in its infancy, the financial viability of many papers depended on subsidies from current or aspiring office-holders, leading to a press that was intensely and unashamedly partisan.[8]

Beginning in the late 1870s, almost every aspect of that picture was transformed. Development of very high speed presses brought enormous advances in the printing process: the maximum daily printing capacity of a press increased 16-fold between 1874 and 1895 before trebling again in the next seven years. In 1870, the largest press made 17 000 impressions per hour; barely thirty years later, it made well over a million. At the same time, a slew of technical improvements reduced the cost of newsprint by about two-thirds and made it efficient to purchase newsprint in extremely large lots. From being artisanal, the production of newspapers became industrial and highly capital intensive, with large circulation papers having much lower unit costs than their smaller rivals.[9]

No less importantly, advertising markets were also transformed. Two factors interacted: on the one hand, urbanisation, income growth and rising literacy laid the foundations for a mass con-sumer base; on the other, consumer good industries such as soaps, processed foods, tobacco products and household fittings them-selves became marked by high capital intensity and vast economies of scale, making them capable of supplying standardised goods in huge quantities at highly affordable prices. Bringing the two together – connecting consumer goods firms seeking sales with consumers seeking inexpensive, reasonable quality goods – was development of systematic marketing, giving birth to national brands that ranged from Singer Sewing Machines to Colgate, Kellogg and Nestlé.[10] Most importantly for the newspaper industry, the rise of national brands created a rapidly expanding market for display advertising in which large circulation papers had enormous advantages.

The most obvious result of the increased importance of economies of scale was a spectacular rise in concentration levels as some newspapers expanded, and came to control a local market, and others collapsed: in the United States, for example, while the number of newspapers continued to grow, the number of cities with two or more daily papers declined by two-thirds in the interwar years; by 1940, for every city which had two daily papers or more, there were nine which had only one. But underpinning that rise in concentration – and the rise to power of the legendary media barons – was intense competition to be the top paper, with the subscription prices for American newspapers, adjusted for inflation, falling by about two-thirds from the 1890s to the 1920s.[11]

Yet prices were only one element in the race for scale – and perhaps not the most significant. For the entire ethos of the newspaper also changed.

While signs of the change can be seen in the pioneering French daily, *Le Matin*, founded in 1884, the great innovator was Adolph Ochs. In 1896 he purchased *The New York Times* as it teetered on the brink of bankruptcy.[12]

Ochs realised that the vast investments required in very high speed printing equipment and physical distribution could only be viable if the paper attracted massive advertising revenues – which was only possible if it had an equally massive readership; and he also realised that the paper would never secure that readership if it remained narrowly partisan. He therefore set down two slogans which its editors were to take as imperative guidance; the first was that the paper would "give the news impartially, without fear or favour." The second was that it was to be a "paper of record," providing "all the news that's fit to print." Thus was born what became known as the "objectivity standard," which was soon adopted as the core ethical norm both by the American Society of Newspaper Editors and by the Society of Professional Journalists, before quickly diffusing abroad.

Objectivity never meant political neutrality: publishers such as Ochs, Hearst, Northcliffe and Beaverbrook had strong views, and wanted to advocate them. But it did mean attempting to draw a line—one sharper than could ever be drawn in reality—between the reporting of facts and the analysis and evaluation of those facts. This partly involved a change in substance: the task of reporters, and the content of news reports, was narrowed to the collection and recording of the four W's and one H: who, what, when, where and how, with the "why" question left to others. At the same time, the shape of newspapers changed: analysis, opinion and editorials were segregated from ordinary reporting and given separately identified pages of their own.[13] Until then, the distinction between reporters, correspondents and columnists was blurred; now, a clear distinction was drawn, including in terms of where they appeared in the paper, between correspondents, who reported facts, and columnists, who stated a point of view, giving the writing of opinion a visibility and prestige it had not previously enjoyed.[14]

At least in principle, this was a happy coincidence of theory and practice. In terms of theory, the Kantian legacy stressed the role of the press in supporting the rational formation of public opinion through objective presentation of facts and through civil but critical analyses; and, in terms of practice, the commercial incentives faced by publishers pushed them to adopt that role as their lodestar. Moreover, for all the slips between the ideal and the reality, it would be fair to say that this unexpected coming together of commerce and philosophy seemed to "deliver the goods."

It is, in effect, a humbling experience to re-read the great columnists of the period from the end of the Second World War to the closing years of the 1970s, when this model was at its height. It is not simply a question of English language writers such as Walter Lippmann and the Alsop brothers in the United States or George Orwell in Britain; even in continental Europe, the leading daily papers carried columns by the likes of Albert Camus and Raymond Aron in France and Norberto Bobbio, Nicola Chiaromonte and Indro Montanelli in Italy, all of whom wrote, week after week, with style, verve and erudition. Set against the great sweep of history, it is hard to think of another period when such depth of insight and civility of tone were brought to huge numbers of readers, helping to create the expectation that this was how what Hobbes dubbed "the conversation of mankind" was to be conducted.

None of these writers confused civility with refusal to take a point of view, even one that was strongly partisan. Their sense of moderation was anything but "une philosophie pour les âmes tendre," – a philosophy for tender souls – as Jean-Paul Sartre dismissively called it. Thus, reflecting toward the end of his life on his intellectual path, Raymond Aron, a man of the centre-right who (unlike Sartre) had been among the first to join the French resistance, wrote that "the liberalism in which I sought and found my spiritual home has nothing in common with a philosophy for tender souls;" what it demands of the writer is a good dose of courage to swim against the current, and to draw, as clearly and explicitly as possible, "the lessons, however uncertain, of historical experience".[15] Equally, Norberto Bobbio, a man of the left also active in the resistance to Mussolini and then Hitler, defined his style as one that combined frankness and directness with "mitezza" or mildness, which he termed the virtue involved in refusing submissiveness without falling into arrogance.

There is, in that sense, considerable truth in Alan Wolfe's 2018 reappraisal of the development of American political culture, where he refers to the first decades after the Second World War as a time when the dominant values in the public conversation were political maturity and the sense of historical irony.[16] Perhaps no one expressed those values better than the literary critic, Lionel Trilling. He asserted that after the horrors of the war and the holocaust, there was, on each and every participant in the public conversation, a "moral obligation to be intelligent," which demanded being "intellectually mature, . . .

willing to judge by reason, observe facts in a critical spirit, and search for the law of things".[17]

None of that is said in the spirit of what would be a misplaced nostalgia. But Hannah Arendt was right when she wrote, echoing the lines in *The Tempest*, that we should relate to the past, "not in order to resuscitate it," but "like a pearl diver who descends to the bottom of the sea" to retrieve lost treasures that, "having undergone a sea change," lie there "in new crystallised forms and shapes that remain immune to the elements," awaiting the intrepid soul "who will bring them up into the world of the living".[18] Viewed from the perspective of 2022, the spirit of that age seems like a lost treasure indeed, lying "full fathom five."

IV

Yet however dazzling that lost treasure may seem, it also had its stern critics.

Writing in a neo-Marxist tradition, the scholars of the Frankfurt School – particularly Max Horkheimer, Theodor W. Adorno, Herbert Marcuse and, in his early work, Jürgen Habermas – cast the media, with its highly concentrated ownership, as pacifying, manipulating and distorting public opinion, narrowing the range of controversy and creating a consensus that was as contrived and repressive in fact as it was tolerant and open-minded in theory. Thus, in his rightly celebrated book, *The Structural Transformation of the Public Sphere*, Habermas argued that in mass communications, "sophisticated opinion-moulding services," operating "under the aegis of a sham public interest," had voided the Kantian process of deliberation of its substance, replacing it with a spectacle in which "the criteria of rationality are completely lacking".[19]

Only slightly later, commentators on the right also lambasted the media, claiming that the few communications channels it offered – including the leading newspapers – had been captured by what Americans call "liberals," who were using their control to spread left-wing propaganda.

It would be easy to show that critics on both the left and the right shared a greatly exaggerated sense of the media's importance in shaping political outcomes. They held what might be termed the hypodermic needle view of media influence: whatever the media said was injected, as if by a hypodermic needle, into the mind of the recipient, altering his or her opinions. Already in the late 1940s, however, research undertaken at Columbia University by the Austrian-born sociologist, Paul Lazarsfeld, had cast doubt on whether the media had anywhere nearly as much impact on opinion formation as the hypodermic needle model implied; and subsequent work, filling many volumes of statistical journals, has only strengthened that skepticism.[20]

Nonetheless, it would be wrong to dismiss the critics entirely. There is, after all, no doubt that media ownership was highly concentrated, reflecting economies of scale involved in assembling mass readerships and delivering them to advertisers. There is equally no doubt that, as C. Wright Mills claimed in his enormously influential book, *The Power Elite*, the media did not provide *public* communications, it supplied *mass* communications. The crucial difference between these, as he articulated the concepts, was that while public communications allowed for give and take, mass communications involved narrow channels that operated in one direction only: far fewer people expressed opinions than received them, and the recipients had no scope to answer back immediately or with any effect.[21] And it is undeniable that the political culture on which this system rested was elitist: indeed, elitism had permeated the model of public deliberation from the outset.

In effect, its core concept of "public opinion" always begged the question: who is "the public"? Or, put slightly differently, whose opinion matters – and whose does not? None of the thinkers who shaped the theory of public deliberation conceived of the public in especially inclusive terms. Kant had wanted to restrict participation in the public debate to property owners; as for Rousseau, he rigorously distinguished the "general will", which should determine the laws, from the mere "will of all," devising mechanisms which limited or even prohibited free association and severely restricted debate.[22]

By the middle of the 19th century, those narrow views of the scope of the deliberative public had, if anything, hardened. The French Revolution, with its descent into the Terror, played a crucial role in that respect. In the Revolution, the Kantian public had met its antithesis – not the autocratic monarch, who the philosophes had elevated into an "enlightened despot," but the mob, in whose "madness," "horrors and crimes," Carlyle saw what he called "the crowning Phenomenon of our Modern Time".[23] Behind the rioter, wrote Hippolyte Taine in his widely read history of the Revolution, lay the savage, with the experience of being in the mob causing its members to revert to a primitive stage of human development.[24]

Little wonder then that Tocqueville, perhaps the most democratic of the century's liberals, opposed every extension of the franchise proposed during his period as a parliamentarian.[25] John Stuart Mill, for his part, saw little merit in popular opinion and rejected the claim that "the multitude [should] … decide according to their own judgement;" instead, Mill advocated

> that political questions be decided not by a direct appeal to the insight or the will of an uninformed multitude, but only by appeal to the views, formed after due consideration, of a relatively small number of persons specially educated for this task.[26]

Finally, Bagehot took it as obvious that a workable democracy required inducing the "self-satisfied, stupid, mass of men to admit its own insufficiency".[27]

But whatever the philosophers may have thought, it was ultimately the technology which determined who had access to communications channels; and if it did nothing else, the rise of the Internet democratised access as thoroughly as the most radical of democrats might have wanted. With the Internet becoming the dominant means of interaction, the mass communications C. Wright Mills had pilloried – in which only the few can communicate to the many – passed away; the age of what he called public communications, in which the many are firmly in control, had arrived.

The dawn of that era was, in its own way, an old dream of the utopians. For example, in his wildly popular *Looking Backwards*, which was first published in 1888, Edward Bellamy imagined that by the year 2000, a technological web would not only allow people to hear the finest music and lectures in their home but also to find, merely by turning a few knobs, some that closely matched their interests. This marvel, he hinted, might even permit many different voices to be heard, inaugurating the happy marriage of democracy and communications.

And a marvel the Internet indeed is. But while the benefits it has brought are beyond doubt, it is equally clear that its rise has left the newspaper industry reeling, while redefining political cultures worldwide.

V

Many economic models, in some cases of great technical sophistication, have been developed to analyse how the newspaper industry might react to the shocks the Internet has unleashed, including the collapse in advertising revenues and the struggle to persuade readers to bear a much higher share of the industry's costs. But those models are inevitably very sensitive to the assumptions on which they rest, and can yield many different outcomes when the assumptions are modified, even slightly.[28] That is not a failing of the models; it is a sign of the fundamental indeterminacy of the reality in which the industry now operates.

There are nonetheless reasons to believe that there remains a substantial demand for a quality press which differentiates its product by scrupulous attention to facts, probing investigative reporting and careful curating of the structure and presentation of the paper as a whole. As many mastheads claw their way back from the precipice, it is becoming clearer that the newspaper, that symbol of modernity, will not disappear from this Earth.

But, as heartening as that is, there are also reasons to believe that the mature, measured analysis which characterised newspapers in the age of the Alsop brothers is seriously threatened – indeed, it was in grave peril even before the Internet arrived. As Matthew Pressman has shown, competition from news magazines – such as

Time and *Newsweek* – and from television led American newspapers to abandon the fact/analysis distinction by the late 1970s; at the same time, their political positioning became more pronounced.[29] Now, that trend has become universal, as newspapers seek readers who are sufficiently interested in news and current affairs to pay for access – and, for better or worse, most of those readers hold firmly defined views.

In and of itself, the trend to greater political polarisation among newspapers might cause little concern: after all, the mere fact that Camus wrote for papers that were clearly on the centre-left, and Aron for papers that were equally clearly on the centre-right, did not undermine the depth of their insight or the civility of their writing. Looking across the advanced democracies as a whole, however there is little doubt that the tone of commentary and of opinion has become increasingly shrill, posing a challenge to what remains of the deliberative ideal.

In part, the shrillness is just a response to the features of the on-line environment. To begin with, consumers are drowning in an incessant flow of competing content. An admittedly rough calculation for 2005 finds that for every minute of mediated content consumed there were some 1 000 minutes of mediated content on offer[30] – but that was before Facebook, Twitter and Instagram brought the real torrents of content to bear. To be heard above the roar one must be loud and piercing – and the pressure on publishers to generate the hits, re-tweets, Facebook likes and the other indicators that determine advertising revenues puts a premium on extreme views, simply presented.

The rise of anonymous comments as the primary form of online interaction has aggravated the problems. It is no accident that in *Genesis*, Adam and Eve acquire names only after the fall: to have a name is to be responsible for one's words and deeds, and hence for the good and evil one's actions cause. Nor is it an accident that for the ancients, the public sphere was where one acted in the open, and hence could be named and held accountable, as against the private sphere where one acted in the secrecy afforded by the walls of one's home. And, if the signature and the full name developed as a mode of personal identification in parallel to the process of individualisation[31], it is because being recognised is so closely bound up with the concept of being free, and hence empowered to act in one's own name, not a serf or a slave. Unburdened by any of those obligations of responsibility, anonymous commentary, if sometimes worthwhile, is all too often mere abuse that has served to push deterioration in public discourse a step further.

But the Internet's features are the not whole story. Rather, it is important also to consider the impacts of the changing composition of the public that newspapers address.

There is, in that, an element of irony. If the thinkers who highlighted the deliberative role of the public sphere were elitist, it was not because they believed in their own inherent superiority; it was because education was only available to the very few. They therefore looked forward to an era in which mass education would lay the foundation for universal participation in reasoned, civil and informed deliberation.

At least as far as newspapers are concerned, that era has presumably arrived: the newspaper reading public has more years of education than ever before. As late as 1966, 48 percent of readers of *The New York Times* had never attended college; by 2016, virtually all had at least a four-year college degree – the exceptions presumably being Bill Gates and Mark Zuckerberg, who are probably wealthier than all its other readers put together. Yet it is these highly educated readers who seem to demand the polarised, dogmatic and petulant expressions of opinion that have become more widespread. The elite, it might be said, have become the mob our intellectual ancestors so anxiously feared.

There is a rich vein of observers who believe that reflects a deterioration in personal character. At least since Tocqueville, Weber and Freud, analysts have forged a link between individual character and social context. Beginning with Christopher Lasch's 1979 bestseller, *The Culture of Narcissism*, which denounced what Lasch called the illiteracy of the highly educated, writers in that tradition have seen secondary narcissism—that is, the narcissism that reduces the world to love and hate – as the dominant personality trait of our era. Incapable of overcoming the wounds of prolonged childhood, narcissists lack the strength required to become independent, free-thinking individuals, says Eli Zaretsky, and hence cannot be "rational coequal participants in creating the binding forces … and resisting the destructive forces" of civilisation.[32] Instead, they act out their passions and frustrations, fluctuating between fury and adoration.

While that is not implausible, how broadly it holds is difficult to say; and it is not clear how its extent and influence might be determined. But what has been shown, notably by Alan Abramowitz, the American political scientist, is that highly educated voters are different. They are not only more politically polarised than less educated voters, but also tend to have a lower tolerance for cognitive dissonance: quite unlike less educated voters, they hold their views as a tightly bound coherent package, rationalising away all discordant facts and never admitting of concessions to the other side.[33] Their belief system is, in other words, tightly bound up both with their personal identity – not merely what they think, but who they are, and how they present themselves to the world – and with their "reference group", making any changes in belief costly. Rather than the open-minded citizens John Stuart Mill had expected universal education to produce, it may therefore have created a public whose salient feature is its unwavering and unquestioning commitment to a fixed point of view.

In short, commentary is affected by three forces at once: the supply side pressure on publishers to obtain the Internet hits that are advertisers' core metric; the demand-side pressures from readers, who are time-starved and politically polarised; and the quality-destroying features of the Internet. Trapped in the cross-fire, civility risks becoming a distant memory.

VI

Or perhaps not. We are, it might fairly be said, moral hypochondri-acs—always worried that the thin veneer of civility which holds so-cieties together is on the verge of collapse. There are good grounds for that constant anxiety: as Norbert Elias, the great scholar of civility, emphasised on the basis of his experience of Nazi Germany, it takes centuries to go from barbarism to civility, minutes to go the other way. The hypochondria, deeply engrained by millennia of natural selection, may help to ensure that when danger looms, we change course. But it is only if we understand what is imperiled, and why it matters, that such a change of course will be possible.

In my view, the ideal of a community which takes political decisions through rational deliberation retains all of its validity; so does the need for it to be informed by thoughtful, civil commentary which helps each and every person fulfill the definition Kant gave, more than two centuries ago, when he asked the question: "What is Enlightenment?" Enlightenment, he answered, is *Sapere aude* – dare to know.

Dare to know: that, I believe, is the essence of the civilisation we have inherited; when the learning is long forgotten, it remains, for each of us, the jewel whose glow illuminates the future. While its future is uncertain, it is only by reaffirming its importance that we will be able to say, like Richard Hooker, the great 16th century Anglican defender of faith and reason, "Posterity shall know that we have not loosely through silence permitted these great things to pass away."

References

Abramowitz, A., *The Disappearing Center: Engaged Citizens, Polarization, and American Democracy*, Yale University Press, New Haven, 2010.

Abramowitz, A., "The New American Electorate: Partisan, Sorted, and Polarized", in J. A. Thurber & A. Yoshinaka (Eds.), *American Gridlock: The Sources, Character, and Impact of Political Polarization*, Cambridge University Press, New York, 2015, 19-44.

Adcock, R., *Liberalism and the Emergence of American Political Science: A Transatlantic Tale*, Oxford University Press, Oxford, 2014.

Arendt, H. (1st publ. by Suhrkamp Verlag, 1955), Introduction to *Walter Benjamin, Illuminations: Essays and Reflections*, Harcourt Brace Jovanovich, New York, 1968.

Aron, R., *Les dernières années du siècle*, Julliard, Paris, 1984.

Broersma, M. J., *Form and Style in Journalism. European Newspapers and the Representation of News 1880-2005*, Peeters, Leuven, 2007.

Chandler, A. D., *The Visible Hand: The Managerial Revolution in American Business*, Belknap Press, Cambridge, MA, 1977.

Elias, N., *The Civilising Process: I. The History of Manners*, Blackwell, Oxford, 1978.

Ergas, H., Pincus, J. J. and Schnittger, S., *Submission to the ACCC Digital Platforms Inquiry*, Sydney, 2018.

Ferenczi, T., *L'invention du journalisme en France: Naissance de la presse moderne à la fin du XIXe siècle*, Plon, Paris, 1993.

Fraenkel, B., *La Signature: Genèse d'un Signe*, Gallimard, Paris, 1992.

Habermas, J. (1962), *The Structural Transformation of the Public Sphere: An Inquiry into a Category of Bourgeois Society*, The MIT Press, Cambridge, MA, 1989.

Hamilton, J. T., *All the News That's Fit to Sell: How the Market Transforms Information into News*, Princeton University Press, Princeton, 2006.

Kaledin, A., *Tocqueville and His America*, Yale University Press, New Haven, 2011.

Koselleck, R. (1959), *Critique and Crisis: Enlightenment and the Pathogenesis of Modern Society*, MIT Press, Cambridge, MA, 1988.

McClelland, J. S., *The Crowd and the Mob: From Plato to Canetti*, Unwin Hyman, London, 1989.

Melton, J. Van Horn, *The Rise of the Public in Enlightenment Europe*, Cambridge University Press, Cambridge, 2001.

Merry, R. W., *Taking on the world: Joseph and Stewart Alsop, Guardians of the American Century*, Viking, New York, 1996.

Mills, C. Wright, *The Power Elite*, Oxford University Press, Oxford, 1956.

Neuman, W. R., *The Digital Difference: Media Technology and the Theory of Communication Effects*, Harvard University Press, Cambridge MA, 2016.

Owen, B. M., *Economics and Freedom of Expression*, Ballinger Publishing Company, Cambridge, MA, 1975.

Pressman, M., *On Press: The Liberal Values That Shaped the News*, Harvard University Press, Cambridge, MA, 2018.

Prochaska, F., *Eminent Victorians on American Democracy: The View from Albion*, Oxford University Press, Oxford, 2012.

Raeff, M., *The Well-Ordered Police State: Social and Institutional Change through Law in the Germanies and Russia, 1600–1800*, Yale University Press, New Haven, 1983.

Riley, S. G., *The American Newspaper Columnist*, Praeger, Westport, CT, 1998.

Sheppard, S., *American Media. American Bias: The Partisan Press from Broadsheet to Blog* (PhD), Johns Hopkins University, Baltimore, Maryland, 2007.

Trilling, L., *The Moral Obligation to Be Intelligent: Selected Essays*, Northwestern University Press, Evanston, 2008.

Urbinati, N., *Representative Democracy: Principles and Genealogy*, The University of Chicago Press, Chicago, 2006.

Ward, S. J. A., *The Invention of Journalism Ethics*, McGill-Queen's University Press, Montreal, 2015.

Wolfe, A., *The Politics of Petulance: America in an Age of Immaturity*, University of Chicago Press, Chicago, 2018.

Zaretsky, E., *Political Freud: A History*, Columbia University Press, New York, 2015.

Endnotes

[1] R. W. Merry, *Taking on the World: Joseph and Stewart Alsop, Guardians of the American Century*, Viking, New York, 1996, 190-2.

[2] M. Pressman, *On Press: The Liberal Values That Shaped the News*, Harvard University Press, Cambridge, MA, 2018, 251.

[3] S. J. A. Ward, *The Invention of Journalism Ethics*, McGill-Queen's University Press, Montreal, 2015, 115, 116, 121.

[4] J. Habermas, (1962) 1989, *The Structural Transformation of the Public Sphere: An Inquiry into a Category of Bourgeois Society*, The MIT Press, Cambridge, MA; R. Koselleck (1959) 1988, *Critique and Crisis: Enlightenment and the Pathogenesis of Modern Society*, Cambridge, Mass, MIT Press; Melton, J. Van Horn, *The Rise of the Public in Enlightenment Europe*, Cambridge University Press, Cambridge, 2001; M. Raeff, *The Well-Ordered Police State: Social and Institutional Change through Law in the Germanies and Russia, 1600–1800*, Yale University Press, New Haven, 1983.

[5] N. Elias, *The Civilising Process: I. The History of Manners*, Blackwell, Oxford, 1978, 42.

6 J. Kant, *Critique of Practical Reason* (1788), trans. Mary J. Gregor, in *Practical Philosophy*, ed. Mary J. Gregor, Cambridge University Press, Cambridge, 1999, A820; B848.

7 J. Kant, 1784, *What is Enlightenment?*, see http://www.columbia.edu/acis/ets/CCREAD/etscc/kant.html (accessed 21 Nov 2020)

8 S. Sheppard, *American Media. American Bias: The Partisan Press from Broadsheet to Blog* (PhD), Johns Hopkins University, Baltimore, MD, 2007.

9 B. M. Owen, *Economics and Freedom of Expression*, Ballinger Publishing Company, Cambridge, MA, 1975, 66, 76.

10 A. D. Chandler, *The Visible Hand: The Managerial Revolution in American Business*, Belknap Press, Cambridge, MA, 1977.

11 B. M. Owen, *Economics and Freedom of Expression*, Ballinger Publishing Company, Cambridge, MA, 1975, 77, 79]

12 T. Ferenczi, *L'invention du journalisme en France: Naissance de la presse moderne à la fin du XIXe siècle*, Plon, Paris, 1993; J. T. Hamilton, *All the News That's Fit to Sell: How the Market Transforms Information into News*, Princeton University Press, Princeton, 2006. (note: text reference was to "Hamilton, 2003" but the only Hamilton on the list was 2006.)

13 M. J. Broersma, *Form and Style in Journalism. European Newspapers and the Representation of News 1880-2005*, Peeters, Leuven, 2007.

14 S. G. Riley, *The American Newspaper Columnist*, Praeger, Westport, CT, 1998, 80-103.

15 R. Aron, *Les dernières années du siècle*, Julliard, Paris, 1984, 81-2.

16 A. Wolfe, *The Politics of Petulance: America in an Age of Immaturity*, Chicago University Press, Chicago, 2018.

17 I. Trilling, *The Moral Obligation to Be Intelligent: Selected Essays*, Northwestern University Press, Evanston, 2008, 390.

18 H. Arendt, (1st publ. by Suhrkamp Verlag, 1955), Introduction to *Walter Benjamin, Illuminations: Essays and Reflections*, Harcourt Brace Jovanovich, New York, 1968.

19 J. Habermas, (1962), *The Structural Transformation of the Public Sphere: An Inquiry into a Category of Bourgeois Society*, The MIT Press, Cambridge, MA, 1989, 195, 249.

20 W. R. Neuman, *The Digital Difference: Media Technology and the Theory of Communication Effects*, Harvard University Press, Cambridge MA, 2016.

21 C, Wright Mills, *The Power Elite*, Oxford University Press, Oxford, 1956, 303-4.

22 N. Urbinati, *Representative Democracy: Principles and Genealogy*, The University of Chicago Press, Chicago, 2006, 97-114.

23 (CFR, I, 17)

[24] J. S. McClelland, *The Crowd and the Mob: From Plato to Canetti*, Unwin Hyman, London, 1989, 132-4.

[25] R. Adcock, *Liberalism and the Emergence of American Political Science: A Transatlantic Tale*, Oxford University Press, Oxford, 2014, 34; A. Kaledin, *Tocqueville and His America*, Yale University Press, New Haven, 2011, 137.

[26] Mill ref.

[27] F. Prochaska, *Eminent Victorians on American Democracy: The View from Albion*, Oxford University Press, Oxford, 2012, 50.

[28] H. Ergas, J. J. Pincus and S. Schnittger, *Submission to the ACCC Digital Platforms Inquiry*, Sydney, 2018.

[29] M. Pressman, *On Press: The Liberal Values That Shaped the News*, Harvard University Press, Cambridge, MA, 2018, 29-44.

[30] W. R. Neuman, *The Digital Difference: Media Technology and the Theory of Communication Effects*, Harvard University Press, Cambridge MA, 2016, 132.

[31] B. Fraenkel, *La Signature: Genèse d'un Signe*, Gallimard, Paris, 1992.

[32] E. Zaretsky, *Political Freud: A History*, Columbia University Press, New York, 2015, 146.

[33] A. Abramowitz, *The disappearing center: Engaged citizens, polarization, and American democracy*, Yale University Press, New Haven, 2010; A. Abramowitz, "The New American Electorate: Partisan, Sorted, and Polarized", in J. A. Thurber & A. Yoshinaka (eds.), *American Gridlock: The Sources, Character, and Impact of Political Polarization*, Cambridge University Press, New York, 2015, 19-44. Note text reference is to Abramowitz, 2012.

PART 3

Parliament, Public Service and Administration

9

The Legislative Council of NSW

A Progressive Conservative Institution

David Clune

The Legislative Council of New South Wales (NSW) is Australia's oldest legislative institution, having been created in 1823.[1] Throughout its long and diverse history, the Council has demonstrated a capacity to change and develop. It has not been a linear, planned growth – more an evolution in response to political challenges and societal change. In its various incarnations, the Council has performed a useful, if mutable, role in the legislative process, growing into a vital one in the 21st century. It has changed from being a conservative gatekeeper to, in the words of former NSW Chief Justice Murray Gleeson, "an essential safeguard against abuses of executive power".[2]

The Council in the 19th century

The rulers of the British Empire in the 19th century had a strong belief that subjects should, as far as practicable, enjoy the rights of those at home. Representation was a key concept in British constitutional practice and it was thus decided that NSW should have a representative institution, although only in a way that stretched the definition to the limit. The first Legislative Council consisted of the Governor, his officials and some leading citizens. It was, nevertheless, a beginning.[3]

In keeping with the philosophy of the Colonial Office at the time, the colonists were given gradual tranches of power in preparation for home rule. In 1843, the Council became Australia's first elected legislature, when a proportion of the members were popularly elected but on a restricted franchise.[4]

With the advent of responsible government in 1856, the newly-created Legislative Assembly had the role of making and unmaking governments. The Council became an antipodean House of Lords, with a membership appointed for life by the Governor on the advice of the Premier.[5] There was, however, continuity in terms of its role in scrutiny of the executive. This was something at which the original Council had excelled under the robust guidance of William Charles Wentworth.[6]

As well as a house of review, the framers of the NSW Constitution intended the Council to be a check on any excesses the popularly elected lower house (Legislative Assembly) might indulge in. This is not quite the revanchist plot that it has been portrayed as. Self-government was a leap in the dark. No-one really knew how it would function. Many feared the "tyranny of the mob" and that the electorate would be bought by the highest bidder. It should be remembered that 19th century electioneering was a disorderly, violent process. Polling day was often the occasion for riots. "Treating" was a common practice and voters were sometimes brought to the polling station in a highly intoxicated state by supporters of candidates.[7] As John Hirst has pointed out, the quality of the membership of the early Legislative Assembly was not high: "To conservatives it appeared as if the government had been debased into a giant system of corruption with needy ministers and members bound together by their joint interest in plunder".[8]

On the whole, democracy did function reasonably well, not-withstanding periods of chronic factional instability that nearly paralysed the Assembly. As well as the larrikins, the 19th century Parliament produced some of Australia's greatest statesmen: Henry Parkes, Edmund Barton, George Reid. The Council was not called upon to defend the gates against the barbarians.

The notion of the upper house as an illegitimate brake on progress has coloured historical perceptions of the Legislative Council's performance. Can it sensibly be argued that NSW would have been a better place if the Parliament had been unicameral? To the contrary, there was a legitimate creative tension between a deliberative, delaying and revising chamber and "the people's house". An upper house can allow interested parties to contribute to legislation and a government to have second thoughts. If it is not bloody-mindedly obstructive, and the lower house is prepared to compromise, better government can result. With some exceptions, such a *modus vivendi* prevailed.

The Council contained a reactionary element but also had members who took the safeguard and review role seriously. An example of this *noblesse oblige* attitude producing beneficial results came during the anti-Chinese hysteria of the gold rush period that resulted in the Lambing Flat riots. In response to public pressure, the Government introduced what can only be described as racist, anti-Chinese legislation. In 1858 and 1861, the Council defeated the Chinese Immigration bills; its members describing them as pandering to the masses, ill-founded, unjust and inhumane.[9]

Charles Cowper, a liberal and the first important Premier of NSW, soon found himself in conflict with the conservative-dominated Council. Demonstrating why he was known as "Slippery Charlie", he realised that transformation of the upper house into an elected institution was not the best way to overcome resistance. Cowper understood that he held the ultimate weapon: being able to ask the Governor to "swamp" the Council by appointing new MLCs. The upper house, in turn, realised that, as it lacked democratic legitimacy, it was not in its self-interest to be overly reactionary. By the 1860s, Cowper and his colleague, John Robertson, had passed key liberal measures to reform the land laws and democratise the electoral system although they lacked a majority in the Council.[10]

Another serious conflict occurred during the premiership (1894-99) of George Reid, a Free Trader and progressive liberal. In June 1895, the Council defeated the Government's land and income tax bills. Reid went to the polls, campaigning on the issue of the powers of the upper house. After he was re-elected, the Council realised it had gone "a bridge too far". A compromise was reached where it bowed to the popular will and passed the disputed measures. In return, Reid quietly shelved his reform bill.[11]

The Council and Labor, 1910-32

As disciplined political parties increasingly dominated the lower house in the 20th century, the need for a house of review became more important. The same forces were, however, at work in the second chamber. The advent of Labor governments with the 1910 election meant that the Council's other role as conservative gatekeeper became more dominant. Labor was in a minority in the Council until 1949.[12]

Labor was a new kind of party. The conference formulated policy, the parliamentarians were directed to implement it, and they voted in parliament as caucus decided. This was anathema to 19th century liberals such as George Reid. Traditional liberals and conservatives in the Council were instinctively wary of the new party. NSW Labor's platform, in fact, consisted mainly of sensible and moderate reforms but it seemed threatening to establishment figures and the perception was enhanced by much wild and windy talk of socialism on both sides.[13]

The legislation of Labor governments was certainly treated more harshly by the Council than that of their conservative predecessors. As it happened, early Labor premiers such as William Holman and John Storey were, on occasion, secretly relieved to have the upper house as an excuse for not proceeding with the more radical demands of the party. The Council was at its most obstructive in dealing with legislation that might adversely affect upper class interests: establishment of state enterprises, regulation of private enterprise, industrial relations, taxation, landlord and tenant. Nonetheless, the upper house was not completely intransigent and compromises were sometimes reached that allowed important parts of the Labor program to pass.[14]

Conflict reached white-hot intensity with Labor demagogue Jack Lang's unsuccessful attempts to abolish the Council in 1925 and 1930. As the political situation became more febrile in the early 1930s, partisanship in the Council became more pronounced. By the time the Governor, Sir Philip Game, dismissed Lang in 1932, NSW was dangerously close to major civil disorder.[15] The Council's guardian role was an important element in preventing this. The fact that it could, and did, defeat or amend some of Lang's more divisive measures was a safety valve against political extremism.

The indirectly-elected Council, 1934-78

By the time of Lang's dismissal – subsequently affirmed by a massive victory for the United Australia Party under Bertram Stevens at the 1932 election – the dynamics of the Legislative Council had been distorted beyond repair. Partisanship was entrenched and the appointment of MLCs at Lang's request had bloated the quantity and diluted the quality of the membership. The first conservative response was an amendment to the NSW Constitution, initiated by the Bavin Government in 1930. The amendments provided that the Council could not be altered or abolished without a referendum. Stevens delivered the next instalment with a reconstitution of the upper house.

The 1934 reconstruction was not, in a philosophical sense, conservative. It was, indeed, based on abstract theory. It was much in the shadow of the Asquith Government's struggle in the United Kingdom against the House of Lords, resulting in the *Parliament Act* of 1911. Nothing ultimately came of subsequent moves to reform the Lords. As part of this, Viscount Bryce produced a report in 1917 that had a major influence on the changes in NSW. The new Council was to have a membership of 60 indirectly elected by all members of both houses. The term of each member of the Council was to be 12 years, with elections for a quarter of the MLCs being held triennially. The aim was to attract members with experience in public life and other important fields such as law and finance who were not up to the rough and tumble of lower house politics. Another aim was to add a non-partisan element that would consider matters impartially and on their merits.[16]

As with many "rational" reforms, the results were nothing like they were intended to be. The low quota needed for election led to bribery and stand-over tactics to obtain votes. As membership was in the gift of the parties, long and faithful service, more than ability, was often the criterion for election. The non-Labor side maintained the pretence of not being an official Opposition but the Council largely operated on a party basis. When Labor, having rid itself of Lang, returned to power under Bill McKell in 1941, it was back to the old game of negotiation and concession to get the government's program through an antipathetic upper house.[17] When the ALP gained a majority in the Council in 1949, non-government amendment of bills virtually ceased. From 1950 to 1959, when Labor had majorities in both houses, only three Opposition amendments were successful.[18]

The Council did, however, maintain a circumscribed scrutiny function. Ken Turner, in his definitive study of the indirectly elected upper house, concluded that it had a "useful record of undramatic tidying up". Writing in 1968 he noted: "Attendance is good, more bills are being amended, more pages of Hansard filled, and greater use of committees is being made".[19]

Max Willis (Liberal MLC, 1970-99; Leader of the Opposition, 1978-81; and President, 1991-98) argues that the 1934-78 Council could be effective as a house of review because some MLCs were true experts in their fields:

> There was nothing people like Sir Edward Warren did not know about the coal industry and the industries allied to it. He only ever spoke on that subject and when he spoke everybody listened. So if there was any kind of legislation relating to the coal industry which required amendment the Government took notice of him, whether it was a Labor government or a Coalition government. Mac Falkiner – the doyen of the Falkiner wool family – spoke if there was anything to do with wool or rural matters. He was a man whose whole life had been spent in that industry and he knew it backwards. For anything on labour and industrial relations you had Fred Bowen, who was the President of the Trades and Labour Council, and John Darling, the Director of the Employers' Federation. People tended to be at the peak of their life or their vocation or their industry. They made very wise and practical contributions. Very often these revisions to legislation, in my observation, occurred behind closed doors. Ted Warren would take the minister

aside and say, "Look, you can't do this", so an appropriate government amendment would be introduced. He would not stand up on the floor and hammer the hell out of the minister and then move an amendment. That was the way it worked. For its time and because of its composition I think it was effective, but in a quite different way to now.[20]

The indirectly-elected Council has the singular distinction of having had its existence affirmed by the people. In 1961, the Heffron Labor Government, reluctantly and under strong party pressure, held a referendum on abolition of the upper house. A resounding 57.6 percent voted in favour of retaining the Council.

The 1978 reconstitution and its consequences

By the 1970s, the Council was widely seen as an anachronism. Its membership was aged, its sitting hours short, its activity limited. A chamber that was not directly elected by the people was no longer defensible. When Neville Wran led the ALP to victory in the elections of 1976, reform of the upper house was high on his agenda; he had previously been a member of the Council, 1970-73. In June 1977, Wran introduced a bill that provided for a chamber of 45 members elected for three Assembly terms. The method of election he proposed was non-preferential proportional representation, where electors would vote for a group of candidates and their votes would then exhaust. The State constituted a single electorate and the quota for election was 6.25 percent.[21]

While more enlightened elements in the Opposition privately agreed that the time had come for reform, they strongly objected to Wran's proposed voting system which they rightly believed would over-represent the party winning a majority of the vote. A compromise was hammered out where, in return for a number of concessions, the Opposition did not oppose a "yes" vote in a referendum on reconstruction of the Council. Wran's most significant compromise was to agree to optional preferential voting. At a referendum held on 12 May 1978, 84.8 percent of those voting supported the proposed reconstitution of the Council.

At the general election in October 1978 Wran won 63 of the 99 Assembly seats. Labor's large vote gave it a majority in the Legislative Council, which it retained until its defeat in March 1988. In terms of legislative review, there was no improvement. Jack Hallam (Labor MLC, 1973-91, Leader of the Government, 1986-88, and Leader of the Opposition, 1988-91) recalls that debate was –

> generally of a partisan nature rather than intrinsic review. The house was discouraged from being a house of review because it had evolved into a partisan house. When one of the major parties had a majority they were not inclined to review legislation unless there was a broad, popular uprising or concern about a particular issue. Amendment was discouraged by the powerbrokers, Askin[22] and then Wran. If they had political control of the Legislative Council, it was legislation by instruction rather than review . . . Of course, it is not the Leader in the Council who is making these decisions – well, certainly not in the Labor Party. They were made by the party executive and the Cabinet. Cabinet would give instructions that the legislation was to be put through in the house and there was no authorisation for the Leader of the Government to accept amendments – sometimes the opposite.[23]

The 1978 reconstruction nevertheless unleashed powerful currents that were to transform the upper house. A major one was that MLCs became younger, full-time, better educated, more professional and more ambitious. They immediately asked the question: how is this new, democratically elected house going to justify its existence?

An obvious answer, looking to the Senate as an example, was an effective committee system. If government control meant little amendment of legislation, committees were a way of investigating and scrutinising in a less confrontational, more bipartisan way. Ron Dyer (ALP MLC, 1979-2003 and a Minister and Deputy Leader of the Government, 1995-2003) has said that –

> interest groups out in the community have the capacity to be consulted if there is an effective and workable committee system. If there is controversial legislation pending, the

upper house, exercising its review function, can institute an inquiry into that particular policy or administrative area, whatever it happens to be, and witnesses can be called representing that particular interest group. So I see that as contributing to an effective committee system, but also as an effective consultation of the people and interest groups via that committee system.[24]

In February 1985, the Government moved, with Opposition support, to establish a select committee, chaired by Dyer, to investigate establishment of a system of standing committees in the Council. The committee's report, tabled in November 1986, recommended establishment of four adequately staffed and resourced committees. Although the recommendations received bipartisan support, nothing eventuated before the 1988 election.[25]

The incoming Coalition Government led by Nick Greiner was committed to the establishment of Council standing committees. The first two, State Development and Social Issues, were established in June 1988. A third committee, Law and Justice, was created by the Carr Government in May 1995. A weakness in the system was that these committees lacked a self-referencing power. They had a government majority, limiting their independence.

Nonetheless, the standing committees have produced a large number of well-researched reports, usually bipartisan, which have had an important influence on the policy process. A notable success was the Social Issues Committee's inquiry in 1989 into adoption of children. In spite of a wide diversity of views among members, the Committee produced a unanimous report that was accepted by the Government and led to a major change in policy. The State Development Committee's inquiries into public sector tendering and contracting and coastal development produced important reforms. An inquiry by the Law and Justice Committee in 2001 into a bill of rights for NSW resulted in establishment of the Joint Legislation Review Committee.[26]

Ministers have increasingly referred issues to the Standing Committees to promote discussion and facilitate reform. In the 2007-11 Parliament, the Attorney-General asked the Law and Justice

Committee to hold inquiries into: adoption by same sex couples; altruistic surrogacy; the naming of children in criminal proceedings; and trials by judges alone. Each report led to legislative reform.[28]

The era of strong bicameralism

The 1988 election was the end of an epoch, as the balance of power moved to the crossbench where it has since remained. In 1991, the Greiner Government reduced the size of the Council to 42 and the term of office to eight years. A consequence was that the quota for election was lowered to 4.5 percent, thus greatly increasing the likelihood of independent and minor party representation. In the 52nd Parliament (1999-2003), there were 16 Government, 13 Opposition and 13 minor party and independent MLCs. The crossbenchers have spanned the ideological spectrum from far left to far right. The first minor parties to win seats were Fred Nile's Call To Australia (later Christian Democrats) and the Australian Democrats, then the Greens and the Shooters. There have also been a variety of micro-party and independent MLCs. The Council was back in business as a house of review in a big way.

When Labor controlled the Council from 1978 to 1988 just one non-government amendment was successful. By contrast, in the Carr Government's first term (1995-1999), when Labor did not have a majority in the upper house, 956 non-government amendments were passed.[27] Lack of control has not meant wholesale obstruction of government legislation. There have been occasions when governments have had to abandon important bills or accept unpalatable amendments. But, by negotiation and compromise, most of their program has been passed. The process has, on the whole, led to better law-making.

John Hannaford (Liberal MLC, 1984-2000; Leader of the Government, 1992-95; and Leader of the Opposition, 1995-99) has said of dealing with the crossbenchers:

> You had to be prepared to listen and to negotiate. What we put in place was a series of meetings with the crossbenchers in the upper house. We met each Tuesday morning in my

office to discuss what was to be the legislative program, and we made certain that the crossbenchers got access to any advisers they needed. I learnt . . . about the need to negotiate and be prepared to give, but maintain your philosophical position in relation to legislation. That had to be sustained, but you could then look at the operating provisions. I took the approach that it is better to get 80 or 90 percent of something than 100 percent of nothing.[29]

Hannaford believes that during the Coalition's period in office (1988–95), crossbench control of the Council resulted in improved legislation:

In that situation you do not get the extreme positions and it means that a government has to look at governing to the middle ground. I think that the enthusiasm of some ministers and the enthusiasm to drive agendas got tempered and we looked for what might be a more moderate reform. If a government without a Council majority wants to drive a significant agenda then it has to be prepared to do a lot more work in conditioning the community and therefore conditioning the crossbenchers.[30]

Michael Egan (Labor MLC, 1986-2005; Opposition Leader, 1991-95; and Treasurer and Leader of the Government, 1995-2005) was also careful to keep the lines of communication open with the crossbenchers:

I used to meet with them every week, only for about 10 minutes, just to take them through what we would be doing that week, seeing if they had any issues of concern. Those meetings used to go well. I would occasionally brief them personally on a bill but generally that would be delegated to either the particular ministers or sometimes even the departmental advisers.

Generally speaking, Egan found the crossbenchers "pretty good" to work with:

At one stage when I was Leader I had 13 crossbenchers to deal with . . . I had to get six of those 13 to support me on anything that we wanted through if it was controversial. And, generally speaking, I could either get the six that were, so to

> speak, on the left to vote for us or the six or seven on the right.
> So you played them off like that . . . Some crossbenchers were
> very good; some used to make me tear my hair out.[31]

The rise of the crossbench also gave the committee system renewed impetus. In May 1997, the Leader of the Opposition, John
Hannaford, moved to establish five General Purpose Standing Committees (GPSCs) each covering a group of portfolios. The motion was
opposed by the Carr Government but passed 21 to 15, with all crossbench MLCs voting in support.

Unlike the standing committees, the GPSCs are not government-
controlled: there are three government members, two from the
Opposition and two crossbenchers. The GPSCs can initiate their
own investigations. They also conduct budget estimates hearings.
The GPSCs tend to focus more on accountability than policy, and
their inquiries are often highly politicised and publicised:

> GPSC No. 3, for example, discomfited the Government with
> its inquiries into policing in the Cabramatta area, which
> prompted a range of changes to police practices. Inquiries
> by GPSC No. 4 into development decisions regarding
> Orange Grove and Badgerys Creek helped prompt an ICAC
> review into the activities of lobbyists in NSW Government.
> The GPSCs continued to trouble the Labor Government to
> the bitter end. Premier Keneally's proroguing of Parliament
> on 22 December 2010 failed to stop GPSC No. 1, chaired
> by Fred Nile, doggedly inquiring into the first tranche sale
> of the state's electricity generators. The Committee reported
> one month before the 2011 election, recommending that the
> sale be rescinded.[32]

The highly partisan nature of estimates hearings has drawn
criticism. Dyer has described them as –

> largely point-scoring exercises. I tended to take the view, as
> a minister and as a member after I ceased to be a minister,
> that the proper role of a member of an estimates committee
> was to go through the estimates, the budget papers, line by
> line and ask constructive questions, for example, saying to
> the responsible minister, "Line so-and-so provides for $X

million to be spent in the ensuing financial year; why was only X minus Y spent, and what were the reasons for that, and why is there such a carryover?" That is just one example. I think that is a perfectly legitimate thing to be asking. However, it is my impression, both when I was a member pre-2003 and since – and it has probably got worse since – that all sorts of extraneous things are obtruding themselves into the estimates process that are highly political.[33]

It is perhaps expecting too much from practitioners of politics which, as Mao Zedong said, is "war without blood", to abstain completely from conflict in committee work. The dichotomy that has evolved of bipartisan policy committees and more partisan scrutiny by the GPSCs is as good a compromise as is likely to be achieved in the real world. It should also be remembered that, while the motives are not pure, point-scoring can be an effective way of enforcing accountability.

In the 21st century the Legislative Council has a well-resourced, active, respected and effective committee system that is producing tangible results. In 2011-12, 32 inquiries were held and 25 reports tabled. Committees received 1 684 submissions, and 94 hearings were held at which 905 witnesses were examined.[34] The Clerk of the Legislative Council, David Blunt, has described the outcomes of upper house committee work in the 55th Parliament (2011-15) as "quite extraordinary" in terms of unanimous cross-party recommendations that were implemented by the government.[35]

The Egan cases

In the 19th century, members of both houses frequently moved for the tabling of State government papers on matters they were concerned with. If passed, such motions were automatically complied with by the government. The procedure fell into disuse in the 20th century.

After the 1995 election, the Liberal-National Opposition in the Council decided to revive calls for papers to aid its investigation of some politically contentious decisions. The flash point came on 18 April 1996 when Hannaford moved that the Government table all papers relating to the approval process for the Lake Cowal gold mine. The motion was passed with the support of some of the crossbenchers. The Leader of the Government, Michael Egan, refused to comply on the grounds that the Council did not have the power to make such an order. Hannaford successfully moved a motion of censure against him. When Egan persisted in his defiance, the Council suspended him. He immediately commenced proceedings in the NSW Supreme Court. Egan argued that, as the Council had no power to compel him to produce documents, the finding of contempt and his subsequent suspension were invalid.[36]

In its decision on 29 November 1996, the Court unanimously held that the Council did have the power to order the production of State papers. In his judgment, Chief Justice Gleeson stated an important principle:

> The capacity of both houses of parliament, including the house less likely to be "controlled" by the government, to scrutinise the workings of the executive government, by asking questions and demanding the production of State papers, is an important aspect of modern parliamentary democracy. It provides an essential safeguard against abuses of executive power.[37]

Egan appealed to the High Court. On 19 November 1998 it ruled in favour of the Council. Justice Kirby said:

> To deny the Council such powers would be to destroy its effectiveness as a house of parliament. The fact that the executive government is made or unmade in the Legislative Assembly, that appropriation bills must originate there and may sometimes be presented for the Royal Assent without the concurrence of the Council does not reduce the latter to a mere cipher or legislative charade. The Council is an elected chamber of a parliament of a State of Australia. Its power to render the executive government in that State accountable, and to sanction obstruction where it occurs, is not only lawful. It is the very reason for constituting the Council as a house of parliament.[38]

In another case, Egan disputed the Council's power to call for privileged documents and lost again. On 10 June 1999, the NSW Court of Appeal held that

> the Council's power to call for documents did extend to privileged documents, on the basis that such a power may be reasonably necessary for the exercise of its legislative function and its role in scrutinising the executive. However, there were different views on the question of the extent of the power to order documents. In particular, Priestley JA found no limitation on that power. Whereas the majority of Spigelman CJ and Meagher JA found that the power does not extend to ordering the production of cabinet documents.[39]

Successful orders for papers have been frequent since the Egan cases. During the 53rd Parliament (2003-06), there were 145. The procedure was used 94 times in the 54th Parliament (2007-10) and 69 times in the succeeding Parliament (2011-14).[40] The capacity to call for papers has facilitated the work of committees, aided scrutiny of the executive, added to transparency in public life, and made a contribution to the policy process.[41]

As a result of the Egan cases, the Council is the most powerful State upper house in Australia. The courts have affirmed that, except as specified in the *Constitution Act (NSW)*, it has powers equal to those of the Assembly. No Australian second chamber makes anything like the use of orders for papers that the NSW Legislative Council does.

A comparative perspective

Steffen Ganghof, Professor of Politics at the University of Potsdam, has identified a new type of governmental system he calls "semi-parliamentarism". It exists when the legislature is "divided into two equally legitimate parts, only one of which can dismiss the prime minster in a no-confidence vote". Such systems balance the conflicting roles of the lower house in maintaining confidence in the government, which Ganghof calls the parliamentary function, and the upper as a deliberative chamber. The part of the legislature with –

> . . . confidence authority can achieve the "majoritarian" values of identifiability, accountability and cabinet stabil- ity, whereas the separated part can allow for proportion-

ality, a multi-dimensional party system and issue-specific deliberation on individual pieces of legislation.

Ganghof describes semi-parliamentarism as "a distinct and neglected type of executive-legislative system that deserves consideration by scholars and constitutional designers alike". It achieves a workable balance between competing visions of democracy.[42] Ganghof has ranked 29 democracies according to how they compare with the ideal definition of semi-parliamentarism. His conclusion is that NSW is "the only case that does not deviate from the ideal type (even though upper house members do serve longer, eight year, terms). The Australian Commonwealth and Japan, on the other hand, deviate most strongly. The other Australian states are in between".[43]

Bruce Stone has identified a number of qualities that he considers desirable in a State upper house.[44] In terms of having enough members to fulfil its role adequately, he assesses the NSW Legislative Council as about the right size. The NSW upper house, like that in Victoria, does not have the power to block money bills. Stone says that there is an argument for restoring such a power if the second chamber has equal democratic legitimacy with the lower house. As he also notes, however, the reverberations from the Senate's blocking of supply in 1975 are still so great that a consensus seems to have developed between parties that "the core, if not the whole, of the budget should not be subject to amendment. It is notable that the blocking of budget legislation, or threats to do so, did not play an obvious role in exposing or resolving governmental crises in WA, SA or Victoria in the early 1990s". Lack of a veto power is thus not a practical impediment to the operation of the NSW Legislative Council as a house of review. In fact, it has much greater input into budget scrutiny through its estimates committees than the Legislative Assembly does.

The effectiveness of the mechanism used to resolve deadlocks between the houses is on Stone's list. In NSW, the absence since the 1934 reconstruction of a budget veto power has reduced the salience of this issue – an argument for not restoring it. The NSW *Constitution Act* provides for a free conference between the houses and a referendum on a deadlocked bill. The former was used effectively to resolve the dispute in 1978 over reform of the Council. The NSW process is not obviously inferior to that of other States and, Stone argues, is superior to the recently introduced Victorian system of a joint sitting after an election which, he says, "clearly weakens bicameralism". Stone acknowledges that lack of major party control reduces the likelihood of deadlocks as governments can negotiate with independents and minor parties to pass legislation. The NSW experience since 1988 is that, on the whole, governments have been able to work effectively with the crossbench to implement their program.

Stone considers the traditional argument that longer terms combined with separate elections can insulate upper houses from the competition to form government and thus enhance their independent perspective. He asks "whether complex rotations and separate elections are intrinsically connected to the old pre-democratic upper houses, or whether there might be a case for them as part of the design of contemporary upper houses". The answer would seem to be that this rather elitist and undemocratic concept has been replaced by the capacity of the second chamber, certainly in NSW, to represent a variety of community opinions, thus tempering potential majoritarian excesses in the lower house.

Stone's final point is the desirability of proportional representation as the electoral system for an upper house. This operates in NSW in a particularly pure form as the quota for election is a low 4.5 percent. Indeed, Stone considers that it is "too small because it facilitates representation of very small communities of opinion, with representatives overly focused upon advocacy of a narrow policy agenda". This does not take account of changes to electoral legislation after the 1999 poll which addressed the question of an unusually large number of micro parties standing, some of dubious provenance, and the consequent manipulation of preference flows. Group voting tickets were abolished and voters were able to allocate preferences "above the line". Tighter registration requirements for parties were introduced. The result is a system that prevents the Council becoming, in Stone's words, "a soapbox rather than a house of review".

In the light of the work of Ganghof and Stone, the NSW Legislative Council would seem to be something of a model for a modern upper house.

Conclusion

The Legislative Council's role as a house of review continues to strengthen and expand. Since 2018, it has appointed four new Standing Committees: Selection of Bills, Regulation, Public Works, and Public Accountability. In 2019, seven GPSCs, now re-named Portfolio Committees, were appointed: Premier and Finance, Health, Education, Industry, Legal Affairs, Transport and Customer Service, Planning and Environment. Changes to the Standing Orders have improved the effectiveness of Question Time and provided more opportunities for private members' business.

In 2019, the Council sat on average for nine hours per day rather than the seven to eight of previous years. There was a substantial increase in the number of successful amendments. In 2019, 140 amendments were agreed to, compared to 90 the previous year, and 59 in 2017. The number of successful orders for the Government to produce State papers increased markedly, from six in 2018 to 52 in 2019.[45]

In the 21st century, the Legislative Council of New South Wales has an effective committee system, promotes accountability through calls for papers, and extensively debates and revises legislation. The Legislative Assembly, by contrast, does few of these things. It does exercise partisan scrutiny, for example, through Question Time. The lower house also has a committee system which does useful work but is largely muzzled by party control. The age of presidential politics, the "ten second grab" and social media has, unfortunately, eroded respect for the Assembly and its traditions. In the past it was where MPs learnt their craft, served an apprenticeship and won advancement. Now members are catapulted into the ministry with little or no experience. Many regard sittings of the Assembly as a quaint old ritual that has to be endured between tweets. As an example, the Assembly now rarely has a committee stage debate (now called Consideration in Detail), where bills are considered clause by clause. In the 1970s, on a major bill, such debates would often go all night. The use of the "gag" is no longer frequent as MPs rarely wish to speak at length.

In the future, a government, either in its own right or with compliant crossbench support, may gain a majority in the Council. In such a situation, the upper house's independent scrutiny function could be severely curtailed. On the other hand, if current trends continue, it may the Legislative Assembly, and not the Legislative Council, which has to justify its usefulness.

Endnotes

[1] (1996) 40 NSWLR 665.

[2] The term is used in the corporate sense. NSW had a legislative institution in the form of the Governor from 1788.

[3] D. Clune, "The Development of Legislative Institutions in NSW, 1823-1843", *Australasian Parliamentary Review*, 25(2), Spring 2010.

[4] D. Clune, "1843: The Year It All Began", *Australasian Parliamentary Review*, 26(1), Autumn 2011.

[5] Initial appointments were made to the Council for five years; appointment from 1861 were for life.

[6] On Wentworth, see A. Tink, *William Charles Wentworth: Australia's Greatest Native Son*, Allen and Unwin, Sydney, 2009.

[7] See M. Hogan, L. Muir and H. Golder (eds), *The People's Choice: Electoral Politics in Colonial NSW*, Federation Press, Sydney, 2007.

[8] J. Hirst, *Freedom on the Fatal Shore*, Black Inc, Melbourne, 2008, 360.

[9] D. Clune and G. Griffith, *Decision and Deliberation: The Parliament of NSW, 1856-2003*, Federation Press, Sydney, 2006, 105-6. Another instance of the Council acting as a safeguard against populism occurred in 1924. In response to a Papal encyclical decreeing that Catholics had to be married by a priest, the Fuller Nationalist Government introduced blatantly anti-Catholic legislation making it an offence to question the validity of a lawful marriage. When the bill reached the Legislative Council, it encountered strong resistance from principled conservatives, who had no time for sectarian rabble-rousing and saw it as an attack on freedom of conscience. They amended the bill in such a way as to neutralise it. See D. Clune, "G Fuller", in D. Clune and K. Turner eds, *The Premiers of NSW, 1856-2005*, vol 2, Federation Press, Sydney, 2006.

[10] A. Powell, *Patrician Democrat: the political life of Charles Cowper 1843-1870*, MUP, Melbourne, 1977.

[11] W. G. McMinn, *George Reid*, MUP, Melbourne, 1989.

[12] Labor was in office: 1910-16, 1920-22, 1925-27, 1930-32, 1941-65, 1976-88, 1995-2011.

[13] On the early Labor Party see N. B. Nairn, *Civilising Capitalism: The Beginnings of the Australian Labor Party*, MUP, Melbourne, 1989.

[14] D. Clune and G. Griffith, *Decision and Deliberation: the Parliament of NSW, 1856-2003*, Federation Press, 2006, 242-270; N. B. Nairn, *The "Big Fella": Jack Lang and the Australian Labor Party 1891-1949*, MUP, Melbourne, 1986.

[15] See A. Moore, *The Secret Army and the Premier*, UNSW Press, Sydney, 1989.

[16] On the indirectly elected Council see K. Turner, *House of Review?: the NSW Legislative Council 1934-1968*, SUP, Sydney, 1969.

[17] D. Clune, "The McKell style of government", in M Easson (ed), *McKell*, Allen and Unwin, Sydney, 1988.

[18] D. Clune and G. Griffith, *Decision and Deliberation: the Parliament of NSW, 1856-2003*, Federation Press, Sydney, 2006, 398.

[19] K. Turner, *House of Review?: the NSW Legislative Council 1934-1968*, SUP, Sydney, 1969, 123.

[20] M. Willis, interview, 2.2.2016, Legislative Council of NSW Oral History Project, https://www.parliament.nsw.gov.au/lc/roleandhistory/Documents/Willis%20 -%20web%20version%20(2).pdf

[21] See D. Clune, *Connecting with the People: The 1978 Reconstitution of the Legislative Council*, Legislative Council of NSW, History Monograph No 2, 2017.

[22] Bob Askin was Liberal Premier, 1965–75.

[23] J. Hallam interview 8.12.2015, Legislative Council of NSW Oral History Project, https://www.parliament.nsw.gov.au/lc/roleandhistory/Documents/Hallam%20 -transcript.pdf

[24] R. Dyer, interview, 6.5.2013, Legislative Council of NSW Oral History Project, https://www.parliament.nsw.gov.au/lc/roleandhistory/Documents/Transcript%20-%20Ron%20Dyer.PDF

[25] On development of the committee system see D. Clune, *Keeping the Executive Honest: The Modern Legislative Council Committee System*, Legislative Council of NSW, History Monograph, no. 1, 2013.

[26] D. Clune, *Keeping the Executive Honest: The Modern Legislative Council Committee System*, Legislative Council of NSW, History Monograph, no 1, 2013.

[27] Information from NSW Legislative Council.

[28] D. Clune and G. Griffith, *Decision and Deliberation: the Parliament of NSW, 1856-2003*, Federation Press, Sydney, 2006, 637-9.

[29] J. Hannaford, interview, 10.12.2015, Legislative Council of NSW Oral History Project, https://www.parliament.nsw.gov.au/lc/roleandhistory/Documents/Hannaford%20-%20transcript.pdf

30 J. Hannaford, interview, 16.7.2013, Legislative Council of NSW Oral History Project, https://www.parliament.nsw.gov.au/lc/roleandhistory/Documents/170904%20Hannaford%20dc.pdf

31 M. Egan, interview, 9.2.2016, Legislative Council of NSW Oral History Project, https://www.parliament.nsw.gov.au/lc/roleandhistory/Documents/Egan%20-%20transcript.pdf

32 R. Smith, "Parliament" in D. Clune and R. Smith (eds), *From Carr to Keneally: Labor in Office in NSW 1995-2011*, Allen and Unwin, Sydney, 2012, 70-1.

33 R. Dyer, interview, 5.7.2016, Legislative Council of NSW Oral History Project, https://www.parliament.nsw.gov.au/lc/roleandhistory/Documents/Ron%20Dyer%20-%20final%20-%20web.pdf

34 Figures from NSW Legislative Council.

35 D. Blunt, 'Parliamentary speech and the location of decision-making', *Australasian Parliamentary Review*, Vol 30 No 1, Autumn/Winter 2015, 94.

36 On the Egan cases see D. Clune, *The Legislative Council and Responsible Government: Egan v Willis and Egan v Chadwick*, Legislative Council of NSW, History Monograph, no. 3, 2017.

37 (1996) 40 NSWLR 665.

38 (1998) 195 CLR 424 at [155].

39 G. Griffith, *Egan v Chadwick and Other Recent Developments in the Powers of Elected Upper Houses*, NSW Parliamentary Library Research Service, Briefing Paper 15/99, Executive Summary.

40 Figures from NSW Legislative Council.

41 For an example of the positive use of the power see S. Reynolds, "Making honey in the bearpit: parliament and its impact on policymaking", *Australasian Parliamentary Review*, 31(2), Spring/Summer 2016.

42 S. Ganghof, "A new political system model: semi-parliamentary government", *European Journal of Political Research*, 26 July 2017, https://onlinelibrary.wiley.com/doi/abs/10.1111/1475-6765.12224.

43 S. Ganghof, S. Eppner and A. Pörschke, "Australian Bicameralism as Semi-parliamentarism: patterns of majority formation in 29 democracies", *Australian Journal of Political Science*, 53(2), 2018, 216.

44 B. Stone, "State Legislative Councils: designing for accountability" in N. Aroney, S. Prasser and J. R. Nethercote, *Restraining Elective Dictatorship: The Upper House Solution?*, UWA Press, Perth, 2008. All quotes in the following paragraphs are from this essay.

45 NSW Legislative Council, *The House in Review*, https://thehouseinreview.com/2019/11/28/2019-in-review-a-year-in-stats/

10

Speaking Truth to Power is No Way to Speak to a Minister

Richard D. French

When in 1979 Aaron Wildavsky adopted the phrase, *Speaking Truth to Power*, for the title of his book on public policy, he introduced into our field the set of preconceptions which went with it. Its coinage invokes moral courage in the public expression of unpopular views to unsympathetic authorities. It was employed in Quaker pacifist and civil rights circles, for example. The importation of the phrase into public administration and policy flatters the adviser that she occupies the moral and intellectual high ground. This is not unconnected to its popularity.

I want to argue that counterposing truth and power in this way is not a helpful way to think about the relationship between policy advisers and their political clients. In the first part of the essay, I shall explore some of the multifold theories of truth and power, and explain my misgivings about the formula. In the second part, I shall change registers and, on the basis of many years of advising and being advised, offer some practical advice to advisers.[1]

Truth and power: a very short introduction

There are two polar extremes in the theory of public policy-making. Foucault popularised the idea that all knowledge is irrevocably compromised by power and claims to truth are stratagems in a battle for domination of the many by the few. This is the sophisticated version of the popular cynicism about "elites" and politics which afflicts democracies today.

On the other hand, there are the rationalists, who believe that behind all the democracies we know and have known, there lies a better, more scientifically informed exercise of government, which would emerge if only the advice of the knowledgeable were taken seriously and systematically by the powerful.

A man like Yehezkal Dror spent a lifetime trying to apply the classic rationalist model to policy-making while accumulating evidence of chronic shortfalls in practice. This was apparently the fault of democracy's decision-makers. For Dror, rulers are both necessary and (Dror's term) "defective"[2]: "There seems to be no basis for assuming that the typical career patterns of rulers bring to the fore persons unusually endowed and equipped to withstand the performance-corrupting factors inbuilt into rulership . . . The game of politics certainly does not assure the high moral fibre of people who reach the top".[3] Dror is representative of the high-minded in academia, at editorial desks, and in many nooks and crannies in the bureaucracy, where "politics" and politicians imply someone intellectually and morally underqualified to be brought home to mother.

Dror's disapproval reminds me of some seminal moments of moral and epistemological self-righteousness in my own experience of Canadian government. I once heard a former secretary to the federal cabinet – the one-time senior civil servant in the land – aver that "The public service is the conscience of the government." At dinner, a former career diplomat and senior ambassador told us that "Every minister I ever worked for was a crook." When I was a provincial minister, I was told by one of my officials, "That may be your position, but it's not the department's position."

Here is Canada's first Parliamentary Budget Officer on the subject of the parliamentarians he was supposed to be advising: "political yes-men and women . . . There wasn't a lot guts in that group of sentries, I thought."[4]

This phenomenon is not confined to Canada, where most of my

experience happens to be. According to Don Russell, Sir Frederick Wheeler's comment that " 'All politicians are bastards' . . . reflected the ethos of the high period of Public Service life in Canberra."[5] I examine below the views of British ministers.

Neither of the extreme theories in question suits the function of policy advice to elected officials. If the emergence of a relationship of sympathy and trust between adviser and client depends upon many contingencies, it is at a minimum necessary to attempt to fashion a relationship of mutual comprehension. The burden of this fashioning lies mostly with advisers.

Can science-organised or propositional knowledge, acquired by qualified persons respecting the various disciplinary standards – help? Of course, but not by any means to the extent that the rationalist dogma of the evidence-based policy movement contends. For any complex socioeconomic problem, we have to "stitch together roughly and prudentially the findings of various pertinent but distinctively specialised studies, filling the gaps with cruder sorts of data and assumptions, and linking them all together with even more disputable normative evaluations." [6]

If this is truth, it is not the imperious "truth" which Hannah Arendt found so inappropriate for political questions, the truth that demands recognition "once and for all."[7] Arendt was concerned to preserve the autonomy of political judgment from the despotism of truth as the philosophers (and scientists) construed it. For her, the truth apposite to politics is to be sought in debate, persuasion, and the sifting of opinion.[8] It is not that there is no truth in public life, but that such truth should not be conflated with empirically grounded scientific evidence. The latter can only be a component of political judgment; it cannot substitute for it.[9]

Bruno Latour expresses a similar thought in other words:

> Political discourse . . . is not indifferent to truth, as it is so unjustly accused of being; it simply differs from other regimes in its judgment of truth . . . true and false, in politics, cannot be compared to the usual type of veracity corresponding to a disfigured version of the scientific reference.[10]

Does empirical research on policy-making in fact support this position? Carol Weiss was for many years the leading student of research usage in public institutions. Her conclusion, expressed early in her career and never revised, was as follows:

> People say that social science research should be used. But many of the people doing the saying are social scientists who . . . expect to speak "truth to power". Such a posture presupposes that (a) there is a clear and single truth, (b) they have it by the tail, (c) it is a whole truth whose revelation is irrelevant to the clash of interests and political stakes, (d) powerful decision makers will heed this truth, and (e) decisions embodying such "truth" will be better and wiser than decisions reached on other grounds.
>
> Few social scientists would make such extravagant claims. Yet, many of them talk as though using social research is a simple and straightforward business: Research is truth and they are the passers of the flame.[11]

Note that we are here only attempting to consider what kind of truth those who wish to speak truth to power are able to mobilise . . . and whether such truth can reasonably claim the moral and intellectual high ground against the "power" allegedly wielded by elected officials. We are trying to provide a realistic perspective for advisers to ministers. We are not trying to suggest that policy advice is political judgment. Perhaps thus far, we have only succeeded in describing what truth in public life is not; how can we get a bit closer to a picture of truth in policy advice which has – at a minimum – a frame?

Let us start by recognising, with Ray Pawson, that "Some knowledge is preferable to no knowledge, and is rather more plausible than 'certain' knowledge."[12] It falls to advisers not to short circuit political judgment by attempting to substitute their certainties for their client's judgment, but to determine what of their knowledge, such as it is, will best serve their client. Paris concluded that "Policy inquiry . . . seeks to stake out a middle ground between claims for unique scientific or normative justification for policy (and associated methodological rules) and the reduction of policy inquiry to relativism or power politics."[13]

The English moral philosopher, Bernard Williams, argued that the practice of truthfulness calls upon two virtues: accuracy ("you do the best you can to acquire true beliefs") and sincerity ("what you say reveals what you believe").[14] An adviser could do worse than think about these as standards for advice. At this point in our discussion, the first virtue asks us to refrain from overstating the accuracy and adequacy of our knowledge/advice as it addresses a complex socio-economic problem which has become a political issue. The second virtue asks us to refrain from the manipulation of our politician-client – a temptation which many an adviser has failed to resist.

Kisby compares advice to a map:

> . . . in order for a map to provide us with a useful model for negotiating the world, it has, despite its selective and simplified nature, to be accurate, if sometimes approximate, in its representations of reality. It is the same kind of accurate, if approximate, representations of reality to which policy-making models and explanatory theories can also modestly aspire.[15]

Ministers, apart from their constitutional role, are pretty much like you or me. The corollary to this is that they learn behaviours and accumulate information more or less like you and me. Advisers have to accept that for politicians, as for most of us,

> Commonly, knowledge, belief, and trust are not things we choose. Rather, they are things that happen to us. We may choose to put ourselves in the way of coming to know, but the knowing finally happens because for some reason, over which we have no control, the apparent fact compels us.[16]

Most politicians, most of the time, will not manifest the analytical reflexes common to the policy analyst and her colleagues in the bureaucracy. This is not a fault, it is a fact of life. It is not a temporary barrier to the arrival of a rationalist utopia, it is a permanent feature of democratic reality. Officials know things ministers do not know – but the reverse is also true, and there is no reason to value one set of knowledge over the other. "The political is not necessarily shabby, nor is technical advice somehow pure."[17]

In particular, advisers must understand that politicians live in a universe of opinion, public attention, competition and conflict, emotion, and chronic uncertainty, calling for skills which are just as critical to democracy as scientific knowledge or professional norms and principles.[18] To achieve public goals, for example, persuasion and rhetoric, not analysis, are the fuel which moves the machinery of the democratic state.

The adviser does well to reflect upon the popular moral intuitions which politicians have to cope with and may well share. They constitute a wider selection of reflexes than those likely to be foremost in the offices of the state. Jonathan Haidt proposes as a hypothesis six foundations for moral intuitions:

1. Harm/care: Concerns for the suffering of others, including virtues of caring and compassion.

2. Liberty/oppression: Concerns about the rights of the vulnerable (by liberals); concerns about the interference of government in individuals' lives (by conservatives).

3. Fairness/reciprocity: Concerns about unfair treatment, cheating and more abstract notions of justice and rights.

4. In-group/loyalty: Concerns related to obligations of group membership, such as loyalty, self-sacrifice and vigilance against betrayal.

5. Authority/respect: Concerns related to social order and the obligations of hierarchical relationships, such as obedience, respect, and the fulfilment of role-based duties.

6. Purity/sanctity: Concerns about physical and spiritual contagion, including virtues of chastity, wholesomeness and control of desires.[19]

Other cognitive psychologists and virtue theorists offer alternative value sets. The point is that if officials naturally gravitate to the first three items on this list, there remains a good-sized tract of the moral landscape essential to political decision-making, but more or less *terra incognita* in the bureaucracy. This is not an injunction to revise policy analysis in the light of criteria other than the traditional economy/ effectiveness/ efficiency/ equality; it is rather an invitation to advisers to accept that when politicians in a democracy fail to respect the letter of such advice, this may not be an occasion to rail against the evils of "politics" and the moral shortcomings of politicians.[20] It may simply be evidence that, as Isocrates is understood to have suggested, in politics, "It is not the discovery of the right course that is so difficult, it is getting other people to accept the right course."[21] Vaughan and Buss advise, "If decisions appear to fly in the face of analysis, they need not devalue either analyst or analysis. The best word of advice to policy analysts is not to take things personally."[22]

So much, here and now, for truth. What about "power"? The first thing to say is that most politicians do not think they have much! Political power withdraws infinitely just beyond the reach of the ambitious politician. Neal Blewett concluded that "The closer one gets to what one thinks is power the more it seems to recede."[23] Or, as an American congressman observed of himself and his colleagues, "For all practical purposes, power doesn't keep people here. They come; they realise they don't have it."[24] Benjamin Barber's experience with the Clinton White House led him to conclude:

> The trouble with speaking truth to power is . . . that intellectuals rarely have the truth while the president rarely has much power – certainly much less than that with which the office is usually credited. In our postmodern era, where no one can claim to speak truth and where there is no one with absolute power to speak it to, the old cliché turns out to have limited traction.[25]

I want, however, to conclude this section on the moral implications of the expression, "power", in the "Speaking Truth to Power." Here we are invited to imagine a politician who has been irremediably tainted by the compromises she has had to make on her ascension to power, advised by a courageous adviser/possessor of the truth. Tell those politicians what they do not want to hear! And of course, there are such moments; call them, all right, "moments of truth." But let us be honest and modest, this is the exception, not the rule. And to begin the advisory relationship with this in mind is to condemn it *ab initio*.

This is probably why Martin Lipsky, a former staffer to the Governor of Massachusetts and lecturer at Harvard, observed:

> Institutionally, the Kennedy School rests on the idea of speaking truth to power. The practical consequence of that is to devalue politics. Students get the message that their role is to squeeze the role of politics out of policy making, that politics gets in the way of good government. That's not the way the real governmental world exists.[26]

One must begin with an assumption of mutual good faith. This, for example, is the only way to win over the new minister who assumes that his department has been intellectually and politically suborned by the previous administration. Just keep trying to help, unless or until experience suggests that the minister is a stranger to good faith. In my experience, there *are* such people in public life and sometimes they *do* become ministers. In that circumstance, which I claim is rare, the adviser is absolved of the obligations I have sketched above. But I insist that only considerable experience can justify such a resignation.

The practice of advice

Much has been written from the perspective of analysis by participants in and around the making of policy.[27] Since there is much less written from the perspective of politics, it is useful to try to see the advisory relationship through the minister's eyes. This helps us to see that the democratic counterpoint to the fear that "politics" somehow pollutes the making of policy is the fear that governments are run by officials with security of tenure and an instinct to evade ministerial prerogative. In short, ministers are frustrated by what they see as official indifference to the electorally legitimated policy aspirations of the political executive – a failure of responsiveness, if you will.

According to Gerald Kaufman, *How to be a Minister*, "The civil service has built-in protective mechanisms for every eventuality and, unless you show them pretty quickly that you do not need them or do not want them, they will in the most benevolent way proceed to turn

you into a pod straight out of the Invasion of the Body Snatchers."[28]
Indeed,

> You should bear in mind that officials are likely to send
> you submissions about subjects that interest them rather
> than those that interest you . . . while acceptance of official
> advice will be followed by instantaneous action, rejection
> will lead to a rearguard action so skilled as to leave you
> breathless with admiration (and fury).[29]

The irrepressible and irreplaceable Alan Clark had his own way of
saying the same thing:

> I have just come from a meeting on "Special Employment
> Measures" (those tacky schemes to get people off the [Un-
> employment] Register). My mind is a maelstrom of nit-
> picking detail, eligibility rules, small print of a kind that
> civil servants relish – not least because they can browbeat
> ministers as a team, with one bespectacled *Guardian* reader
> in sole charge of each "scheme" and thus in complete com-
> mand of its detailed provisions. The unfortunate Minister
> blunders about like a bull on sawdust with the picadors gal-
> loping round him sticking in their horrid barbed *banderillas*
> (if that's what they are).
>
> "But no, Minister, in that case the eligibility requirements
> would have lapsed . . ."
>
> "Ah yes, Minister, but there is no provision under the Order
> for . . ."
>
> "Mmm, Minister, it would have to be discretionary and that
> could only be exercised in exceptional circumstances . . ."[30]

For Clark:

> Civil servants . . . can't bear Ministers making announce-
> ments on any topic unless the idea originated with them.
> I often think that in their ideal world the "Line to Take" is
> prepared before the policy concept itself. No program, but
> *none* is so true to life as *Yes, Minister*.[31]

Richard Crossman's *Diaries* are full of such frustration.[32] Officials
conspire to control ministers:

My Minister's room is like a padded cell, and in certain ways I am like a person who is suddenly certified a lunatic and surrounded by male and female trained nurses and attendants. When I am in a good mood they occasionally allow an ordinary human being to come and visit me; but they make sure that I behave right, and that the other person behaves right.[33]

Every ministerial committee has a shadow committee of officials to give "support" – that is, concert on an official line to impose on ministers. Every department has a Treasury spy. Cabinet minutes are taken to reflect what officials think ministers should have said rather than what they actually said. His "Private Office is the Department's way of keeping a watch on me, of making sure I run along the lines they want me to run on, of dividing my time and getting the Department's policies and attitudes brought to my notice."[34] His policies are relayed to middle-level and junior officials, whom he is not allowed to see, in forms unlikely to gain their support. "Broadly speaking, the civil servants will run the Ministry the way they want; and if I am determined to have something changed it will take me a long time."[35]

I offer these comments not because they are the only reasonable characterisation of the context of the policy-advisory relationship, but because they provide a counter to the high-minded assumption of many officials that they are the only protection in executive government that democracy enjoys. Governments are elected to make policy; this is their burden and their democratic prerogative.

Are there any guidelines as to how advisers might help in that endeavour? We take it for granted that we are here dealing with advisers who have superior knowledge of their domain of responsibility, who know that implementation does not happen by magic, who understand that their (reputation for) integrity is sacrosanct, who are prepared to put forward the awkward facts regardless of the client's inclinations, and who wish to present complex information and evaluation in a form assimilable by decision-makers.

As to superior knowledge, this does not imply feigning omniscience. As Robert Solow has put it, "Hard as it is to say, sometimes 'I don't know' is the best answer."[36] As to awkward facts, an Australian official said, "If a minister wants to do something stupid, 'to object once is obligatory, twice is desirable, and three times is suicidal.'"[37]

It bears repeating that recognition that public life imposes limits on the rationalist ideal does not mean that policy advisers should attempt to factor into their analysis the political context of a policy decision. It is impossible to eliminate politics from policy advice, but advisers should not assume that the onus is on them to undertake the balancing act required. Rather, their role is to tailor their synthesis of the factors of economy/ effectiveness/ efficiency/ equality to the kind of presentation which a politician can absorb.

Let me begin with some general observations. Analysts search for a compelling account of the substantive architecture of an abstract problem. Politicians, with few exceptions, seek the political meaning of a concrete issue. They will imagine themselves explaining the policy to the interested publics. Neither party should expect an account of "law-like regularities" allowing sound prediction of the results of specific actions.[38] Both parties should recognise that the posing of the appropriate question is much the most important step in the advisory process.[39]

For advice, it is above all a matter of finding images, metaphors, charts, figures, and narratives in the issue context (which may well derive in part from empirical evidence, but) which appeal to the decision-maker's cognitive style, and permit reasoning from the familiar to the unfamiliar. It is this recognition that analysis is only a first step in the communication at the centre of the advisory relationship that should differentiate the policy adviser from the academic.

A former British minister put it this way:

> Analytical data is useful, but yes, it would certainly be true that anecdotal evidence about how things worked from people that you came to trust was strongly influential, and the more abstruse the academic evidence, the less you tended to rely on it.[40]

Research says that politicians prefer oral briefing over the written word. This, and the fact that a good deal of discussion of this nature occurs when the minister is "on the run" (even if she may be sitting down) implies a kind of dialogue rather than a set-piece presentation. We train students for the latter, and rightly so, but much of what really counts happens less formally. Such dialogue brings tacit knowledge to the surface. "The most brilliant advice may go wholly unheeded if it's not fitted to the social context of decision makers, the psychology of people making decisions in a hurry and under pressure, and the economics of organisations often strapped for cash."[41]

None of this implies that anything goes. There are better and worse policy narratives. They have to be coherent, internally consistent, and be "grounded in the real experience of policy actors."[42]

After focusing as much on the recognition of meaning as on analysis, and on communication as on ratiocination, advisers should think about accuracy in labelling what they are offering. In particular they should try to separate established facts, defensible in public, from personal evaluations or departmental preferences. For example, in the office of the German Chancellor, regulations require that information and evaluation must be explicitly separated in advisory practice.[43] Furthermore, advisers should be careful not to oversell the validity and robustness of any research upon which they base recommendations. There is testimony by students of policy as to academically trained advisers moving rapidly without notice from the relatively firm ground of scientific knowledge ("the data" or "the evidence") to the swampy ground of personally preferred "solutions".[44]

Advisers must make the assumptions underlying advice explicit. They must avoid the "Nirvana Fallacy": the illusory comparison of an idealised future program with today's tattered reality.[45] They must make an honest attempt to unlearn the disciplinary blinders they were socialised into at university, and use any form of knowledge which may be helpful to the issue at hand. They must acknowledge risk and the possibility of unintended consequences, not just with lip service, but in the depth which knowledge, experience and the occasion permit. Whenever possible, assumptions should be tweaked and sensitivity analyses employed to provide maximum clarity as to future scenarios. This does not necessarily require quantitative data.[46]

Advisers should always remember that the *distribution* of benefits and especially costs (in the broadest sense) consequent upon a policy decision will be of vital importance to decision-makers. Any attempt to identify and weigh these issues will be of great significance to ministers. So will attention to means as well as to ends. Citizens will take the means for the policy and, where means impose upon them without adequate public defence, will be obdurate. Many a plausible policy has come to grief because the prospect of a tasty omelette has obscured the necessary breaking of eggs. As Stilgoe and others say, "The old model of expertise – truth to power – talks to the public. It does not listen. The new model of expertise needs to listen and learn to listen differently."[47]

Conclusion

I have argued that the adage that policy advisers should "Speak Truth to Power" is unhelpful because it connotes a relationship of moral and intellectual inequality between the adviser and her political client. Political theory provides some alternative conceptions of such a relationship which help to sketch a more equitable and, I claim, more effective, approach for policy advice. In particular, policy advisers have to come to terms with the reality that elected officials play as legitimate and important a role in democratic government as officials. The habits, folkways, and intellectual culture inherent in democratic public life are not going to change without, at a minimum, dramatic constitutional upheaval. This is unlikely. Policy advisers would do well to accept and engage with that reality instead of trying to work around or against it.

The role of policy adviser can be immensely rewarding. Some of the things I was able to be involved in as a young man in a policy role remain among the most satisfying memories of my career. Participation in issues of public importance has its own unique thrill, at least for some of us. I am sorry to say that at times it seems to foster a form of moral and intellectual complacency on the part of public officials, which is healthy neither for them nor for Westminster democracy.

In discussing these issues, I have intentionally avoided what has become a standard response to the various ills of democratic policy-making – the resort to one or another form of "public engagement." This is another story, but let me simply say that I do not see the erosion of the importance of confidential policy advice by officials of the state to elected officials as likely any time soon. I do not believe that "the cure for the ills of democracy is more democracy," if more democracy implies a transfer of some or all of policy-making responsibility to groups of citizens under the tutelage of academics. Nor do I believe for a moment that there is widespread demand among citizens to spend time in church basements, community centres, school classrooms, or hotel ballrooms debating public policy.

There is no limit to the practical advice that can be proffered to policy advisers. I have largely focused on the relationship with the client rather than the epistemological issues (on which there is a large literature) because I think that many policy advisers come to the job with little useful preparation of a practical nature. My attempt here has been to distill – if that is not too ambitious a word – from experience and the literature the things I would like to have understood when I began to work in the secretariat to the cabinet of the Pierre Trudeau government in Canada. The point, I guess, is that the kind of academic preparation which universities offer is just the beginning of the learning process for a policy adviser. Some of the subsequent learning will come, if he or she is fortunate, from politicians in need of advice (whether they know it or not).

Endnotes

[1] The author would like to acknowledge his debt to James Mitchell: James Mitchell, *"Can I Really Speak Truth to Power?"* Notes for Remarks to the Strategy and Coordination Branch, Canadian Border Services Agency, 14 June 2007, Montebello Quebec.

[2] Yehezkal Dror, "Conclusions', in William Plowden (ed.), *Advising the Rulers*, Blackwell, Oxford, 1987, 185-215.

3 Ibid., 191, 196.

4 Kevin Page, *Truth and Lies on Parliament Hill: Unaccountable*, Viking, Toronto, 2015, 4.

5 Don Russell, "The Role of Executive Government in Australia, Parliament of Australia", Canberra, *Papers on Parliament No. 41*, December 2003, 5.

6 Rogers M. Smith, "Reconnecting Political Theory To Empirical Inquiry, Or, A Return To The Cave?" in E. D. Mansfield and R. Sissons (eds), *The Evolution of Political Knowledge: Theory and Inquiry in American Politics*, Ohio State University Press, Columbus, OH, 2004, 60-88, at 68. See also Giandomenico Majone, "An Anatomy of Pitfalls" in G. Majone and E. S. Quade (eds.), *Pitfalls of Analysis*, Wiley, Chichester, 1980, 7-22, at 16.

7 Martin Jay, *The Virtues of Mendacity: On Lying in Politics*, University of Virginia Press, Charlottesville, VA, 2010, 160.

8 See also Wendy Brown, "Speaking Power to Truth", in *Truth and Democracy*, J. Elkins and A. Norris (eds.), University of Pennsylvania Press, Philadelphia, 2012, 87-94, at 94.

9 Richard Bernstein, "Judging–The Actor and the Spectator", in his *Philosophical Profiles: Essays in a Pragmatic Mode*, University of Pennsylvania Press, Philadelphia, 1986, 221-237; Mauricio Passerin d'Entreves, "Arendt's Theory Of Judgment", in Dana Villa (ed.), *The Cambridge Companion to Hannah Arendt*, Cambridge University Press, Cambridge, 2000, 245-60; Jay, op. cit., 160-1; Rob Watts, "Truth and Politics: Thinking About Evidence-Based Policy in the Age Of Spin", *Australian Journal of Public Administration*, 73(1), 2014, 34-46, at 42-3; Linda M. G. Zerilli, "Truth and Politics", in J. Elkins and A. Norris (eds), *Truth and Democracy*, University of Pennsylvania Press, Philadelphia, 2012, 54-75.

10 Bruno Latour, "What if We *Talked* Politics a Little?" *Contemporary Political Theory* 2(2), 2003, 143–64, at 147.

11 Carol H. Weiss, "Introduction", *Using Social Research in Public Policy Making*, Lexington, MA, Lexington, 1977, 1-22, at 7.

12 Ray Pawson, *Evidence-Based Policy: A Realist Perspective*, Sage Publications, London, 2006,180.

13 David C. Paris, "Policy Inquiry and Rational Ideologies" in E. B. Portis and M. B. Levy (eds), *Handbook of Political Theory and Policy Science*, Greenwood Press, NY, 1988, 75-89, at 87.

14 Bernard Williams, *Truth and Truthfulness: An Essay in Genealogy, 2004*, quoted in Matt Sleat, "On the Relationship Between Truth and Liberal Politics", *Inquiry – An Interdisciplinary Journal of Philosophy* 50, 2007, 288-305, at 292.

15 Ben Kisby, "Interpreting Facts, Verifying Interpretations: Public Policy, Truth and Evidence", *Public Policy and Administration* 26(1), 2011,107-27, at 121.

16 Russell Hardin, *How Do You Know? The Economics of Ordinary Knowledge*, Princeton University Press, Princeton, 2009, 41.

[17] Patrick Weller, "Types of Advice," in William Plowden (ed.), *Advising the Rulers*, Blackwell, Oxford, 1987, 149-57, at 154.

[18] Richard D. French, "The Professors on Public Life", *The Political Quarterly* 83(3), 2012, 532-40.

[19] Jonathan Haidt, *The Righteous Mind: Why Good People are Divided by Politics and Religion*, Pantheon Books, NY, 2012.

[20] Theodore Sorenson, "Presidential Advisers", in Thomas E. Cronin and S. A. Greenberg (eds), *The Presidential Advisory System*, Harper and Row, NY, 1969, 3-10, at 6, and Sorenson, *Decision-Making in the White House: The Olive Branch or the Arrows*, Columbia University Press, NY, 2005 [1963], 65.

[21] Allan Bloom, "An Introduction to the Political Philosophy of Isocrates", in M. Palmer and T. Pangle, (eds), *Political Philosophy and the Human Soul*, Rowman and Littlefield, Lanham, MD, 1995, 15-34, at 20.

[22] Roger J. Vaughan and Terry F. Buss, *Communicating Social Science Research to Policymakers*, Sage, Thousand Oaks, CA, 1998, 108. See also Alain C. Enthoven, "Ten Practical Principles for Policy and Program Analysts', *Benefit-Cost and Policy Analysis: An Aldine Annual on Forecasting, Decision-making, and Evaluation*, [Volume 3], 1975, 456-65, at 456.

[23] Neal A. Blewett, *A Cabinet Diary: A Personal Record of the First Keating Government*, Wakefield Press, Kent Town, South Australia, 1999, 206.

[24] Burdett A. Loomis, *The New American Politician: Ambition, Entrepreneurship, and the Changing Face of Political Life*, Basic Books, New York, 1990, 243.

[25] Benjamin R. Barber, *The Truth of Power: Intellectual Affairs in the Clinton White House*, Columbia University Press, New York, 2001, 14.

[26] Quoted in Lisa Anderson, *Pursuing Truth, Exercising Power: Social Science and Public Policy in the 21st Century*, Columbia University Press, New York, 2003, 37.

[27] Some good examples are Henry J. Aaron, *Politics and the Professors*, Washington, DC, Brookings Institution, 1978; Meredith Edwards, *Social Policy, Public Policy: From Problem to Practice*, Allen and Unwin, Sydney, 2001; Philip B. Heymann, *Living the Policy Process*, Oxford University Press, NY, 2008; Richard P. Nathan, *Social Science in Government: The Role of Policy Researchers*, Rockefeller Institute Press, Albany, 2000; Peter Schuck, *Why Government Fails So Often and How It Can Do Better*, Princeton University Press, Princeton, 2014; Alex Stevens, "Telling Policy Stories: An Ethnographic Study of the Use of Evidence in Policy-making in the UK", *Journal of Social Policy* 40 (2), 2011, 237-55.

[28] Gerald Kaufman, *How to be a Minister*, London, Faber and Faber, 1980, 23.

[29] Ibid., 30-1.

[30] Alan Clark, *Diaries*, Phoenix/Orion, London, 1993, 22.

[31] Ibid., 218, italics in the original.

[32] Richard Crossman, *The Diaries of a Cabinet Minister: Minister of Housing, 1964-66*, Hamish Hamilton and Jonathan Cape, London, 1975; *The Diaries*

of a Cabinet Minister: Lord President of the Council and Leader of the House of Commons, 1966-68, Hamish Hamilton and Jonathan Cape, London, 1976.

[33] Ibid., 1975, 21.

[34] Ibid., 1975, 385.

[35] Ibid., 1975, 273.

[36] Clinton J. Andrews, "Giving Expert Advice", *IEEE Technology and Society Magazine*, Summer, 1998, 5-6, at 6. See also Walter Heller, "Economic Policy Advisers", in Thomas E Cronin and Sanford D. Greenberg (eds), *The Presidential Advisory System*, Harper and Row, NY, 1969, 29-39, at 35.

[37] Anne Tiernan, and Patrick Weller, *Learning to be a Minister: Heroic Expectations, Practical Realities*, Melbourne University Press, Melbourne, 2010, 159.

[38] Mark Bevir and Rod A. W. Rhodes, *Governance Stories*, Routledge, London, 2006, 25-6, 164. See also Enthoven, op. cit., 458.

[39] Henry Kissinger, "The Intellectual and the Policymaker", in Thomas E. Cronin and Sanford A. Greenberg (eds), *The Presidential Advisory System*, Harper and Row, New York, 1969, 156-68, 164 and Enthoven, op. cit., 460.

[40] Michael Hallsworth, with Simon Parker and Jill Rutter, *Policy Making in the Real World: Evidence and Analysis*, Institute for Government, London, 2011, 90.

[41] Geoff Mulgan, "Experts and Experimental Government", in R. Doubleday and J. Wilsdon (eds), *Future Directions for Scientific Advice in Whitehall*. Cambridge, 2013, 32-8, at 34. Accessed 10 October 2017 at http://www.csap.cam.ac.uk/media/uploads/files/1/fdsaw.pdf .

[42] Raul Perez Lejano,. "Postpositivism and the Policy Process", in E. Aralal Jr., M. Howlett, M. Ramesh, and X. Wu, (eds.*), Routledge Handbook of Public Policy*, Routledge, Oxford, 2013, 98-112, at 108.

[43] Renate Mayntz, "West Germany", in William Plowden (ed.), *Advising the Rulers*, Blackwell, Oxford, 1987, 3-18, at 11 and R. Kaiser, "Comment," in William Plowden (ed.), *Advising the Rulers*, Blackwell, Oxford, 1987, 18-21.

[44] Sorenson, op. cit., 1969, 6; Vaughan and Buss, op. cit., 116; Carol H. Weiss, "The Haphazard Connection: Social Science and Public Policy", *International Journal of Educational Research* 23(2), 1995, 137-50, at 148.

[45] Schuck, op, cit., 62.

[46] Enthoven, op. cit., 456-7, 463-4; Majone, op. cit., 18.

[47] Jack Stilgoe, Alan Irwin, and Kevin Jones, *The Received Wisdom: Opening Up Expert Advice*, Demos, London, 2006, 51.

11

The New Zealand Public Service

Reflections on the Past Century

Don Hunn, John R. Martin and Elizabeth McLeay

New Zealand has had a public service since 1840. With the exception of a period of provincial government between 1852 and 1876 the New Zealand government has been truly a "national" government. For all of this period public servants have administered the policies and services of the executive government. From 1840 they were serving the Governor and the British Colonial Office (and, later, the provincial superintendents as well). With the granting of responsible government in 1856, ministers took over the staffing and administration of the public service; but there was "a complete lack of consistency in appointments, pay and promotion".[1] Political patronage was common. Similarly, the business of government was carried out by a range of agencies marked by a lack of organisational uniformity. Despite royal commissions in 1866 and 1880, and a very significant growth in the number and size of departments under the Liberal governments in office between 1890 and 1912, the case for reform of the systems of recruitment, promotion and classification was not substantively acknowledged until 1912.

The Royal Commission (the Hunt Commission)[2] and the Public Service Act of 1912 established the foundations of the New Zealand Public Service (NZPS). As we discuss later, questions can legitimately be raised about the extent to which some aspects of the fundamental values enacted in the 1912 Act are still in place today. Nonetheless, the description of the NZPS as "unified, career and politically-neutral" was unlikely to be challenged between 1912 and at least

1988. During that period New Zealand experienced two world wars, the depression of the 1930s and, as a country dependent on a limited range of pastoral exports, the exigencies of the world economy. Throughout, the public service played an important role.

This essay sketches the historical context of the modern NZPS, reviews its constitutional position, and reflects on its present state.

The "Old" Public Service

The issues that led to the establishment of the 1912 Royal Commission (comprising businessmen); on which it reported; and on which it made balanced recommendations were widely acknowledged. Although the Commission was given a short reporting period of three months, it reported to a different government from that which had set it up, a general election having intervened. Indeed, by the time the Commission delivered its report, a Public Service bill had already been introduced by the new (Reform) government. This bill foreshadowed in major aspects the recommendations of the Royal Commission. From these beginnings emerged a broad consensus in Parliament (with support from the employee organisation, the Public Service Association) around the removal of "politicisation" from the NZPS. That consensus would continue until the 1980s.[3]

The Public Service Act 1912 applied to the NZPS (43 government departments) and, until 1919, the Post and Telegraph Department but not the railways, the defence force, police or the education or hospital boards. Staffing of the public service at 1 April 1912 was just under 5,000; the Post Office and the railways employed some 19,000 staff.[4] The principal characteristics of the NZPS that were to endure until 1988 were:

- independent, non-political staff management vested in the Public Service Commissioner – including the selection and appointment of heads of departments (with a few exceptions);

- a "career service" from cadet on school-leaving until retirement (at 65 or at 60 after 40 years of service);[5]

- the Commissioner's statutory responsibility for efficiency and economy within the NZPS subject to the overall control of the Cabinet;
- the classification of staff in the service;
- implicit acceptance of the notion of "fair relativity" in pay with the private sector;
- the opportunity for appeal against non-appointment and non-promotion; and
- the publication of the Public Service Official Circular (PSOC) as a means of communication between the Commissioner and employees.

The permanent staff of the NZPS grew from just on 5,000 as at 31 March 1913 to 6,500 in 1919 – with a further 2,100 temporary staff and to 8,100 – with 2,100 temporary in 1931. By the first year of World War II the numbers stood at 12,200 plus 8,600 temporaries. As at 31 March 1947 there were 23,100 permanent and 5,000 temporary staff. By 31 March 1987 – the last year of the "old" public service – the number had grown to 70,500 plus 2,000 temporary employees.[6]

Several features stand out from these raw numbers. The growth in the public service over three decades was five-fold; the population grew by only 60 percent (1914: 1.1 million; 1947: 1.8 million). Temporary staff, not surprisingly, were employed during the First World War to meet the new wartime functions and to replace public servants serving in the armed services. They were sharply reduced in the 1920s, a decade of relatively slow growth followed by several years (1932–35) during the depression in which permanent staff numbers fell. The doubling of numbers (including a large number of temporaries) by the early years of the Second World War was largely attributable to the expansion of government services by the first Labour government that took office at the end of 1935. The post- war period of thirty years was one of consistent increases whichever government was in office.

The "old" public service until the 1960s was essentially a "career" service. Except for several years in the early 1930s, the service gave a high priority to recruitment of school-leavers as "cadets" – until 1945 through the competitive Public Service Entrance exam. From the 1940s, for several decades competition with the private sector resulted in a low level of recruitment of cadets to the clerical division. Graduate recruitment (except for professional positions: science, engineering, health and so forth) was not favoured and did not become widespread until the 1960s. Part-time study (particularly accounting) was encouraged and in 1939 and in 1940 a full-time, two-year post-graduate program, the Diploma of Public Administration, was established at Victoria University College, Wellington.

Appointments in the "old" public service were generally from within the service. Indeed, many remained within one department for most of their careers. Appointments from outside the public service were required to be able to justify that they were "in great degree" or "clearly more suitable" (*State Services Act 1962*) than an internal applicant. The strong emphasis on a career within the public service – from cadet to permanent head – saw individuals remaining as permanent heads for many years. Notable examples are Dr C. E. Beeby (Director of Education, 1940–60); Bernard Ashwin (Secretary to the Treasury, 1939–55); and A. R. Entrican (Director of Forests, 1939–61), all of whom played very significant roles in New Zealand's development.

Until after the Second World War, the public service was overwhelmingly male. Women appointed as temporaries during the First World War were quickly dispensed with and those who remained were subject to severe discrimination: pay ceilings, superannuation rights, appeal rights. An Economies Commission of 1921 reported permanent heads as of being of the "almost unanimous opinion [that] women clerks were 'not as serviceable as men.'"[7] Such prejudices were, if anything, reinforced by the depression; and "the situation of women changed very little" through the 1920s and '30s. Nor was there any rapid change after Labour came to office late in 1935. But during and after the Second World War there was a marked demand for women. Nonetheless, "[a]s far as career opportunities were concerned, the public service continued to present a dead end for women".[8] Over the post-war years successive measures were implemented to support equal opportunities for women in the public service, for example, flexible working hours and extended maternity leave. Concurrently, there was a long campaign for equal pay for women public servants doing equal work under equal conditions. Eventually the passage of the *Government Service Equal Pay Act 1960* introduced equal pay into the public sector, covering all government employees and recognising the need to implement equal pay in occupations performed exclusively by women.

Pay-fixing has always been a central issue in the public service. Although not initially recognised in statute, New Zealand implicitly followed the British "fair relativity" approach from 1912. The salary scales and pay rates were determined by the Public Service Commission (PSC) (with a right of appeal from 1948 to the Government Services Tribunal), increasingly after negotiation with the employee unions, and under the control of Cabinet. Such mechanisms as the "ruling rates survey" in respect of tradespeople gave effect to the fair relativity principle. In practice fair relativity – later "external comparability" – was difficult to translate into pay scales. From the 1960s the Commission was preoccupied with development of "occupational classes",[9] uniformity across the state agencies, and half-yearly surveys of private sector earnings. An important factor was the strength of the unions – the Public Service Association (and in concert with the Post Office and Railways organisations, the Combined State Services Organisations (CSSO)). To over-simplify the process, public service pay was adjusted by application across the sector of average movements in the private sector supplemented by negotiated settlements for individual occupational classes often associated with industrial action, threatened or actual.

The notion of the "Crown", as distinct from successive governments, is central to the bureaucracy. It underlines the continuity of the "New Zealand Government" and its unity. In respect of staffing this emphasises the importance of, from 1962, the State Services Commission (SSC) and from 2020 the Public Service Commission. The Commission, with a chair and multi-members until 1988, was the employer of *all* public servants (irrespective of agency), the fixer of pay (see above), and a body independent of the political executive in individual staff matters.

The 1988 "Revolution"

The fourth Labour Government, led by David Lange, came into confront a major economic crisis. Fuelled by its apparent success in measures to encourage productivity in manufacturing, reduce subsidies to agriculture and radically change the taxation system, as had also happened in Australia, the Government embarked on reform of the public sector.[10] The first major initiative was the *State-Owned Enterprises Act 1986*, which corporatised state trading activities (including the railways, the Post Office and forestry).[11] The *State Sector Act 1988* applied the same reforming zeal to the NZPS. And in 1989 this was complemented by the *Public Finance Act* that brought much of the philosophy of private sector financial management – and accrual accounting – into the public sector.

The thrust of the reforms is captured by Geoffrey Palmer, then Deputy Prime Minister and one of their architects:

> The *State Sector Act* . . . was based on . . . the relative lack of responsiveness of large bureaucracies. It acknowledged the very considerable difficulties in ensuring that these bureaucracies used resources in a way that was efficient, responsive and flexible, and also the need to reduce the rigidities in the public sector so that there could be greater responsiveness and greater flexibility.
>
> A group of young, vigorous and able Ministers saw for themselves what it was like. They acted accordingly.[12]

The authority of the State Services Commissioner over the unified public service was greatly reduced by the 1988 Act. Essentially the Act devolved the management of the public service to individual departments leaving the Commission with a responsibility to protect the political neutrality of the public service, to issue codes of conduct, to investigate government departments, and to advise the government on the organisation of the public service. Departmental chief executives (formerly permanent heads) assumed the role of employer – formerly with the Commission – and determined pay scales for the departmental employees. The Commissioner continues to have a statutory duty to act independently of ministerial direction. The Commissioner continues to select chief executives, but the Cabinet can reject the Commissioner's recommendation and instruct him/her to appoint someone they nominate. Although this has not happened, it is an issue to which we return later in this essay.

During the three decades since the *State Sector Act 1988* the service changed in many ways – as was intended by the reforming Labour government. One obvious change is that it is very much smaller. The extent to which these changes were warranted, and the degree to which they fundamentally modified the pillars of the "old" public service – unified, career, politically neutral – indeed altered the service's constitutional status, are questions to be addressed in the remainder of this essay.

The "New" Public Service: influences and structure

As can be seen, the contemporary public service has been shaped by, on the one hand, its own historical traditions of political neutrality, professionalism and public service and, on the other, by successive reforms, especially those influenced by the public management theory that was part of the neo-liberal reforms of the 1980s and 1990s. We now explore the wider influences on the public service.

New Zealand's non-codified constitution is derived from Westminster although it has been modified over the years.[13] One of its inheritances from Westminster was the doctrine of parliamentary sovereignty (or supremacy). Thus, while the courts adjudicate on administrative actions, Parliament's policy decisions are not judiciable. Since abolition of the ineffective Legislative Council in 1950, there has been no upper house to constrain the actions of governments when secure in their majorities in the House of Representatives. Furthermore, New Zealand's political executives have historically been strong, commanding the loyalty and cohesion of their

party teams. Hence, the radical nature of the structural and ideological changes the public service experienced during the 1980s
was enabled by constitutional characteristics that allowed governments to implement structural and policy changes with ease. It can,
indeed, be argued that those reforms were unconstitutional since
they were not heralded by inclusion in the Labour Party election
manifesto, thus lacking an electoral mandate.

Until the change to the Mixed Member Proportional electoral
system [MMP] in 1993 after two referendums, New Zealand's two-
party parliamentary system fostered adversarialism, with one party
making changes and the other opposing them and often, later, un-
doing them. This meant that not only was the NZPS vulnerable to
swift restructuring but also public servants had to be sensitive to
rapidly changing policy cycles. The pace of change was and is exacerbated by the triennial parliamentary term, which has not encouraged forward planning by political executives—although their
policy advisers in the core government agencies fill this vacuum to
the extent they are able.

Changes to the electoral system also affected the public service.
Between 1996 and 2020, when the Labour Party was elected with
a significant parliamentary majority, a series of coalition and minority governments held office. Legislative changes have had to be
negotiated within governing coalitions and, also, with government
support parties, thus slowing down and complicating the policy-
making process.[14] MMP also has led to governments using executive
orders instead of legislation in order to implement their policies.

Public servants had to adjust to policy change negotiated by two
or more political parties instead of simply implementing the manifesto commitments of a single party. Even before the introduction
of MMP governments, political advisers were being employed by
ministers to enhance policy contestability, as happened in other
Westminster polities. MMP accelerated this trend, involving an increased number of political advisers on short-term contracts whose
loyalty and tenure were linked to ministers, not the public service.
Overall, then, the public service has had to adjust to a more complex policy environment, with more players involved in decision-
making.

As well as acquiring a largely uncodified constitution, New Zealand inherited the Westminster convention of ministerial responsibility: ministers are responsible to Parliament and voters for their own actions (policies and personal behaviour) and those of their ministries and departments.[15] With the erosion of the convention that it is the ministers who face the public, not their once anonymous public servants, the latter are now more likely to be named as responsible for particular actions. That ministers must resign when things go badly wrong in the agencies for which they are responsible has never been the practice in New Zealand (and scarcely ever was the case in the United Kingdom). Ministers generally argue that they are responsible for putting right the situation and thus remain in office. (In contrast, many ministers have resigned or been dismissed on the grounds of their inappropriate personal behaviour.) Senior public servants in contemporary New Zealand are vulnerable to public and media criticism, a process in which Opposition MPs are also happy to engage.

No liberal-democratic state includes all aspects of its constitution in one document (or even several): important practices are set out in other written sources; and even codified constitutions depend also on conventions – unwritten rules – for their effective and democratic functioning. Indeed, there has been a trend in Westminster systems to increase the documentation of rules in recent years.[16] Even so, New Zealand's constitutional sources are particularly diverse, scattered and dependent on conventions (as is also the UK constitution). One consequence for the public service is that its guiding principles and powers are defined in a range of different documents. These include the brief *Constitution Act 1986*, which outlines the main features of New Zealand government, defining each of its major branches. Apart from the triennial term of the House of Representatives, which can only be amended with the approval of three-quarters of the House of Representatives or a majority of voters at a referendum, the *Constitution Act* is not entrenched and could thus be simply amended or repealed.[17]

Two of the most important statutes have been the *Public Finance Act 1989* and the *State Sector Act 1988*. Both acts have been significantly amended since. Indeed, the latter was replaced by the *Public Service Act* in 2020.

The rules dictating public accountability are to be found not only in the *Public Finance Act*: the *Public Audit Act 2001* outlines the responsibilities of the Audit department and, importantly, confirms the Comptroller and Auditor-General as an Officer of Parliament. Other major statutes are the *State-Owned Enterprises Act 1986*, the *Crown Entities Act 2005*, the *Crown Research Institutes Act 1992*; and the *New Zealand Public Health and Disability Act 2000.*

Some public servants are governed by specific pieces of legislation: for example, the role of the head of the public service, the State Services Commissioner, now the Public Service Commissioner. The wider state sector is governed by two main statutes: the *State-Owned Enterprises Act 1986* and the *Crown Entities Act 2004.* Apart from the Ombudsman and Official Information acts (see below), other important constitutional documents are the *Cabinet Manual*, and the *Standing Orders of the New Zealand House of Representatives.*[18]

The public service expanded its roles and responsibilities in the post-war period, as pointed out above. Particularly notable were the several movements to enhance citizens' rights and environmental rights that emerged in the 1960s and 1970s. For example, the *Ombudsman Act 1962* encouraged public service responsiveness to citizens' problems while the *Official Information Act 1982* (OIA), which stressed citizen participation, encouraged openness. The effectiveness of the OIA is under challenge in the 21st century. Not only did these and other social changes alter how the public services operated but they also involved appointment of specialised agencies and staff.

Other important results of the move to improve the rights of citizens were the influential *Bill of Rights Act 1990*, the Office of the Privacy Commissioner (1993), and the enhanced recognition of the principles of the Treaty of Waitangi 1840.[19] In 1975 the Waitangi Tribunal was created and was granted extended powers in 1985. It hears claims from iwi and hapu for compensation (at least in part) to Maori for the land and other possessions taken from them during the Pakeha settlement period from 1840 onwards. The Tribunal is not part of the public service, but public servants, with their ministers, are involved in responding to the Tribunal and recommending action to government. There had always been a department to deal with Maori issues. Subsequently other small public sector ministries were created to respond to the needs of women and, also, residents from the Pacific Islands. As can be seen, the public service has had to respond to rights-based movements both in developing and implementing relevant policies and in terms of acquiring specialist staff.

Governments have responded to other imperatives concerning the role of the state by creating a myriad of bodies beyond the public service (for example, the Crown Research Institutes). As in Australia, there has been increasing use of consultants and "expert" inquiries. Documenting the wider state would involve a list of many statutes and enter the whole problematic area of the risks involved in contracting out the state's functions, an example of which has been the politically contestable and arguably unethical privatisation of some of New Zealand's prisons.

Parliament itself has affected how the public service operates. Since 1979 all bills except money bills and those being hurried through the parliamentary process under "urgency" (at times even skipping the committee stage) have been referred to subject select committees. In 1985 the committees were reformed and given more powers, including the capacity to conduct inquiries without the permission of the House itself. The emphasis on the work of the committees has meant that ministers must be well-briefed before they face them and public servants themselves must answer questions from MPs (on behalf of their minister). These processes expanded the work of public servants and have also made them public figures, given that committee hearings are normally held in public. Guidelines for MPs and public servants have been drawn up for these purposes.[20] Less publicly obvious, at least so far as the public servants are concerned, has been the rising numbers of parliamentary questions addressed to the responsible ministers, especially written questions, which are even more work intensive.

The contemporary public service has, in turn, helped to shape the constitution and political culture. Treasury officials, for example, were key to the implementation of the public management reforms, both in terms of providing ideas and instituting new policy processes. Public servants in the Cabinet Office were crucial advisers during the transition to MMP. Indeed, they rewrote the *Cabinet Manual* to reflect the new policy environment, a manual that, in turn, influenced the UK government when it entered its era of "hung" parliaments.

The Secretary to Cabinet is also Clerk of the Executive Council, the formal body chaired by the Governor-General that officially approves bills and executive orders. The Cabinet Secretary advises the Governor-General during post-election periods when parties are negotiating coalition and support agreements. The Cabinet Secretary, furthermore, has a key role in advising prime ministers on constitutionality and core executive processes. Crown Law also has an important role as guardian and interpreter of the constitution, as does the Public Service Commissioner. The Auditor-General is another constitutional guardian, a watchdog over public expenditure and an investigator of poor and corrupt financial decisions. The Secretary to Treasury is also crucial in protecting constitutionality. Public servants are vital guardians of the New Zealand constitution.[21]

Naturally, also, public servants have played a vital part in adding to and writing the new rules that have been the consequence, to a lesser or greater degree, of the developments traced above. Codes of conduct and behavioural guidelines have been developed.[22] The *Cabinet Manual* and its associated document[23] has become increasingly elaborate in response to the complications of multi-party government as well as the complex public and state sector; parliamentary institutionalisation has led to guidelines being created for each side of the constitutional fence; and ministers have been issued with statements of how they should behave with their public service advisers.[24] Thus much that defines the contemporary public service and its relationship with the political branch of government is now to be found in documents that write down the conventions and set out principles for appropriate and constitutional behaviour. The constitution exists beyond its statutes.

Throughout the 21st century New Zealand has debated its future constitutional development (including the possibility of becoming a republic, which would change the language of the "Crown", among other adaptations). One question that closely affects the NZPS is whether or not the parliamentary triennial term inhibits foresight and long-term policy development. In 1967 and 1990 voters resoundingly defeated proposals for four-year terms in non-binding referendums.

There is also the more fundamental question of whether New Zealand should continue on its pathway of incrementally and relatively easily amending its constitutional arrangements or adopt a codified and entrenched constitution.[25] This in itself might not affect the public service: much would depend on its position within a written constitution.

Geoffrey Palmer and Andrew Butler are sufficiently concerned by some of the problems of the contemporary public service to propose that the following principles become part of their constitution:

- The public service is a career-based service driven by a culture of excellence and efficiency, where appointment and promotion is on merit.
- The first duty of the public service is to act in accordance with this Constitution and the law.
- The public service must act in a spirit of service to the community and with commitment to open democratic government.
- The public service is politically neutral and impartial and serves loyally the Government of the day.

- The public service must provide ministers with free and frank policy advice.
- The public service upholds the concept of stewardship, that is, active planning and management of medium- and long-term interests, along with associated advice.
- The public service and all other institutions of the State must maintain high standards of integrity and conduct.[26]

To the above we would add an eighth principle: The public service must be a unified instrument of support for executive government and not a federation of independent fiefdoms.[27]

In the following section we explore some of the issues that face the future of the NZPS.

The New Zealand Public Service: recent changes and contemporary concerns

In the years following the so-called "decade of reform" (1985–1995), the search for managerial perfection took on the aura of the quest for the Holy Grail and, some would say, with equal lack of success. Others viewed this period as one of a natural process of trial and error as a radical new approach to governance was implemented and a new culture developed.

There were four major analyses undertaken within the public service itself: the Schick Report produced in 1997 by an eminent American professor retained by the SSC and the Treasury; and three major reviews by public servants.[28] All four endorsed the view that improvements had been made, particularly in financial control and decentralised management, but pointed to significant deficiencies in the system and, in the case of the Schick Report, it was suggested that the reforms created new problems.

A new code of conduct was promulgated in 1990 by the State Services Commission followed by its comprehensive revision and re-issue in 2007. The *Public Finance Act* introduced the concepts of "outputs" and "outcomes" as describing the respective responsibilities of public servants and ministers and as the basis for departmental expenditure votes. While the definitions were useful in improving financial management, they were not helpful in focusing organisations on results; and the term, "outcome", was redefined so that it lost its political implication. Departments were expected to give more emphasis to achieving specific objectives as defined in their Statements of Intent.

There were two attempts at introducing strategic management systems. The first was in the 1990s when, in putting together their performance agreements with their ministers, departments were committed to achieving Key Result Areas (KRAs) in order to contribute to the government's broader Strategic Result Areas (SRAs). The system was managed by the three central agencies (the SSC, the Department of the Prime Minister and Cabinet, and the Treasury) and involved discussions with ministers in Cabinet to ensure that the final document did in fact assist the government to achieve its medium-term strategies within the agreed budget allocations.

The second attempt followed the "Better Public Services" review when, in 2012, the government agreed to focus the public service on ten over-arching goals, defined so as to ensure that concrete results were obtained in those areas which ministers considered to have the highest priority and that departments could contribute to one or more of them. Both systems were introduced by National Party governments and, despite ministers in those administrations considering the processes to have been successful in obtaining the results they wanted, both were abandoned by their Labour successors.

The above moves were but a few examples of processes that have been tried in order to implement the reform philosophy and either abandoned, modified or substantially amended during the past 30 years. At the same time the political landscape has been transformed by introduction of proportional representation. And the electorate, disillusioned with the failure of successive governments to deal successfully with pressing social issues, made clear its distaste for the neo-liberalism with which the new public management has been associated.

Fragmentation has been a persistent problem. As already noted, the number of public servants had been drastically reduced by the mid–1990s. This was probably the largest cut in any developed country. Successive governments have accepted that this reduction had too severe an effect on delivery of services. The 2017 SSC report on the public sector workforce showed that the public service as defined in the *State Sector Act* employed 48,900 people representing around 16.5 percent of the state sector and 1.9 percent of the country's workforce. By December 2021, however, the number of full-time equivalent employees had risen by 3,950 (6.9%) during 2021 to 61,100. This rise was attributed to the demands of dealing with Covid 19 and "to delivering on the Government's priorities".[29]

Of even greater significance than the reduction in numbers and services, much of which was most severely felt in rural areas, has been the profound difference in the employment regime. Prior to 1988 the SSC was legally the largest employer in the country, albeit that most public servants below the second and sometimes third level were hired by their departments under delegated authority. This was the core of the concept of a unified public service that the electorate had endorsed since 1912. As at June 2017, the state sector as a whole (excluding local government employees) employed 295,000 people in more than 2,800 agencies, all of them their own employers. Central government was managed by 29 public service departments, six non-public service departments, three Offices of Parliament, the Reserve Bank of New Zealand, 20 District Health Boards, 27 tertiary education institutions, 2,416 School Boards of Trustees, 70 Crown Entities, 150 Crown Entity subsidiaries, 56 organisations under the *Public Finance Act* and 16 State-Owned enterprises and mixed ownership companies.[30]

For many years, going back well before the reforms, there has been talk of "one-stop shops" and "joined-up government" and this was something the two attempts at strategic management, referred to above, were intended to promote. In practice the emphasis on managerialism and "letting the managers manage" has moved in the opposite direction. As all of these agencies have their own separate accountabilities and performance requirements, it is not to be wondered at that they are organisationally- and not nationally-centric. In a world in which the social and economic problems we face are multi-layered and inter-disciplinary, a great deal more attention has to be given to a governmental structure which reduces structural complexity and enables cooperation and coordination among agencies. This may well require rethinking current concepts of accountability and performance measurement.

An examination of its leadership must be at the heart of any attempt to arrest the perceived decline of the NZPS. One of the intentions of the reform was to break the power of the "College of Cardinals", the combination of the State Services Commissioners and the departmental chiefs who formed the panels to select their fellow Permanent Heads – so-called because they usually remained in their positions until retirement.[31] The name was changed to "Chief Executive", they were chosen by panels still selected by the State Services Commissioner but from representatives of the general public, and they were placed on term-bound individual contracts.

The 1988 Act set out this procedure. The Act also provided, for the first time, that the government could decline to agree to the candidate chosen by the Commissioner and could appoint its own nominee but on condition that this was notified in the *Official Gazette* so that the public (that is, the media) could be aware of the nature of the appointment. It is of particular significance that not once since this provision was available to them have ministers taken advantage of it, even in cases where they were not pleased with the State Services Commissioner's choice. The politicians know only too well that the public's determination to maintain a politically neutral NZPS would lead to an outcry if they began appointing their own supporters.

In addition to changing the appointment process, the ministers of the day made it clear, as they were entitled to do, that they would expect the Commissioner (by 1989, the four-person Commission had been replaced by a single Commissioner) to cast the net for chief executives much more widely than previously when they most often came from within their own departments. The Commissioner was asked specifically to bring in "new blood" from the private sector and from abroad. In the event, this approach has not worked well. On the whole, international appointees have not been successful, while the most able candidates in the private sector have shown considerable reluctance towards working in an environment dominated by politics. As a result, many fewer chief executives originated from within their own agencies, preference being given to senior officials who had demonstrated their management capability in other NZPS departments. One effect has been that more often ministers have sought expert advice from below the heads of their departments or elsewhere altogether.

The contrast between this situation and the past could not be greater. In preparing this essay we have looked back over the past 50 years and recollected the leadership group before the reforms. Without difficulty we have recalled the names of 30 permanent heads from that period (one sign of the times being that they were all male). Virtually all had personal qualities that enabled them to provide strong leadership to their departments, even if they were not always good managers. Very often they were experts in their field who could not only provide sound technical advice to their ministers but also lead their profession within the wider community.

It would not be as easy to recall the same number of chief executives over the past 20 years, and certainly few have impressed the public with their professional authority. It is a telling commentary on the attempts to instill greater accountability that it is easier to remember the names of departmental heads from a period when public servants were supposed to be anonymous than it is now when they are subjected to much more public examination and rigorous performance assessment. It is neither desirable nor possible to return to the past, but it is open to question whether the practice of looking for chief executive appointees outside the field of expertise and experience demanded by the position, is meeting the need for stronger leadership of the public sector.

The question of leadership also raises that of policy advice. It is a fundamental precept that the two prime functions of a departmental head are, first, to provide his or her minister with free and frank professional advice; and second, to implement the government's decisions under the supervision of their minister. During the 1990s the State Services Commissioner became concerned that the concentration on management at that time had led to a falling away in the quality of policy advice, particularly after being informed by the Prime Minister that, in a cabinet committee, one senior chief executive had declined to answer questions of policy on the grounds that his responsibility was for the management of his department; it was up to his minister to respond on matters of policy. The result was the launching of a service-wide project described as "The Policy Initiative" to re-emphasise the importance of departmental policy capability.[32] This appeared to have had little effect. Only five years later the then Minister of State Services, Jenny Shipley (subsequently prime minister, 1997-99), in a major address to senior public servants, complained about the quality of their policy advice.[33]

In 2010, a report prepared by a group chaired by Graham Scott, former Head of the Treasury, argued that, in spite of some examples of good practice, there were serious problems with the overall ability of the NZPS to provide the government with high quality advice.[34] Some ministers had questioned whether their departments had the capability to tender the advice they needed. This review led to further detailed work resulting in a final report to ministers in 2014 and a Cabinet direction that improvements had to be made. Commenting on the fact that only 18 of 31 chief executives had "had past experience in policy management", the Scott Report noted that they had been told "that multiple candidates for Chief Executive and Deputy Chief Executive positions were unable to address substantive policy questions relating to the relevant sector in job interviews". The report recommended that, "where the provision of policy advice is combined with operational arms, it is preferable for the Chief Executive to have policy advice experience".[35]

The Scott Report led to "a suite of actions"[36] and subsequently to the appointment of the chief executive of the Department of the

Prime Minister and Cabinet to the additional role of "Head of the Policy Profession" and to a program of improvement throughout the NZPS which is ongoing. But the question remains whether the problem of policy advice is solely one of quality.

An issue that has had a much greater public airing is whether NZPS advice is any longer as "free and frank" as in the past. Both Labour and National prime ministers have strongly endorsed the principle, as have successive State Services Commissioners and at least two chief executives of the Department of the Prime Minister and Cabinet. The bible on these matters, the *Cabinet Manual*, is explicit in its guidance to ministers that they "have a duty to give fair consideration and due weight to free and frank advice provided by the public service".[37]

Notwithstanding all these assurances that the principle persists and is alive and well, there remains considerable doubt among commentators whether departmental advice in practice is as free and frank as tradition and theory suggests.[38] The clearest support for the anecdotal evidence that is widespread, especially among junior public servants, has been given by the findings of research undertaken in 2005 and 2017. Chris Eichbaum and Richard Shaw report that, although officially the principle of free and frank advice was being maintained by ministers and senior officials:

> [T]he problem is that that's not the view of the women and men in the engine room of public administration in New Zealand. What they tell us is that things have changed, and not for the better. They tell us that too many Ministers no longer want free and frank advice and they tell us that Ministerial staff interject themselves into administrative processes to filter out advice that a Minister may need to hear but that she or he . . . deems unhelpful or potentially embarrassing.[39]

The essence of the research findings is that, while ministers have always been able to obtain advice from a number of sources, the increase in the influence of the political advisers in their offices, particularly since the advent of MMP, has led to a countervailing reduction in the influence of the ministers' departmental advisers. If that is the case, the system clearly needs a fresh look to ensure both sets of advice are available to ministers and that the professional stream of advice, based on sound evidence and analysis and giving them a range of viable options, reaches them without interference.

Reports in the media also have suggested that the doctrines of "no surprises" and "responsiveness", which have gained greater currency over the past 20 years, developed to the point that senior officials tended to play it safe and tailor their advice to their ministers in order to ensure its acceptability.[40] That is in keeping with other observations that requests to departments under the *Official Information Act* are more routinely than formerly (and not in accordance with the legislation) referred to the minister's office for reply.[41] All of these indicators have persuaded at least the editorial writers that the NZPS has become more politicised than the public interest (and the constitution) requires.

The NZPS has assisted successive governments during the past century in achieving policies that were often radical and in delivering services through difficult times. While the reforms of the 1980s and later picked up ideas which were widely (but not universally) accepted throughout the developed world, and included the notion that successful countries would have to break free from centralised rules and bureaucracies, they were essentially an attempt to solve pressing economic and financial issues, not to reform the constitution. As the country became even more critical of the neo-liberal ideas which impelled the reform (and some of the most trenchant criticism has come from former ministers who were responsible for it), too often the focus has been on the perceived failures and lapses of the public sector and insuffient credit has been given to its successes. Criticisms of the NZPS intensified as the country struggled, mostly successfully, with the impact of the Covid pandemic.

The reputation of the Office of the State Services Commissioner itself suffered even though the scope of responsibility of the Commissioner was considerably broadened by the *State Sector Amendment Act 2013*. The situation has not been improved by the attitude of some ministers. At the height of the restructuring, when the NZPS was fully extended in implementing the government's instructions, Minister Richard Prebble would tell anyone who would listen that the immensely popular BBC show, *Yes, Minister*, was "not a farce but a documentary".[42] (Admittedly the ground had already been well prepared by the brilliant New Zealand television series, *Gliding On*, written by Roger Hall. This portrayed the NZPS as a conglomeration of cardigan-wearing time-servers.)

In January 2018, the former Prime Minister, Bill English, commenting on the new Labour/New Zealand First Government's announcement that it was dropping the "Better Public Services" targets, said that this would lead to "dumb and lazy government" and to public servants "putting their feet up around the country because now they don't have to worry too much about achieving much or being accountable".[43] It is to be hoped this was more a reflection of Mr English's disappointment over his inability to continue in government following the 2017 general election and not a judgment of the performance of a public service which had played a major role in assisting him to weather the strains on the economy of the Global Financial Crisis and two devastating earthquakes.

2018 marked the thirtieth anniversary of the *State Sector Act 1988*, an appropriate occasion for its review. The Minister of State Services in the Labour-New Zealand First Coalition Government (supported by the Green Party) initiated the review, involving public consultation. The result was the *Public Service Act 2020*.[44] Its full impact has yet to be seen.

The 2020 Act set out to deal with the problem of lack of coordination and restated the principles under which the NZPS is to operate, including a renewed emphasis on the "spirit of service". It remains to be seen, however, whether it has created an environment in which those matters that do not depend on legislation can be dealt with successfully – some, among others, being the public acceptance of the appropriate role of public administration in the 21st century; the quality of NZPS leadership; the professional competence of NZPS staff; the loss of the unified service; the move away from a career Public Service; the increasing use of external consultants; ministers' reliance on other sources of advice, including political advisers; the provision of free and frank advice; and the effect on the attitudes of NZPS Chief Executives of the new requirements by ministers for "responsiveness" and "no surprises".

Advice given by John Nethercote to the New Zealand Senior Executive Service when he addressed them in 1989 might well be kept in mind:[45]

> It is of primary importance that policy should return to a central place in public service life. All the talk about management has its usefulness but in the end it is a servant, not a substitute, for good policy. Management only works when policy is sound – how else can objectives be defined, performance evaluated? Public servants should not fall for the trap of confusing technique for thinking.
>
> The fortunes of public services . . . have always waxed and waned . . . . Each generation has the duty to shape its own destiny and, if it is lucky, it will have plausible opportunity to do so. The wise will do so with respect, but not veneration, for the past . . . . Public services unwilling, or unable, to take the lead in diagnosing their own ills, and developing their own cures, are unlikely to be able to provide governments with the support to which they are entitled.[46]

Whether or not public servants apply the Nethercote doctrine, the outcome will depend largely on the reaction of their political masters, as it is they who have the political power and the demo-cratic responsibility to tackle the problems we have highlighted here.

References

Advisory Group, "Better Public Services: Advisory Group Report" (State Services Commission, Wellington, 2011). At http://www.ssc.govt.nz/sites/all/files/bps-report-nov2011_0.pdf. Accessed 17 August 2018.

Advisory Group on the Review of the Centre, "Report of the Advisory Group on the Review of the Centre", State Services Commission, Wellington, 2001. At: http://www,ssc.govt.nzupload/dowloadable_files/review_of_centre.pdf. Accessed 17 August 2018.

Boston, Jonathan and John Uhr, "Reshaping the Mechanics of Government", in Francis Castles, Rolf Gerritsen and Jack Vowles, eds., *The Great Experiment: Labour Parties and Public Policy Transformation in Australia and New Zealand*, Auckland, Auckland University Press, 1996, 48-67.

Butler, Andrew and Geoffrey Palmer, *A Constitution for Aotearoa New Zealand*, Victoria University Press, Wellington, 2016; and *Towards Democratic Renewal: Ideas for Constitutional Change in New Zealand*, Victoria University Press, Wellington, 2018.

Cabinet Office, *CabGuide* (Cabinet Office, Wellington, 2017). At: www.dpmc.govt.nz/cabguide. Accessed: 12 January 2018.

Cabinet Office, *Cabinet Manual*, Department of the Prime Minister and Cabinet, Wellington, 2017. At: https://www.dpmc.govt.nz/sites/default/files/2017-06/cabinet-manual-2017.pdf. Accessed 1 December 2017.

Committee appointed by the Government to Review Expenditure on Policy Advice, "Review of Expenditure on Policy Advice", The Treasury, Wellington, 2010. At: https://treasury.govt.nz/sites/default/files/2011-04/report-repa-dec10.pdf. Accessed 17 August 2018.

Cooke, Henry, "Bill English Slams Government for Getting Rid of Public Service Targets", *Stuff*, 23 January 2018. At: https://www.stuff.co.nz/national/politics/100801792/bill-english-slams-government-for-getting-rid-of-public-service-targets. Accessed 21 August 2018.

Dowding, Keith and Elizabeth McLeay, "The Firing Line: When and Why do Prime Ministers Fire Ministerial Colleagues?", in Paul 't Hart and John Uhr (eds), *How Power Changes Hands: Transition and Succession in Government*, Palgrave Macmillan, Houndmills Basingstoke, 2011, 157-73.

Dunne, Peter, "No Surprises Risks and Responsibilities", *Public Sector*, December 2017.

Eichbaum, Chris and Richard Shaw, "Frankly we're not as free and frank as we were", *Newsroom*, 8 December 2017. At: https://pro. newsroom.co.nz/articles/authors/2739-chris-eichbaum. Accessed 17 August 2018.

Furphy, Samuel (ed.), *The Seven Dwarfs and the Age of the Mandarins: Australian Government Administration in the Post-War Reconstruction Era*, ANU Press, ACT, 2015.

Henderson, Alan, *The Quest for Efficiency: The Origins of the State Services Commission*, State Services Commission, Wellington, 1990.

Hunt, William D., "Report of Commission Appointed to Inquire and Report on the Unclassified Departments of the Public Service of New Zealand", *Appendices to the Journals of the House of Representatives* [AJHR], H.34, Wellington, 1912.

Keith, Kenneth, "On the Constitution of New Zealand: An Introduction to the Foundations of the Current Form of Government", in Cabinet Office, *Cabinet Manual*, Department of the Prime Minister and Cabinet, Wellington, 2017, 1-6. At: https://www.dpmc.govt.nz/ sites/default/files/2017-06/cabinet-manual-2017.pdf. Accessed 1 December 2017.

Louisson, Simon, "An Inside View of the Politicisation of the Public Service", *Dominion Post*, Wellington, 8 September 2017. At: https:// www.stuff.co.nz/dominion-post/comment/96522159/simon-louisson-an-inside-view-of-the-politicisation-of-the-public-service. Accessed 21 August 2018.

Martin, John R., "An Age of the Mandarins? Government in New Zealand, 1940-51", in Furphy, *The Seven Dwarfs*, 81-110.

Martin, John, *Public Service and the Public Servant*, State Services Commission, Wellington, 1991.

McLeay, Elizabeth, *In Search of Consensus: New Zealand's Electoral Act 1956 and its Constitutional Legacy*, Victoria University Press, Wellington, 2018.

McLeay, Elizabeth, *The Cabinet and Political Power in New Zealand*, Oxford University Press, Auckland, 1995.

Nethercote, John, "Policy: Centre of Good Public Administration", Part 2 of an edited text of an address to the New Zealand Senior Executive Service, Wellington, 28 September 1989, see also *The Canberra Times, Canberra,* 9 October 1989.

New Zealand House of Representatives, *Standing Orders of the House of Representatives,* Wellington, 2017. At: https://www.parliament.nz/ en/pb/parliamentary-rules/standing-orders. Accessed 12 December 2018.

New Zealand Treasury, "Review of Policy Expenditure and Advice", The Treasury, Wellington, 30 January 2014. At: https://treasury.govt. nz/information-and-services/state-sector-leadership/cross-agency-initiatives/review-policy-expenditure-and-advice. Accessed 23 August 2018.

Palmer, Geoffrey and Matthew Palmer, *Bridled Power: New Zealand's Constitution and Government,* 4th edn., Oxford University Press, Melbourne, 2004.

Palmer, Geoffrey, "Political Perspectives", in John Martin and Jim Harper (eds), *Devolution and Accountability: Studies in Public Administration,* Government Printing Office, Studies in Public Administration, No. 34, Wellington, 1988, 1-7.

Palmer, Matthew S. R., "What is New Zealand's Constitution and Who Interprets it? Constitutional Realism and the Importance of Public Office Holders", *Public Law Review,* Vol. 17, 2006, 133-62.

Palmer, Matthew S. R., *The Treaty of Waitangi in New Zealand's Law and Constitution,* Victoria University Press, Wellington, 2008.

Polaschek, R. J., *Government Administration in New Zealand,* New Zealand Institute of Public Administration, Wellington, 1958.

Prebble, Richard, "Address to Chairs of State-Owned Enterprises", Unpublished, Wellington, 1989. Source: Don Hunn's notes.

Rhodes, R. A., John Wanna and Patrick Weller, *Comparing Westminster,* Oxford University Press, Oxford, 2009, 88.

Schick, Allen, "Assessment of the State of the New Zealand Public Service," Occasional Paper No 1, State Services Commission, Wellington, 1998. At: http://www.ssc.govt.nz/upload/downloadable_files/occasional-paper-1.pdf. Accessed 17 August 2018.

Schick, Allen, "The Spirit of Reform: Managing the New Zealand State Sector in a Time of Change", State Services Commission and The

Treasury, Wellington, 1996. At: http://www.ssc.govt.nz/upload/downloadable_files/spirit_of_reform_all.pdf. Accessed 17 August 2018.

Shaw, Richard and Chris Eichbaum, *Public Policy in New Zealand: Institutions, Processes and Outcomes*, Pearson, Auckland, 2005.

State Services Commission, *Annual Report 1997-98*, State Services Commission, Wellington, 1998, 40. At: http://www.ssc.govt.nz/AR98. Accessed 19 August 2018.

State Services Commission, *Officials and Select Committees – Guidelines*, State Services Commission, Wellington, 2008. At http://www.ssc.govt.nz/node/6340. Accessed 12 December 2018.

State Services Commission, "Policy Advice Initiative: Opportunities for Management", State Services Commission, Wellington, 1992.

State Services Commission, *Reform of the State Sector Act 1988: Directions and Options for Change*, State Services Commission, Wellington, September 2018.

State Services Commission, *Report on Public Service Workforce Data: Human Resource Capability Survey*, State Services Commission, Wellington, 2017, 2. At http://www.ssc.govt.nz/2017-public-service-workforce-data-hrc-report. Accessed 17 August 2018.

State Services Commission, *Standards of Integrity and Conduct*, State Services Commission, Wellington, 2007. At: http://www.ssc.govt.nz/sites/all/files/Code-of-conduct-StateServices.pdf. Accessed 12 December 2018.

Te Kawa Mataaho Public Service Commission, "2021 Public Service Workforce Data", Te Kawa Mataaho Public Service Commission Wellington, 2021. At https://www.publicservice.govt.nz/resources/2021-public-service-workforce-data-published/. Accessed 16 March 2022.

The Treasury, "Review of Policy Expenditure and Advice", The Treasury, Wellington, 30 January 2014. At: https://treasury.govt.nz/information-and-services/state-sector-leadership/ cross-agency-initiatives/review-policy-expenditure-and-advice. Accessed 23 August 2018.

Wintringham, M. C., "Annual Report 1997-98", State Services Commission, Wellington, 1998. At:http/www.ssc.govt.nz/AR98. Accessed 19 August 2018.

Endnotes

[1] R. J. Polaschek, *Government Administration in New Zealand*, New Zealand Institute of Public Administration, Wellington, 1958, 97.

[2] William D. Hunt, "Report of Commission Appointed to Inquire and Report on the Unclassified Departments of the Public Service of New Zealand", *Appendices to the Journals of the House of Representatives* [AJHR], H.34, Wellington, 1912. William Hunt, a successful businessman, chaired the Commission.

[3] The recommendations of the Hunt Commission and the passage of the 1912 Act are discussed in Alan Henderson, *The Quest for Efficiency: The Origins of the State Services Commission*, State Services Commission, Wellington, 1990, 43-55; and Polaschek, *Government Administration in New Zealand*, 109-11.

[4] For discussion of the meaning of "department" and the number of government departments see Polaschek, *Government Administration in New Zealand*, Appendix A, 293-9.

[5] Public servants were members of a contributory superannuation scheme. Women retired at 55 or with 30 years service.

[6] The figures are from Henderson, *The Quest for Efficiency*, Appendix II, 397-8.

[7] Henderson, *The Quest for Efficiency*, 252.

[8] Ibid., 254.

[9] By 1974 the previous five divisions – General, Clerical, Professional, Administrative and (very small) Educational – had been transformed into a fine-tuned 137 occupational classes.

[10] For the differences and similarities, see especially Jonathan Boston and John Uhr, "Reshaping the Mechanics of Government", in Francis Castles, Rolf Gerritsen and Jack Vowles, eds, *The Great Experiment: Labour Parties and Public Policy Transformation in Australia and New Zealand*, Auckland University Press, Auckland, 1996, 48-67.

[11] Most were later privatised.

[12] Geoffrey Palmer, "Political Perspectives", in John Martin and Jim Harper, eds, *Devolution and Accountability: Studies in Public Administration*, Government Printing Office, *Studies in Public Administration*, no. 34, Wellington, 1988, 1-7.

[13] For a brief summary of New Zealand's constitution see especially: Kenneth Keith, "On the Constitution of New Zealand: An Introduction to the Foundations of the Current Form of Government", in Cabinet Office, *Cabinet Manual*, Department of the Prime Minister and Cabinet, Wellington, 2017, 1-6. At: https://www.dpmc.govt.nz/sites/default/files/2017-06/cabinet-manual-2017.pdf. Accessed 1 December 2017. See also Matthew S. R. Palmer, "What is New Zealand's Constitution and Who Interprets it? Constitutional Realism and the Importance of Public Office Holders", *Public Law Review*, Vol. 17 (2006), 133-62; and Geoffrey Palmer and Matthew Palmer, *Bridled*

Power: New Zealand's Constitution and Government, 4th edn, Oxford University Press, Melbourne, 2004.

14 See, for example, Richard Shaw and Chris Eichbaum, *Public Policy in New Zealand: Institutions, Processes and Outcomes*, Pearson, Auckland, 2005.

15 Keith Dowding and Elizabeth McLeay, "The Firing Line: When and Why do Prime Ministers Fire Ministerial Colleagues?", in Paul 't Hart and John Uhr, eds, *How Power Changes Hands: Transition and Succession in Government*, Palgrave Macmillan, Houndmills Basingstoke, 2011, 157-73; John Martin, *Public Service and the Public Servant*, State Services Commission, Wellington, 1991, 21-42; and Elizabeth McLeay, *The Cabinet and Political Power in New Zealand*, Oxford University Press, Auckland, 1995, 186-204.

16 R. A. Rhodes, John Wanna and Patrick Weller, *Comparing Westminster*, Oxford University Press, Oxford, 2009, 88.

17 Some provisions of the *Electoral Act 1993* are singly entrenched and have been since 1956. It has become a constitutional convention that the single entrenchment is respected. See Elizabeth McLeay, *In Search of Consensus: New Zealand's Electoral Act 1956 and its Constitutional Legacy*, Victoria University Press, Wellington, 2018.

18 Cabinet Office, *Cabinet Manual* (2017). The Standing Orders of the House of Representatives (2017) are at: https://www.parliament.nz/en/pb/parliamentary-rules/standing-orders. Accessed 12 December 2018.

19 See especially Matthew S. R. Palmer, *The Treaty of Waitangi in New Zealand's Law and Constitution*, Victoria University Press, Wellington, 2008.

20 See State Services Commission, "Officials and Select Committees – Guidelines", State Services Commission, Wellington, 2008. At http://www.ssc.govt.nz/node/6340. Accessed 12 December 2018.

21 See Palmer, "What is New Zealand's Constitution and Who Interprets it?"

22 See State Services Commission, "Standards of Integrity and Conduct", State Services Commission, 2007. At: http://www.ssc.govt.nz/sites/all/files/Code-of-conduct-StateServices.pdf. Accessed 12 December 2018.

23 The "how to do it" guide is: *CabGuide*, Cabinet Office, Wellington, 2017. At: www.dpmc.govt.nz/cabguide. Accessed: 12 January 2018.

24 Cabinet Office, *Cabinet Manual*, Section 3.

25 Andrew Butler and Geoffrey Palmer, *A Constitution for Aotearoa New Zealand*, Victoria University Press, Wellington, 2016; and *Towards Democratic Renewal: Ideas for Constitutional Change in New Zealand*, Victoria University Press, Wellington, 2018.

26 Butler and Palmer, *Towards Democratic Renewal*, 80.

27 In August 2018, the responsible minister, Chris Hipkins, announced the end of performance bonuses for chief executives. He stressed that the aim

was "to put the brakes on the growth rate of chief executive pay", also noting the Government's "belief that performance pay is counter-productive to achieving the *collaborative team-based leadership* that is critical to achieving better outcomes for New Zealanders", "Minister of State Services Press Release", Wellington, 21 August 2018. Emphases in the original.

[28] Allen Schick, "The Spirit of Reform: Managing the New Zealand State Sector in a Time of Change", State Services Commission and The Treasury, Wellington, 1996. At http://www.ssc.govt.nz/upload/downloadable_files/ spirit_of_reform_all.pdf. Accessed 17 August 2018; Schick, "Assessment of the State of the New Zealand Public Service", Occasional Paper No 1, State Services Commission, Wellington, 1998. At: http://www.ssc.govt.nz/ upload/downloadable_files/occasional-paper-1.pdf. Accessed 17 August 2018; Advisory Group on the Review of the Centre, "Report of the Advisory Group on the Review of the Centre", State Services Commission, 2001. At: http://www.ssc.govt.nz/upload/downloadable_files/review_of_centre. pdf. Accessed 17 August 2018; Advisory Group, "Better Public Services: Advisory Group Report", State Services Commission, Wellington, 2011. At https://www.ssc.govt.nz/sites/all/files/bps-report-nov2011_0.pdf. Accessed 17 August 2018.

[29] State Services Commission, "Report on Public Service Workforce Data: Human Resource Capability Survey", Wellington, State Services Commission, 2017, 2. At http://www.ssc.govt.nz/2017-public-service-workforce-data-hrc-report. Accessed 17 August 2018. The 2021 figures are in: Te Kawa Mataaho Public Service Commission, "2021 Public Service Workforce Data", Wellington, Te Kawa Mataaho Public Service Commission, 2021. At https://www. publicservice.govt.nz/resources/2021-public-service-workforce-data-published/. Accessed 16 March 2022.

[30] State Services Commission, "Report on Public Service Workforce Data", 1. By December 2021, however, the number of full-time equivalent employees had risen by 6.9%, in part due to the Covid pandemic demands.

[31] The "College of Cardinals", although a different notion, may be seen to share some characteristics with the Australian "Seven Dwarfs", namely length of tenure of some of its departmental heads and their contribution to the New Zealand public interest. See Samuel Furphy, ed., *The Seven Dwarfs and the Age of the Mandarins: Australian Government Administration in the Post-War Reconstruction Era*, ANU Press, ACT, 2015. See also John R. Martin, "An Age of the Mandarins? Government in New Zealand, 1940-51", in Furphy, ed., *The Seven Dwarfs*, 81-110.

[32] State Services Commission, "Policy Advice Initiative: Opportunities for Management", State Services Commission, Wellington, 1992.

[33] This was noted by the State Services Commissioner, M. C. Wintringham, in his "Annual Report 1997-98", State Services Commission, Wellington, 1998, 40. At: http://www.ssc.govt.nz/AR98. Accessed 19 August 2018.

[34] Committee appointed by the Government to Review Expenditure on Policy

Advice, "Review of Expenditure on Policy Advice", The Treasury, Wellington, 2010. At: https://treasury.govt.nz/sites/default/files/2011-04/report-repa-dec10.pdf. Accessed 17 August 2018.

[35] Committee appointed by the Government to Review Expenditure on Policy Advice, 41.

[36] See the Treasury's press statement on the Scott Review, "Review of Policy Expenditure and Advice", The Treasury, Wellington, 30 January 2014. At: https://treasury.govt.nz/information-and-services/state-sector-leadership/cross-agency-initiatives/review-policy-expenditure-and-advice. Accessed 23 August 2018.

[37] Cabinet Office, *Cabinet Manual*, 43. See also the State Sector Act 1988, Section 32(1) (f). At: http://www.legislation.govt.nz/act/public/1988/0020/latest/DLM129548.html. Accessed 17 August 2018.

[38] For example, see Palmer and Butler, *Towards Democratic Renewal*, 79-80.

[39] Chris Eichbaum and Richard Shaw, "Frankly we're not as free and frank as we were", *Newsroom*, 8 December 2017. This report summarises their research findings on political neutrality in the public service in 2005 and 2017. In 2017, Eichbaum and Shaw surveyed 417 public servants. At: https://pro.newsroom.co.nz/articles/authors/2739-chris-eichbaum. Accessed 17 August 2018.

[40] Peter Dunne, "'No Surprise': Risks and Responsibilities", *Public Sector*, 40(4) 24, 2017.

[41] Simon Louisson, "An Inside View of the Politicisation of the Public Service", *Dominion Post* (Wellington, 8 September 2017). At: https://www.stuff.co.nz/dominion-post/comment/96522159/simon-louisson-an-inside-view-of-the-politicisation-of-the-public-service. Accessed 21 August 2018.

[42] Richard Prebble, "Address to Chairs of State-Owned Enterprises", Unpublished, Wellington, 1989. Source: Don Hunn's notes.

[43] Henry Cooke, "Bill English Slams Government for Getting Rid of Public Service Targets", *Stuff*, 23 January 2018. At https://www.stuff.co.nz/national/politics/100801792/bill-english-slams-government-for-getting-rid-of-public-service-targets. Accessed 21 August 2018.

[44] State Services Commission, "Reform of the *State Sector Act 1988*: Directions and Options for Change", Wellington, State Services Commission, September 2018. At: https://www.havemysay.govt.nz/option-2/the-case-for-change/. Accessed 17 September 2018. See the *Public Service Act 2020*. At: https://www.legislation.govt.nz/act/public/2020/0040/latest/LMS106159.html. Accessed 10 March 2020.

[45] The *State Sector Act 1988*, at the request of the State Services Commission, provided for the Senior Executive Service. The aim was to retain a unified public service after the introduction of the decentralised management system. After a promising start the experiment failed. NZPS chief executives

saw the SES as undercutting their own authority over their own departments and increasingly declined to nominate members of the SES, which was in effect abandoned. It was removed from the legislation in the *State Sector Amendment Act (No 2) 2004.*

[46] John Nethercote, "Policy: Centre of Good Public Administration", Part 2 of an edited text of an address to the New Zealand Senior Executive Service, Wellington, 28 September 1989; and see *The Canberra Times*, Canberra, 9 October 1989.

12

The Independent Expert as Arbiter

The Australian Case

William Coleman

He is no metaphysician, but that does not worry Australians; he is ... expert, and therefore much admired in our homeland.
– Vincent Buckley 1983

John Nethercote's first direct acquaintance with how Australia is governed came in the mid-1970s in assisting the Royal Commission on Australian Government Administration. Thus at the beginning of his career Nethercote encountered a phenomenon highly characteristic of Australian government: the officially-sponsored report of the "independent expert" on some matter of policy. The Royal Commission on Australian Government Administration was indisputably "expert": the presiding and pre-eminent figure of the Commission, Dr H. C. Coombs, was an economics adviser of decades standing, a retired career official and former Governor of the Reserve Bank of Australia. And the Royal Commission was "independent"; four of the five commissioners, including Coombs, held no post in the executive arm of government. How real were the apparent benefits of this expertise and independence is, however, a less definite matter. Nethercote has provided his own retrospect on what became known as the "Coombs Commission".[1] This essay takes up the question in more general terms. It identifies several pathologies of the independent expert inquiry, and draws on Australian experience to illustrate them.

The scope of the phenomenon

The inquiry that is independent, expert, and policy-focused needs to be distinguished from inquiries of other familiar sorts.

Many are the inquiries that are both expert and policy-focused, but not independent. Isolating these conclusively from the subject of the present essay is problematic because independence comes in degrees. But the fact that the *perception* of independence is an essential desiderata of the governments that establish such inquiries provides a sharpening of the criteria of "independence". Any permanent government entity – however independent of the executive government in law – will likely suffer the perception of lack of independence. This essay, therefore, avoids the reports of "statutory authorities", such as, for instance, the National Health and Medical Research Council, and restricts itself to *ad hoc* bodies created specifically for an inquiry.

One may also distinguish the independent, expert, and policy-focused inquiry from the inquiry which, however independent, is not policy-focused, but is, instead, tasked with establishing some culpability or responsibility. These inquiries may be indirectly concerned with policy, but are primarily judicatory in purpose, and born of an apprehension of some wrong-doing or delinquency. Such inquiries include royal commissions that have left some crater impacts on Australian public life; including the royal commissions into *Misconduct in the Banking, Superannuation and Financial Services Industry* (Commissioner: Kenneth Hayne), 2019; *Certain Australian Companies in Relation to the UN Oil-For-Food Program* (Commissioner: Terrence Cole) 2006; *Espionage* (Commissioner: Justice William Francis Owen) 1954; *Certain Matters Relating to Mungana, Chillagoe Mines [etc]* (Commissioner: J. J. Campbell) 1930; and *Administration of Lands Department* (Commissioner: Justice William Owen) 1906.*

Finally, the subject of this essay may be distinguished from the inquiry which is independent and policy-focused, but not expert. A moderate example is the arbitral body that makes some decision

---

* See Hagger and Montanelli (1980) and Prasser and Tracey (2014).

that amounts to a policy, upon the basis of its inquiries. Such arbitral bodies do not presume to be expert in the subjects they rule upon. Thus the various courts and commissions of arbitration and conciliation that have made policy decisions about wages never purported to be economic experts; and they never even pretended to a research capacity. What they knew was no more than the evidence that was submitted to them. But it is post-war Britain that provides the most decided, and successful, examples of inquiries that were independent and policy-oriented but, virtually by intention, inexpert. The epitome of this was the string of inquiries that Cyril Radcliffe was charged with undertaking. A chancery barrister by training, Radcliffe's career as an "inexpert" began late in the 1940s when commissioned lead the body to determine the border between India and Pakistan, despite – or, perhaps, because of – his total lack of any background in the sub-continent. He later conducted a royal commission on the working of the monetary system (1957–9).[2] The appeal of such "inexperts" presumably arises from the thought that expertise may actually conflict with still more desirable properties such as disinterestedness and open-mindedness. Further, the extant expertise may not be coincident with the highest intelligence available. But the Radcliffe formula is a chancy one: a lack of expertise is hardly a guarantee of lack of interestedness, or of the best intelligence. And Australia has – with some significant exceptions – stuck with expertise.

Rationale

It is easy to identify *bad* reasons for the establishment of an independent expert inquiry. The executive government may seek to distance itself from contentious political decisions by interposing an "expert and independent inquiry" between themselves and that decision. Or governments may establish an inquiry as a substitute for action: they are "a means of doing something by doing nothing".[3] More than a century ago G. B. Barton complained of Australian governments' "anxiety to shirk its proper responsibilities on every matter of importance by appointing a select committee, a board or a Royal Commission".[4]

The good grounds for invoking expert inquiries presumably

rest on the existence of an intense division of knowledge in modern society. The historical record, however, suggests that in Australia the independent expert report is often born of a tangled relationship to the division of knowledge. Sometimes it has not been the division of knowledge as such, but the division of knowledge between an informed bureaucracy and an uninformed executive that has occasioned utilisation of independent outside experts by the executive government, as an antidote to monopolisation of knowledge by bureaucracies.

A second popular foundation for deployment of outside experts has been, not so much an exploitation of the division of knowledge, as a taming response to it. Consider the familiar case of the spontaneous but unrelenting expansion of legislation on some subject. This will produce experts in various corners of the legislative/regulatory thicket; but it will also call for experts who comprehend the labyrinth, and so can rationalise it, and so make it simpler, less anomaly ridden, and more transparent.

But whatever favourable grounds may plainly exist for the use of experts, three critiques may be advanced.

1. The market success critique of expertise

In this critique, decentralised decision-making "succeeds". The "market" pools and makes maximal use of the extant dispersed knowledge, so as to leave no potential gain in economic welfare unexploited.[5] So who needs experts? This "market success critique" of expertise holds that experts are redundant.

The classic case for the market success critique of expertise is supplied by the allocational problem. We assume there is a stock of sugar to be allocated amongst billions of consumers. A sugar planning commission can be conceived. But the throngs of sugar experts could not acquit the allocational task better than a competitive market for sugar. The example can easily be duplicated for production: stock of capital is to be allocated amongst billions of households. No capital allocation commission will cope, but each user will know what productive uses they can put capital to;

and a market for the purchase and sale of capital will result in the capital ending up in the hands of those who can use it best. In this scenario the futile resort to "experts" is a pathology arising from the inferiority of regulation and planning to the market. These resorts are an ineffective antidote to the diseases of too little market.

The market success critique of expertise may in turn be subject to critique.

Market success propositions obviously presuppose that a competitive market is possible; but markets are inhibited in situations with natural monopolies and public goods. Even within a market context the simple Hayekian demonstration of the success of the allocation proposition assumes a particular specification of the division of knowledge: each person has an "intimate knowledge" of how they may use sugar in ways beneficial to themselves. Suppose, instead, the good in limited supply is antibiotics; that would suggest a very different division of knowledge, one in which the market itself will summon experts ("doctors"). Or suppose, instead, that there is no such thing as "sugar", but millions of different "sugars" each with a different level of impurity or adulteration, and only the owner of a given batch knows that level. This situation of "asymmetric information" reveals situations when a less than omniscient state may be able to increase welfare by means of regulation devised by experts.

2. The government failure critique of expertise

Any conclusion that a certain hypothetical government action would be welfare-improving is no warrant for the contention that actual government action is generally improving. This simple observation is the starting point of all criticisms of "government failure"; and, specifically, of the "government failure critique of expertise".

The "government failure critique of expertise" does not rely on the market making government and its experts redundant; neither does it rely on some inadequacy of experts themselves. It supposes instead that government misuses, or misrepresents, what experts have to offer.

An ingenious illustration of the "Government Failure Critique of Expertise" is the critique of the precepts of orthodox public finance that have been advanced by the strain of thought known as Public Choice. In particular, James Buchanan and Geoffrey Brennan have argued with élan that the theorists of orthodox public finance have (unwittingly) made themselves experts in goose-plucking for the benefit of the state. These two authors have shown that the rules of "optimal taxation" – that minimise the welfare cost of a given amount of tax revenue – bear an unnerving degree of equivalence to the rules that maximise tax revenue for a given amount of welfare cost. Thus, in their telling, public finance expertise has amounted to a resource that assists the exploitation of the public by the state.[6]

A second type of "government failure critique" of expertise arises from government misrepresentation to the public of the problem that experts are supposedly summoned to solve. In this criticism all policy issues are bound up with values, leaving experts in only an auxiliary, if still necessary, capacity. Governments, however, find debates over values disturbing, so favour presenting the issue to the public as purely objective, and so properly left to experts.

3. The expert failure critique of expertise

In "expert failure critique of expertise", experts are not made redundant by the market; nor is their expertise misused by government. Rather, experts themselves are at fault.

It is this type of failure that the critics of expertise fall on with greatest relish. And the greatest target is the expertise that is not expertise: the pretence to knowledge paraded as possession of knowledge; the passing off of opinion as knowledge. The history of science provides numerous succulent examples of such impositions. In 1865, midway between *The Origin of Species* and *The Descent of Man*, 716 Fellows of the British Association of the Advancement of Science publicly affirmed the equal standing of the Bible with science in regard to the investigation of nature: "It is impossible," the signatories declared, "for the word of God as written in the book of nature, and the word of God as written in the holy scriptures to contradict one another". The company included 72 Fellows of the Royal Society and 111 Fellows of the Geological Society.[7]

Topical events of recent decades provide further examples.

Consider the (surely justified) decision of the British Government in 2002 not to join the Euro. A British journalist has recently recalled:

> In 1999, *The Economist* wrote to the UK's leading academic practitioners of the dismal science to find out whether it would be in our national economic interest to join the euro by 2004. Of the 165 who replied, 65 per cent said that it would. Even more depressingly, 73 per cent of those who actually specialised in the economics of the EU and monetary union thought we should join – the experts among the experts were the most wrong.[8]

Such failures of expertise may, with generosity, be construed as mistakes, not about the existence of the superior knowledge of experts, but about the extent of that superiority. Yes, the experts know more, but not as much as they think they do; they may be right on average, but mistaken in believing they are right all the time. Experts, to put the point leniently, suffer "over confidence" or, to put it more harshly, "arrogance". Such over-confidence might be deemed an occupational hazard; a downside of an inevitable amour-propre. But Levy and Peart develop the thought that there is something more essential about the over-confidence or arrogance of expertise. Expertise is a hierarchical thing; and this imparts an authoritarian accent to its investigations and inquiries. A commission of inquiry is not a discussion club, nor a debating society.[9]

Further, expert failure extends beyond "mere" conceit to encompass bias. Bias has many sources; personal biases (against others, or for yourself); biases of enculturation; and the bias of credal commitment, seen most palpably in the religious convert. Levy and Peart (2017) pursue this last form of bias in experts with two telling examples. They do not choose the easy targets, but two brilliant scientific minds; Karl Pearson and Paul Samuelson. They target Samuelson's repeated public forecasts that the Soviet GDP would probably overtake GDP of the United States in a little more than 20 years; and Karl Pearson's elaborate statistical case against admitting Polish Jews to Britain in the inter-war period. Their contentions were not only

wrong with the wisdom of our hindsight; they constituted *ex ante* irrational judgments, consisting of a near absence of updating of their
priors in the face of extending information, that may be traced to an
irrational commitment to their priors.*

These non-rational commitments of experts pass beyond the
positive into the normative. And thus experts have passed off their
values as expertise. A palpable example is parole boards, in Australia as elsewhere. A gaol sentence is a reflection of values if anything
is. But parole boards, whose values differ so distinctly from much of
the Australian public, would have it that their decisions reflect an
expertise.[10]

Australian experience

None of the critiques canvassed above will annihilate the value of
expertise. "Truth is not manifest". It takes an expert to realise that a
cubic metre of air weighs (about) 1.22 kgs; or that a uniform tariff of
10 percent on imports is equivalent in its effects to a 10 percent tax
on exports (Lerner's theorem); or that a reduction in the amount of
electricity required to produce a given amount of illumination may
increase the amount of electricity consumed for illumination (Jevons
paradox.) It is expertise that acquires and sustains such knowledge.

For all that, the canvassed critiques of expertise do have some
force. This essay undertakes to supply a few illustrations of them
from Australian experience. The pathologies below may not
actually be typical, nor is it contended that they are so. But they are
recognisable.

Thomas Bigge and *Inquiry into the State of the Colony of New South Wales*, 1822

In 1992 a historian of Australian agriculture imagined,

> What if bureaucrats in a late-eighteenth century Ministry

---

* Thus, in 1961, Samuelson forecast that the GDP of the Soviet Union could
  surpass that of the United States by 1984, an interval of 23 years. Nineteen
  years on, in 1980, Samuelson now forecast that the Soviet Union's GDP could
  surpass that of the United States by 2002, an interval of 22 years.

of Central Planning in London had devised a system of arable farming for Australia, rather than farmers responding to market imperatives? . . . Who would have sat on the interminable inter-departmental and parliamentary sub committees . . . and which "independent, outside" experts would have been paid huge consultancy fees for their advice? As earnest civil servants concerned about their career advancement, the planners would have sought to give their masters . . . a solid, technical, preferably impenetrable report . . . mindful of the politicians' capacity to deal with original challenging thoughts . . . The technical fashions of the day would get a lot of attention . . . the best and latest would be recommended . . . when it came to implementing the recommendations, the budget would then matter and those on the spot would have to make do with half a loaf – perhaps a plough with nothing with which to pull it.[11]

This flight of imagination is not as whimsical as it might seem. Before there existed trial by jury, a free press, or a legislature of any kind in Australia, the independent expert trod the land. In 1819 three extensive inquiries into almost every dimension of New South Wales were undertaken by Thomas Bigge at the behest of the Secretary of State for War and the Colonies.

Bigge's commission was born of the frustrations arising from an acute asymmetry of knowledge between an expensive dependency and her parent society. The outlay of the NSW apparatus had risen from £95,291 in 1815 to £558,101 in 1820. How much was waste? What was going on?[12] Whitehall could wait 10 months before receiving a response to a communication to Sydney. It needed a man on the spot.

Bigge would have been deemed to be "expert" on colonies. He was well-versed in agriculture, including the doctrines of the "new farming". He had been the chief justice in Trinidad, a colony with definite parallels with New South Wales: a population of about 30,000, composed of a free elite, a freedman class and a mass in bondage. "In Trinidad he was called to leave his bench, gown and wig and conduct inquiries into many branches of the colony's administration other than law"[13] including financial mismanagement and corruption, slave emancipation, "emigration, land sales, agriculture, the public stores, public works and labour supply".

And Bigge could be judged as independent as could be hoped of any appointee: he had no position at the Colonial Office; he was not some favourite of faction.

But, however useful to later historians, his New South Wales report did little to further the general welfare under the heads he was assigned to investigate.

Bigge's report is vulnerable to the market success critique. What NSW clearly needed was a great deal more market, and Bigge's inquiry was in part a response to that need. But he only went the other way and tended to more control. Thus, he favoured the elimination of wage earnings by convicts. It may be that Bigge, in the words of one even-handed critic, was "trying to discover what economic activities he should advise the government to promote", but, by the lights of the market critique, he should not have been advising the government to "promote" any particular activity at all. He should, instead, have advised it to establish "competitive neutrality", and let the market determine the allocation of resources between alternative activities. To illustrate the point more specifically; in censuring the pursuit of arable agriculture by smallholders on the supposed grounds that it was "exhaustive", Bigge surely overreached his capacity to know: perhaps the rate of return on the amount of capital required to make arable agriculture "non-exhaustive" was less than the rate of return on that capital in alternative uses. What individual could claim to know this particular of hundreds of thousands of acres? Only "the market" could know. "He did not consider if established practice might have been developed to suit local conditions, rather than merely being a reflection of the brute ignorance of smallholder farmers".[14]

But the Bigge report is perhaps most vulnerable to "expert failure" critique of expertise, given that the distinct tendency of both contemporaries and historians is to judge Bigge's inquiry to be biased against Macquarie and smallholders, and in favour of large landowners. According to Raby, "His close association with the large landowners during his sojourn, if anything, probably reinforced his biases. Bigge relied mainly on this group for his information about smallholder farming".[15]

To illustrate: Bigge pressed for transfer of convicts from government works to private agriculture on account of a supposed excess demand for skilled labour in private agriculture, and an excess supply of skilled labour in public works. But some historians have argued the very facts recorded in his reports confirm the opposite. "Bigge's evidence established this point with great clarity, although his Report argues the opposite case . . . It is hard to escape the conclusion that Bigge first decided on his thesis and then looked for evidence to support it".[16] The questionnaires and examinations look less like inquiry than case-building: "The thousands of pages of the transcript of evidence form an interesting but often specious chronicle".[17]

Bigge's report also exemplifies the latent authoritarianism of the "expert inquiry". One contemporary sought to trace Bigge's dogmatism to his "long career of presiding [in Trinidad] where the dictum of the court was not to be controverted".[18] But, as Levy and Peart stress, any investigation is, by its nature, not a discussion, nor a debate. It grants no equal time, no right of reply. Bigge's commission brings out well the authoritarian potential of the officially sanctioned expert inquiry. As one historian observes of his remit:

> He was also to disclose confidences of the private or public lives of servants of the Crown and leading citizens and officials "however exalted in rank or sacred in character". He thus left England in the dual guise of public commissioner of the Crown and of private inquisitor for the government.[19]

One hostile historian suggests Bigge "deliberately refrained from administering the oath to witnesses, since that might impose some restraint on them".[20] Even a less aggressive appraisal avers that Bigge's report was based on "unsworn statements of a large body of persons, to most of whom lying was not even a peccadillo".[21]

A final point: Bigge lacked vision. He had much less of this grace than such men of executive action as the governors, Arthur Phillip and Lachlan Macquarie. The recommendations of his report were many, precise and mostly minor. An unsympathetic critic deems that his "mountain of labour brought forth, not one mouse, but a whole swarm of mice".[22] A sympathetic student of Bigge's life allows that "He had not been endowed with imaginative gifts . . .".[23] Is expertise bound up with an analytical "left hand brain"?

H. C. Pearson and the report on the state of public education in Victoria, 1874-1876

There was no lack of vision in H. C. Pearson; or sensitivity or seeming candour; or an ability to perceive several sides of a question, and yet take an emphatic position. In all these attributes there was something of John Henry Newman about Pearson. It is hardly surprising that Pearson was an idol of the youthful Alfred Deakin. Or that Edmund Barton's own biases were encouraged by the racial antipathies – articulated by Pearson at some length[24] – in someone so apparently elevated.

The occasion that saw Pearson materialise as an outside expert was the same as that which brought forth Bigge: an executive government seeking to get a grip on new, expensive and seemingly out of control bureaucratic structure.

Victoria's *Education Act 1872* had effected the de facto nationalisation of schools in Victoria. Free (to user) state schools had put hundreds of fee-charging schools out of business. To the same effect, Pearson noted, "The state makes it practically impossible for private persons to establish primary schools",[25] since government aid to church schools was now abolished. A new Department of Education was instituted. Regrettably, "The Department was plagued by seemingly insurmountable difficulties",[26] that included a burgeoning of bureaucracy, requiring the employment of a host of clerks (including a youthful J. F. Archibald); acute allocational problems; disaffection at its "arbitrary acts"; exploding costs per pupil (from £3-0-5d in 1871-72 to £5-4-0d in 1884-85); and an "orgy" of school construction which left, as in NSW, many handsome school buildings, but also excited the misgiving that a needless expense was being incurred for the benefit of building contractors.

Pearson could be described as expert for this problem: he had briefly been Headmaster of a prominent fee-charging secondary school in Melbourne; and had been a professor at King's College, London. He had attended Rugby School as freshly remade by Thomas Arnold, and he possessed an abiding interest in education, manifested by his inquiry into education in Ontario, and his later appointment as Minister of Education of Victoria. And he was independent, even if "there was no hiding the political character of the appointment" in 1878 to report on "the state of public education in Victoria".[27]

For all these apparent merits, Pearson's report is vulnerable to market success critique. He was tasked to deal with the frustrations and burdens brought by a great bureaucracy. But he proposed to deal with the ills of bureaucratic control with more bureaucratic control. He wished to remove parents' right to choose school; he wanted to eliminate merely "licensed" teachers; he believed there was an "overwhelming case in favour of absolute and universal compulsion"[28]; and he recommended instituting, by my reckoning, 202 pay classifications. Moving in the other direction, he favoured schools having more control of the hiring and firing of teachers.

His report also manifests a certain kind of "expert failure", as it is suffused with unacknowledged normative presumption. Pearson was essentially a secularised Anglican divine. He was the grandson of one founder of the Bible Society; the son of John Norman Pearson, a chaplain to an older brother of the Duke of Wellington; and a nephew of Reverend Richard Puller, who, as "Piercy Ravenstone", had breathed fire against the liberalism of political economy. He was a student at King's College, London, "a home of Anglicanism", and an undergraduate in the Oriel College of Tractarian John Henry Newman and "the Noetics". He maintained a public antipathy to (in his words) "Catholics, Jews, publicans and Scots clergy".[29] In adulthood he lost a Christian theology, but he acquired a "secular theism", in which God was replaced by Reason, the Church by the State, and the priesthood by a Millian clerisy, composed of such as himself. Under such a vision it was logical enough that children would be in tutelage to those who were, in his own words, under "infinite obligation" to the State; it was Pearson's view that "Much of the progress of Civilisation consists of limitation of parental right".[30] Until the early 1840s the Church of England had fought to maintain a preeminent place in education in Australia: to Pearson, a generation later, a secularised state system would assume that mantle. This yearning was not the fruit of his knowledge, but of his own peculiar – and alarming – religion of the state.

Brigden and *The Australian Tariff: an Economic Enquiry*, 1929

Unlike the reports of Bigge or Pearson, the "Brigden Report" of 1929 was not occasioned by a political executive seeking an antidote to bureaucracy's monopolisation of information; but as a means to rationalise unforeseen but unceasing profusion of one species of legislation: tariffs.

From the *Tariff Act* of 1902, Australia's tariff barriers had burgeoned. And the years following the Great War saw no halt. The average tariff rate rose from about 10 per cent in 1918 to about 20 per cent by 1927.[31] The Prime Minister, Stanley Melbourne Bruce, neither a free trader nor a protectionist, put some trust in the expert to tame this inexorable profusion. Shortly before, Bruce had brought to fruition a council of scientists and industrialists in the form of the Council for Scientific and Industrial Research. A council of economic scientists might promise to be equally useful. In this spirit, in 1927, he asked L. F. Giblin; C. H. Wickens (the Commonwealth Statistician); the "businessman-ideologue" E. C. Dyason; J. B. Brigden; and D. B. Copland to undertake an investigation of the effects and success of tariff policy.[32]

The inquiry was independent: unlike the Tariff Board, which, by law, was presided over by the head of the Trade and Customs department, the Comptroller-General of Customs and Excise. And it was expert: Brigden had studied economics under F. Y. Edgeworth; Giblin was taught statistics by Karl Pearson; Copland was a professor of economics; and Wickens lectured on monetary economics at the University of Melbourne. They had the benefit of 150 years of theorising on tariffs; torrents of data; and the Tariff Board's quasi-legal inquiries.

But the proceedings of the Inquiry exposed any pretension that these experts were possessed of objective knowledge sufficient for their purposes, as they were significantly split between a free trade "Melbourne group" (Copland, Wickens and Dyason) and a more protectionist "Hobart group" (Brigden and Giblin). True; it managed to secure a common proposition that could be seen to give something to both sides – free trade would increase mean income but decrease median income. But other "experts" could dispute both: Leslie Melville[33] dismissed the model of the inquiry as "ingenious fantasy". And other experts could also contend against both mean income and median income as a superficial metric of welfare.[34]

The report did prove an important, perhaps key, stimulus to the development in the 1940s and '50s of the theory of the distributional implications of international trade[35]; but this stimulus was only possible on account of that theory being so underdeveloped in 1929 when the authors encountered the questions the report dealt with. They experienced the predicament endemic to economists: their knowledge was partial. They knew the road south was wrong; but between east and north they differed amongst themselves, inconclusively. Such expertise is valuable – the south road is wrong! – but far from decisive. And here lies perhaps the key inadequacy of characterising the expert as the custodian of complex, and therefore recondite, objective knowledge; it is not that they do not possess any, but what they possess is often not decisive to the question in hand, and, in consequence, "experts" diverge according to their "point of view".

Niemeyer and his *Review*, 1930

Sir Otto Niemeyer's *Review* was something of a repeat of Bigge's report; the antipodean portion of the Empire was again in financial crisis; and Niemeyer, representing the Bank of England, was to "observe" the economic situation in Australia. As a Bank of England official, he was independent of the Prime Minister of Australia who had (ostensibly) tasked him. And he was expert in international finance: he had advised Churchill on restoration of the gold standard, was a director of the Bank of International

Settlements (1931-65), and was, in the 1930s, to make reports on Argentina, Brazil, China and India.

But Niemeyer could not be said to be very expert on Australian particulars: "It would be ridiculous for him to say anything about Australian conditions", he wrote in *The Advertiser* on 19 July 1930, on account of his "present limited knowledge of Australia". And Niemeyer hardly had the conscientiousness of Bigge. During his four-month junket of port drinking and golfing, he floated a series of astringent judgments about his host country that were at best dubious. Productivity per head in Australia had fallen six percent in 20 years; Australia was "overpopulated"; Australia was a "poor" country. Finally, the Commonwealth Bank's own suggestion that Britain would soon leave the gold standard was "staggering".

Overall, Niemeyer seems in the grip of "City" prejudgments about Australia. Consonant with this, during his lengthy stay Sir Otto did not so much observe as decree. His advice was stark, peremptory and commanding: the Premiers were to balance their budgets immediately.

There is a temptation to judge, in retrospect, how right or wrong was this advice; and from such a judgment to infer how valuable or harmful his "expert" inquiry was. But Niemeyer's case threatens the very notion of the expert as custodian of objective knowledge. True: taking Niemeyer's advice was probably for the best of Australia in 1930. But what made Niemeyer's advice good advice for Australia was simply the fact that British investors thought it so. Since Niemeyer had their confidence, to do anything other than what he favoured would be to starve Australia of capital inflow. So if Niemeyer recommended balancing budgets, that becomes advice worth following. If Niemeyer, however, had favoured a looser fiscal policy, then that would have been appropriate. Niemeyer thus illustrates what is not infrequently encountered in capital markets: that truth is not one, and there are plural "belief equilibria", each belief making for events that justify it. Experts "knowing" contrary propositions might both be granted a useful credence.

Sydney and the *Planning Scheme of the County of Cumberland*, 1948.

The period following the Second World War provides an example of the expert report being invoked, not as a response to an asymmetry between bureaucracy and executive, but in an attempt to give, or impose, a rationale to a previously spontaneous growth: the cityscape of Sydney.

Since Governor Phillip's time, Sydney's fretwork of bays and dimpling hills have impeded implementation of rectilinear visions of the city. Various governors had effected some straightening out, but the first concerted attempt to "remodel Sydney on an intelligent plan" came with the 1909 *Royal Commission for the Improvement of the City* and *Sydney and Its Suburbs*.

The commission was independent. And it was expert, if only in the etymological sense of "skilled through experience", being largely composed of public sector practitioners; the Lord Mayor, a former lord mayor, a former police chief, a former public works chief, two members of parliament, an architect, a civil engineer, and a councillor. Yet it was not all practice: notions of town planning by then hung thick in the air; and the Commission's favourite architect, Sir John Sulman, was to found Australia's planning association in 1913.

The Commission did some useful work. It mooted the King's Cross underpass; it recommended the City Circle schema of railways and, above all, it settled the site of the Sydney Harbour Bridge.

But the Commission can be criticised for aspiring to impose its own aesthetic values across the city, as Eric Irvin observed.[36] A critic might deem these values to be those of the lid of a Quality Street chocolate box. A defender might instead invoke Sydney's Central Railway Station. Whatever value in the Commission's aesthetics, it was heavy in presumption for it to recommend, in effect, that the city of Sydney be remade in "Federation Classical Academic" style.

But the Commission was only the prologue to the hay day of

experts in planning of Sydney. This was ushered in by *The Local Government (Town and Country Planning) Amendment Act 1945*. This created the Cumberland County Council, an assembly of delegates of the local councils of the Sydney area. Its remit included preparation of a plan for Sydney that they could recommend to the NSW Government. The Council duly appointed a Chief County Planner, S. L. Luker, of the Town and Country Planning Institute, and his team got to work. The resulting *Scheme* of 1948 was given some heed and many genuflections by Labor governments, before it was euthanised by a Liberal government late in the 1960s. By that date the *Scheme* had become a relic, totally overwhelmed by the post-war boom.

The *Scheme* had been hopelessly wrong in its population forecasts of the post-war period, upon which the plan was predicated.

Australia's Population in the Post-War Period (millions)

	Scheme estimates and forecasts	Actual
1947	7.58 e	7.64
1972	8.91 f	13.09
1980	9.19 f	14.07
1990	circa 9.0 f	17.17

Sources: Scheme, 50; ABS, Australian Population Statistics, 310.5.65.001

The *Scheme* supposed Australia's population would increase by 18 percent between 1947 and 1990; and would be in actual decline by the latter date. In the event, Australia's population increased by 125 percent between 1947 and 1990, and would increase another 11 percent in the following decade. Thus the *Scheme* of 1948 assumed that the stagnation of the preceding 20 years would endure. Here we have one of the great historical ironies of the age of "town planning": gazing out from the balcony of 1948 towards the blue horizon of the post-war world, they resolutely planned for a 1930s Sydney.

The *Scheme*'s population predictions were not arrived at in a cavalier way. On the contrary, they were built on the 1944 projections of the National Health and Medical Research Council overseen by two mandarins, H. C. Coombs (Department of Post-War Reconstruction) and Roland Wilson (Department of Labour and National Service). Neither did the *Scheme* unthinkingly adopt these. The *Scheme* deemed the fertility rate of 0.925 children per woman assumed by the 1944 projections to be a touch "conservative"; so it allowed for the possibility it would recover to 1.0 by 1970. The 1944 projections ignored immigration; the *Scheme* allowed for what it described as a "liberal allowance" for migration, 30,000 per annum. In the event these careful prognostications were quickly exploded: in the ten years, 1948-49 to 1958-59, permanent and long-term arrivals averaged 125,300 per annum; the fertility rate leapt and, in 1970, still stood at 1.415.

As with so much expert failure, the *Scheme*, in making these projections, ignored the Socratic lesson: "The only thing I know is that I know nothing".[37]

Further, a market success critique may be applied to the *Scheme*'s hapless attempts to predict population. Put simply, any given household may have been as clueless as the *Scheme* regarding Australia's population 30 years hence, but they probably had a better sense than the *Scheme* of their own future fertility. And that better sense would be reflected in the pricing by capital markets of future consumption relative to current consumption. Bureaucrats cannot know the productive uses of capital in future relative to today. Each household, with its own hunch of its future size, would have a better estimate of what they could do with the capital in the future ... and the capital market will respond with higher rates of return on saving, and a resources flow into long investment.

Beyond its lack of success in its positive contentions, the *Scheme* can be criticised for insinuating its values in the guise of expertise. Perhaps the pre-eminent value of the *Scheme* is planning itself. Planning is not a means to an end, but is an end in itself; the alternative is dismissed by pejoratives – "piecemeal", "chaotic", "promiscuous", and, worst of all – "unplanned".

But the values of the *Scheme* extend to what are best described as "aesthetic"; it does not shy away from invoking the "aesthetic point of view". A leading strand of its aesthetics is orderliness. This value can be detected in its concern to segregate townscapes and countrysides carefully into a kind of TV dinner landscape; where each activity was neatly assigned to a certain regular portion of the terrain. You can also see it in a kind of Classicism that it adopts with respect to the Country part of "Town and Country" planning: the nature it takes pleasure in is what it refers to as "picturesque" and "sylvan"; the countryside it favours is a quilt of farm houses, silos, and orchards.

With respect to the Town part, the value of orderliness pre-disposed it to a Modernism of straight lines and simplicity. The Parliament House, the Mint, and Sydney Hospital are consequently deemed "obsolete"; and yet are to be preserved as relics. It is with respect to vernacular architecture that the Plan reveals not only a lack of imagination, but the planner's belief that all progress must be planned, and, if necessary, uncompromisingly so. The housing of inner Sydney is judged "obsolete". And the "slum clearance" that had been taking place since the 1880s is deemed inadequately piecemeal. It therefore advocates "clearance" (that is, demolition) of 47,000 dwellings, covering 3,000 acres. The *Scheme* does not flinch at recommending this horrifying vision be put into "immediate" effect with respect to Paddington, Redfern, Balmain and Surry Hills. With the housing "cleared", the street pattern would be laid down anew. Thus Paddington, Redfern, Balmain and Surry Hills were to be razed. In accordance with this enjoinder, within a few years the City of Sydney had prepared specific plans for the levelling of Paddington and Woolloomooloo, and the construction, over the shards, of a complex of freeways, "open spaces" (that is, empty spaces) and blocks of state housing.

That this appalling act of mass destruction never came to pass was partly due to the City of Sydney's lack of finance. And partly due to "the contradictions of *dirigisme*". In the same year as the *Scheme* was delivered, the *Landlord and Tenant Act 1948* established rent maxima for the post-war period. An upshot of the consequent below-market rents was that owner-occupation of any property now realised a greater property value than ownership by landlords;

and the ownership of inner-city suburbs consequently shifted from landlords to owner-occupiers. Thus was created a population of owners in the inner city so numerous that resumption of their property for "clearance", *Scheme* style, was to be both logistically and politically forbidding.

The decline of the expert report?

This essay amounts to a warning regarding the potential pathologies of the independent expert report. Clearly the significance of such a caution will decline to extinction if the "expert review" dies. Is the outside and expert report an endangered species?

The Rudd Labor Government was busy commissioning expert inquiries. And the decision of the subsequent Liberal-National Government, amid a crisis in electricity prices, to commission an "Independent Review into the Future Security of the National Electricity Market", presided over by the Chief Scientist, Alan Finkel, might suggest the "independent expert report" is as lively as ever in Australia.

But other indications are that the independent and expert report is in some decline.

I refer to the *Review of Funding for Schooling*, universally known by the moniker, "Gonski", presided over by a person without any pretence to expertise in the subject-matter, but which, for all that, has acquired a peculiar power of fetish. This document cleaves tightly to the seemingly unalterable formula for Australian education since the Acts of the 1870s – more centralisation and more "funding" – in spite of the evidence of failure of this formula, and in the face of ever more drastic applications of it. Thus a UNICEF report in 2017 on performance of 15-year-olds in reading, maths and science, in 41 European Union and OECD countries, measured Australia to be third worst. UNICEF's Australian director of policy and advocacy – an "expert" presumably – stated: "There's certainly a decline in real terms in the education space in Australia, partly because we have yet to see education reform that goes beyond funding-model debates". "Gonski" is no more than another funding-model scheme to increase "funding" substantially. For all that, the *Review* promptly won a pledge of support from all major parties.

Any decline of the "expert review" would be part and parcel of the well-known emptying out of expertise of the Australian public service; and the burgeoning perception of a more general decay of depth, acumen and scholarship. Perhaps a future age will yet rue that the vices of the (genuinely) expert were moderate relative to those of the oracular amateur.

References

Australian (*The*), "Queensland parole scandal", 14 November 2017.

Australian (*The*), "Justice system "now at turning point", 16 October 2017.

Ashton, Nigel, "Nigel Ashton interview", *Planning Sydney. Nine Planners Remember*, P. Ashton (compiler), Council of the City of Sydney, Sydney, 1992.

Ashton, Paul, *The Accidental City: Planning Sydney since 1788*, Hale and Iremonger, Sydney, 1993.

Barton, G. B., *The Troubles of Australian Federation*, Australia, 1901.

Bennett, J. M., "Bigge, John Thomas (1780–1843)", *Australian Dictionary of Biography*, Volume 1, Melbourne: Melbourne University Press, 1966.

Bigge, Thomas, *Report of the Commissioner of Inquiry into the State of the Colony of New South Wales*, Libraries Board of South Australia, 1966.

Brennan, Geoffrey and James M. Buchanan, *The Power to Tax: Analytical Foundations of a Fiscal Constitution*, Cambridge University Press, Cambridge, 1980.

Brigden, J. B., D. B., Copland, E. C. Dyason, L. F. Giblin and C. H. Wickens, *The Australian Tariff: An Economic Inquiry*, Melbourne University Press, Melbourne, 1929.

Buckley, Vincent, *Cutting Green Hay: Friendships, Movements and Cultural Conflicts in Australia's Great Decades*, Allen Lane, Melbourne, 1983.

Cumberland County Council, *The Planning Scheme for the County of Cumberland*, Cumberland County Council, Sydney, New South Wales, 1948.

Dennis, J., "Bigge versus Macquarie", *Journal and Proceedings of Royal Australian Historical Society*, 23(6), 1937, 411-65.

Department of Education and Training, *Review of Funding for Schooling: Final Report*, Department of Education and Training, Canberra, 2011.

Dollery, Brian and Stuart Whitten, "An empirical analysis of tariff endogeneity in Australia, 1904–1974", *Economic Analysis and Policy*, 28(2), 1998, 213-30.

Economist, The, "Economists for EMU", 15 April 1999, https://www.economist.com/node/199382

Ellis, M. H., 'Some Aspects of the Bigge Commission of Inquiry into the Affairs of New South Wales 1819-1821', *Journal and Proceedings Royal Australian Historical Society*, 27(2), 1941, 93-126.

Ergas, Henry, "Australia's Defence: A Review of the 'Reviews,'" *Agenda – A Journal of Policy Analysis and Reform*, 19(1), 2012, 63-74.

Fine, G., "Does Socrates Claim to Know that He Knows Nothing?" *Oxford Studies of Ancient Philosophy*, 35(2), 2008, 49-86.

Hagger, Jean and Tina Montanelli, *Consolidated index to the Checklists of Royal Commissions, Select Committees of Parliament and Boards of Inquiry, Held in the Commonwealth of Australia, Queensland, New South Wales, South Australia, Tasmania and Victoria, 1856-1960* La Trobe University, Bundoora, Vic.,1980.

Hayek, F. A., "The Use of Knowledge in Society", *American Economic Review*, 35(4), 1945, 519-30.

Irvin, Eric, *Sydney as it Might Have Been*, Alpha, Sydney, 1974.

Irwin, Douglas A., *Against the Tide: An Intellectual History of Free Trade*, Princeton University Press, Princeton, NJ, 1996.

Jones, Ross, "The Rogers-Templeton and Pearson Royal Commissions: Contemporary Views of the 1872 Victorian Education Act", *History of Education Review*, 27(2), 1998, 50-66.

Levy, D. M. and S. J. Peart, *Escape from Democracy: The Role of Experts and the Public in Economic Policy*, Cambridge University Press, Cambridge, 2017.

Lloyd, Peter, "100 Years of Tariff Protection in Australia", *Australian Economic History Review*, 48(2), 2008, 99-145.

Melville, L. G., "The Australian tariff: a review of the report of the committee appointed by the Prime Minister", *Australian Quarterly*, 1(3), 1929, 54–63.

Millmow, Alex, "Niemeyer, Scullin and the Australian economists", *Australian Economic History Review*, 44(2), 2004, 142–6.

Nethercote, John, "Forty years on: the Coombs royal commission on government administration", *Canberra Times*, 1 July 2014.

Parsons, T. G., "Does the Bigge Report follow from the evidence", *Historical Studies* 15(58), 1972, 268-275.

Pearson, Charles H., *National Life and Character: A Forecast*, Macmillan, 1893.

Pearson, Charles H., *Public Education: Royal Commission of Enquiry: Report on the State of Public Education in Victoria and Suggestions as to the Best Means of Improving it*, Government Printer, Melbourne, 1878.

Pearson, Karl, "The problem of alien immigration into Great Britain, illustrated by an examination of Russian and Polish Jewish children," *Annals of Eugenics*, 1(2), 1925, 56-127.

Prasser, Scott and Helen Tracey (eds), *Royal Commissions & Public Inquiries: Practice & Potential*, Connor Court, Ballarat, 2014.

Raby, Geoff, *Making Rural Australia: An Economic History of Technical and Institutional Creativity, 1788-1860*, Oxford University Press, Melbourne, 1996.

Radcliffe, Cyril John, Report of the Committee on the Working of the Monetary System, H.M.S.O., London, 1959.

Reader, John and P. A. Hill, *Missing Links: in Search of Human Origins*, Oxford University Press, Oxford, 2011.

Ritchie, John, *Punishment and Profit*, Heinemann, Melbourne, 1972.

Ritchie, John, "John Thomas Bigge and his Reports on New South Wales", *Journal of the Royal Australian Historical Society*, 60(1), 1974, 12-27.

Stebbing, William and C. H. Pearson, *Charles Henry Pearson, Fellow of Oriel and Education Minister in Victoria: Memorials by Himself, his Wife, and his Friends*, Longmans, Green and Co., 1900.

Sydney Morning Herald, "UN agency ranks Australia 39 out of 41 countries for quality education", 16 June 2017.

Tregenza, John, *Professor of Democracy: the Life of Charles Henry Pearson, 1830-1894, Oxford Don and Australian Radical*, Melbourne University Press and Cambridge University Press, 1968.

Viner, Jacob, "The Australian tariff", *Economic Record*, 1929, 5(2), 306–15.

Endnotes

1   John Nethercote, "Forty years on", *Canberra Times*, 1 July 2014.

2   Report of the Committee on the Working of the Monetary System, H.M.S.O., London, 1959.

3   See, for example, Henry Ergas "Australia's Defence: A Review of the 'Reviews'", *Agenda: A Journal of Policy Analysis and Reform*, 2012.

4   G. B. Barton, *The Troubles of Australian Federation*, 1901.

5   F. A. Hayek "The Use of Knowledge in Society", *American Economic Review*, 1945.

6   See Geoffrey Brennan and James M. Buchanan, *The Power to Tax: Analytical Foundations of a Fiscal Constitution*, Cambridge University Press, 1980.

7   See John Reader and P. A. Hill, *Missing Links: in Search of Human Origins*, Oxford University Press, 2011, 4.

8   Alistair Heath, [London] *Daily Telegraph*, 18 May 2016.

9   See D. M. Levy and S. J. Peart, *Escape from Democracy: the Role of Experts and the Public in Economic Policy*, Cambridge University Press, 2017.

10   See *The Australian*, 16 October 2017 and 14 November 2017, for controversy over parole board decisions.

11   Geoff Raby, *Making Rural Australia: An Economic History and Technical and Institutional Creativity*, Oxford University Press, 1996, 68.

12   See N. G. Butlin, J. Ginswick and P. Statham, 1986, "Colonial Statistics before 1850", *Source Papers in Economic History*, no. 12, Australian National University, 40.

13   John Ritchie, "John Thomas Bigge and his Reports on New South Wales", *Journal of the Royal Australian Historical Society*, 1974, 22.

14   Geoff Raby, *Making Rural Australia*, Oxford University Press, 1996, 68.

15   Ibid.

16   T. G. Parsons, "Does the Bigge Report follow from the evidence", *Historical Studies*, 1972, 274.

17   J. M. Bennett, "Bigge, John Thomas (1780–1843)", *Australian Dictionary of Biography*, Melbourne University Press, 1966.

18   John Ritchie, "John Thomas Bigge", *Journal of the Royal Australian Historical Society*, 1974, 23.

[19] Bennett, op. cit.

[20] J. Dennis, "Bigge versus Macquarie", *Journal and Proceedings of Royal Australian Historical Society*, 1937, 442.

[21] See M. H. Ellis, 'Some Aspects of the Bigge Commission of Inquiry into the Affairs of New South Wales 1819-1821', *Journal and Proceedings Royal Australian Historical Society*, 1941, 112.

[22] Dennis, op. cit., 442.

[23] John Ritchie, "John Thomas Bigge", *Journal of the Royal Australian Historical Society*, 1974, 22.

[24] See Charles H. Pearson, *National Life and Character*, Macmillan, 1893.

[25] Charles H. Pearson, *Public Education: Royal Commission of Inquiry*, 1878, 55.

[26] Ross Jones, "The Rogers-Templeton and Pearson Royal Commissions", *History of Education Review*, 1998, 50.

[27] John Tregenza, *Professor of Democracy*, Melbourne University Press, 1968.

[28] Charles H. Pearson, *Public Education*, 1878, 39.

[29] William Stebbing and C. H. Pearson, *Charles Henry Pearson*, Longmans, Green and Co., 1900.

[30] Pearson, op. cit., 39.

[31] Brian Dollery and Stuart Whitten, "An empirical analysis of tariff endogeneity in Australia", *Economic Analysis and Policy*, 1998.

[32] J. B.Brigden, D. B. Copland, E. C. Dyason, L. F. Giblin and C. H. Wickens, *The Australian Tariff*, Melbourne University Press, 1929.

[33] L. G. Melville , "The Australian tariff", *Australian Quarterly*, 1929, 1.

[34] Jacob Viner, "The Australian tariff', *Economic Record*, 1929, 5.

[35] Douglas A. Irwin, *Against the Tide*, Princeton University Press, 1996.

[36] Eric Irvin, *Sydney as it Might Have Been*, Alpha, 1974.

[37] G. Fine, "Does Socrates Claim to Know that He Knows Nothing?" *Oxford Studies of Ancient Philosophy*, 2008, 35.

13

Canberra Knights

The Rise and Fall of the Public Service Mandarins 1936-86

J. R. Nethercote

Two stories

The narrative of the Canberra knights is epitomised by two particular episodes of Australian history. The first, in 1947, the second, 27 years later, in 1974, with some overlapping cast.

On the afternoon of Friday, 15 August 1947, following a meeting of the Cabinet which had taken up most of the day, Ben Chifley, Prime Minister and Treasurer, was in his office in the north-eastern corner of what is now called Old Parliament House with four of the most influential officials in the land. Three of them were officers of what was then known as the First Division of the public service. They were Dr Roland Wilson, the Statistician and Economic Adviser to the Treasurer who had been, from 1940 to 1946, secretary to the Department of Labour and National Service; Dr H. C. Coombs, generally known as Nugget, Director-General of Post-War Reconstruction; and Professor Kenneth Bailey, Solicitor-General and secretary, Attorney-General's Department since 1946. The fourth was Mr F. H. Wheeler, the ranking officer in the Treasury at the helm of the General Finance and Economic Policy Branch.

None was a shrinking violet and only Coombs had something of an inclination in these circumstances to wait to be spoken to before speaking.

Two days earlier, the High Court of Australia had delivered judgment in what is known as the *Melbourne Corporation* case. In that case, the Melbourne City Council had successfully challenged a provision in the Banking legislation of 1945 compelling public authorities to bank with the government-owned Commonwealth Bank, then the central bank as well as a trading bank.

During a pause one of the officials present at the meeting asked the Prime Minister what he intended to do about the Melbourne Corporation judgment. Chifley, who had already arranged for the Cabinet to meet again the next day, replied: "I'm going to nationalise the banks."

The four officials present were struck dumb. After a further pause discussion of the matter in hand resumed.

One of those present, the youngest and most junior at the gathering, Wheeler, reflected, many years later, on this brief interlude as a moment of great shame in his long career as an official.

His view simply reflected his well-known and dogmatic insistence on due process, and, following Thomas Hobbes (not necessarily consciously), an opinion that good advice centred on consequences. In his view, the High Court's decision should have been thoroughly examined from all angles; was it fatal to the Government's policy?; were there other possibilities open to the Government to achieve its purposes?; would public ownership of all banks accomplish the Government's objectives?

Instead, the Cabinet met the next day with little expert briefing or analysis. Late in the afternoon the Government's decision to nationalise the banks was contained in a 45-word press release. The era of spin was yet many decades away.

Chifley's next step was to summons the Economic Adviser to the Commonwealth Bank, Leslie Melville, to Canberra on the following Monday for advice about how the takeover might be effected.

The rest is history: the new legislation easily passed both the House of Representatives and the Senate; the Government had comfortable majorities in each House (33 to three in the Senate!). The High Court held the new legislation invalid and, when it went to the Judicial Committee of the Privy Council, it again failed notwithstanding advocacy over many days by the Deputy Prime Minister and Attorney-General, Dr H. V. Evatt, himself a former justice of the High Court.

While the case was in progress, two Law Lords died.

The Leader of the Opposition, Mr R. G. Menzies, asked the Prime Minister one day how many more jurists would have to die before the Attorney-General concluded his case!

Twenty-seven years later, in mid-December 1974, there was another similar meeting in the same neighbourhood of Old Parliament House, with a much larger cast but including, in some cases in absentia, survivors of the 1947 meeting. Among those present were the Minister for Minerals and Energy, Mr R. F. X. Connor, and the Attorney-General, Senator Lionel Murphy, shortly to be elevated to the High Court.

The Treasurer, Dr J. F. Cairns, was already in receipt of some compelling advice, an exemplary piece of public service drafting, from the Deputy Secretary (Economic) in the Treasury, John Stone.

The matter under discussion was a proposed US $4 billion loan from Middle Eastern sources. One question was whether the loan required the approval of the Loan Council, a Commonwealth-State body which for many years oversaw government borrowings in Australia. The Attorney-General assured those assembled that Loan Council approval was not needed when the loan was for "temporary purposes." That a 20-year loan could be considered to be for "temporary purposes" surprised even the Prime Minister, Gough Whitlam, when he arrived. Hitherto, "temporary purposes" had been regarded as a matter which could be finalised during the financial year.

Wheeler, by now Sir Frederick and himself secretary to the Treasury (since 1971), was also taken aback by the view that a loan for a 20-year period could be deemed to be for "temporary purposes." There was no reticence on this occasion: he simply contended that the idea would not be accepted by "informed public opinion."

The Prime Minister, with at best a tenuous grasp of financial and economic questions, grew impatient with Wheeler's interventions, which had something of an air of a viva voce about them, and addressed him directly: "Fred, you are on the skids."

But, as many people present, including two principals, have attested, this was not the last word. With a clarity no-one could mistake, Wheeler responded: "Prime Minister, I simply seek to inform you of facts your ignorance of which will bring you down."

Later in the afternoon Wheeler convened a largish meeting of senior Treasury officers to brief them on the day's excitements. It was a feature of Wheeler's administrative practice to keep "the team" informed. As the meeting closed Wheeler, not usually thought of as a person of prayerful disposition, put his hands together and said: "Lord, forgive them, for they know not what they do."

Early in the evening he accompanied the secretary of the Attorney-General's Department, Clarrie (later Sir Clarrie) Harders, to the Prime Minister's Lodge where two meetings were in progress: in one room a smaller group of ministers and officials was still discussing the US $4 billion loan for "temporary purposes." In another room, the Federal Executive of the Australian Labor Party was in session. There was some overlap in membership between the two gatherings.

When the time came to constitute a meeting of the Federal Executive Council to authorise the Minister for Minerals and Energy to raise the loan, Wheeler advised the Treasurer, Dr Jim Cairns, who was also at this time Deputy Prime Minister, not to sign the relevant minute as neither he nor the Treasury could expect any control over its implementation and management. This struck Connor as an impertinence. He confronted Wheeler: "I am a Minister of the Crown," he said as they reportedly went toe to toe. "And I am the Permanent Secretary to the Treasury," Wheeler responded. When, in later years, he was asked the meaning of this exchange, he explained it was "a mutual exchange of pomposities."

Cairns did sign the documentation, as Deputy Prime Minister. It is thought that this is the only time Executive Council proceedings have carried four signatures instead of the customary three.

In the ensuing twelve hours, by a process of which Charlie Chaplin,

Buster Keaton or the Marx brothers would have been proud, the Governor-General, Sir John Kerr, whose approval for the previous evening's meeting of the Federal Executive Council had not been sought, was brought into the action. Meanwhile, the Prime Minister and a sizable entourage headed off on a mission to Europe. It was a sojourn interrupted but certainly not terminated by Cyclone Tracey's devastation of Darwin on Christmas Day, 1974.

Canberra Knights – the great age

The three-and-a-half decades between the Second World War and the Fraser Government marked the great age of public service mandarins in Australian government. They were formidable presences during all prime ministerships from Curtin to Fraser inclusive but, after the drowning of Harold Holt on Sunday 17 December 1967, they were increasingly under challenge.

They were almost unknown to the public (though Coombs and Wilson for 15 years had their signatures on the banknotes as Governor of the Bank and head of the Treasury). This was an era when the public service was expected to be anonymous. Some clearly had a flair for publicity, described by Sir Paul Hasluck as a talent for being conspicuously inconspicuous, but most wore their anonymity as a badge of honour.

When they joined government service, mostly at or following outbreak of war in 1939, they were relatively young men, highly educated by the standards of the time and the standards of a public service dominated by clerks with school-leaver qualifications and a diminishing number of veterans of the Great War.

It is relatively easy to date the start of the mandarin era – the appointment of Roland Wilson as Commonwealth Statistician in 1936. It occasioned a strike (in public service terms, a stoppage) among the staff, which epitomised deep-seated hostility to university graduates and an unhealthy attachment to seniority in promotions. Outbreak of war immediately brought Wheeler and Len Hewitt to Canberra to assist the Prices Commissioner, Douglas Copland, one of their professors at Melbourne University. Another of their fellow students was intended to come but did not – Bruce (later Sir Bruce) Williams, vice-chancellor of the University of Sydney from 1967 to 1981 and a member of the board of the Reserve Bank for most of that time. Coombs was already in tow as an officer of the Commonwealth Bank under the supervision of the afore-mentioned Professor Leslie Melville; he was temporarily seconded to the Treasury.

Another important source of graduate strength was the Economics Division of the Bank of New South Wales, from whence came people such as Arthur Tange and James Plimsoll and a number of other luminaries, several of these later collected accolades of knighthood.

John Crawford from the Rural Bank of New South Wales was perhaps the most significant of others attracted from banking. By slightly more regular paths came Allen Brown, Jack Bunting, Fin Crisp, Peter Lawler and Geoff Yeend; all served in the Department of Postwar-Reconstruction; all became department heads; and, apart from Crisp, who became Professor of Political Science at Canberra University College in 1950, all were knighted.

Not all the stars saw the public service as the place to spend the war: one notable exception was Richard Randall, who was already on the strength; he insisted on serving in uniform as a private.

All these men, and others of comparable quality, mainly worked in new organisations or new units of established bodies concerned with higher level policy of the war and, above all, with planning for the post-war world, domestically and internationally. The leitmotif, generally, was qualification in economics and commerce. But three of the most famous had degrees in law – Professor Bailey, in his mid-40s when he came to Canberra as an adviser to the Attorney-General's Department; Allen Brown; and Henry Bland.

These men rose rapidly to senior posts and eventually to top posts in departments and agencies. For most of their careers they worked either for very senior officials or for ministers; they had little experience of hierarchy in any ordinary sense.

Another prominent figure in this phase of public service development was Dr J. W. Burton. He was the first person to win a public service post-graduate scholarship which he used to take a doctorate in economics at the London School of Economics. He returned to work in the Department of Labour and National Service and then Post-War Reconstruction. His rise really started when he became private secretary to Dr H. V. Evatt, the Minister for External Affairs, and thence, in 1947, at age 32, secretary of the Department of External Affairs. It was a controversial appointment made the more controversial the following year when he unsuccessfully sought Labor pre-selection for the newly-created House of Representatives seat of the ACT (limited voting rights).

Burton was hardly alone in having studied abroad – Coombs, on a Hackett Fellowship from the University of Western Australia, took a PhD, also from the LSE (with a thesis on central banking); Wilson, a Rhodes Scholar and Harkness Fellow, had doctorates from Oxford and Chicago; Bailey and Crisp had been Rhodes Scholars; and Crawford had done research in the United States.

Paul Hasluck's career follows some of the same paths as Burton's but is otherwise a contrast. After graduating from the University of Western Australia where he had studied part-time, he embarked upon a career in journalism. Early in the 1940s, with encouragement from the Labor leader, John Curtin, also a journalist, he joined the infant Department of External Affairs where he worked on planning for the post-war world. Unhappy with the Evatt regime, especially after Burton had been appointed secretary, he joined the History Department at UWA. He had already been engaged to write the civil history of the war but before he had moved much beyond the first volume, he was endorsed by the Liberal Party to contest the new seat of Curtin which he held until 1969. In less than two years he was a Cabinet minister – Minister for Territories.

After nearly twenty years as a Cabinet minister he was appointed Governor-General and, in time, held several knighthoods including in the most illustrious order of all, the Garter.

Quite a number of these luminaries were, physically, of modest stature and they have become known as the Seven Dwarfs. There is no canonical list but Wilson, Coombs, Bailey, Brown, Crawford, Bland and Randall are on almost everyone's short-list; some lists omit Bland and include Fred Shedden. A related topic of dinner party conversation is the question of who is Snow White. On the latter matter, both Chifley and Menzies have claims.

The old guard

It is misleading to be totally pre-occupied with the Canberra knights, the Seven Dwarfs and their peers and contemporaries. There was also an old guard to which laurels rightly attach. In the conduct of the war itself, the pre-eminent official was Fred Shedden, head of Defence since 1937 and secretary to the War Cabinet, born in 1892. Shedden, who had strong and long relations with Whitehall, is one of the few individuals to have been nominated for a knighthood by a Labor prime minister. In 1943 Shedden was heading to Washington, DC, for important negotiations. The Prime Minister, John Curtin, sought advice from General Douglas MacArthur about whether anything could be done to ensure the success of the mission. MacArthur suggested a knighthood.

Curtin took the advice. In the King's birthday honours list of 1943, Shedden became a Knight of the Most Distinguished Order of St Michael and St George, the highest honour ever conferred on an Australian public servant except for Sir Robert Garran, a Knight Grand Cross in the same order (and possessing a couple of other knighthoods as well).

The Treasurer, Chifley, when informed of Shedden's elevation, shook his head in disbelief: "I could never have done it!"

Shedden was still in the saddle in the mid-1950s when he was finally persuaded to retire a year or so early, the Prime Minister, Menzies, being among those who had concluded it was time for him to go. He spent the rest of his life in his office at Victoria Barracks, St Kilda Road, Melbourne, writing a history of Australian defence policy; it has never been published.

Two old Treasury hands, successively secretaries to the department, S. G. McFarlane (Misery Mac) and G. P. N. (George Percival Norman Bloody) Watt, were not, in the fashion of the time, knighted. Another of the old brigade was the Chairman of the Public Service Board reconstituted in 1947, William Dunk. He was a veteran of the Audit Office who, in 1945, found himself head of the Department of External Affairs in succession to Lieutenant-Colonel W. R. Hodgson, a Gallipoli veteran, with qualifications in both accountancy and law. Apparently there was some optimism that he might be able to bring some order to the department (and its minister, Dr Evatt). In what is one of the earliest known contests between a department and a minister's private office, Dunk was hardly a match for the two doctors, Evatt and Burton.

Dunk guided the public service through the difficult years of the 1950s, a time of marked parsimony. He was acutely alive to the seemingly intractable problems confronting the public service as it developed – a combination of statutory and industrial relations complexity. Accordingly, over several years, he set about persuading Wheeler to return to Canberra from Geneva where he was Treasurer of the International Labour Organization since 1953. He succeeded in the face of the Treasury's strong support for Harry Bland's claim to the post. Wheeler took over as Chairman in the final days of 1960.

Dunk presided over introduction of computing into the public service – it was one of the first organisations in Australia to apply ADP to its operations. Convinced that the public service could not be efficient while it was divided between Canberra and Melbourne, and dispersed around Melbourne, Dunk successfully added his weight to the case of developing Canberra as the national capital and headquarters of government.

Transfers from Melbourne to Canberra were resumed in the late 1950s; reinvigoration of Canberra's development was signalled by establishment of the National Capital Development Commission.

On another front, he guided through and effected important changes in recruitment, opening the door a little further for graduate recruitment. The vehicle for this change was the Prime Minister's Committee on Public Service Recruitment chaired by Sir Richard Boyer and whose most influential member was R. S. Parker of the Australian National University (he would have liked to be more influential).

Dunk was knighted in 1957.

Sir George Knowles, Solicitor-General until 1946, is another who warrants inclusion in any list of distinguished officials of the pre-mandarin period.

The redoubtable Alf Rattigan, Chairman of the Tariff Board from 1963 and tireless campaigner against protection, was another who in style was more reminiscent of older traditions and practices. He had succeeded Sir Frank Meere as Comptroller-General of Customs and Excise in 1960; Meere, by contrast, was an unapologetic of the tariff, which accounts for his knighthood prior to retirement and his appointment to the Temporary Assistance Authority in 1962.

Back to the Canberra knights

In this generation of officialdom, 1936 until the early/mid-1980s, though they may in short-hand be described as the Canberra knights, the full story is more complex.

It is now almost impossible to recapture fully the ambience of government in this era, the era of the typewriter and the file, of the trunk call, the telex and the stencil. STD and photocopying were well in the future; the Internet and the mobile phone had not yet entered the imagination.

Until the 1950s, the highest levels of Commonwealth administration were centred on Parliament House, East Block and West Block. West Block itself housed the Treasury, Attorney-General's and External Affairs, among others. In the 1960s the Administration Building, now the John Gorton Building, was completed, used first by Defence and later by External Affairs, Trade and Attorney-General's. All were nevertheless still in the parliamentary triangle within easy walking distance of Parliament House.

In the late 1960s the Administration Building was matched on the western side by the Treasury Building where, in addition to the Treasury, the Tax Office and the Bureau of Census & Statistics could be found.

On the eastern side of King's Avenue, in temporary buildings since demolished, the departments of Immigration, Customs & Excise, and Primary Industry, and the Public Service Board (itself!), were housed.

Most department heads and other senior officials would see their ministers every day if they were in Canberra. It was a short walk from the office to Parliament House. Apart from travel to Melbourne and less frequently Sydney, officials rarely travelled from Canberra which, until the 1960s, was located in the central basin.

The knights were largely to be found in the parliamentary triangle – Treasury, External (now Foreign) Affairs, Defence (located at Russell Hill from the 1960s), the Prime Minister's Department, Trade (later Trade and Industry), Attorney-General's and, because of its Defence connections, Repatriation (now Veterans' Affairs). They were sometimes, essentially for personal reasons, to be found elsewhere – Immigration; National Development; Customs and Excise; Education and Science; Health; and Aboriginal Affairs come to mind. It was only in later times that they would occasionally be found, geographically, elsewhere, mainly Woden, but certainly not Belconnen or Tuggeranong.

The public service knights were not all to be found in Canberra. At a time when significant departments were still based in Melbourne, knights could occasionally be found in the Post Office; Labour and National Service; Works and Housing; and Civil Aviation. (Indeed, after the war, Shedden himself was based in Melbourne.)

Not all the knights were in the public service. The chiefs of the fighting services stand out in this category. In Sydney, heads of the Commonwealth Bank and the Reserve Bank (the Governor of which was usually created a Knight Commander of the British Empire (KBE) rather than the more humble Knight Bachelor); also in Sydney was the General Manager of the Australian Broadcasting Commission and the Managing Director of QANTAS. One knight could even be found in Cooma – Sir William Hudson, chief executive of the Snowy Mountains Hydro-Electric Authority.

Not everyone took a knighthood. The most conspicuous abstainer was Dr Nugget Coombs, notwithstanding Prime Minister Billy

McMahon's offer of a KCMG. (A few people have claimed to have turned down offers of knighthoods or lesser Imperial honours but it is not invariably clear that the offer ever actually came their way!)

Knighthoods generally went to heads of department and other chief executives. Sir Richard Randall was knighted whilst still Deputy Secretary at the Treasury. Most public service knights who were not First Division officers were senior diplomats. It was necessary to ensure Australian diplomats were not too obviously seen to be of lower rank than their British counterparts. Even so, a knighted Australian ambassador in Washington was invariably of lower rank than the UK ambassador but it is unlikely that many people in DC would have been sufficiently acquainted with the nuances of the pecking order to realise this.

As the 1950s drew to a close, the public service elites were prominent in foundation of the Commonwealth Club. In the late 1960s, when the Gorton Government, perceived as anti-establishment, was in office, the Commonwealth Club was something of a symbol of establishment resistance to the new regime. This owed something to appointment of Len Hewitt as secretary to the Prime Minister's Department, replacing Sir John Bunting who had been ousted. Hewitt was reportedly not a member of the Commonwealth Club; in more recent times he listed the Melbourne Club, the Union (Sydney) and Brooks's (London) in his *Who's Who in Australia* entry.

Everything was thus in place for colourful portrayal of Gorton, the Tory larrikin as John Howard portrays him, and the forbidding secretary of his department, against Sir Frederick Wheeler, the dour proponent of due process and frank and fearless advice, chairman of the Public Service Board and President of the Commonwealth Club, 1966-69. It was fertile territory for the gossip angle on government and, as such, readily exploited.

The end of the era

Deciding when this discernible era comes to an end is less clear-cut than working out its commencement. It will be obvious that the era is very much the Keynesian ascendancy, of government growth in general and the Commonwealth in particular, in many senses it was under challenge if not in decline by the early 1970s.

The protracted removal of Sir Arthur Tange from External Affairs, over four years, 1961-65, is an important sign that what the Public Service Act then called Permanent Heads were not as permanent as they may have looked. In Tange's case, the Cabinet was advised that, except where misconduct was involved, he could only be removed by abolishing the department! In the 1970s, this expedient was threatened on a number of occasions and employed at least once.

Eventually Tange went to India where he replaced Sir James Plimsoll as high commissioner; Plimsoll in turn returned to Canberra to replace Tange as head of the department.

The removal of Sir John Bunting as secretary to the Prime Minister's Department in 1968 by the newly-appointed prime minister, John Gorton, was certainly a decisive moment in the erosion of high office in the public service. So, perhaps more so, was the even swifter removal of his successor, Sir Lenox Hewitt, when Gorton lost the prime ministership in March 1971 and was replaced by William McMahon. In 1968, Bunting had remained formally in situ for two months; Hewitt had little more than two days. Hewitt himself described his removal as "the first public execution of a permanent head."

In both these instances the displaced department head was accommodated in a new department – the Department of the Cabinet Office in Bunting's case; what eventually became known as the Department of the Environment, Aborigines and the Arts in Hewitt's.

Arrival of the Whitlam Government in December 1972 definitely brought upheaval. The Minister for Labour, Clyde Cameron, simply refused to work with the inherited head of the department, Dr Hal Cook, whom he had never met; it had been his occasional practice as Opposition spokesman on industrial relations to complain that employment figures had been "cooked". Cook took an ambassadorial post in Geneva, as did another displaced department head, George Warwick Smith, who lost his post when the Department of the Interior was dismembered.

The department heads were unsettled in the Whitlam years by which time abolition of a department was now seen as a viable option whenever an unwanted department head hesitated. The appointment late in 1973 of Alan Renouf as secretary to the Department of Foreign Affairs ruffled quite a few feathers. Sir Paul Hasluck, Governor-General at the time, recorded in his notes of discussions with the Prime Minister, Whitlam:

> He[Whitlam] said that the whole of the "public service es-tablishment" (Bunting, Waller, Cooley, Tange, et al) had been against Renouf and in favour of Shann and had tried to keep him from making the appointment. He took responsibility for it. I repeated that I thought Renouf a better man than Shann, who, in my view, was a bit too shrewd, too partial to his own favourites, and apt to talk too freely. Renouf, however, would need underpinning on the administrative side. Whitlam said that an attempt had been made to get him to take either Plimsoll or Tange back as Secretary to Foreign Affairs instead of Renouf.

A major assault came in mid-1975, in the wake of the Loans affair referred to earlier. Whitlam determined to dislodge Sir Frederick Wheeler from the Treasury on the basis that he had lost confidence in both Wheeler and the Treasury. A bid to activate disciplinary action against Wheeler failed after vigorous counter-argument from Clarrie Harders, secretary at Attorney-General's.

Whitlam then tried a carrot – in this case, an offer of appointment as Governor of the Reserve Bank. Wheeler still resisted, not least because he was not keen on the person most mentioned as a likely replacement at the Treasury. He wondered if he was the only person ever to turn down an appointment to the governorship of a central bank!

The Fraser Government's arrival in 1975, though there was some rhetoric about restoring traditions, as there had been when

McMahon became prime minister in 1971, also brought continued institutional weakening of the top public service offices. Ministers and, more particularly, prime ministers, were becoming more restive and more assertive.

Whitlam had appointed three of his private secretaries as heads of department – John Menadue to Prime Minister and Cabinet; Peter Wilenski to Labor and Immigration; and Jim Spigelman to Media. Fraser kept Menadue at Prime Minister and Cabinet until the spring of 1976 when he left to take up the ambassadorship in Tokyo. But the other two were left to find new assignments immediately. Wilenski, after an interval, went to the Australian Graduate School of Management, from which base he conducted a review of the New South Wales Public Service commissioned by the recently elected Wran Government; Spigelman spent some time at the Law Reform Commission before eventually going to the Sydney bar.

Fraser went a step further. On the advice of Sir Henry Bland, who headed what was called the Administrative Review Committee, he secured amendments to the Public Service Act to ensure that any future appointment of a department head had to be vetted by the Public Service Board. Anyone, official or otherwise, not designated "an established candidate" by the Board, could only be appointed for the period of the appointing government. The legislation also made provision for appointments to be made on the basis of recommendation by a panel headed by the chairman of the Public Service Board.

This legislation ran effectively from 1977 until 1984. All department head appointments in this period were of "established" candidates. The Bland system was, thus, only ever partially activated. It was probably never intended that it would be used more than very sparingly.

The new procedures had the effect of diminishing the power of the Board chairman who now had to operate within a statutorily prescribed structure instead of having great flexibility. This new, more formal procedure provided the means for the head of the Department of the Prime Minister and Cabinet to forge an enlarged role in relation to the public service; he was almost invariably a member of the selection panels.

During 1979, both Wheeler and Sir Arthur Tange retired. Tange had made a big comeback after leaving India. Following the 1969 Federal election he found himself with three offers: returning to External Affairs as secretary; going to Defence as secretary; or moving to Washington as ambassador. He chose the Defence post. Over nine years he became the architect of a unified Defence administration.

It was the fate of Wheeler, by contrast, to preside over the division of the Treasury in 1976. Henceforth, public expenditure management functions were handled by a new Department of Finance. The only satisfaction which Treasury traditionalists could derive from this course of events was that it did not entail adoption of a proposal of the Royal Commission on Australian Government Administration to establish a Department of Industry and the Economy.

In 1984 the *Public Service Act* was again amended, removing the procedures incorporated in 1976 but also further loosening the tenure provisions for department heads; department heads, henceforth to be called secretaries, could now be readily removed, the only safeguard, if it can be so described, being requirement of a report (note: not a recommendation) from the chairman of the Public Service Board.

The Act was also amended to underline the subordination of secretaries to ministers by addition of the words in italics:

> The Permanent Head of a Department shall, *under the minister*, be responsible for its general working and for all the business thereof, and shall advise the Minister in all matters relating to the Department.

Michael Keating, head of Prime Minister and Cabinet, 1991-96, has explained that: "Although this change might appear to be mainly symbolic, it clearly meant a lot to ministers at the time." Later on, Gareth Evans, a senior minister in the Hawke and Keating governments, has shed important new light on the meaning of the new phrase:

> But it does not necessarily imply "subordination" in practice, and is not remotely at odds . . . with the notion of the

departmental head-minister relationship being a flourishing "partnership."

Towards the end of 1984, John Stone, head of the Treasury since 1979, left the Treasury, registering strong dissent about what he described at "Public Service Reform (sic!)." Stone accepted no honours and disclaimed description as a mandarin (as did most department heads, especially after *Yes, Minister* reached Australian TV screens).

In 1981 and 1982 the last department heads were knighted – Sir William Cole (Chair, Public Service Board) and Sir Peter Lawler (Administrative Services); and Sir Neil Currie, secretary of various departments in the preceding decade and Australia's ambassador in Tokyo, 1982-86.

Following election of the Hawke Government, Lawler went to Dublin as ambassador (he was also accredited to the Holy See). Very much more seriously, the Hawke Government did not reappoint Cole when his term as chairman expired in October 1983 – the first occasion this had happened to a chairman; there was, indeed, only one previous instance of a commissioner not being reappointed as recognition of distinguished service. Peter Wilenski was appointed in his stead. Cole eventually went to Defence as secretary until retiring in 1986. He was the last knight to occupy a head of department post. Sir Geoffrey Yeend, secretary of Prime Minister and Cabinet since 1978, had left earlier in the year.

The age of the Canberra knights was certainly now over, in every sense. Their successors were no longer knights and all but a few have to settle for appointment as in Officer of the Order of Australia. A few – Prime Minister and Cabinet; Treasury; Defence; and sometimes Foreign Affairs – become Companions of the Order of Australia, but not invariably.

Tenure is uncertain and can be brief. The Governor of the Reserve Bank outshines his Treasury counterpart who now also stands second in the public service pecking order even to the secretary of the Department of the Prime Minister and Cabinet. This is a bad move. The Treasury remains the fount of business, as it has been historically. Moreover, capable heads of Treasury are must harder to come by than capable heads of Prime Minister's. The short list for the latter is much longer than the long list for the former.

The Solicitor-General is a larger figure than the secretary of the Attorney-General's Department.

The main employee enhancements have been in arrangements for superannuation and redundancy pay!

Canberra knights in context

Other public services in the Westminster tradition had similar but far from identical experience to that of Australia recounted in this essay; in important respects there are contrasts. Each responded to comparable circumstances but in its own character and style. The circumstances shaping developments were similar: general growth of government and range of services, sharpened in the first instance by efforts to combat the Depression, and, post-war, the tasks of what has generally been termed reconstruction. Policy in these fields was extensively influenced by the economic doctrines of Keynes, especially as enunciated in *The General Theory of Employment, Interest and Money*. A second influence in the welfare field took its inspiration from what is known as the Beveridge report on social insurance; both had an influence well beyond the United Kingdom.

Building a graduate workforce for general administration was a major challenge in several jurisdictions but one hurdle Whitehall did not have to overcome. It had been recruiting graduates, very largely from the ancient universities, Oxford and Cambridge, for more than eight decades, a consequence of the Northcote-Trevelyan report and the distinction it drew, for purposes of organising the civil service, between intellectual and mechanical work.

Whitehall itself nevertheless recognised by the mid-1930s, certainly after militarisation of the Rhineland in 1936, that were there to be another war, substantial changes would be necessary; reassignment of existing staff and bringing retired officials back to work would not be sufficient. In particular, it was contended, "to meet the inevitable expansion of bureaucracy that war would involve, some steps had to be taken to identify and safeguard professional men of administrative experience whose services might be a valuable asset to the Civil Service."

Progress was initially slow but, after Munich, the pace of activity increased. In matters of personnel, it centred on, but was not confined to, what was called the Central Register branch of the Ministry of Labour, headed by a formidable ex-suffragette, Beryl Power. People especially sought were those with qualifications in economics, statistics, and all sorts of science and technology. When war commenced in September 1939 there was a card index of 80 000 potential recruits, starting with an already identified top group of "100 Principals who will be required on the outbreak of war."

The names of many of those brought into the Civil Service at this time were, or became, famous. At the very top was Keynes himself at the Treasury. Others became durable if not necessarily permanent presences in Whitehall: Lord Helsby, Head of the Home Civil Service, 1962-68; others, if less permanent, nevertheless frequently paced its corridors, such as future Lords Franks, Redcliffe-Maud and Plowden; some, including future leaders of the Labour Party, Hugh Gaitskell and Harold Wilson, went on to careers in politics. Numbers were such that security clearances were not always thorough; it was thought likely that "the most dangerous element would have taken the trouble to obtain first rate references"; these included Kim Philby and Anthony Blunt. Ironically, one person for whom there did not seem to be a place was Beveridge himself, deemed the "least congenial of social scientists." Eventually the Minister for Labour, Ernest Bevin, found a backwater for him: chairmanship of the Committee on Social Insurance. "The rest, as the saying goes, is history," according to Peter Hennessy, the illustrious historian of Whitehall.

For Hennessy, this was a conspicuously, arguably uniquely innovative period of government. He colourfully recorded: "The last person truly to reform Whitehall was that well-known expert in public administration, Adolf Hitler. He obliged the British Government to find new men and new methods almost overnight."

The impetus did not outlive Hitler, however. One of the newcomers, Richard Clarke, later a permanent secretary, lamented in 1946 upon the death of Keynes, that "it will be interesting to see whether the Treasury relapses into habitual slovenliness and complacency or whether some new man is found for providing stimulus."

In Hennessy's account, "The answer was depressingly swift in coming," and it was seen to be closely linked not only to the departure of the so-called irregulars, returning to their universities, their companies, their law practices, their old professions, but to the loss of economists notwithstanding creation in 1947 of a new Central Economic Planning Staff under Plowden.

Ottawa, too, had a highly distinguished historian, Jack Granatstein. He regarded this era, that of Liberal Party government from 1935 to 1957, as "the greatest period of the [Canadian] civil service. Canadian government essentially embarked on a strengthening of policy capacity during the Depression. In Ottawa the professors took charge, unlike in Australia where they were essentially advisers, albeit of a notably influential cast. The big names, both from Queen's University at Kingston, were Oscar Skelton, an historian, at External Affairs; and Clifford Clark, at Finance. Major figures in External Affairs usually had degrees in history; Arnold Heeney, recruited by Prime Minister Mackenzie King to perform for him what Maurice Hankey did for prime ministers at Westminster, had a background in law.

But otherwise it was economists in the lead, and they consolidated their place in government in institutions which they assisuously developed – the Department of Finance itself, which in these years housed the secretariat to the Treasury Board, a statutory committee of Cabinet overseeing public expenditure; the Bank of Canada, established in 1934; and the Department of Industry and Commerce. The place of the economist in government was fostered by a prominent protégé of Keynes himself, Robert Bryce; Schumpeter reportedly observed, Keynes is Allah and Bryce is his Prophet. Bryce became Secretary to the Treasury Board in the late 1940s; was appointed Clerk of the Privy Council and Secretary to the Cabinet in 1954; and deputy minister at the department of Finance in 1965, moving to the International Monetary Fund in 1969.

The preeminenece of economics was reinforced and given a leftward twist in the 1960s when a number of economists shifted to Ottawa from Saskatchewan following defeat of the New Democrat Government in 1964. One, Tom Shoyama, became deputy minister for finance and another, A. W. Johnson, became secretary to the Treasury Board and then deputy minister of Health and Welfare.

Canberra knights in retrospect

This generation of senior public servants, 1936-1986, was significant for a good deal more than the fact that, having reached the highest levels of the bureaucratic greasy pole, they joined the knightly ranks of an order of chivalry. The comparable generation in Ottawa had similar distinction but it was not signalled by any titles and only, eventually, by very sparing post-nominals.

Indeed, the distinction does not especially attach to the individuals or the group of individuals. But it does have much to do with the stage of Australia's development, including governmental and administrative development, and the circumstances of the time, especially the war. It related, most particularly, to the opportunities of the times.

So, just what was the distinction of the knights and their generation apart from academic accomplishment of a high order. First, it was the nature of academic accomplishment. Many of these men – and they were pretty well all men – took their university degrees part-time. For them, following school, and sometimes, as for Wheeler, even before, higher education and formative vocational experience went hand-in-hand.

The education they received was likewise distinctive. Classes were small and, above all, they were educated before text books had established an iron grip over learning. Those who read economics, as so many did, it was still in the Adam Smith mould, before mathematics became so important. A number read galley proofs of Keynes's *General Theory*. If they studied ancient history, they often read Thucydides, Cicero and Tacitus (sometimes in original languages).

Second, when they entered government they filled a vacuum. They did not augment policy capacity; they were, in large measure, the policy capacity. They did not, in any ordinary sense, work their way up the hierarchy. Almost immediately, as has been observed, they worked either directly for ministers or for department heads and other top officials.

They created a new form of organisation, not simply an instrument for executive action but one with thinking and research capacity.

A special feature of this era is the huge canvas on which they worked, both domestically and internationally. They were in new fields and many of the old puritanical/parsimonious inhibitions were starting, if fairly slowly, to drop away.

What marked out the era were the opportunities. Nationally, the Commonwealth was claiming its ascendancy in the federation in economic, industrial and social terms; nothing symbolised this so much as Commonwealth assumption of the income tax and the powers over public expenditure thus acquired.

Internationally, Australia was establishing itself, regionally and in international organisations, the United Nations being most notable. It was increasingly a direct participant in international relations instead of, as previously, usually working within the umbrella of Empire. (It was with the outbreak of war in 1939 that Australia established its first missions abroad (apart from London) – in Washington, DC, Tokyo and China, and also in Ottawa.

This generation, to repeat, had unusual opportunities and the participants of the time made much of them. Later generations can convincingly claim to have taken advantage of opportunities available in their time, but these opportunities have been more modest in scope.

The officials of the war and post-war era worked in particular fields of policy for long periods and had long tenure at the top. Shedden headed Defence for 19 years; Coombs was Governor of the Commonwealth Bank, then the Reserve Bank, from 1949 until 1968; Wilson had 15 years at the Treasury and another eight as chairman of the Commonwealth Bank (and seven at QANTAS); Bailey was

Solicitor-General for 19 years; Bland, 16 years at Labour; Sir Edwin Hicks, 12 years at Defence after five at Air; Tange, 11 years at External Affairs and, later, nine at Defence; Sir Giles Chippendall, nine years at the Post Office; Dunk, 13 years at the Public Service Board; Wheeler, 11 years at the Board followed by eight at the Treasury; Randall, five years as Secretary to the Treasury preceded by 13 as the ranking officer; Brown, nine years at Prime Minister's; Bunting, Cabinet Secretary for 17 years, preceded by four years as deputy secretary in the department; Crawford, a decade at Commerce and Agriculture, then Trade; Sir Alan Westerman, 11 years at Trade.

Simply to list these long tenures should not be read as advocating this as good practice. Certainly, Shedden eventually tried the patience of many, including the Prime Minister. And Bland admitted that he was getting bored half way through his time at Labour (partly accounting for his very strong interest in appointment as chairman of the Public Service Board when Dunk retired).

Nowadays, very occasionally, a secretary will have a decade in a job, but not often; not too many even have a decade at secretary level. The more astute, after five or six years as a secretary, will find a comfortable perch among statutory offices.

Canberra was not a Camelot but the Canberra knights had some similarities with the Knights of the Round Table. They informally had a code of behaviour for they saw themselves not as clerks but very much as professional as doctors and lawyers, and certainly as engineers. The essence of the code was political impartiality; ethical conduct; frank and fearless advice to ministers based on intensive and exacting analysis; due process; administration based on law; and what amounted to frugality in deployment of public funds. They were specialists in governmental, ministerial and parliamentary business.

Insights into this feature of the mandarin age can be found in the Garran Orations of Paul Hasluck (1968); Wheeler (1979); and Tange (1981), as well as Roland Wilson's Giblin lecture of 1976 and articles by Crawford.

And, like the Knights of the Round Table, there were rivalries, compelling rivalries. Apart from those with a personal element, of which there were quite a few, the rivalries were over policy (no doubt, in some instances, with a perceptible measure of what is now called empire-building).

The big clashes were between those concerned with growth and those who gave priority to distribution and fostering equality. There were also related arguments about the extent of government intervention in economic matters, and those who preferred greater reliance on markets. As the 1950s proceeded, some officials eyed the activities of the Commissariat du Plan in France with envy; as time went on, others also saw the Ministry of International Trade and Industry in Japan as a model which might be adapted for Australian use.

In the public domain, these rivalries came to a head in the 1960s, in the aftermath of the credit squeeze of 1960 which caused the Menzies Government so much angst at the 1961 Federal elections. The Government, after a period, appointed a committee of enquiry into the economy. It was headed by Dr (later Sir James) Vernon, Managing Director of CSR. The members were Sir John Crawford (deputy chair), D. W. Molesworth and Kenneth Myer (Melbourne businessmen), and Professor Peter Karmel, an academic economist and university administrator.

The committee, very well resourced for the time, contested Treasury views on a number of matters (for example, foreign investment). It was notably timid (even evasive) on the tariff, perhaps having judged that the time was not ripe for an assault on this icon of public policy. And it proposed an advisory council on economic matters, repudiation of which was the centrepiece in Prime Minister Menzies' rejection of the report. The report, something of a manifesto for interventionists, was a significant episode in the now long-running competition between the Treasury and those seeking to clip its wings.

Another contemporaneous clash at the time centred on the bid by Trade and Industry to secure a second First Division post, an Associate Secretary. The Public Service Board resisted the proposal on the basis that all staff of a department should be subject to the Secretary who was appointed by the Governor-General. As tensions mounted it was proposed, early in 1965, that the question be considered by a meeting of various senior ministers (the Prime Minister, the Deputy Prime Minister, the Treasurer as well as their departmental heads and Wheeler, the chairman of the Board).

Wheeler successfully resisted the suggestion, writing to the Prime Minister on 9 March 1965:

> The Chairman of the Board is, of course, properly available to Cabinet or to any group of Ministers for the purpose of informing Ministers of the Board's exercise of its statutory powers or for the purpose of assisting Ministers in their consideration of any matter such as the proposal for the creation of a statutory officer.
>
> However, I feel that in principle any debate on a matter of Public Service administration between the Board and a Permanent Head should take place in our Board Room rather than in the Cabinet Room or a Ministerial Office. Both in principle and in practice I feel it important to avoid any situation which would have the appearance of a Permanent Head hailing the Board before Ministers.

That was the end of the matter for many years.

Above all, the circumstances of government in the 1940s, '50s and into the '60s and those half a century later were markedly different. Officials were advisers most proximate to ministers and they often had exclusive access to what information was available, but recall that this was essentially not only the pre-computer age but virtually the pre-photocopy age.

Comparison with recent decades is neither easy nor clear-cut. Certainly, contemporary department secretaries have much to contend with – ministerial staff; the 24-hour media cycle; the burdens of administrative review; and maybe no longer have an advantage concerning information.

On the other hand, government is now vastly better resourced. Departmental staffs are much larger, better educated and not nearly so occupied with "mechanical" work (to use Northcote-Trevelyan terminology). A contemporary public service should be superior in many respects, just as the word processor is indisputably superior to the quill.

Questions also arise concerning the accountability and power of officials in the war and war-time period. Ministerial control was exercised at two levels. Prime ministers can be formidable presences. This was certainly so with Chifley and Menzies. Both were endowed with a sense of strategy, purpose and priority, not qualities of which every successor can boast. Menzies had a Rooseveltian gift for fostering internal competition, advocates and opponents of particular approaches acting as checks on one another. It was a governmental variant of adversarial practice with which he was familiar in the courts.

Any government which survives must have a complement of senior ministers who understand the basic role of ministers is tell officials what the public will not stand (a precept first enunciated by the late 19th century Liberal minister in the United Kingdom, Sir William Harcourt).

An appropriate note on which to conclude is the question of whether the mandarin age was a golden age? This long agitated major figures in the succeeding management age. An apprehension arose in the early years of the Hawke Government that the emerging generation lacked the eminence and gravitas of their knighted predecessors. Though a contrived apprehension, mainly promoted by disappointed fans of the Whitlam Government, there was much heat in what was, of sorts, the public service history wars (and also a curious case of intergenerational public service bashing).

Even those familiar with the life and times of what one of the earliest of the new generation of departmental secretaries disparagingly called the "good old days" would be circumspect about lauding war and post-war period as a golden age. The reasons for such reticence have been extensively covered in this essay. Shakespeare has provided wise counsel which these protagonists should have heeded: "all that glisters is not gold."

PART 4

Political History and Biography

14

How Prime Ministers and Number 10 Understand History

Anthony Seldon

On 13 June 2016, Theresa May became prime minister of the United Kingdom, with one major historic task for her to fulfil: Britain's exit from the European Union (EU). She set about the task knowing next to nothing about the history of the EU or of Britain's relationship with it, and neither did she consult historians or retired civil servants who could have given her the vital background. After three years of abortive negotiation, she left office, with Britain still inside the EU, more divided as a country than at any point in the previous hundred years.

This essay examines the way that prime ministers and No 10 Downing Street have understood and been influenced by history. Given that decisions taken by British prime ministers have often had such a sweeping influence on the history of the world, and that many other nations have modelled their heads of government on the British prime ministership, this question is of more than parochial interest.

Puzzlingly, some other Whitehall departments have historical sections, but not Number 10, where it is most needed. The Foreign Office (FCO) has the largest, run by a "Chief Historian", which provides historical background when required, assists historians with their research, and produces books bringing together annotated documents on key topics. It does outstanding work, but, until recently at least, has generally steered clear of offering policy advice. The department whose historical section is most policy-oriented is the Navy within the Ministry of Defence. The Cabinet Office's historical section keeps a beady eye on publications by those who have signed the *Official Secrets Act (UK)*, and polices the propriety and ethics of what appears in print. It also oversees the official history series, and the release of official documents. The Treasury had a flourishing history section which fell victim to cuts after the UK's financial crisis in 1976, but has since given birth to a "history network" which organises lectures, tours and liaises with academics teaching and studying the Treasury and economic policy. Most Whitehall departments though, like Number 10, do little historically.

This is a shame and a loss because history matters. It can help avoid repetitions of past mistakes, can provide context, understanding and nuance, and allow for a clearer appreciation of the sensibilities of key players in major decisions and tasks. All too often, however, the arguments against taking stock of history win out. Yes, it can be expensive, it does take time to comprehend properly when ministers often need or want to act quickly, political priorities often trump academic considerations, and mistakes can be made when politicians draw on the wrong historical parallels. Anthony Eden (Prime Minister, 1955-57) saw Egyptian leader Gamal Abdel Nasser's nationalisation of the Suez Canal in 1956 as akin to Hitler's land grabs in 1938-39. But this and other such follies are arguments not against history but against bad history. Historians at Eden's elbow would, we hope, have pointed out the very obvious differences. Perhaps he might have listened. But prime ministers have been denied the chance of listening to historians at their elbows. Advisers, often hot-headed, have been there. Not reflective historians.

Britain has had 55 prime ministers in the 300 years since Robert Walpole became the first holder of the office in 1721. Not for another 14 years, until 1735, did he move into Number 10 Downing Street, the building that has been synonymous with prime ministerial power ever since (even if it was not until 1902 that prime ministers started to live regularly as well as to work there).

In the last 300 years, the office of prime minister has changed fundamentally. Britain in those three centuries became a great power, and ceased to be a great power. It moved from an agrarian to an industrial to a post-industrial economy. It acquired an empire and lost an empire. Its monarchy waxed and waned in importance, while the power of Parliament steadily grew. The House of Lords lost authority while the House of Commons gained it, as Britain moved from an aristocratic government to a popular democracy. Cabinet rose in influence and lost its influence. Political parties proliferated in power and number, while the influence of the established church and the ancient universities declined. Ireland joined the United Kingdom in 1800 and southern Ireland left it in 1921. The size of government grew, and grew, and grew and, with it, the expectation that the prime minister would preside over it all, with a bespoke policy for every department.

The office of prime minister had to adapt through these and many other profound changes, accomplishing it by constant change through five distinct phases. The "Treasury" prime minister (1721-1815) saw the job emerge from being the First Lord of the Treasury to one overseeing a range of departments bound together by an emerging caucus of ministers which morphed from the King's Council into Cabinet. The "Imperial" prime minister (1815–1914) saw the prime minister's responsibilities grow to overseeing the vastly expanded British possessions abroad. In the "Total War" (1914–1945) phase, the office of prime minister acquired yet more new powers as Britain strained every sinew to fight and win two world wars.

The "welfare state" prime minister (1945–1970) saw the powers of office expand domestically as the reach of government broadened out in peacetime over the economy and social policy. Finally, the "European" prime minister (1970–2021) phase saw the prime minister's time and priorities increasingly being taken up by the European Union, which Britain entered in 1973 and left in 2020.

The prime minister had very different roles, powers and staffing in each of these five separate phases. In 1721, the job essentially was to ensure a majority in Parliament or, more specifically, the House of Commons, liaise with the Monarch of the day, oversee the national finances, and keep the country safe. By 2021, the job had expanded beyond these to include being the chief executive, the national leader, chief policy formulator, chief appointing officer, chief diplomat, and the chief communicator.

Not everything changed. Some continuities can be found over the 300 years, including a lack of time for the prime ministers for reflection, and a disregard or a highly subjective reading most had for history. The 20th century saw professions coming to government, with chief scientists, chief economists and chief accounting officers. But no chief historians were appointed to inform the leaders about what had happened in the past, and how to avoid the same pits into which predecessors had fallen.

Long before 1721, history was being taken seriously in the country. King Henry VII requested that a history of England be written, published in 1534 long after his death; and an office of Historiographer Royal was appointed in England in 1660 and in Scotland in 1681.

The professionalisation of government in the latter 19th century coincided with a growing interest in the writing of "official" accounts of key episodes, notably wars. The South African War (1899-1902) precipitated the emergence of a Historical Section in Whitehall and a more systematic approach to the writing of official history. Lessons learnt included the importance of gathering contemporary accounts, which informed the series, the British Official History of the Great War, which ran to an incredible 109 volumes. This was trumped by the official histories of the Second World War, with the first volume published in 1949, and the final one in 1993.

What is less clear is whether contemporary politicians absorbed the lessons learnt, or even read the volumes. Official histories continued to be written up to the present day, with the expense a regular concern of the Treasury and of Parliament. Overly long and laborious official histories began to be written on narrow subjects such as the national parks, not always of prime learning potential, while institutional memory was being thoughtlessly squandered. As if to compensate for the lack of historical thinking present in decision-making, the British government compensated by setting up official enquiries, the most ponderous and egregious of which was the Chilcot Inquiry into British involvement in the Iraq War, which took over seven years, found little new and which hardly anyone read in its entire 2.6 million words. The cost ran to several millions of pounds which could have been much better directed to historical work where it would have born value.

Errors meanwhile were being needlessly made by politicians and officials, month by month, because no one knew the relevant history. Various studies have appeared about this phenomenon of avoidable error, few better than Ivor Crewe and Anthony King's, *The Blunders of our Governments* (2013).

So concerned was I by the lack of historical awareness within government, specifically at Number 10, that fellow historian Peter Hennessy and I established The Institute of Contemporary British History in 1986 to stimulate greater study of the recent past and to provide opportunities for the makers and the researchers into recent history to meet and debate together. Among other activities it has organised a series of "witness seminars", based on what I had seen in the Presidential libraries in the United States, bringing together some dozen key participants in key events with researchers posing questions. The first was on the "winter of discontent" of 1978-79, the 115th, 25 years later, was on Britain and the 1991 Gulf War.

Then, in 2011, I began, with the future Cabinet Secretary, Jeremy Heywood, the history program at Number 10 including a series of historical talks by former senior staff who had worked with earlier prime ministers or by historians, and a drive for Number 10 to take its own history more seriously. Prime Minister Henry Campbell-Bannerman (1905–08) had been responsible for suggesting the main staircase in Downing Street be adorned by images of all previous prime ministers. The practice continues to this day whereby, within months of a premiership ending, the photograph of the departed prime minister appears at the top of the staircase, with all the earlier prime ministers shuffled down the wall one place. Yet despite this daily reminder of history as they walk up and down, prime ministers have been largely oblivious of the importance of history.

This essay argues that, even though prime ministers might not consciously think about history, their every action is informed by two very different kinds of historical impulse. We will call these the interior and the exterior. Both these forces come into play and reinforce each other, driving the prime minister to take the courses of action they do.

The exterior impulse is the easier to observe. This consists of the understanding of history that each prime minister brings to the office. Regardless of whether they studied history at university, and some 10 did, they all studied history at school (or, at the very least, read history books where they were home schooled, as some early prime ministers were). They have all had their historical heroes, who will have guided their thinking and shaped their entry into politics, and their subsequent rise up the greasy pole. For some, like Harold Macmillan (1957–63), or Boris Johnson since 2019, the classical world was a major inspiration. For Winston Churchill, it was the life of one of his ancestors, the Duke of Marlborough, the hero of military campaigns in Europe in the early 18th century, about whom he wrote a four-volume biography. To some, the Bible was a key historical as well as a religious inspiration, as was the case with Tony Blair (1997-2007), who justified British involvement in the US invasion of Iraq in 2003 by reference to the parable of the good Samaritan. For other prime ministers, it was very recent history. Anthony Eden (1955–57), as shown above, saw the Egyptian leader, President Nasser, as another Adolf Hitler or Benito Mussolini, and he saw it as his job to ensure that he was stood up to rather than appeased.

The interior impulse is formed of the historical experience that the prime minister has had on a personal level, the key events of their life which have gone to make them the people that they are, and to go on and become prime minister. For some prime ministers, it has been a father who has been a vicar and imbued their child with a strong sense of social purpose: this was the case with Gordon Brown (2007–10), and Theresa May (2016–19). For other prime ministers, it has been a sense of escaping poverty and acquiring power to improve the lot of ordinary people. This helps to explain the premierships of the first Labour Prime Minister, Ramsay MacDonald (1924, 1929–35), and John Major (1990–97). For others, it was a sense of aristocratic duty to serve, which helps explain the emergence as prime minister of Lord Salisbury (1885–86, 1886–92, 1895–1902) and Alec Douglas Home (1963–64).

For some, the sense of inner conviction is so strong that it can lead them to misread a position which a deeper sense of history would have illuminated. Margaret Thatcher (1979-90) had a reading of history that suggested to her that a strong, unified Germany would be a menace again and a severe challenge to British interests, and was thus at best lukewarm to German reunification after 1989. Blair's reading of British history, that the United Kingdom should always stay close to the United States, encouraged him to back President George W. Bush's invasion of Iraq in 2003. He was cautioned by the President of France, Jacques Chirac, who told him over lunch: "I have fought in the Algerian War, I know what war is like, I know about the delicate balance of power inside Iraq. Tens of thousands will die if the country is invaded". "Poor Jacques", said Blair after the meal: "he really doesn't get it".

The strongest sense of history that most of the 55 prime ministers have had in the last 300 years has been of their own importance, and how history will judge them. Winston Churchill (1940–45, 1951–55) famously said: "history will be kind to me because I intend to write it". From roughly the halfway point of their premiership, a light goes on in the head of the incumbent prime minister illuminating a question: "What will be my legacy?" We can observe them yanking the direction of government policy from that point forward in the direction of legislation and decisions that will build their own personal legacy, not unlike pharaohs in ancient Egypt directing the building of their pyramid. Vast resources of money and time would be devoted to these vanity projects which benefited the lives of Egyptians not an iota.

Lest anyone missed the brilliance of the prime minister's achievement, almost all since 1900 have then added to the record by writing memoirs, few longer than Harold Macmillan, who wrote six long volumes. We cannot say thus that prime ministers are unaware of their own history: but it is often their subjective sense of their own legacy rather than the contribution they make to their country.

Historians in Number 10 would help the British prime minister factor in the national story and needs, alongside their own interior needs. Many thousands of books will be written about Britain's shambolic exit from the European Union and, yes, inevitably there will be official inquiries too. The one lasting legacy that would make a positive difference, however, would be something else. Britain should in its wake establish the office of "chief historian", with equal rank to the government's chief scientist, chief medical officer, chief economist, chief statistician and more.

The chief historian would oversee not the publication of more official histories: there is a three volume history of Britain's history in the European Union written by former diplomat Stephen Wall. May did not trouble to read them. Instead, the chief historian will oversee the steady supply of accurate historical information to prime ministers and their key advisers, inclining, indeed especially when history suggests they are taking the wrong decisions. They would also oversee a network of historians in each department throughout Whitehall.

History matters as much as economics, statistics, and, yes, even science. Many recent events show this conclusively.

15

Stanley Melbourne Bruce and Robert Gordon Menzies compared

David Lee

At Sir John Cockroft's installation as Chancellor of the Australian National University, the Prime Minister of Australia, Robert Gordon Menzies, paid a generous tribute to Stanley Melbourne Bruce. Bruce, Cockroft's immediate predecessor as Chancellor of the ANU, had been Prime Minister of Australia from 1923 to 1929 and High Commissioner in London from 1933 to 1945. Menzies referred to the outgoing Chancellor as "probably the outstanding Australian of our time".[1] When Menzies made these remarks about Bruce, he himself had served continuously as prime minister from 1949 and would not retire until 1966.

Few could see the merit in Menzies' elevation of the older man and less successful prime minister over himself. The *Sun-Herald*, for example, commented that Menzies' remarks would be neither popular nor historically endorsed. Bruce's six years and 255 days as prime minister were "averagely successful", the paper judged, but "wrecked by a gross miscalculation in 1929" and "the fact remains that the greater part of his career had been spent abroad".[2] This essay compares two prime ministers who worked closely together from 1939 to 1941, one as prime minister, the other as high commissioner in London.[3]

Both Menzies and Bruce had Scots forebears. Menzies was born on 20 December 1894 at Jeparit, Victoria, the son of the Australian-born storekeeper, James Menzies, and his wife Kate, née Sampson. Menzies' forebears were Scots on the paternal side and Cornish on the maternal. James Menzies, as well as being the town's storekeeper, was a lay preacher in the local, non-conformist church. Stanley Melbourne Bruce was born in Melbourne in 1883, the youngest of five children of John Munro Bruce and Mary Ann née Henderson. John Munro Bruce had been born in 1840 in County Leitrim in Ireland but his forebears were Scots and he was educated at Madras College in St Andrews in Scotland. Like James Menzies, he was a non-conformist who had settled in Victoria and established himself as a partner in a thriving soft goods business. John Munro Bruce and James Menzies, both rising men, sent their gifted sons to good schools, Stanley Melbourne Bruce to Melbourne Church of England Grammar School and Robert Gordon Menzies to Wesley College.

Success at Wesley College set Menzies on the road to the University of Melbourne, a degree in law, admission to the Bar and a brilliant career as a lawyer and politician. Bruce followed a somewhat different path. Following the tragic suicide of his father in Paris in 1901, Bruce borrowed money to put himself through a degree at Cambridge University. After graduating with a BA from Cambridge, he trained with a leading British commercial law firm, Ashurst, Morris and Crisp, and read for the Bar in England. Although Bruce became chairman of the Anglo-Australian family company, Paterson, Laing and Bruce, and visited Australia from time to time in that capacity, he made England his home until the circumstances of the Great War, during which he fought at Gallipoli with the British Army, brought him back to his country of birth in 1916.

Bruce's attitude to Britain and to the British Empire differed from that of Menzies, whose experiences of the British Empire as a young man were imagined and idealised. Menzies would not make his first trip to England until 1935 at the age of 39. In contrast, Bruce experienced Britain first-hand from just after leaving secondary school until his enlistment in the British Army. One Australian journalist remarked that these years of expatriation so moulded Bruce that he acquired "that quality of aloofness from the Australian man in the street that forever separated him from the heart of his own country; it left him even in his political heyday a foreigner in his own land, a man out of touch with the people he was leading".[4] Unlike his predecessors as prime minister, Alfred Deakin,

Andrew Fisher and William Morris Hughes, Bruce had a different approach to presiding over what Australian historians have called the "Australian settlement", partly because of his absence during the formative years of the Commonwealth of Australia.

The Australian settlement was a set of long-standing policies agreed in the first decade after Federation.[5] The settlement consisted of the White Australia policy, and policies of industry protection and wage arbitration. Protectionism and centralised wage-fixing were settled policies by 1923, but Bruce, as a man from the world of commerce, was vitally concerned with trade and the better marketing of Australian exports, so that Australia could earn more income to pay off its burgeoning national debt and continue to borrow to support population growth by attracting greater numbers of migrants. Bruce was never comfortable with the amount of Australian protection, thinking that it was squeezing the internationally efficient export trade. In 1929 he would test his views by appointing a committee to investigate the tariff headed by the Australian economist, J. B. Brigden. Brigden's report agreed with Bruce that Australian tariffs had reached a "dangerously high" level and that Australia should adopt a more scientific tariff that would not place such a heavy burden on the rural exporting sector.

The Great War affected Bruce and Menzies in different ways. The Bruce family agreed that Stanley, who happened to be in Australia when war broke out, would return to England and enlist, while Ernest, the oldest brother, having served as a younger man in the Boer War, would remain in Australia to manage the family business. Stanley duly enlisted in the Inns of Court Regiment, went to Cornwall to join the 12th Worcestershire Regiment and then sailed to Egypt to join the Royal Fusiliers. In 1915 Bruce fought with the British Army in Gallipoli, was twice wounded and won the Military Cross and Croix de Guerre avec Palme. The Bruce family agreement on military service went awry, however, when Ernest Bruce decided to enlist in the Royal Field Artillery despite being about 40 and having a shattered left arm. Ernest went through the worst of the fighting in France and Belgium, won the Military Cross and rose to the rank of Major.

It was the brave and impulsive decision of Ernest to enlist that saw Bruce, while convalescing, return to Australia to take care of the Australian side of the family business, a duty that had been assigned to Ernest. While managing Paterson, Laing and Bruce, Bruce spoke at recruiting meetings in Australia. These brought him to the attention of the Prime Minister, Hughes, and to Nationalist Party power brokers who persuaded him to contest a by-election for the seat of Flinders in 1918. Later, the weakness of Hughes's government saw Hughes co-opt Bruce, a decorated war veteran and successful businessman, into the government as Treasurer in 1921. This set him on the path to the prime ministership.

The Menzies family made a similar wartime pact when it agreed that Robert's older brothers, Les and Frank, would join the Australian Imperial Force while Robert stayed at home to finish his university studies. One biographer, Kevin Perkins, has commented that while the decision not to enlist was finally Robert's, "it was based on the general wish of almost the whole Menzies family, and in such a close group, that carried weight".[6] Menzies would not emulate Ernest Bruce in making an impulsive decision to enlist but dutifully stayed to finish his law examinations. A scholarship helped to meet some but not all his expenses; such were the family bonds that Frank Menzies helped to save the Menzies family (and Robert) from financial embarrassment by making an allotment from his army pay of £200 per year that contributed to the expenses of Robert's education.[7] Bruce's rise to the prime ministership was aided considerably by his distinguished military service. By contrast, Menzies' political career would suffer from his failure to enlist, most conspicuously in 1939 when Earle Page, Leader of the Country Party (and briefly prime minister), sought to block his elevation, citing his failure to serve his country during the Great War. Page's accusations were ironic in view of the Country Party leader's own war service.[8]

At the General Election of 1922 the Nationalist Government in which Bruce was Treasurer lost its majority in the House of Representatives. Its support fell from 38 to 28; representation of the Australian Labor Party rose from 26 to 30; the recently formed Country Party had 14, giving it the balance of power. The overall result of the election was a slight gain for Labor offset by an increase in Country Party and independent Liberal members at the expense of the Nationalists.

Earle Page, the Leader of the Country Party, refused to enter into a coalition arrangement with a government led by Hughes. Many expected that Hughes would meet the House of Representatives with a reconstructed minority Nationalist government and defy the House of Representatives to vote no confidence in it. Hughes, however, astonished his own party by informing it that he intended to resign. Hughes's reasoning was that if he faced the House and lost a vote of confidence, the Governor-General might have sent for the leader of the Australian Labor Party, Matthew Charlton. He promised his party to manage political affairs so that his old political party, the Labor Party, did not come to power.

Hughes therefore recommended that Bruce should make an effort to form a coalition government with the Country Party. Bruce first protected his flank from Hughes by keeping Senator George Pearce, formerly in the Labor Party and a close associate of Hughes in the ministry. He then agreed with Page that five of the eleven portfolios in the government would be assigned to ministers drawn from the Country Party. In reaching the agreement with Page, Bruce helped to establish an entity, the non-Labor coalition, which would dominate politics at the Commonwealth level for most of the next 100 years. Preferential voting and the coalition government established by Bruce and Page helped to make coalition part of Australian political culture in contrast to the situation in Canada where the existence of three major parties, Conservatives, Liberals and Progressives, and a first-past-the post electoral system, led to minority governments being much more frequent.[9] The practice of coalition government was a key feature of Menzies's long post-war ministry which he managed adeptly between 1949 and 1966.

Bruce was a significant actor in Menzies's accession to the prime ministership in 1939. By then, the United Australia Party-Country Party coalition government headed by Joseph Lyons and including Robert Menzies as Attorney-General was in trouble. Early in 1939, Bruce, now High Commissioner in London, learned this first hand when he visited Australia. While in Australia a deputation from the influential National Union informed Bruce that the Lyons Government was losing ground because of its inability to make decisions and asked Bruce, four years Lyons's junior, to return to Australia to strengthen it. Lyons also asked for Bruce's help. Bruce responded that Lyons should immediately see the Governor-General, recommend to him that Bruce be commissioned to form a government, and agree to serve under Bruce, allowing Bruce three months to find a seat. After initially agreeing to these all-or-nothing terms, Lyons later demurred, informing Bruce that he thought them impracticable in a time of peace. Had Bruce been more flexible and agreed to serve under Lyons, perhaps as Treasurer, he may have put himself in a position to succeed Lyons as prime minister, especially in the event of war. After Lyons's death in April 1939, Bruce again flirted with the idea of making a comeback to Australian politics but Page's maladroit intervention against Menzies rallied the United Australia Party behind Menzies. Bruce later wrote to Menzies that:

> There is no doubt that Page was your fairy godfather, if you had the slightest desire to become Prime Minister. Apparently he had a considerable objection to your becoming one and promptly took the only possible course which would make the job a sitting certainty for you. The working of Page's mind is still a complete mystery to me notwithstanding my very considerable experience of its vagaries.[10]

Until the 1920s the High Court had held that the Commonwealth arbitration system could not legally intervene between the States and their employees. However, in 1920, in the *Engineers' case,* it had widened the power of the Arbitration Court to include employees of State instrumentalities such as railways. The Court's verdict brought much fame to Menzies as the leading advocate in the case.

Six years later, Bruce, unhappy with divided control over industrial matters, submitted at a joint meeting of the Nationalist and Country parties a proposal for a referendum on industrial issues. He aimed at root and branch reform of the arbitration system by amending the Constitution to empower the Commonwealth Parliament to establish "judicial authorities" with jurisdiction over all industrial disputes–whether interstate or intrastate–and with powers to enforce their decisions, make common rules for industries and delegate their functions to subordinate State tribunals.

Bruce duly prepared referendum proposals to expand the Commonwealth's power over industrial relations and essential services. In the second reading speech on the referendum bill in the House of Representatives, Bruce explained that these reforms would address major ills in the Commonwealth. They would alleviate the uncertainty caused by overlapping of Commonwealth and State awards in industry and promote industrial peace; they would redress the limitation whereby the Commonwealth Arbitration Court could not make a common rule applicable to all in a particular industry; they would stop unions being able to "pick the eyes" out of the awards available to them by going back and forth between Commonwealth and State jurisdictions; and they would remedy the "almost hopeless" position under which the Arbitration Court had no judicial power and thus could not impose penalties or even interpret its own awards.

In commenting on the second referendum proposal on essential services, Bruce declared flatly: "I cannot think it possible for any person to raise any objection to it".[11] One who did was a young lawyer and aspiring Nationalist Party member of the Victorian Parliament, Robert Menzies. Menzies was concerned about a proposal which, he believed, could not be properly defined and might well justify Commonwealth interference in State affairs under the guise of preventing disruption to essential services. Menzies joined forces with Arthur Robinson, a leading businessman, to bring together various interests opposed to the referendum. The organisation opposed greater Commonwealth control over corporations and argued that there were good reasons to maintain State control over industrial relations, one of which was that State upper houses, in which employers were well represented, were in a good position to block measures from more democratic lower houses. Menzies, a leading supporter of Robinson, cast doubt on whether the legal institutions of the Commonwealth of Australia were more conducive to industrial peace than State instrumentalities: "The old methods of strikes", he declared, had in "their favour that everything was above board; there was no hypocrisy. Strikes were admittedly costly and clumsy, but were they any inferior to the present system of litigation, in which employers and employees were made parties to a dispute in a court".[12]

Despite Bruce's strenuous efforts, the referendum proposals of 1926 failed. Continuing industrial turbulence in the late 1920s and the onset of troubled economic times saw Bruce take an impulsive decision. He forewarned his friend, R. G. Casey, Australian Liaison Officer in Whitehall, that:

> I am also "going over the top" and saying definitely that the present system of dual control in industrial matters is impossible, and that either the Commonwealth or the States must be the sole authority. I am indicating that if the States are prepared to refer the necessary powers to the Commonwealth we are prepared to undertake the task, but failing their doing this I am stating that the Commonwealth proposes to get out of the field of industrial arbitration. This will unquestionably cause the biggest turmoil we ever had in Australia. It is, however, essential to face the position unless disaster is to come to us.[13]

Accordingly, in September 1929, he introduced the *Maritime Industries Bill* leaving industrial relations to the States, with only a few exceptions. As a consequence of manoeuvres organised partly by Hughes, it was amended in committee in the House of Representatives to provide that there should be no action to give effect to the legislation until it had been approved in a referendum. Although only seven months had elapsed since a general election, Bruce took the opportunity to call a fresh election in a bid to strenghen the Government's position in the House. It was the first time that there was an election for the House alone. Bruce's tactic failed; the Scullin Labor Government came to office with a handsome majority but found itself at the mercy of Nationalist numbers in the Senate.

It need not have been so but Bruce, unlike Menzies, found it difficult to cope with ambiguity and felt compelled to take decisive action to correct it.[14] One of the reasons for Menzies' longevity in office was a willingness to live with ambiguity and particularly the ambiguity of the federal system.

In paying tribute to Bruce in 1962, Menzies acknowledged that he had learned from Bruce's successes and his mistakes. Following the disagreement between the Country Party and Menzies in 1939,

Menzies followed Bruce's example in taking great care to cultivate good relations between the Liberal and Country parties when he became Leader of the Opposition in 1943, and particularly as prime minister between 1949 and 1966. Menzies also learned from Bruce's political failure in 1929 to live with the ambiguity and frustrations of the federal system.

References

Lee, David, *Stanley Melbourne Bruce: Australian Internationalist*, Continuum, London, 2010.

Martin, A.W., *Robert Menzies: A Life, Vol. 1, 1894–1943*, Melbourne University Press, Melbourne, 1993.

Martin, A.W., *Robert Menzies: A Life, Vol. 2, 1944–1978*, Melbourne University Press, Melbourne,1999.

Nethercote, J. R. (ed.), *Liberalism and the Australian Federation*, Federation Press, Sydney, 2001.

Perkins, Kevin, *Menzies: Last of the Queen's Men*, Rigby, Adelaide, 1978.

Endnotes

[1] "Forgotten Man", *Sun-Herald*, 15 April 1962.

[2] Ibid.

[3] This essay draws on the two-volume biography of R. G. Menzies by A. W. Martin and my *Stanley Melbourne Bruce: Australian Internationalist*, Continuum, London, 2010. John Nethercote greatly assisted both authors.

[4] Quoted in Lee, *Stanley Melbourne Bruce*, 9.

[5] See Paul Kelly, *The End of Certainty*, Allen & Unwin, Sydney, 1992.

[6] Kevin Perkins, *Menzies: Last of the Queen's Men*, Rigby, Adelaide, 1868, 31.

[7] Ibid., 32.

[8] See "Sir Earle Christmas Grafton Page (1880-1961)" in Geoffrey Serle (ed.) *Australian Dictionary of Biography*, Volume 11, Melbourne University Press, Melbourne, 1988, 118-22.

[9] I am grateful to John Nethercote for this insight.

[10] Quoted in Lee, *Stanley Melbourne Bruce*, 131.

[11] Quoted in ibid., 63.

[12] Quoted in ibid., 64.

[13] Quoted in ibid., 85.

[14] I am indebted to John Nethercote for this insight.

16

Curtin 1942, Morrison 2018 – Two Declarations on Australia's National Interests

John Edwards

Eight months after President Donald Trump's announcement in March 2018 that he would begin to impose penalty tariffs on China's exports to the United States (US), Scott Morrison, the Prime Minister of Australia since 24 August 2018, gave what one day may come to be seen as a remarkable statement. Asked at a doorstop with reporters in Singapore about how he would handle the "delicate balance" between China and America, Morrison said firmly that "Australia doesn't have to choose and we won't choose." He added:

> We will continue to work constructively with both partners based on the core of what those relationships are. We don't choose between the issues–we don't choose between the partners–we get on with the relationships.

Morrison's statement did not cause any controversy. On this issue there was no great difference between the two major Australian political parties. If there had been a significant difference between the prime minister and the Department of Foreign Affairs and Trade or powerful members of his Cabinet, it would probably have been floated somewhere. It was not. Even the national security community, deeply suspicious of China, raised no public alarm over Morrison's statement. To Australian political commentators, foreign policy analysts, business leaders, political leaders, what Morrison said was self-evidently Australia's attitude. It was not news – though it had not hitherto been so plainly nor so succinctly put.

Yet given Australia's foreign policy since the end of the Second World War, it was a notable marker. For more than sixty years the ANZUS alliance has been the bedrock of Australian security policy. It remains so today. But while this once also implied support for the US in most aspects of global economic and strategic leadership, it was now qualified when China and the US were at odds. Choices once easy to make were harder. With nearly one-third of its goods exports going to China, with Chinese nationals now the preponderant share of both foreign students and foreign tourists in Australia, with free trade agreements with both America and China and with Australia eagerly negotiating membership of a regional trade agreement which includes China but which the US did not wish to join, with a history of amicable relations with China for half-a-century and with both countries now describing their relationship as a "comprehensive strategic partnership", with Australia's economic future far more linked to China than to the US, it was not in Australia's interests to declare for one side or the other in their trade dispute.

Morrison's statement registered a change so long in the making, so obviously appropriate to Australia's national interests, it took no one by surprise. It made manifest a view long immanent. Short of something much closer to actual hostilities between the two, Australia was neutral in what could become a serious and prolonged economic crash between these great powers.

In the record of Australian foreign policy, Morrison's Singapore comments may well prove to be analogous to Prime Minister John Curtin's statement on 27 December 1941, that Australia "looks to America, free of any pangs as to our traditional links or kinship with Britain." Both statements registered changes in the interpretation of Australia's national interests by its national leadership. Both declarations had been preceded by changes within Australia's region which forced Australians to realign attitudes. Both statements recognised the centrality of a more recent relationship to Australia's national interest, without repudiating the importance of an older relationship. Neither statement was regarded by its author as new or shocking or unexpected.

Might Morrison's statement be merely provisional, one that might easily be reversed or varied? Evidently annoyed by a crackdown on Chinese influence on Australian politics and by Morrison's call for an independent investigation of the China origins of Covid, in 2020 China cut imports of Australian wine, barley, beef, lobster, cotton, copper and coal. By February 2022 Morrison was describing Labor deputy leader Richard Marles as Beijing's 'Manchurian candidate' for the forthcoming federal elections, criticising Marles for a 2019 speech in which Marles called for Australia to continue to build strong relationships with China. It was pre-election attempt by Morrison, the *New York Times* reported (10 March 2022) "to exploit rising fears of China". Morrison's 2019 affirmation of a 'strategic partnership" with China was not repeated. Was Morrison's 2018 refusal to choose between the United States and China declaration already disavowed?

Tracing the causes and consequences of Curtin's iconic 1941 statement shows how this kind of declaration might be amended. But it also shows that if the underlying circumstances continue to affirm its appropriateness, the declaration becomes harder and harder to repudiate. Facts do, in the end, prevail.

The importance of Curtin's 1941 declaration, the guarantee of its durability, was that it, too, made manifest what was long immanent. The declaration was not, as is sometimes supposed, a major shift in either Australian or British policy. It had long been assumed by Britain that if Japan entered the war, the United States would probably also enter and would be Australia's military ally. At the time Curtin wrote his declaration Churchill was negotiating with Roosevelt in Washington. One agreement he communicated to Curtin early in January 1942, was that the US accepted Allied responsibility for fighting the Pacific War, including Australia's defence. It was evident to Curtin as 1941 drew to a close that British Empire troops were being thrown back in Malaya towards Singapore, and that Britain could not muster either the air or naval power to hinder the Japanese advance. In turning to America at the end of 1941, Curtin like Morrison was recognising facts.

But the declaration was also momentous, or has come to be seen so. Since European settlement over 150 years earlier, as a group of colonies and then as a nation, Australia's defence had explicitly been a British responsibility. Even more, Britain in 1941 was still "home" to most Australians, and the centre of an immense and powerful empire to which Australia was proud to belong. For all that, coming as Japan swept south, the controversy in Australia over it was restrained and easily managed. Churchill was certainly irritated by the declaration, but not because Australia looked to America. That, after all, was his own advice to Australia. The problem was that Churchill, too, looked to America. Churchill was in Washington and claiming to speak for the Empire at the same time that Curtin was seeking direct talks with the Americans over the Pacific War. Not least because it threatened to diminish the priority of the war against Germany, Churchill resisted Curtin's demand for direct discussion with Washington.

Like Morrison's Singapore statement, Curtin's December 1941 declaration recognised the importance to Australia of a new power without discarding the existing power. In February 1942, Curtin refused Churchill's request that the 7th Division, returning to Australia from the Middle East, be diverted to Burma. More than the declaration itself, that decision instanced Curtin's insistence that Australia's national interests prevail over those of Britain. Shortly after refusing the 7th Division for Burma, however, Curtin agreed to assignment of elements of the returning 6th Division to reinforce Ceylon temporarily. The 9th Division was not retrieved from the Middle East until 1943. The Imperial tie remained.

Even in 1941 and early 1942 Curtin had himself walked back from some of the boldness of his declaration. He mischievously told the credulous British High Commissioner, Sir Ronald Cross, that the statement really withdrew Australian objections to America's separation from the Empire. A few days after the declaration, Curtin told the Secretary of the Department of Defence Co-ordination, Fred Shedden, that he had not intended any departure from existing policy, and none had been made.

Yet Curtin's 1941 statement, however qualified, was of the utmost

330 POWER, POLITICS AND PARLIAMENT

significance, one that became a more important marker as time went by. It explicitly recognised that the interests of Australia and Britain, so closely aligned for so long, had now been separated by the Pacific War.

The width of this separation was not apparent even to its exponent, Curtin. He suspected but could not document Churchill's ceaseless endeavours to draw American resources away from Australia's strategic interests, and towards those of Britain. Curtin did not at first know that when Australia was at most risk of subjugation to Japan, in April 1942, Churchill had sought to have powerful remnants of the United States Pacific fleet moved to the Indian Ocean to interdict what he supposed might be a Japanese landing in Ceylon and India. Roosevelt himself was appalled by Churchill's panic over India and refused the ships. In a secret speech to the House of Commons that same month, Churchill deprecated the likelihood of danger to Australia and thought a Japanese attack on India far more likely.

Curtin was unaware that, in July 1942, US Army Chief of Staff, General George C. Marshall, and his fellow service chiefs had proposed a Pacific offensive, a proposal beaten back by Roosevelt. Curtin was not informed of the British fury at Admiral King's successful insistence on a Pacific offensive at the Casablanca Conference in January 1943–nor was Curtin informed at the time that the conference had altered the whole Allied strategy to the Pacific War. During that conference Marshall accused the British of preferring to hoard Allied forces in Britain rather than allowing more resources to flow to the Pacific War. Curtin did not know of that disagreement, either. Given what he did not know, it is remarkable that so many of Curtin's decisions were right.

In any consideration of how the national interest may be abruptly revised when circumstances change, how the revision is announced and received, how applied, and how sustained, it is useful to observe how Curtin's thinking continued changing after declaring that Australia looked to America. That examination is a reminder that sharp turns in interpretation of the national interest may not be quite as sharp as they sometimes appear, and that older relationships, older styles of thinking and behaving, may often continue to run alongside the new. That was the case with Curtin's thinking about Britain and America. It is also evident as three quarters of a century later Australia picks its way between the competing claims of America and China. After turning to America, Curtin worked earnestly to turn back to Britain.

Despite the 1941 declaration, despite the British leaving the Pacific War, despite the close relationship with MacArthur and the Americans, Australians of Curtin's time continued to think of themselves as British. Whether or not he shared it, and to some extent he evidently did, this sentiment limited Curtin's options and the breadth of his thought.

By the middle of 1943 Curtin revived Australia's interest in the British Empire. In a speech in November 1936, Curtin, as Leader of the Opposition, had been a perceptive critic of the strategy of relying on a British fleet and the Singapore naval base to deter Japan from war. Were Britain in a war with Germany, he warned, it would find it difficult to send a fleet of sufficient power to Singapore. Curtin's warning proved correct. Yet through the 1943 election campaign, Curtin, as his press secretary Don Rodgers later recalled, "draped himself in the Union Jack." He called for a "Fourth Empire", a union of sovereign states loyal to the British throne that would aid each other in war. In this Fourth Empire, Australia would determine policy for the Empire in the Pacific, backed by British naval power. At the beginning of 1944 he called on Britain, post-war, to make Singapore once again the base for naval power in the Pacific.

The Fourth Empire and Australia's proposed role as its leader in the Pacific was a fantasy, strongly supported by his civilian advisers but of no interest to Britain, Canada or South Africa. To Curtin it made sense because he imagined a victorious Britain would be powerful after the war. He knew the Dutch, French and Portuguese colonial powers in Australia's region had offered no serious resistance to Japan. He was concerned with a post-war Pacific world in which Australia would find itself alone among the "teeming millions of coloured races." Curtin pressed his proposal through to the May 1944 meeting of Commonwealth Prime Ministers in London where it was met with hostility by Mackenzie King, Prime Minister of Canada, and indifference by Churchill.

After turning to America at the end of 1941, Curtin appeared to have turned back to Britain. But that was not quite so. Curtin discovered there was no going back. The demands of Britain and America collided, and Curtin chose America.

America had Allied responsibility for directing the Pacific War. With Curtin's agreement, Australian military forces were under the control of General Douglas MacArthur, Allied Commander in Chief for the South-west Pacific. He and MacArthur had a cordial relationship, one very useful to both leaders. MacArthur was deeply suspicious of British intentions in the Pacific, partly perhaps because he did not like British colonialism but, more importantly, because he did not want his command diluted. Before he left for Washington and London in April 1944, Curtin visited MacArthur. They agreed MacArthur's command arrangements should not be changed.

While Curtin was reaffirming MacArthur's command over Australians troops, Churchill was planning otherwise. Since the collapse of its defence of Burma early in 1942, Britain had been absent from the Pacific War. By early 1944, with Allied troops fighting up the Italian peninsula, and preparing for the landing in Normandy, Churchill was eager to rejoin the Pacific War. If America won the Pacific War without Britain, it would determine which colonial powers came back to the region, and in what form. It would determine the peace treaty with Japan and build the American alliance with China. This Churchill was determined to prevent. But while he could now spare ships for the Pacific War, he could not spare major formations of troops or planes until the defeat of Germany. He looked to Australia to provide the troops for operations on MacArthur's left. In one of Churchill's many conceptions, Australian troops would help capture the tip of Sumatra, a possible jumping off point for the recapture of Singapore and Malaya. It would, Churchill told his advisers, redeem the stain of Singapore's surrender.

Though General Sir Thomas Blamey eagerly joined in the British plans, Curtin affirmed and reaffirmed in meetings with and cables to Churchill that he would not agree to a change in the command arrangements in the South-west Pacific. He would stick with Mac-Arthur. It was not the only reason Churchill's plan was finally abandoned, but it was certainly one of them. Curtin's 1941 declaration had recognised America's responsibility for the Allied war against Japan.

By 1944 the logic of Australia's relationship with America remained implacable.

No Labor leader challenged Morrison's 2018 declaration. An important difference between the 1941 declaration and the 2018 declaration is that in the earlier period there was no agreement between the major political parties. One reason perhaps is that Australians have had several decades to get used to the ideas of Morrison's declaration. Between Pearl Harbor and Curtin's declaration they had three weeks.

Billy Hughes, leader of the United Australia Party and Deputy Leader of the Opposition, initially objected to Curtin's declaration. He was soon mollified, but loyalty to Britain coloured subsequent decisions by the UAP and its Country Party ally. The deposed former prime minister, Robert Menzies, was, through that period, the political force Curtin had to watch. Menzies lost no opportunity to accuse the Labor Government of lack of loyalty to Britain. He wanted the 7th Division landed in Burma, as Churchill demanded. He told Churchill's private emissary in Australia that he opposed the island-hopping strategy the Americans had adopted, and wanted instead a land attack on Singapore and Malaya. In the House of Representatives he called for Australian troops to invade Malaya.

Morrison's Singapore statement, unnoticed in November 2018, may be entirely forgotten. If Morrison is remembered only as an interim leader, his public announcement that Australia did not have to choose and would not choose between the United States and China, may be recorded here and not elsewhere. Much depends on whether the strategic competition between China and the United States continues for decades to come. If it does, and it is surely likely it will, if Australia's economic interests remain focused on an economic community of which China is by far the biggest member, then Morrison may be remembered for this declaration, and perhaps little else.

17

In Search of Sir Robert Menzies

Paul Kelly

John Nethercote is steeped in the ethos of public administration, the institutions of parliamentary government, the value of proportion and practicality in statecraft, a passion for cricket as a pastime and, above all, in political leadership as a project in artistry. It is no surprise that Nethercote was drawn to the study of Sir Robert Menzies. It is also not surprising that, as John matured, his fascination with Menzies deepened. The common ground and outlook they shared – across different generations – laid the foundations for one of John's most enduring and productive preoccupations.*

At a time when most of his generation found Menzies to be largely uninteresting or of little relevance, Nethercote reached the opposite conclusion. While a baby boomer, born in Sydney in 1948 with his undergraduate years spanning 1965 to 1968 – the era of the so-called "sixties revolution" – John defied cultural fashion and saw the Menzies story as a significant door to wisdom and insights. His instincts would be vindicated. As the decades rolled forward and the 21st century revealed the sorry saga of Australian prime ministers struggling to survive beyond one election – where Menzies had managed seven in succession – the notion that lessons were to be drawn from his unparalleled statecraft was irrefutable.

---

* This essay draws upon the author's contact with John Nethercote since 1970. The quotes are based upon an interview conducted with Nethercote in 2018, supplemented by extensive written material provided by John about his own career, his assessments of Menzies, and his view of the historiography surrounding Menzies.

Nethercote looked at and listened to Menzies and saw and heard things that others missed. "His white hair gave Menzies a brightness," he said. "His voice was never old. His accent is so distinctive, distinguished but also clearly Australian." The voice was the essence of Menzies's magnetism. Nethercote was introduced to Menzies on the wireless during the late 1950s as were millions of Australians. John began listening to ABC broadcasts of Question Time in the House of Representatives along with major parliamentary speeches from about the age of 10 years.

The family lived in the St George area of Sydney and John's bedroom overlooked Tom Ugly's bridge. His family was political in a 1950s fashion, enough to have in the home books on British kings and queens, 19th century British prime ministers and, inevitably, Winston Churchill's war history, volume 1, *The Gathering Storm*. His father admired Menzies and disliked his 1950s Labor rival, Dr H. V. Evatt, the local member. The Menzian voice echoed in John's brain – he identified Menzies with "presence." Nethercote told me: "Menzies always spoke to his audiences while Churchill spoke to the ages." John recalled the remark of ALP parliamentary veteran Clyde Cameron: "Menzies looked like a PM, he behaved like a PM and he had the presence of a PM." For Nethercote, it was "as high a tribute as could be paid."

After completing his honours year in Government and Public Administration at Sydney University, Nethercote, after a year teaching in Papua New Guinea, became part of that wave of young idealistic graduates pulled towards the public sector that surged to Canberra each year. The Treasury took many of the best economics graduates. Others entered one of the two special training programs – the External Affairs Department had its annual course for aspiring diplomats and the Public Service Board had a year-long Administrative Trainee scheme that prepared graduates for careers in policy departments. John subsequently joined the latter in 1970 and worked at the Public Service Board.

The shadow of Menzies loomed over the Canberra of the early 1970s. He had retired only in 1966. There were many senior public servants who had worked with Menzies or had some brief contact with him. It was a stimulating place at the time. The Gorton Government had narrowly survived a general election in October 1969. Especially after a half-Senate election late in 1970, the capital steadily readied itself for arrival of the Whitlam Government that its admirers felt would extinguish the remaining Menzies mythology. Some of the giants formed in an earlier age of public administration were still in harness – Sir Frederick Wheeler at the Public Service Board, Sir Arthur Tange at Defence, Sir Richard (Dick) Randall at Treasury, with Whitlam about to recall former Reserve Bank Governor, Dr H. C. (Nugget) Coombs, as his special adviser.

This was the environment that fashioned John's mind. He had read many of the great texts – J. A. La Nauze on Alfred Deakin, L. F. Fitzhardinge on Billy Hughes, Cecil Edwards on S. M. Bruce and Fin Crisp on Ben Chifley. The ethics of the public service reinforced his natural outlook: "Intense partisanship was never part of my political education," he said. Much of John's work focused on inter-action between the public service and the ministerial system, initially before the arrival of ministerial staff. For several months in 1974 he worked closely with Whitlam's former private secretary, Dr Peter Wilenski, at the Royal Commission on Australian Government Administration chaired by Dr Coombs.

John's skill was perspective: to adapt to new intellectual currents but never to succumb to them. He found the Whitlam era exhilarating but he never became a disciple. He noted that Whitlam thrived as a political leader in the vacuum created by Menzies's departure. The public service opened doors to a global perspective as Nethercote expanded his intellectual range and worked in London and Ottawa examining at first-hand the workings of comparable Westminster systems.

Nethercote had a keen sense of the Liberal Party and the nation wanting to move quickly beyond Menzies after his retirement:

> What seemed to be clear from a very early stage was that many people, on both sides of politics, wanted to see it not simply as a retirement but as the end of an era. Whatever

people, not least senior ministers, thought of the era, there appeared to be relief that it was over. Apart from Harold Holt, the main ministers who spoke up for the Menzies Government were Paul Hasluck and Malcolm Fraser, one of the two new ministers in the Holt Government. [The other new minister was Dame Annabelle Rankin, the first woman to head a department.]

John met Menzies only twice. The first, very briefly, at an Australia/West Indies test cricket match. The second occasion arose when John was working for Sir John Bunting who had been Secretary of the Prime Minister's Department under Menzies and was a Menzies confidant. Sir John had organised a small gathering for afternoon drinks. Menzies was in retirement and Nethercote recalled that "he charmed those present with stories of John Monash and Tom Playford." John had been instructed by Dame Pattie about how much scotch Menzies was to be offered. When freshening up his glass, Menzies' finger moved up the glass. Much to Dame Pattie's apparent chagrin, John readily obliged. As he departed, Menzies paused: "Thank you, young man, you have been most kind."

The key to history is to see the past beyond the prism of the present. As John read about Menzies, absorbed the stories and studied his speeches (especially when writing about Menzies's time as Leader of the Opposition), he saw a politician of immense yet almost overlooked ability, guided by principle, purpose and understanding of the Australian temper:

> In politics and government Menzies masters institutions from within rather than without – whether parliament, cabinet or the public service ... Menzies treats senior officials as though they are instructing solicitors, a relationship he knows well. Evatt knows it well, too, but seemed to want to do the solicitor's job as well as that of the barrister.

John became convinced that Menzies's "foundational strength" lay in philosophy. He saw "a broad philosophy woven around central convictions such as individual responsibility and industry, self-reliance, prudence, frugality, looking after oneself and those for whom one is responsible, starting with family." For Nethercote, much of this was common ground. He felt in harmony with Menzies, saying, "I was broadly sympathetic with much that Menzies stood for. Like him, nonconformist churches had had a pronounced impact on my upbringing". But, on matters of government, John feels he was keener than Menzies on federalism and probably more sympathetic to bicameralism.

If philosophy and conviction were Menzies's strengths, Nethercote also realised that implementation was the key – here Menzies had a deep grasp of the practical. Menzies made change only on an incremental basis: a political leader must possess a "mind for practical purposes" and he knew the usefulness of under-statement, an art nearly every subsequent prime minister has abandoned.

Nethercote said: "Menzies's great insight is the need for reassurance. Even as he presides over enormous developments in population and society, his contribution is to stress continuity. If anything, he underplays a good deal of progress in Australian society and is wary of excessive expectations; he is circumspect in claiming credit for his government; only that it has created conditions for the people to improve their own lot."

The Menzies method was so successful it fooled a number of historians and commentators into thinking nothing much happened in Australia from 1949 to 1966 when, in fact, the nation was transformed and the condition of its people enhanced to an astonishing degree. Menzies understood his times, usually, if perhaps not invariably. "Menzies never craves public attention and certainly not any form of adulation," Nethercote said. He operated long before the electronic media changed the role of high office and leaders saturating the public with constant television and radio appearances. Menzies, in a sense, controlled the tempo of politics. It is, however, unlikely his style would be as successful in the current age of inflated demands, expanded agendas for individual rights, and the cult of narcissism.

Menzies was middle brow in his tastes, never the cultural aristocrat. John observes:

> Menzies is mainstream. He had an instinctive affinity with

ordinary Australians of his era. He reads books of the sort that many of his compatriots would (Dickens, Ngaio Marsh), at the theatre he loves musicals, in painting he eschews surrealism and abstraction, and his sports are cricket, VFL (Carlton) and tennis. While exceptionally intelligent and well-educated, Menzies does not wear his learning on his sleeve notwithstanding the famous retort to an interjector: "Bob, what are yer gonna do about 'ousing?" "Well, first of all, I would put an 'h' in front of it!"

As a young man of the 1960s generation, Nethercote was sympathetic to the post-Menzies mood for change. It was reflected conspicuously in the effective end of the White Australia policy and the 1967 referendum on Aboriginal advancement, steps Menzies had resisted in office in the first case. The other deeply practical change was removal of the so-called marriage bar on permanency of married women in almost all Australian Government employment. John followed the late 1967 controversy over the use of the VIP squadron – a major issue at the time – and saw this as definite confirmation that the Menzies era was over; "it demonstrated an indulgence and indiscipline in government which would not have occurred under RGM."

During 1967 Menzies published a volume of memoirs, *Afternoon Light*, to a cool reception and, several years later, *The Measure of the Years*. John notes: "whatever disappointments some readers may have initially had, they were at least quintessentially Menzies." The post-Menzies age was dominated by public discussion about "the future" and idealism vested in greater government programs, more centralisation of power and huge increases in spending on health and education. John's assessment was surely correct that Menzies's reputation "waned" in this immediate period. This was compounded by the failure of the Vietnam War and the changing outlook towards conscription, two of the defining issues towards the end of Menzies's time as prime minister.

During the 1980s and 1990s Nethercote's experience in a wide range of areas of public administration and parliamentary activities provided a broad foundation for his historical assessment of the Menzies age. This involved work with the Defence Review Committee, as secretary of the National Inquiry on Local Government Finance, directing the Public Service Board's research agenda, serving as Secretary of the Senate Standing Committee on Finance and Public Administration, research into decision-making in the central government agencies, lecturing at the ANU on government and public policy, preparing various chapters for the 7th edition of Harry Evans (ed.), *Odgers' Australian Senate Practice* (1991), and papers for the Parliamentary Library on the mandate doctrine in Westminster governance, and another on changes in departmental machinery of government post-1987.

At the turn of the millennium, Nethercote left the public service and went to work for the Liberal Party at the Menzies Research Centre. This inaugurated an intense phase of his career focused around historical research, editing books, writing on government and public administration and providing appraisal of an exceedingly long list of Australian books and many classics in the fields of government and politics. John held various visiting appointments at Griffith University, the ANU and, after 2009, as an Adjunct Professor at the Australian Catholic University. He edited a collection of essays organised by the Liberal Party to mark the Centenary of Federation, *Liberalism and the Australian Federation*, published in 2001, and, to mark the 50th anniversary of Menzies's retirement, *Menzies: The Shaping of Modern Australia* (2016).

Nethercote developed close collaborative partnerships with Allan Martin, author of the two volume biography of Menzies published in 1994 and 1999; with Ian Hancock who has written extensively on the Liberal Party and Liberals including a biography of John Gorton; John Edwards, biographer of Paul Keating and John Curtin; and John Howard (serving as fact-checker on Howard's *The Menzies Era*).

Integral to John's life was following and participating in the evolving historiography surrounding Menzies. John identified the signs of a "turnaround" in views of Menzies with the 1978 publication by Percy Joske, a former Liberal MP and friend of Menzies, of his book, *Sir Robert Menzies: 1894-1978*; and Cameron

Hazlehurst's *Menzies Observed*, published in 1979. He felt the associated Hazlehurst essay on Menzies in the book, *Australian Conservatism*, edited by Hazelhurst himself, was "among the first, thoughtful, researched pieces on RGM."

But Nethercote identified Judith Brett's *Robert Menzies' Forgotten People*, first published in 1992, as influential in reigniting interest (not invariably friendly) in Menzies and, in particular, in his "neglected radio broadcasts in 1942 of which *The Forgotten People* was justly the most famous." Brett's thesis offered a fresh insight into Menzies's political and cultural depth and gave him a new relevance for another generation. "Brett's is in many ways an admirable study but its psychological orientation was viewed by a number of readers as idiosyncratic," Nethercote said.

Brett's book was the first of several published as the centenary of Menzies's birth in 1894 and the 50th anniversary of the formation of the Liberal Party approached. Others included Gerard Henderson's *Menzies' Child* and an edited collection, *The Menzies Era* (edited by Scott Prasser, Nethercote himself and John Warhurst).

Nethercote saw publication of the Martin biography as the "most important." He reported that Martin felt Menzies warranted three volumes but felt his own age precluded it. "Martin's volumes were well received if not, perhaps, with a great deal of enthusiasm," John said.

> Especially during the writing of volume two I met frequently with Martin and I was reading drafts of the work as it proceeded. Some of our discussions were very robust but the main result was usually an expansion of the account. Generally I saw in Menzies a much tougher practitioner of politics than Martin did; Allan Martin had a more benign view of human nature than I have.

The Labor Party would agree with Nethercote. Menzies possessed a deadly precision in lancing its vulnerabilities. John tried unsuccessfully to persuade Martin to write more on Menzies's relations with the senior public servants. Like Martin himself, he was aware of gaps in Martin's account, for instance, concerning ASIO, women and Aborigines. But he applauded Martin's disposition, believing that "the first duty of the historian was to find out what happened and why, a precept Martin often repeated."

The author launched Martin's second volume in King's Hall at Old Parliament House and said that volume two "completed the most authoritative account" of Menzies's life. This included the observation that assessments of Menzies were bedevilled by three factors – the impression his success was due more to Labor failure; the paradoxical view that, while Australia thrived under Menzies, somehow this had nothing to do with him; and the sheer longevity of his rule which meant there were so many manifestations of Menzies in office that it was easier to seize upon a stereotype than attempt to understand the entire man in his complexity.

John told me over dinner in 2018 that Martin had said to him: "You were the first person who told me I was doing important work rather than wasting my time on Menzies." In the introduction to volume two Martin thanked John for his "erudition and interest in Menzies" that had enlivened their discussions. Nethercote believes that over time "the foundations for a fuller appreciation of Menzies's life and career have progressively emerged."

John said the richer understanding of Menzies was assisted by the publication in 2011 of letters he periodically wrote to Heather Henderson in *Letters to My Daughter* and Heather Henderson's 2013 memoir, *A Smile for My Parents*, offering an insight into the lives of Menzies, Dame Pattie and the Menzies family – the forgotten people made manifest. In 2014 Anne Henderson released a compelling account of the first Menzies prime ministership with her book, *Menzies at War*. John considers Ian Hancock's 2000 publication of *National and Permanent? The Federal Organisation of the Liberal Party of Australia 1944-1965* was a decisive contribution.

A contribution that Nethercote valued highly and which was, however, dismissed by some critics, was the deeply revealing account of how Menzies functioned as prime minister in the book, *R G Menzies: a Portrait*, by Sir John Bunting, a senior officer in the Prime Minister's Department and Secretary from 1959 to 1968. John said: "Its strength was precisely that it gave anyone interested in the period an unrivalled first-hand insight into the personality of the central figure. Bunting restricted himself to telling readers just, and only, what he knew."

Consider a couple of many examples. Bunting said his normal interviews with Menzies took 30 minutes and covered many items but Menzies valued the "two minute" process, saying that only Bunting could be relied upon to state a problem and get the response within two minutes. Bunting says Menzies championed the "single word and the simple word." He quotes from a note Menzies prepared for ministers:

> English is a great language. In the present century the scientists have given it a dreadful mauling, of a polysyllabic German kind … Why should we all fall victims to the jargon of economists or journalists? … The greatest proof of literacy is the capacity to use simple English.

Nethercote said valuable material about Menzies came from the many political autobiographies and biographies by or about Arthur Fadden, Harold Holt, Percy Spender, Richard Casey, Garfield Barwick, Paul Hasluck, John Cramer, John McEwen, John Gorton, Jim Killen, Bill Hayden along with the diaries of Peter Howson. Also shedding important light are autobiographies by Sir Alan Watt and H. C. Coombs and biographies of Arthur Tange and James Plimsoll. In 2011 the Victorian Division of the Liberal Party published a new edition of *The Forgotten People*, with a penetrating introductory essay by David Kemp.

John pays a special tribute to a book from an "unlikely source" – *The Menzies Era* – by the second longest serving PM after Menzies, John Howard. "It is an extraordinary book and, in Australian politics, almost unique," John said. "It stands alongside Deakin's two memoirs, *Crisis in Victorian Politics*, and *The Federal Story*, as major works of history by Australian statesmen." Nethercote was fact-checker for the book and held long discussions with Howard on the project. He said:

> Howard's book gains added strength by not being a biography and by having a "life and times" quality. What

he brings to the subject is a notable feel for the dynamics, rhythms and momentum of politics.

The Howard book, launched by the author in September 2015, also at Old Parliament House, is a remarkable perspective on one PM by another prime minister who sat in the same chair. Howard identifies the 1949 election as a pivotal point for Australia – if Menzies had lost and Labor won a mandate for bank nationalisation, then history would have been "fundamentally different", with Australia likely to have followed the "dismal British path" after the war, leading to a growing and inefficient state sector that culminated in Britain's economic paralysis of the mid- and late-1970s.

For Howard, the enduring Menzies achievement is that "the great Australian middle class" emerged during his time and "preserving it remains a constant national aspiration." Howard said Menzies "embodied the sense of security and optimism" that was a hallmark of the Australia "that I grew up in." The tangible results are uncontested: consistent economic growth, low unemployment, rising home ownership and, in Howard's words, "an egalitarian enjoyment of the fruits of economic success." In his conclusion, he commented on Menzies's resilience – a lesser leader would have been broken "by the indignities that were heaped upon him by some treacherous colleagues." Yet Menzies emerged stronger and learnt from his mistakes.

Nethercote followed the reviews of Howard's book closely. He said there was the "usual criticism" about the attempt to ban the Communist Party, Petrov, Suez, conscription and Vietnam (a not insignificant list, by the way) but little that was new. "It suggested to me that Menzies's reputation as a considerable prime minister to be respected if not admired is now entrenched and continues to grow," John said.

In 2016, to honour the 50th anniversary of Menzies's retirement, Nethercote edited *Menzies: The Shaping of Modern Australia*. Those contributing essays included David Kemp, Anne Henderson, John Howard, Henry Ergas and J. J. Pincus, Anne Twomey, Graeme Starr and John himself, among others. In the first chapter Kemp wrote that Menzies was "the most influential Australian political leader of the twentieth century" and that all governments in the four decades that followed him "built upon the foundations he set in place." Kemp continued:

> Through the Liberal Party of Australia Menzies set out to reset the course of Australian history, to expose the fantasies of the Left utopians and to build a new political culture on a rescued liberal tradition – one not based on class, sectarian or nationalist hatreds, but on mutual respect and faith in the ability of people, making their own choices in life, to create a good society.

Nethercote's final assessments of Menzies are praiseworthy yet anchored in realism. He sees Menzies as pre-eminent. He was also a delegator with many of era's policy hallmarks tied to a particular minister: McEwen and the Commerce Treaty with Japan; Barwick and trade practices or matrimonial causes; Hasluck and Papua New Guinea. Another example is Spender and the Columbo Plan along with the ANZUS Treaty.

Menzies did not assume merit was its own reward. "Menzies's interest is only partly in whether an idea is good," John said:

> Menzies's more pointed concern is what will be the consequences? Menzies knows always to have attention to the state and tide of public opinion. He is not afraid to be tough but, not least with the passing of the years, he realises he must be sparing. Menzies followed his own aphorism that democratic leadership requires the support of half the people and the respect of a goodly number of the rest.

His second prime ministership is assisted by a share of luck, notably the Labor split and emergence of the DLP. Yet Menzies also makes his own luck with his measured approach to policy development, ever watchful for the convenient opportunity.

Another example is astute courting of the Catholic vote exemplified by his initiatives in education. John suggests Menzies recognised this potential a long way out. He had "no difficulty" in luring Joe Lyons away from Labor in 1931. Contrary to many views, John believes that by the 1950s Menzies felt the protective tariff was "excessive"; he discreetly oversees a sustained challenge under Sir Leslie Melville and Alf Rattigan.

On economic policy more generally, Menzies arbitrates the contest between economic advisers "as a judge watches competing barristers" – this usually produced favourable results, the great exception being the credit squeeze of 1960 and his near-death experience at the 1961 election. In the contests between the Treasury and its various challengers, the Commonwealth (later Reserve) Bank, and later, more flamboyantly, the Trade Department, and the duels between Roland Wilson and Nugget Coombs, Menzies displays an astuteness, and a deftness which even Franklin Roosevelt might have envied. Nethercote offers an acute "big picture" summary:

> A key element in his long prime ministership is that Menzies interpreted, as post-war reconstruction got underway, the type of society that would emerge. Labor was entrenched in its ways whilst Menzies had a better sense of the world emerging, in part, I suspect, from his interest in America. Britain is still important but the United States is ascendant in so many aspects of Australian life, white goods, movies, television, shops, foreign policy and defence.

"RGM was never, for me, a messiah," Nethercote told me:

> I certainly saw him as a principled politician, certainly more principled than most, but never one for whom all that mattered was to be morally right or on the right side of history.

John said "the essence of Menzies's greatness as a statesman" derives from Menzies's own analysis in *The Measure of the Years*:

> As we look back over the panorama of history and select (as even the least of us have the privilege of doing) the political giants, we find ourselves identifying them as, above all, great artists.
>
> For the artist is the man who knows how to use his materials; who has a sensitiveness to his environment and an understanding of humanity, and a great skill in execution.

18

Australian Political Biography and Psychohistory

Tom Frame

I am an accidental devotee of political biographies. In my teenage years when I first contemplated a career in the Royal Australian Navy (RAN) and hoped to sound knowledgeable at the selection boards, I was drawn to authors that gave their readers a glimpse of the personal and professional lives of naval officers in the exercise of command. The subjects were initially those who served in wartime. As many of these officers subsequently occupied positions of national leadership, my interests slowly extended to political biographies – mostly British, American and Australian. Since then I have been accumulating life stories because they give an insight into two things: first, the evolution and expression of human nature; and, second, the contexts in which leadership is expected and the constraints bearing upon its exercise. I gain most from biographies conveying a sense of the subject's character, emotions and personality so that, when the last page is turned, I feel that I know the subject and understand the influences shaping their actions and attitudes.

This essay is inspired by John Nethercote's long-standing interest in the careers of public administrators and their vastly understated place in the writing of general Australian history. From my reading of his published work, Nethercote argues consistently that the foremost challenge is ensuring that an account of the politics of public life does not exclude the more personal dimensions of everyday living. Politicians and civil servants are, of course, people whose preferences and prejudices, strengths and weaknesses, fears and anxieties bear upon the philosophies that undergird their attitudes and the priorities that shape their actions. A biography that was indifferent to a person's inner being would be inadequate and rather boring. In commenting on the public service of luminaries such as Sir Robert Garran, Dr H. C. "Nugget" Coombs, Sir Frederick Wheeler, Sir Roland Wilson and Dr Peter Wilenski, Nethercote observes that none were functionaries who merely managed well-established and clearly defined bureaucratic systems.[1] Each in his own way was involved in the political contest of ideas that is conducted before public policy is finalised and government decisions are made. They were creative thinkers and expansive leaders whose contributions to national life reflected the complexity of their characters. Their personalities influenced their handling of complicated questions associated with policy and administration. Reflecting on the holistic approach that he commends, I want to reflect on the biographer's approach to their subject's inner life (as much as it can be known) and the extent to which judgements about character should inform assessments of conduct. I will use Nethercote's critique of a biography of H. C. Coombs and my own work on Harold Holt to consider the claims of psychohistory as a mode of biography and as an approach to writing life stories.

Private, personal and public intersections

Nethercote has produced and reviewed a number of biographies. As a keen observer of human beings attentive to their frailties and failings as well as their strengths and successes, he has drawn attention to the place of what I would call the "inner life" in the careers of prominent Australian politicians and public administrators. He has pointed to interactions with families and friends because what happens at home can shape what occurs at work. Did the subject have a supportive family or did domestic demands bear upon the performance of their official duties? Work habits are also revealing. Was the subject disciplined and methodical in how they approached their responsibilities or were they erratic and disorganised? When commentary on the inner life is absent, when formative interactions with family and friends are ignored and when destiny defining emotional struggles with ambition and disappointment are overlooked, the reader has an incomplete, if not inaccurate, picture of the subject. They are essentially one or, at best, two-dimensional figures lacking definition and depth. The reader is usually left to guess at their motivations and to surmise the values and virtues that drove their careers. These concerns provoked Nethercote's criticism of Tim Rowse's biography, *Nugget Coombs: A Reforming Life*, published in 2002.[2]

Several reviewers have noted that Coombs's own account of his life published in 1981, *Trial Balance*, is protective of his private life.[3] The economic historian, Evan Jones, claimed it was "guarded and misleading".[4] Like most personal apologias, *Trial Balance* is Coombs's preferred portrait and how he wishes others would see him. This is the posed "publicity shot" usually circulated to the media. As Tim Rowse began his research, the man behind the myth remained in the background. In reviewing *A Reforming Life*, Nethercote explained that "in the private politics of Australian government Coombs is a major figure" but lamented that much of Coombs's private life was notably absent from Rowse's book. Nethercote commented that Coombs "possessed a charm and wit that set him apart from many of his peers. His company had a relaxed quality that made him attractive to most of his political masters". Coombs apparently "yearned for recognition" and had, according to Coalition minister and Viceroy, Paul Hasluck, a talent for being "conspicuously inconspicuous". Nethercote noted that Coombs was said to be "the greatest self-publicist in the history of the Australian public service". Nethercote then asked: this is "a fascinating book, but is it a biography of Coombs?" The absence of material not on the public record was a function of Coombs's request that the author not "intrude on 'personal space' – attitudes, beliefs, relationships which I have tried to protect as private". Nethercote responds:

Rowse's acquiescence in Coombs' terms seem least satisfactory because they have such a highly inhibitory effect to the extent that Coombs loses much of his humanity. It is ironical that Coombs, so often the advocate of accountability and research, should, in his own case, seek a dispensation. Why could such matters not have been left to Rowse's discretion?

These omissions are notable because, according to Nethercote, Rowse has not produced a "conventional biography" but depicted Coombs's life as a "series of attempts to answer the question: how can liberal government draw heavily on the expertise of policy intellectuals while continuing to honour popular sovereignty". This is an entirely worthwhile exercise but, Nethercote contends, it could have been more effectively completed with the inclusion of personal and private material. Hence, he concludes, "the abstract cloak of this volume obscures rather than enlightens". Coombs remains a mythic figure. Nethercote knew Coombs and observed him over several years, believing his personal disposition and professional demeanour helped to explain the approach he adopted on a number of policy issues. For instance, Coombs's dislike of conflict and confrontation led him to avoid hard decisions and to delay difficult choices. It might also have led to conciliation and compromise on matters requiring firmness or resolution. There was much to commend Nethercote's interest in the "whole" person as a vehicle for understanding the public figure.

Harold Holt's inner life

I read Nethercote's review of *A Reforming Life* while working on my biography of Harold Edward Holt (1908-1967), the seventeenth prime minister of Australia.[5] I started work on the book after leaving the Navy and moving away from naval history. But why write about Holt? After completing a detailed study of the tragic sinking in 1964 of HMAS *Voyager*, in which 82 men perished,[6] I became interested in the prime minister who ordered the second of two royal commissions into the disaster – Harold Holt. He had been a leading member of the Menzies Government for more than a decade, holding the key portfolios of Immigration, Labour and National

Service, and the Treasury. Holt had been the subject of two works – both highly misleading. The first was *My Life and Harry* by Dame Zara Holt (later Bate).[7] There were fabrications and falsehoods throughout the book as Holt's widow offered a distorted account of their relationship. The second was *The Prime Minister was a Spy* by the British novelist Anthony Grey.[8] Based on the allegations of a former naval officer, Ronald Titcombe, Grey accused Holt of spying for the Chinese Communist regime over a thirty-year period. The book was completely fanciful and the publisher pulped most of the unsold print run. I thought Holt deserved better. He was the longest-serving parliamentarian to become prime minister. He was the nation's leader for 692 days and initiated many reforms across a range of portfolios until his disappearance off Victoria's Cheviot Beach on 17 December 1967. Yet Holt was remembered for only two things: his unscripted remark on the White House lawn in June 1966 that Australia would be "all the way with LBJ" in South Vietnam; and the apparently mysterious manner of his death by drowning. I knew Holt deserved better.

As a first time biographer, I thought long and hard about the tone and tenor of the book I wanted to write. The key question concerned the amount of material to include about Holt's private life as the basis for interpreting his political career. Being born late in 1962 and having only early childhood memories of his disappearance, I knew very little about his character or personality. What made him "tick" was almost entirely unknown, at least to me. As I read his official papers and the volumes of newspaper clippings he created, my subject continued to be a veiled figure. Because Holt did not keep a private diary, wrote very few personal letters and clearly had no interest in assembling material for a future biographer, getting a sense of the man could only be derived from unscripted speeches and the recollections of those who knew him well. I then heard his voice on audio recordings and this revealed how he projected ideas and insights to others. I looked at countless photographs and these helped me to gain a sense of the man as well. The most revealing was probably taken in the first half of the 1960s when Holt was the Federal Treasurer. Sadly, the place and date were not recorded. He was sitting at one edge of what looked like a bench at a bus stop reading the morning paper, wearing unfashionable glasses, dressed in a plain suit accompanied by suede boots. Sitting at the other end of the bench was a small boy looking bored. He had no idea who the man was and Holt appeared completely unconcerned. This revealed a great deal about the man. Holt was unpretentious and in many respects rather ordinary. Unlike his imposing predecessor, Sir Robert Menzies, Holt was unassuming and easy-going. He did not try to be someone he wasn't. But he would become the prime minister of Australia – a feat only sixteen others had managed before him in the nation's history. He was not everyman.

As I met his family and friends and assembled the fragments of his life from the papers that remained, I began to gain a sense of the enduring consequences of his unsettled childhood. He was sent away to boarding school before he was aged eight. This was followed by the collapse of his parents' marriage and the early death of his mother. There were hints of the loneliness he felt as a teenager starved of affection and the sense of isolation that flowed from spending most school holidays with extended families or the families of school friends because his father, Tom, was either unavailable or busy. [His father would later marry the girl Harold was dating – Viola Thring, half-sister of the legendary Australian actor Frank Thring.] A series of cryptic but telling comments revealed that Holt craved the company of others and loathed being alone, that he needed the personal reassurance of romantic love, that he disliked hurting people, even his political opponents, that he was affected emotionally by the suffering of others, that mixing with people from the theatre and the race track undergirded his sense of human equality, and that the opportunities he had enjoyed ought to be shared by others. His natural inclination was to include rather than to exclude people from a conversation and he disliked confrontation when consensus was within reach. Holt's personal credo was Rudyard Kipling's 1895 poem "If". He kept a copy near to hand throughout his adult life and commended its sentiments to others.

Without a sense of Holt's early life, and an appreciation of his character and personality, it would have been impossible to explain why, as prime minister, he promoted the aboriginal referendum in May 1967 and established the Council for Aboriginal Affairs within the Prime Minister's Department, dismantled the White Australia policy and instituted Australian passports, created the Australia Council for the Arts and promoted the National Fitness Campaign, increased Australia's contribution to the Vietnam War with the deployment of national servicemen, and so on. Many of these reforms were later mistakenly attributed to his successors – John Gorton and Gough Whitlam. Drawing on my time as a naval officer and on my training as an Anglican priest, I was confident that I knew something of human nature and personal experience, and how one influenced the other. None of my assessments of Holt's character or my judgments of his personality required or depended upon specialist knowledge of psychology. Was this a deficiency that I should, however, have addressed?

Psychohistory and its possibilities

The late Professor Patrick O'Farrell (1933-2003) introduced me to the possibilities of "psychohistory" during a tutorial for history honours students at UNSW in 1984. The application of psychology to history had been suggested by the historian William Langer in his 1957 presidential address to the American Historical Association entitled "The Next Assignment"[9] and Stuart Hughes in a 1961 address, "History and Psychoanalysis: an explanation of motive", later published in *History as Art and Science* in 1964.[10] Langer believed his colleagues would gain deeper insights into human conduct through "the exploitation of the concepts and findings of modern psychology". His interest was not in classical or academic psychology but in psychoanalysis and "its later developments and variations as included in the terms 'dynamic' or 'depth' psychology". Other proponents of psychohistory, principally the American social thinker and founder of the *Journal of Psychohistory*, Lloyd deMause, have drawn attention to the emotional origins of social and political behaviour in the way a nation raises its children and orders family life. He contends that both bear upon public life.

> As a division of scientific psychology, psychohistory is simply the psychology of the largest groups. It is based on psychoanalysis because this is the most meaningful depth psychology of the twentieth century – as opposed to sociological theory, which is based on eighteenth-century associationism, or its nineteenth-century variant, behaviorism. Yet, as psychohistorian Rudolph Binion constantly stresses, psychohistorical laws are *sui generis*, not derivable from clinical practice, but only from historical observation. For while they draw upon sound principles of individual psychology, they go beyond them to dynamics peculiar to large groups, and are no more reducible to clinical psychology than astronomy is to atomic physics. Thus my work envisions a full "history of the psyche" rather than just "using psychology in history". This means that the kind of psychohistory written by those of us associated with the Institute for Psychohistory derives less from William Langer's famous "Next Assignment" for historians to "use psychoanalysis in history" than from Freud's initial hope that "we may expect that one day someone will venture to embark upon a pathology of cultural communities".[11]

These claims are bold if nothing else.

Our prescribed tutorial reading was *Style for Historians* by Peter Gay and the discussion question concerned Gay's claim that "all history is in some measure psychohistory".[12] Gay later wrote *Freud for Historians* and *Freud: A Life for Our Time*.[13] We were also encouraged to read *Civilisation and its Discontents* in which Freud offered a general theory of history based on psychoanalysis although his focus was on the influence of social structures on individual psyche and not the reverse.[14] O'Farrell was careful not to criticise psychohistory before we had formed our own views but it was plain he was far from persuaded. After discussing Gay, I recall the class being divided. Some were intrigued by the possibilities of psycho-history; others (including me) thought it fraught with insurmountable difficulties including the problem of applying psychoanalytical theory to individuals whose early life experiences were little known and poorly documented. Gay conceded that the two principal deficiencies of the practice of psychohistory over the two decades since Langer commended its embrace were the "pressure towards reductionism [and] … its cavalier way with the evidence". Notwithstanding these serious methodological flaws, Gay believed the chief impediment to wider appreciation of psychohistory was the animosity of historians towards Freud as an historical figure and their lack of interest in gaining some expertise in psychoanalytical theory. Three decades later, Australian historians appeared to be no better disposed to psychohistory.

In a survey of recent Australian political biography, the late Professor Geoffrey Bolton made mention of the few Australians to have explored the possibilities of applying psychology to history.[15] He noted that Allan Martin, author of the highly regarded two-volume biography of Sir Robert Menzies, had been attracted to the work of Erik Erikson. Bolton observed: "Although traces of his approach lingered in the final version of his biography of [Sir Henry] Parkes, Martin came largely to discard Erikson's model in favour of a more empirical approach to the evidence". Bolton thought that James Walter's use of psychology in a 1980 study of Gough Whitlam, *The Leader*, produced many "valid and plausible" findings.[16] The "interface between private and public character", remarked Bolton, "keeps coming back to me in attempting the biography of Paul Hasluck". The former Liberal minister and Viceroy had a very different persona in public than in private. He seemed cold and aloof in public but was warm and engaging in private. Bolton thought there was, however, "a recognisable continuum between the personality on or off duty". Bolton also noted the influence of family and friends, physical health and mental well-being on the performance of a public leader's official duties. He suggested that historians needed to grapple with the private lives of public figures to empathise with, and then to explain, their struggles and successes. But does this mean that biographers need to attend closely to the claims of psychohistory?

Biography and the mysteries of human nature

There are many ways to approach biography, each with its own particular merits. No single approach is entitled to assert supremacy given the complexity of the biographical task. Diametrically opposed are approaches focusing exclusively on the private lives of their subjects and those concentrating entirely on the public lives irrespective of whether the decision to focus on one at the expense of the other is intentional or inadvertent. In many respects, the exclusion of either personal or public material is unfulfilling to the reader. Does the need to blend private and public necessitate the embrace of psychohistory?

Thirty years after first deciding that psychohistory was problematic, most of my objections remain unresolved. There are two distinct schools of psychohistory drawing on different traditions with psychology that cannot be readily harmonised. Nor is it clear whether the psychohistorian requires expertise in psychology or mere acquaintance with its key concepts. The task is not simply one of depicting the subject's private life, portraying their public life and then asserting the correlation of emotional conditions and behavioural consequences. Historians are required to explain how they interpret their subject's conduct in general terms: Why does this person behave as they do? How do they assess particular actions in specific terms? Why did this person make this decision?

While I am unwilling to dismiss psychohistory because I do believe there is a need to consider the influence of the inner being on external behaviour, my main concern is the frequent absence of enough evidence for the psychohistorical approach to have cogency or consistency. Few historians ever have sufficient material before them relating to their subject's early upbringing, relationships with family and formative schooling experiences to make informed judgments about how these things bear on adult decision-making. Further, I am not convinced that the historian needs to embrace psychology's methodological commitments in order to comment on character or personality. After all, what is the point and purpose of historians attempting biography? Would we really want to limit biography to psychologists? When the subject is a politician or a senior public servant, we want to know the details of their life, how their attitudes and actions shaped the conduct of government, and whether the reader can draw on their life as an example to greatness or goodness, on the one hand, or draw inspiration and insight from their life in dealing with contemporary issues, on the other.

I am, therefore, commending the need for a conscious commitment to finding the right balance between explanations of the inner life and interpretations of public careers. I am not sure that many biographers begin their research with a sense of where that balance might lie in handling their subject.

In sum, the proponents of psychology oblige its opponents to do better when it comes to accounting for the personal dimensions of public life and to show greater honesty in disclosing the basis upon which character and personality are judged. The challenge, as ever, is striking a balance and finding the right fulcrum. Whether or not they are drawn to psychohistory, biographers cannot ignore this challenge.

While he has not addressed the claims of psychohistory directly, Nethercote's work is an echo of these concerns and we are indebted to him for placing them before us.

Endnotes

[1] John Nethercote, "Anonymous in Life, Anonymous in Death: Memoirs and Biographies of Administrators", in Tracey Arklay, John Nethercote and John Wanna (eds), *Australian Political Lives: Chronicling Political Careers and Administrative Histories*, ANU E-Press, Canberra, 2006, 87-90; accessible at http://press-files.anu.edu.au/downloads/press/p69061/mobile/ch01.html

[2] Tim Rowse, *Nugget Coombs: A Reforming Life*, Cambridge University Press, Melbourne, 2002; and John Nethercote, Review of *A Reforming Life*, *Australian Journal of Public Administration*, 60(4), 103-6.

[3] H. C. Coombs, *Trial Balance*, Macmillan, Melbourne, 1981.

[4] Evan Jones, "Nugget Coombs and his place in the postwar order", *The Drawing Board: An Australian Review of Public Affairs*, 4(1), July 2003, 23-44.

[5] Tom Frame, *The Life and Death of Harold Holt*, Allen & Unwin, Sydney, 2005.

[6] Tom Frame, *Where Fate Calls: the HMAS Voyager Tragedy*, Hodder & Stoughton, Sydney, 1992.

[7] Zara Holt, *My Life and Harry: An Autobiography*, Rigby, Melbourne, 1968.

[8] Anthony Grey, *The Prime Minister was a Spy*, Coronet, Sydney, 1983.

[9] A copy is accessible at https://www.historians.org/about-aha-and-membership/aha-history-and-archives/presidential-addresses/william-l-langer

[10] H. Stuart Hughes, *History as Art and as Science: Twin Vistas on the Past*, Harper Collins, New York, 1964.

[11] Lloyd deMause, *The Foundations of Psychohistory*, Creative Roots, New York, 1982.

[13] Peter Gay, *Freud for Historians*, Oxford University Press, Oxford, 1985, and *Freud: A Life for Our Time*, J. M. Dent, London, 1988.

[12] Peter Gay, *Style in History*, W. W. Norton, New York, 1974.

[14] Sigmund Freud, *Civilisation and its Discontents*, originally published in German in 1930 and later translated by James Strachey. A full copy is available at: http://www.stephenhicks.org/wp-content/uploads/2015/10/FreudS-CIVILIZATION-AND-ITS-DISCONTENTS-text-final.pdf

[15] Geoffrey Bolton, "The Art of Australian Political Biograph", in Tracey Arklay et al, *Australian Political Lives*, ANU Press, Canberra, 1-12.

[16] James Walter, *The Leader: A Political Biography of Gough Whitlam*, University of Queensland Press, St Lucia, 1980.

19

The Full Set

Writing the Life of William McMahon

Patrick Mullins

I was once told a story that began with William McMahon telephoning the Treasury and demanding that an urgent briefing be delivered to his Bellevue Hill home. An official duly set out for Drumalbyn Road. On arrival, he was told that McMahon was in the pool. The official went outside and, seeing the Treasurer swimming laps, made to leave the briefing file on a chair. But McMahon broke off and told the official to give him the briefing orally. Then McMahon resumed swimming. The retired public servant telling me this story began chortling: "To think – he was doing freestyle while this poor bugger walked up and down the length of the pool, reading the file aloud. And Billy was deaf, too, remember – what on earth would he have heard?"

I doubt whether this story is true, but it has nonetheless remained with me – largely because, while writing my biography of McMahon, I often felt like that official: speaking to an audience able to hear little but the effluxion of bubbles and static, deaf to my suggestion that McMahon might be a figure of some substance and interest.

For, where he has not been forgotten, McMahon is known as a disreputable character. During his career, there was considerable, if private, scorn for him. Menzies would refer to McMahon as "that little bastard" or "Little Willie", and, during one Cabinet meeting, interrogated him so forcefully that McMahon demanded to know why he was being picked on.[1] Garfield Barwick regarded him with considerable disdain; Arthur Fadden called him "Billy the flea".[2] Complete distrust prompted John McEwen to veto McMahon's candidacy for the Liberal Party leadership after the death of Harold Holt in 1967; John Gorton's dislike was such that, after he was toppled as leader of the Liberal Party and prime minister, he promised that he would "smash" McMahon even if he had to "smash the party too".[3] Subsequently published autobiographies and reminiscences confirm the low opinion that McMahon's contemporaries had for him, with Paul Hasluck's the most caustic and memorable:

> The longer one is associated with him [McMahon] the deeper the contempt for him grows, and I find it hard to allow him any merit. Disloyal, devious, dishonest, untrustworthy, petty, cowardly – all these adjectives have been weighed by me and I could not in truth modify or reduce any one of them in its application to McMahon. I find him a contemptible little creature.[4]

The regard among academics for McMahon's short-lived prime ministership is no less damning. He is widely thought to be Australia's worst prime minister.[5] Historians of all colour have concurred in this. "His name is a byword for decay, folly, and defeat," wrote Don Watson.[6] He "was one of Australia's worst prime ministers," according to Ian Hancock.[7]

A citation of the above was the invariable response when I told people I was writing McMahon's biography. The question behind it was implicit: why write the biography of a man of such little worth, a man so disreputable, so disliked, so ignominious? Why spend time on him? The consensus regarding McMahon was evident; so, too, was the value of a biography of him. As one journalist wrote dismissively, upon hearing of my book, "I'm not sure that we need a biography of Billy McMahon."[8]

And yet I did it anyhow. Why?

It started with a question. All biographies must be about a question, James Walter argues: the question is the *raison d'etre*. "Political biography surely has to be about answering some sort of question about how politics works, how institutions work, how policy is made".[9] My question was simple: If he was such an incompetent, when he was so derided, when he was so disliked, *how* did McMahon become Australia's prime minister? *How* did he rise to the point where becoming prime minister was even possible? Yes, there had been answers: McMahon's propensity for treachery, his relentless leaking, his penchant for good homework. But no one had considered the question closely enough to provide answers adequate for the twenty years that McMahon had endured in the ministry, rising relentlessly, with apparent success in each portfolio. As I came to see it, the inadequate answers were the consequence of there being no detailed, biographical study.

The advantage and opportunity of a biographical study is, in part, its simplicity. The focus on an individual – to the point that some call biography a cousin to the novel – offers the researcher and reader a path, a way to make sense of events, people, institutions, culture, and historical context. The narrative form that is the invariable backbone of a biography is especially conducive to this. Though it may lead to some distortion of the role of the individual – what the historian Edward Hallett Carr called "the bad King John heresy" – the rigorous and well-told biography facilitates an understanding of the individual, the past, and the individual's role in it.[10] Inhabiting a space between history and literature, biography draws on both: it builds from the historical record, evaluating and showing character, to tell the story. A biographical study of McMahon, therefore, offered the opportunity to answer my question, to trace the events and actions that led to him succeeding John Gorton in March 1971.

I put this into practice while studying McMahon's pre-selection, in the lead-up to the 1949 election. Ian Hancock's pioneering history of the Liberal Party noted that its pre-selection committees all but had a checklist when assessing putative candidates: "A Protestant male in his thirties or forties, who had a war record, professional qualifications, a commitment to the public good, and a loathing of socialism".[11] Biographical research showed that McMahon checked all these boxes. While a teenager, he had converted from his paternal family's Catholicism to the Church of England. He was forty-one by the time of the 1949 election. He had served, with a modest record, in the Army during the Second World War. He had degrees in law and economics from the University of Sydney, and had worked as a solicitor. Although there is no notable evidence of his commitment to the public good in the years preceding his entry to politics, McMahon certainly had a loathing of socialism: he had travelled abroad after the war and seen communism in operation in Eastern Europe.

This certainly meant McMahon checked the basic boxes – but, amid the many candidates who vied for pre-selection for Lowe at the 1949 election, why choose McMahon? An interview with a Liberal Party elder pointed to the importance of biographical study again. "McMahon went to the right schools. He was a member of the right clubs. He knew the right people," this man said. McMahon had attended Sydney Grammar School, an incubator for much of the NSW political elite. His study at Sydney University was under the tutelage of the leaders of the NSW Bar and Australia's foremost economic experts. He had lived at St Paul's College. He was a partner at Allen Allen & Hemsley, Australia's oldest law firm. He was a member of the Royal Sydney Golf Club, of the Royal Sydney Yacht Club, of the Australian Club, and the Melbourne Club. He had grown up a ward of Sir Samuel Walder, a vice-president of the United Australia Party and Lord Mayor of Sydney. He had known, since his youth, non-Labor premiers Sir Thomas Bavin and Sir Bertram Stevens. He had been an articled clerk to Sir Norman Cowper, an influential figure in non-Labor politics. He had a long acquaintance with Billy Hughes, who had crossed swords with his grandfather, James "Butty" McMahon, when Hughes was a union official on the make. The importance of these connections was obvious. McMahon could draw upon the networks that mediate and distribute social influence. The Liberal Party elder I was speaking to admitted this bluntly. "We relied on the fact that he was from Allen Allen & Hemsley, that he came from a wealthy family. We took him at face value," he said. He looked embarrassed, even pained as he said this. "What else were we to do?"

That allowed me to understand how McMahon entered politics.

But how did he rise from the backbench to the ministry, and from there to the prime ministership? Biographical research again pointed the way, and McMahon's first promotion, in 1951, suggested how the patterns of behaviour that aroused anger in his colleagues had been established early.

Three weeks after the re-election of the Liberal-Country Party coalition to its second term in office in May 1951, Menzies announced his desire to appoint a twentieth minister of state. He would reveal the identity of that minister, he said, once Parliament had passed an amendment to the Ministers of State legislation allowing for expansion of the ministry. Speculation about who would be appointed was rife. Astute observers quickly surmised that, owing to the composition of the ministry and the Liberal Party's strength in NSW, the new minister would be drawn from MPs of that state. With a narrowed range of potential candidates, a consensus emerged that Frederick Osborne, MP for Evans, was the likely appointee.[12] A solicitor and ardent anti-communist who had commanded a destroyer in the Royal Navy in the Battle of the Atlantic in the Second World War – "If you wandered the world looking for a finer fellow . . . " one Liberal said to me – Osborne heard enough of the rumour to check, and receive confirmation of, its veracity. But the gap left between Menzies's announcement of his intention to appoint a minister and his actual appointment of that minister – some three months – left a crucial gap where, as Osborne was to say, "axes were sharpened and knives were ground."

Three NSW Liberals went in secret to Eric Harrison, in his capacity as the senior minister in the state, to voice their objections to Osborne's promotion. They told him that Osborne did not enjoy their confidence. They thought him too arrogant. A surprised Harrison dutifully reported the meeting to Menzies, who, though also surprised, noted the objections. Thus, when he announced the identity of the new minister in July, he did not name Osborne. He named McMahon.

A disappointed and humiliated Osborne now learned of the deputation that had waited on Harrison. He went to see Harrison to ask if it was true. Harrison confirmed it. "I want to ask one thing only," Osborne said to him. "Was Bill McMahon a member of that deputation?"

Harrison looked down his nose and said that he was.

Osborne regarded it as an act of treachery. Before this, he and McMahon had been friendly. "In those days we used to talk to each other quite freely," he recalled. McMahon had given Osborne a lift down to Canberra after the 1949 election, so that they could both go into the House of Representatives and see where they would sit. They were both solicitors, both from Sydney. This changed that. A journalist told Osborne that although it was not uncommon to have your throat cut in politics, it was unforgiveable that he had been allowed to walk around for three weeks without knowing it had been cut. Osborne agreed. "That experience had a profound effect on me," he said later. "I had gone into Parliament full of what I would call an ebullient self-confidence. It destroyed that. It altered my political bearing. I became very unsure of myself for a while and a bit cagey. [...] After that I found it very difficult to have anything to do with McMahon at all."[13]

McMahon never spoke of this incident in these terms. He had no regrets about his actions. He believed that Menzies had promised him the appointment long before the 1951 elections. It was his spot, and friends and colleagues had helped ensure that he received it.[14] As he was to say:

> I had to wait some weeks, during which time I was informed on a couple of occasions that somebody else might be appointed in my stead. Then I received advice from a Cabinet minister. I went to Ezra Norton of the *Daily Mirror* and sought his support. Within a couple of days I became a member of Cabinet. [...] I learned in those days that there always is someone able to give us guidance of a very helpful kind.[15]

The appointment as Minister for the Navy and for Air gave McMahon his first step on the ministerial ladder; it also established that McMahon was willing to undermine and manipulate for his own advancement. Plainly, there was no moral transgression in betrayal or embarrassment in self-interest. The episode pointed to a method of behaviour, one that might very well have been encouraged by the failure of colleagues to muster any kind of adverse consequence for it.[16]

How McMahon became prime minister was not the only question my biography aimed to answer. It was also directed at discovering what exactly McMahon did in the office he had striven for so long to attain – and to explain why he lost it at the 1972 election.

Answers to the latter have never been in short supply, but to the former there has been precious little. But for a few partial accounts, McMahon's actions and those of his government have never been the subject of a sustained study that could identify successes and failings. The silence left and the drama that followed allowed for the pervasive and mistaken sense that nothing had happened under McMahon. And yet an inspection of the legislative record, Cabinet papers and chronology showed a government and a prime minister wrestling with substantial issues. As Donald Horne – in one of the few partial accounts of the McMahon Government written – was to argue:

> [The McMahon Government] opened a way towards reform of the Australian constitution, dismantled much of the censorship of film and books, required a timetable for the decolonisation of New Guinea, recognised the need for planning for the "environment", withdrew Australian troops from Vietnam, downgraded the five-power Malaysia-Singapore alliance, further diversified the immigration program, foreshadowed the paramountcy of consumer rights and spoke of sweeping new laws against monopolies and restrictive trade practices, began phasing out the means test on pensions, encouraged discussion on a national superannuation scheme, set up a poverty enquiry, adopted an ambitious new framework for urban growth and proclaimed a new policy to control foreign investments.[17]

Directed, in no small part, by McMahon, the government's at-tempts to grapple with the social, economic, and political changes flowering in Australia were undoubtedly reactive. But those attempts were, at times, successful. The biography allowed me to bring those successes into focus; it also facilitated an understanding of why McMahon and his government failed – on China, on apartheid, on the economic challenges, on Vietnam, on land rights for Aborigines, and on poverty – and how these failings led to its defeat at the 1972 election.

In doing so, it became clear that the value of a biography of McMahon was not merely to be found in the information it could provide on McMahon alone; it was also bound up in the wider arc of history that the biography could explore. Leon Edel's argument that biography "reveals the individual within history, within an ethos and a social complex", points to this compelling characteristic of biographical writing: although the spotlight of a biographical study remains fixed on the individual, its sweep takes in much more.[18] Biography illuminates place, culture, and society, contextualising the life as it has been lived, drawing events together as they have been experienced.

The biography allowed a greater exploration of Australian history: from the Menzies governments to McMahon's, to those of Whitlam and Fraser. It extended beyond the government that McMahon had led, allowed a way to connect disparate events together, make them intelligible. Studying constitutional law at the University of Sydney in 1929, for example, McMahon came under the tutelage of Sir John Peden, the dean of the Law School. Peden was an advocate of the theories of A. V. Dicey, the English jurist who had promoted monarchical powers as a bulwark against the Home Rule movement in Ireland in the 1880s. Regarding Dicey's *Introduction to the Study of the Law of the Constitution* as "almost sacred", Peden set it as a class text and would expound on the unwritten powers that could regulate governments. Three of Peden's other students absorbed and reacted to this: the future attorney-general and chief justice of the High Court, Garfield Barwick, agreed that the power to withdraw a commission was "always available as a last resort". Justice of the High Court and leader of the parliamentary Labor Party, Herbert

Vere "Doc" Evatt, agreed that the powers existed but argued that they should be set down and codified. Future governor-general John Kerr absorbed all these arguments and views: as he would say later, the question of the reserve powers was a "reality" for him from his early student days.

Knowledge of McMahon's study under Peden allowed me to link his life with seminal events in Australia's history. The line from Peden's arguments to Sir Philip Game's dismissal of Jack Lang could be extended to the dismissal of the Whitlam Government in 1975, in which Barwick and Kerr would both play a part. The link was not merely one of convenience, either: McMahon had disagreed with Peden's argument about the existence of the reserve powers. He did not believe that they existed.

That McMahon's life could illuminate events and elements of Australia's history was a point that his one-time publisher, Richard Smart, had noted. In the 1980s, Smart had agreed to publish McMahon's autobiography. Although McMahon hardly had the stature of Menzies or Whitlam, his life was an interesting one, touching on a sweep of important events and moments in Australian history. "There's a bloody good story in there," Smart would say. McMahon would never finish that autobiography, nor see it published, but the example was telling. A study of his life could illuminate far more than people might think.

When I first contacted John Nethercote to seek his advice about a book on McMahon, he apprehended all of the above immediately. Meeting over coffee at his home, he noted the gap that existed in the historical record, and the questions that arose from McMahon's becoming prime minister. It was signal to his interest in seeing this gap filled and those questions answered that, before the first cup of coffee was gone, John had offered to read and comment on the manuscript. "I did this for Allan Martin, who wrote on Menzies," he said to me, "and I did the same for Tom Frame when he wrote his biography of Harold Holt. I also did this for Ian Hancock's John Gorton." Then John said, with a smile of satisfaction, "Now, with Billy McMahon – I think I'd like to get the full set."

Endnotes

1 Paul Hasluck, *The Chance of Politics,* ed. Nicholas Hasluck, Text, Melbourne, 1997, 133; Sir Garfield Barwick, interviewed by J. D. B. Miller, NLA Oral History, TRC 499/1, 37; Dudley Erwin interviewed by Robert Linford, NLA Oral History, TRC 4900/7, 5:10; Peter Howson interviewed by Jonathan Gaul, NLA Oral History, TRC 229, 4:1/22.

2 Arthur Fadden to Ulrich Ellis, 17 March 1971, NLA MS1006, Box 30.

3 Paul Hasluck, "The prospects of the McMahon Government", 5 April 1971, NAA: M1767, 3.

4 Hasluck, 1997, 185.

5 Strangio, in Strangio, 't Hart, and Walter (eds), 2013.

6 Don Watson, *Recollections of a Bleeding Heart: A Portrait of Paul Keating,* Viking, Sydney, 2012, 132.

7 Ian Hancock, *The Liberals: The NSW Division 1945–2000,* Federation Press, Annandale, 2007, 7.

8 Troy Bramston, "Prime ministers and their biographers: it's better to get along", *The Australian,* 18 November 2017.

9 James Walter, "The 'Life Myth', 'Short Lives', and Dealing With Live Subjects in Political Biography", *Australian Political Lives: Chronicling Political Careers and Administrative Histories,* eds, Tracey Arklay, John Wanna and J. R. Nethercote, ANU E-Press, 2006, 29–34.

10 E. H. Carr, *What is History?,* Penguin, Australia, 2008, 45.

11 Ian Hancock, *National and Permanent? The Federal Organisation of the Liberal Party of Australia, 1945–1965,* Melbourne University Press, Melbourne, 2000, 97.

12 "Field narrows for final Cabinet post", *Northern Star,* 2 June 1951, 5.

13 Frederick Osborne interviewed by Ron Hurst, NLA Oral History, TRC 4900/108. The quote Osborne attributes to a journalist may also be found in Hal Myers, *The Whispering Gallery,* Kangaroo Press, Brisbane, 1998, 112. According to Osborne, Menzies later remarked that colleagues had betrayed him.

14 Evan Whitton, "Mr Prime Minister: Jeff Bate, MHR, rates the 4 he served under", *Daily Telegraph,* 24 October 1972, 8.

15 McMahon, *CPD HoR,* 109, 23 May 1978, 2232–34.

16 McMahon and Hurford, *CPD HoR,* 76, 22 February 1972, 7.

17 Donald Horne, *Time of Hope: Australia 1966–72,* Angus and Robertson, Sydney, 1980.

18 Leon Edel, *Writing Lives: Principia Biographica,* W. W. Norton, New York, 1984, 13–14.

20

Biography of a Mandarin

Writing about Sir Arthur Tange

Peter Edwards

John Nethercote has contributed notably to several areas of Australian political history, but in none is his pre-eminence more obvious than the politics of the upper reaches of the Commonwealth public service (now the Australian public service) and the interactions of departmental heads with ministers. From the 1940s to the 1980s, what we now call the "governance" of Australia centred on these interactions. One way into a better understanding of that process is to research and write biographies of the leading mandarins, as the top officials are semi-respectfully known, to be read alongside studies of prime ministers and ministers, as well as studies of policy.

In the late 1990s I was ending my formal role as Official Historian of Australia's involvement in South-east Asian Conflicts 1948-1975 – that is, the Malayan Emergency, the Indonesian Confrontation and the Vietnam War. When seeking a topic that would build on my experience of working on this area, but would also be a distinctly fresh approach, I recalled something that Frank Crowley had said to a tutorial of undergraduates taking his Australian history course at the University of Western Australia in the 1960s: "Every historian at some stage should write a biography." Crowley was at the time engaged on his two-volume *magnum opus* on Sir John Forrest.

I linked this observation with my own longstanding interest in the importance of public servants and their relationships with politicians. My first job after completing my doctoral thesis was helping

Professor R. G. "Bob" Neale to establish the historical section of the Department of Foreign Affairs. One task that Neale assigned me was to write what appears as Appendix II in volume I of *Documents on Australian Foreign Policy 1937-49*, on the early history of attempts to found a foreign office and diplomatic service.[1] The topic engaged me and I expanded it into my first book, *Prime Ministers and Diplomats: The Making of Australian Foreign Policy 1901-1949*.[2]

Combining these two areas, it occurred to me that a number of historians had referred to the "formidable" public servant, Sir Arthur Tange, but without elucidating that adjective. I had interviewed Sir Arthur for the official history, and been impressed by his ability to recall the events in which he had been engaged and to put them into context. Perhaps, I wondered, here was a subject who could open up a new line of inquiry into the period I had been studying. The gods smiled on the idea. The Department of Defence was willing to support the project, without directing its judgments. No less importantly, Tange himself was willing to collaborate. Well into retirement, he was happy to get his recollections, and his views, on the record. He had started work on his own memoir, and he had a collection of personal papers in the study of his home in Manuka. Thus began what became a three-part project. I would write a traditional, cradle-to-grave biography;[3] I would edit and prepare for publication his memoir, a rough draft of which he had written by the time he died;[4] and I would sort and catalogue his papers for the Manuscripts Section of the National Library of Australia.[5] The three-in-one nature of the project made possible a more thorough examination of the man and his work than would any single part of it.

The personal papers were held in two filing cabinets in the study at his home. I was given access to one. Much of the early work on the project consisted in my going to his house and working through the material, often having a light lunch which he prepared and over which we talked much more candidly than would have been possible in a formal interview. Often I was researching in his study while he was writing his memoir, sitting at his dining-room table and tapping away on an aged typewriter. It seemed to me that, as I gained his confidence, more material appeared in the filing cabinet to which I had access.

The personal papers complemented the vast amount of official archival material. I was reasonably familiar with much of this, having spent many years on the official history, but the volume of papers that had crossed Tange's desk during his eleven years as Secretary of the Department of External Affairs (1954-65), and then another ten as Secretary of the Department of Defence (1970-79), was enormous. Lack of material was never a problem. Achieving some sort of mastery of the vast mass was a problem, as was seeking to ensure that I saw what was truly significant in assessing his personal role.

The aim of the book was not just to tell an individual's story, but to show what effect the personality of a long-serving departmental head had on major policy developments. The frequent description of Tange as "formidable" denoted a personality and style of administration that inspired devotion from some and deep hostility from others. Admirers and detractors alike told many stories about him. The wider question was whether this mattered. Were those stories merely gossip, of interest only to denizens of Canberra, or did they have important implications for the making and implementation of policy? Did Tange's personality influence major decisions of foreign and defence policy in the 1950s, 1960s and 1970s? More broadly, how and why did the Menzies Government come to rely heavily on senior public servants, including those known in the 1950s as "the seven dwarfs"? How did that translate into the era of Tange and Sir Frederick Wheeler, the last two great mandarins of the era? What really was the significance of the Commonwealth Club, and those who referred to themselves as "the sergeants' mess" within the Club?

Most of the stories about Tange that resonated for years afterwards arose from his final position, as Secretary of the Defence Department from 1970 to 1979. One of the lessons that emerged from a biographical approach was the importance of his earlier, eleven-year term as Secretary of the Department of External (later Foreign) Affairs, from 1954 to 1965. A second lesson was that, in both cases, relations between the departmental head and the minister, and often the prime minister, were crucially important. While politicians and journalists often focus on diplomats and other public servants in terms of their assumed partisanship, in fact the personality of the minister and his (in Tange's day, ministers and permanent heads were all male) attitude to public servants was far more important. In External Affairs, Tange's relations with his ministers ranged from the near-filial (R. G. Casey) through warm and constructive (Percy Spender, before Tange became Secretary, and Garfield Barwick) to formal (Menzies, as his own foreign minister for two years) to frigid (Paul Hasluck). Did this matter? It seemed to me no coincidence that the best and most enduring policy decisions, such as the ANZUS treaty and the Colombo Plan, emerged when the minister and the department, especially the permanent head and the senior officers, were working well together; while the most damaging decisions, such as the Suez crisis of 1956 and the commitment of combat forces to Vietnam, arose when the department was sidelined or overruled.

Tange's relations with successive ministers in his decade at Defence were similarly varied, again owing more to personality than to party. Tange had a poor opinion of David Fairbairn, for example, not least because the former RAAF officer showed too much deference to his former Air Force colleagues. By contrast, after a very rocky start, he established an excellent relationship with the minister who appointed him, the young and assertive Malcolm Fraser. Together they set about jolting the clumsy Defence machinery into a more effective body. Fraser's departure, in the manoeuvre that brought down John Gorton as prime minister, was one of the few occasions when Tange was visibly moved by the fate of a minister. Fraser later said that Tange was the public servant he most admired in his time in high office, and apparently regretted not appointing him as Secretary of the Department of the Prime Minister and Cabinet. A Fraser-Tange combination at the head of the ministry and the public service would have struck fear into the hearts of many in Canberra at that time.

For rather different reasons, Tange thought that Lance Barnard, Whitlam's first Minister for Defence as well as his loyal Deputy

Prime Minister, was too often underestimated. When Barnard departed for a diplomatic post, some observers expected fireworks with his successor, Bill Morrison, knowing that as a young diplomat, Morrison had incurred the wrath of his then departmental head – Tange. In fact, Morrison was more than happy to leave Tange in place, as he was not only implementing Labor's organisational and policy reforms in Defence, but was also taking the brunt of the criticism for them, when the Government had more than enough political battles on other fronts.

Tange came to be known more for the reforms of Defence organisation than for any other role in the public service. His report on the reorganisation of what had been the Defence group of departments, *Australian Defence: Report on the Reorganisation of the Defence Group of Departments*, AGPS, 1974, was generally known as the Tange report, and the major reforms that followed, including merging the service departments and the Supply department into the Defence Department, abolishing the boards that had administered each service, and creating the "diarchy" of the civilian Secretary and the uniformed Chief of the Defence Force at the head of the organisation, were commonly called the Tange reforms. To some degree, this was the focal point of the whole biography, and its principal *raison d'être*. A biography of the public servant at the centre of the project was, it seemed to me, the best way to understand and explain how and why these controversial but enduring reforms came into existence. One needed to understand Tange's personality, as well as the political and administrative context, to comprehend how and why the inquiry, and the subsequent report, took the shape that they did.

So much attention has been given to Tange's role in the reform of the structures and administration of Defence that it has sometimes been overlooked that he had a real interest in strategic policy and what he liked to call "higher defence policy." A major theme in strategic policy during his time in Defence, and a probable reason why senior people in Defence, notably the then Deputy Secretary (Strategy), Hugh White, were interested in supporting the project, was the emergence of the concept of "the self-reliant defence of Australia" as the basis of Australia's strategic posture. Tange claimed to be the author of the term, "self-reliance", in this context, and it emerged in the first Defence White Paper, prepared in his time as Secretary. It was only by examining the preceding years, especially tracing Tange's interaction with departments and ministers, that one could see how this idea, associated with a more nuanced approach to the Australian-American alliance, came to dominate official thinking.

When embarking on the biography, I had not realised the extent to which many of the reforms and concepts for which Tange was renowned, sometimes revered and sometimes reviled, when in Defence in the 1970s had been based on his experience in External Affairs, in the late 1950s and early 1960s. Tange's attitude to Australia's relations with the nations that Menzies liked to call "our great and powerful friends," Britain and the United States, and his emphasis on the importance of Australia's growing relationships with the newly independent nations in Asia, all emerged in a policy document, a sort of personal White Paper on foreign policy, that Tange wrote in 1955, soon after becoming head of External Affairs. The attitudes revealed there were reinforced by developments in Australia's near north, especially the Dutch New Guinea dispute, which brought home the difference between Australian and American policies towards Indonesia. An important part of his role as Secretary of External Affairs was to sit on the Defence Committee alongside the service chiefs and other senior civilian public servants. It now seems clear that Tange was the moving force behind the attempt by the Defence Committee (which was chaired by the Secretary of the Defence Department, the position he would later assume) to persuade the government to adopt a more self-reliant posture in defence policy, reducing the heavy reliance on allies.

Similarly, Tange's experience in External Affairs was the origin of his views on the importance of a closer relationship between the services, and of educating senior officers of all three armed services to realise that they were not only warriors but also public servants, expected to give sound advice on policy options to the government of the day. Tange was a strong supporter of the creation of the Australian Defence Force Academy, which would give young officers of the three services not just training in military skills but also a broad and liberal education in such fields as the history and politics of the region. These views emerged not only from Tange's experience in External Affairs, but also from his subsequent diplomatic post as High Commissioner to India and his visits to Vietnam, where he saw American generals discussing the intersection of political and military concerns. The troubled history of the proposal to form what we now know as the Australian Defence Force Academy also illustrated the importance of a close relationship between a departmental head and a minister or prime minister. The concept of a tri-service academy had many opponents from within the services and from members of the coalition parties. ADFA only came into being because Tange and Fraser were able jointly to keep the project alive in a hostile environment.

As for any biographer, a central challenge was to get as close as possible to one's subject while also seeking to achieve some distance, in order to make judgments with a degree of objectivity. I had constantly to remind myself that this elderly man, who welcomed me into his home and facilitated my work, was also the most feared departmental head of his day, the man whose rages were the stuff of legend. Inevitably I was drawn into seeing issues from his perspective. Time after time a matter of foreign or defence policy, or of the role of the public service, would surface in a news bulletin and I would think – or say, to the understandable frustration of my wife – "I know what Arthur would think about this", or "Tange always used to say . . . ". The more I came to see of his personal life, and came to know his family, the more difficult it was to establish a degree of distance. It is a sad fact that his death, while I was in the midst of the project, probably enabled me to write with greater objectivity than would have been been possible with a subject still alive.

The process of entering his mind was gained largely, not in formal interviews with Tange so much as in informal conversations. These conversations were made possible because for much of the time, while I was working on his papers, arising from whatever topic I had just been researching, I was in his study, or at table with him during occasional breaks. These informal conversations could often be unguarded and revealing, not least on the importance of interpersonal relations and their impact on major and minor decisions. I supplemented the conversations with Tange himself with as many interviews as possible, of widely varying degrees of formality, with those who knew him or had worked with him in whatever capacity. For any subject, but especially for someone whose personality was as prominent as Tange's, a biographer had to seek as many perspectives as possible – those of fervent admirers, harsh critics, and every shade in between. He was a man of strong opinions, and a man who generated strong opinions, and it was a biographer's task to explain why.

The importance of getting this right has hit me with considerable force as I subsequently wrote a biography of Robert Marsden Hope, the judge who conducted two Royal Commissions on the intelligence and security services.[6] A major theme of this latter book is that the most significant critic of the reforms proposed by Hope's first Royal Commission in the mid-1970s was Tange. They clashed over the respective roles in assessment of the Joint Intelligence Organisation (now the Defence Intelligence Organisation), an important agency within Tange's department, and the new organisation proposed by Hope, the Office of National Assessments (recently upgraded to the Office of National Intelligence). Hope was also highly critical of the directive under which the Australian Secret Intelligence Service (ASIS) operated – a directive that had been drafted by Tange as Secretary of External Affairs. There is no little irony in the situation. In two important fields of national security policy, defence and intelligence, Whitlam entrusted the preparation of major structural and policy reforms to individuals he respected outside the political sphere, a public servant and a judge. Each tackled the task with great energy and skill; each produced results that have proved of enduring value to governments of all persuasions for several decades; each owed his success to his personality as much as to his intellect and experience. But far from respecting their similar tasks, they clashed in one of the most important conflicts in the structural reform of

Australia's national security agencies in the last fifty years. As the biographer of both, I faced the unexpected challenge of being fair to each. There will be no more astute judge of whether I meet that challenge than John Nethercote.

Endnotes

[1] "The Organisation of Australia's External Relations", Appendix II, R. G.Neale (ed.), P. G. Edwards and H. Kenway (asst. eds), *Documents on Australian Foreign Policy 1937-49, Vol. I, 1937-38*, Australian Government Publishing Service, Canberra, 1975, 544-55.

[2] P. G. Edwards, *The Making of Australian Foreign Policy 1901-1949*, Oxford University Press, Melbourne, 1983.

[3] Peter Edwards, *Arthur Tange: Last of the Mandarins*, Allen & Unwin, Sydney, 2006.

[4] Sir Arthur Tange (ed. Peter Edwards), *Defence Policy-Making: A Close-up View, 1950-1980*, Canberra Papers on Strategy and Defence No. 169, ANU E-press, Australian National University, Canberra, 2008.

[5] MS9847, Manuscripts Collection, National Library of Australia.

[6] Peter Edwards, *Law, Politics and Intelligence: A Life of Robert Hope*, NewSouth, Sydney, 2020.

21

Biography of a Diplomat

Jeremy Hearder

Diplomats write memoirs if they are prepared to do the necessary work. Many more would have a tale worth telling but a sense of discretion leads them to hesitate to lift the veil a little on what they knew and saw. Or memoirs become a project that gets put off, and never done. Memoirs vastly outnumber biographies, and those that do come to fruition often make a valuable contribution, especially if written not long after their authors' period of service, and with all the authority of first-hand knowledge and feel for situations.

Biographies of diplomats take longer to complete, with the research into official records and personal papers, and interviewing contemporaries of the subject. But with the passing of time a biographer can be more objective, and more frank, than the diplomat's memoir, and can explain better the wider significance of a diplomat's contribution.

Among the biographer's sources are interviews with those still around who knew or worked with the subject. Valuable information can emerge that is not recorded elsewhere or known to others. In the course of a diplomatic career, however, with postings in many different countries, this can amount to an enormous number of potential interviews. In my biography of Sir James Plimsoll[1], the number ran into hundreds.

Pioneers

In writing a biography it is often difficult to find out about the early life and formation of the subject: especially where there is little in the way of written material, and reluctance to disclose much about early lives even to close friends. But the search is essential and rewarding, because upbringing, formation and early experiences are usually critical to understanding the character, capacity and motivation that come to the fore in a person's later life. And this is especially the case in trying to understand how many pioneer Australian diplomats managed on their first assignment abroad, in learning to adapt to a profession hitherto unknown in the Australian Government.

During the period just before the Second World War, and in the years immediately after, people of Plimsoll's generation took up the task of establishing Australian diplomatic missions abroad, and the role of representing Australia internationally. This was at a time when the Department of External Affairs in Canberra was tiny and struggling with added responsibilities and expectations of successive governments.

A constant problem was to manage a growing diplomatic network. Postings often happened in an ad hoc fashion, with little notice of a move. There was little capacity to train and brief officers embarking on postings. In 1924 Prime Minister S.M. Bruce had taken advice from a member of the UK Foreign Office, and decided not to set up an Australian foreign service at that time.[2] But, later, towards the end of the 1930s, there seems to have been no attempt to get some expert advice from the United Kingdom about actually setting up some Australian missions overseas when the decision was taken to do so: perhaps with the approaching war in Europe no such adviser could have been made available to go to Australia. But many of those posted for the first time were thrown in at the deep end and had to fend for themselves.

The following is a brief outline of the early background and experience of James Plimsoll and of Tom Critchley, two of Australia's most distinguished diplomats. In the 1940s few Australians had had any international experience. For both Plimsoll and Critchley it was such experience that came their way at, or towards, the end of the War, that was an important element in motivating them in each case to become diplomats and to be able quickly to perform in an outstanding way.

Plimsoll's background

Plimsoll's qualities of self-discipline and hard work developed in the era of the Depression – full-time work in a bank for five and half days a week, and university studies in the evenings.

Over eight years as an evening student at the University of Sydney he earned degrees in Economics and then Arts, while at the same time involving himself in student affairs, eventually becoming President of the Union, during which he experienced working with fellow students and professors, and learned to speak without notes.[3]

In the ensuing three years, 1942-45, he worked as an Army captain in the intellectually high-powered Army Directorate of Research in Melbourne, which included many who were or would become professors. His work involved discussions and recommendations about Australia's future role in post-war policy towards Papua and New Guinea and the region to Australia's north, and a written study of United States current affairs.[4]

Then, early in 1945, came a life-changing move. He went to the United States to attend a military training course, mainly about Japan, for hundreds of US and British army officers. Plimsoll finished second overall. This, in turn, led to him working in the Australian Military Mission in Washington. But it took three months for the appointment to be formally approved. Plimsoll spent the time on an intensive personal study trip, getting to know some of the USA, travelling through New England and the Midwest.[5]

In October 1945, with the War over, Major Plimsoll, like many others in the Australian Military Mission, was expecting to return to Australia, demobilise and resume his career as a bank economist in Sydney. Out of the blue the short-staffed Australian Legation in Washington asked Plimsoll to help an officer from Canberra prepare for the imminent arrival of Dr Evatt, Australia's Minister for External Affairs, for the inaugural meeting in Washington of the Far Eastern Commission (FEC). This was being set up following the Potsdam Agreement, to facilitate allied coordination of post-war policy towards Japan.

Plimsoll adapted to the task, working day and night for three days, particularly helping prepare a speech for Dr Evatt to deliver; and then through the three weeks of the meeting. Dr Evatt was impressed with Plimsoll and arranged with the Australian Army for Plimsoll to remain in Washington in a diplomatic role as Australia's Representative on the FEC for the next two years. Evatt subsequently persuaded Plimsoll to join External Affairs.[6]

In 1950, after only three years, mainly spent at Australia's Mission to the United Nations in New York, Plimsoll achieved rapid promotion to ambassadorial level. This was as Australian representative in the United Nations Committee for Unification and Rehabilitation in Korea (UNCURK), stationed in Korea during the 1950-53 war there, where his performance so impressed the Americans that, months after he returned to Canberra, Washington asked Canberra to send him back to Korea.

It was the beginning of a most distinguished diplomatic career.

Tom Critchley's background

To some extent Plimsoll's early life mirrors that of Tom Critchley, another pioneer diplomat who served Australia with great distinction. Like Plimsoll, Critchley worked in a bank, the Rural Bank of NSW, and studied economics in the same evening classes as Plimsoll at Sydney University. A similarly disciplined worker, Critchley was a much more able economist than Plimsoll, and was promoted to work in the Bank's research department while still an undergraduate. Following graduation he worked in the NSW State Treasury and the Premier's Department, and was invited to join a small group to do research leading to a book, *Australia Foots the Bill*, about wartime economic policy. Others in the group included Arthur Tange and Syd Butlin.

Unable to become a pilot in the RAAF owing to colour blindness, he transferred to the Army as a captain while, at the same time, working as an economic adviser in the Federal Department of War Organisation of Industry in Melbourne. In the Bank, at university and, in later work, his supervisors included people of considerable significance: John Crawford,[7] H. D. Black and Ronald Walker.[8]

Critchley wanted to do something a little closer to the action in the war. By chance, early in 1944, an opportunity for him to work in New Delhi arose. He seized it with both hands; it was an experience which would have a critical influence on him. Critchley's role was as Director of Research and Information as part of the Far East Bureau, an offshoot of the UK Ministry of Overseas Information. He supervised 12 people who worked on producing weekly reports on the situation in Japanese-occupied areas of Asia, and in Japan itself. He reported to a UK Foreign Office representative, Esler Dening, who was also Chief Political Adviser to Admiral Mountbatten, UK Supreme Allied Commander, South East Asia Command.

Dening had an unusual background. He was born in Japan of a British father and Australian mother. In 1915, at the age of 18, with his father having died and his mother having returned to Australia, he went to Australia from Japan to enlist in the Australian Imperial Force (AIF), in which he served with distinction in the campaigns in France.[9] On demobilisation he joined the UK Consular Service, in which he served for 18 years in Japan, Korea, the Philippines and Manchuria, accumulating considerable first-hand knowledge of the area.

With his AIF experience, Dening would have had some understanding of Australians. But he was some 20 years older than Critchley, and he was in favour of the UK and other colonial powers holding on to their possessions in the area.[10] Further, he was "not very happy in the post. He was impatient with the workings of the military mind".[11] These factors may have led to a much less close working relationship for Critchley with his chief, compared with those which Critchley enjoyed with his staff.

They were of similar age to him, 12 were graduates, most had specialised knowledge of conditions in particular [Asian] countries and at least 10 different nationalities were represented.[12] He socialised and played tennis with them, many of whom he would meet again elsewhere. Many "had either held , or were destined to hold, influential positions in their own countries". An example was Thanat Khoman, later a long-serving Foreign Minister of Thailand. He absorbed from them "a good understanding of neighbouring Asian countries, which I had only known about vaguely from Australia".[13] From them Critchley became aware of the mood for change in the Asian region, how the region was changing with rising nationalism and opposition to continued colonial rule. He doubtless would have been influenced by the final years of movement for Indian independence that was playing out around him in Delhi.

All this experience had a major influence on Critchley. At the end of the War he chose to take up an offer to join External Affairs in Canberra, over a number of other job offers in India and Australia. He became head of the Economic Section in the Department.

Late in 1946 he saw an advertisement for an ANU Social Science Research Fellowship. He applied, with a proposal to work on the economic implications of the current Australian immigration policy. He had thought a lot about the issue before leaving India, where he had written a pamphlet on Australia and New Zealand at the invitation of Oxford University Press there, in which he had been encouraged to include as much as possible about immigration in response to likely interest of Indian readers.[14]

In his ANU application Critchley expressed the view that it would be necessary in the years ahead to be prepared for the need for some change, if not in the overall policy. He foresaw that "in the not too distant future we shall be forced to make concessions. Important factors working in this direction are the resurgence of Asia . . . and the need for Australia to orient her economic and political policy towards her neighbours".[15] Such thinking would have been rare in Australia at the time, especially from a junior public servant. It was indicative of the impact his time in India had had on his thinking. His application was not, however, successful.

After about 18 months in Canberra, late in 1947, he was sent abroad to a job, in retrospect, almost tailor-made for him, given the experience he had had in India. This was to assist Judge Richard Kirby in the Australian delegation to the United Nations Good Offices Commission to Indonesia. Indonesian independence advocates had nominated Australia to assist them in their negotiations with the Dutch who were unwilling to let go. Also involved were delegations from Belgium, assisting the Dutch; and the United States.

Negotiations were difficult and protracted. After a few months Kirby was summoned home and, contrary to his own expectations and advice, was not replaced. Instead, despite his comparative youth and inexperience, it was Critchley who became the principal Australian representative, assisting the Indonesians in their negotiations with the Dutch.

Australian policy was to give sympathetic support to the Indonesian leaders in their quest, both as a matter of principle but also in Australia's national interest as a near neighbour. In the course of two years, Critchley saw this through to a successful conclusion. A remarkable feat, and his name was made among Indonesian leaders, including President Sukarno. It was a stepping-stone to a distinguished career in the region as an Australian diplomatic representative.

There were some similarities. Neither Plimsoll nor Critchley originally had any intention of becoming a diplomat, not so much out of lack of interest but from lack of prior knowledge. This came to them by chance, through opportunities to work abroad in the Indo-Pacific region during the later part of the war – the first journey outside of Australia for each.

During their respective careers neither was keen to work in Canberra. It was working abroad that motivated them. Plimsoll tolerated two long stays in Canberra; Critchley avoided any lengthy stays.

For relaxation Plimsoll could be absorbed in art or examining old buildings, or reading works of literature. But he rarely took holidays: "His mind was always churning".[16] Critchley's was a more rounded approach. Good at sport at school, he had a lifelong enthusiasm for tennis, golf and surfing. And his mother insisted that he learnt the piano, which led to another life-long enthusiasm for playing jazz piano in bands – which helped him pay his way through university, and gave him another relaxation away from work.[17] He also learnt to fly after the war. Thus he had a number of ways of getting right away from work.

Critchley also become adept at using sport, especially golf, as a means of developing close contacts with local ministers and others wherever he was posted.

For Plimsoll and Critchley, as for others of that generation, in going about their business as Heads of Mission they tended to be loners – especially with high level work. This came of being used to working either in very small posts or being very much on their own. This would be accentuated by two factors: Increasing self-confidence, and – given the poor communication with Canberra – if they felt confident they understood the Government's views (for example, Plimsoll/Spender/Korea, and Plimsoll, Menzies and the United Nations).

The careers of both Plimsoll and Critchley spanned a period that saw the evolution of Australia into a credible member of the international community, with a professional foreign service.

Endnotes

[1] Jeremy Hearder, *Jim Plim Ambassador Extraordinary. A Biography of Sir James Plimsoll*, Connor Court, Brisbane, 2015.

[2] David Lee, *Stanley Melbourne Bruce Australian Internationalist*, Continuum International Publishing Group, NY, 2010, 47.

[3] Hearder, op. cit., 15-18.

[4] Ibid,, 29.

[5] Ibid., 34-7.

[6] Ibid., 39-40, 46-7.

[7] Later Sir John Crawford, a leading figure in Canberra and overseas in the decades after the War as Secretary, Department of Commerce and Agricultuire, then Trade; Vice Chancellor the ANU.

[8] Later Sir Hermann Black, Chancellor, University of Sydney, and Sir Ronald Walker, prominent economist and Australian diplomat.

9 Entry for Dening in "Discovering Anzacs.naa.gov.au". Also article about Dening's father in Hamish Brain "Walter Dening (1846-1913) and Japan" in Hugh Cortazzi (ed.), *Britain and Japan: Biographical Portraits* , Vol. vii, Brill, Leiden, Netherlands, 2010, 384-5.

10 "Dening was a "stolid imperialist" in outlook and convinced that the British Empire would be an 'essential factor' in the maintenance of Far Eastern peace". Christopher Baxter, *The Great Power Struggle in East Asia*, 1944-50. *Britain, America and Post-War Rivalry*. Palgrave Macmillan, London, 2009, 10.

11 Sir Norman Brain, Obituary on Dening in *Asian Affairs*, 8(2), 1977, 241.

12 Critchley letter of 28 November 1946 to Secretary of Interim Council of the ANU. EA folder BW 4795 Critchley Papers.

13 Critchley, Oral History, ANU, 5.

14 Letter of 13 March 1946, from OUP Madras, India. Critchley Papers.

15 Critchley letter of 28 November 1946, to Sec Interim Council ANU. Critchley Papers.

16 Lt-Cdr. R. J. Griggs, later Vice-Admiral Griggs, Deputy Chief, Australia Defence Forces, conversation, 2 March 1998.

17 Laurie Critchley (daughter), conversation, 7 November 2017.

22

Gaudron's Law
A Tool for Change

Pamela Burton

The Nethercote effect

John Nethercote mentored my writing of *From Moree to Mabo: the Mary Gaudron story*.[1] He was an unlikely mentor for a judicial biography of a radical woman lawyer who did not want her story told, and written by another woman lawyer, who did. John was, however, the best person for the job of, what Professor Jonathan Pincus cheekily calls, "the midwifing process". Nethercote defined his role early in the piece: "Can't have it read as a feminist whinge", he would say, and "Must not be a hagiography", and "Just because she is a woman, and a left winger, does not mean she is to be applauded."

That set the tone for our writing relationship. Importantly, I am grateful for his sharp eye for factual errors, his memory for historical detail, and the guidance he gave me.

Introduction

This essay aims to illustrate the value of biography in capturing aspects of the social and political landscape of the times. In Mary Gaudron's case, her life story is set primarily in New South Wales, from the 1940s and into the present century.

I highlight some social, cultural and religious influences that I found helped to shape her world-view and how, in turn, the values she developed and her thinking ultimately influenced aspects of those same landscapes. I also consider the extent to which her working-class origins, her gender, and party-political leanings, posed obstacles to her career advancement and, on the other hand, the serendipitous circumstances that allowed them to work to her advantage.

My research into the Gaudron story started after her appointment to the High Court in 1987. It was not completed until after she retired from the Court in 2003. Thus, to an extent, I was able to observe her, and how others perceived her, in "real time". I approached the task, first, by considering the environments in which she grew up and worked, then locating her in that context, before carrying out an investigative process to fill in personal information.

Not having direct access to my subject necessitated digging deep in the search for information and, in so doing, I unearthed material which might have remained buried had I received and relied on information from the subject herself. In Gaudron's case, the picture unearthed, which I write more about below, turned out to be lively and colourful. It was the picture of a humble but extraordinary Australian who is now part of Australia's legal history.

Moree – the wrong side of the tracks

Mary Gaudron's political and legal life started at age eight when she met "Doc" Evatt in the hot, dusty and flood prone rural town of Moree in NSW, during his campaign for the "No" vote on the constitutional referendum to ban the Communist Party. She wanted to know what a "Constitution" was. The exchange between the driven man and the young girl resulted in Evatt sending her a copy of the Constitution. She waved it around at school, telling fellow pupils that she "knew" what she was going to be when she grew up – a lawyer. Not just a lawyer, but a barrister.

John Nethercote, reading an early draft of my book, seemed taken with my description of Evatt in 1951, campaigning with a loudhailer from the back of a blue Holden Ute in Moree. I told him that, like Mary Gaudron, I had met "the Doc" at the same age as she had, and I used my recall to try and project how she might have perceived the man. "It couldn't be any other party leader, but Evatt," Nethercote said, and encouraged me to plough on confidently with the work.

Gaudron was literally raised on the wrong side of the tracks, in a unionised community of shacks, tin sheds, tents and cottages of Moree railway workers neighbouring a camp of dispossessed Aboriginals on the banks of the Mehi River. Both communities held the status of battlers, somewhat alienated from the rich white community on the other side of the river.

I was impressed, not only by this unlikely start for the person destined to be first woman to be appointed a justice of the High Court of Australia, but by the symmetry to her story: she became one of the justices who decided Eddie Mabo's landmark case on indigenous land rights,[2] participated in the related *Wik* decision,[3] and gave a separate majority decision in favour of the waterside workers in the *Patrick Stevedores* case.[4] My book's sub-title, *From Moree to Mabo,* encapsulates this – but much happened in between, driven by various contemporary political events.

An interesting thing about Gaudron is that she did not see her childhood as underprivileged. Apart from some impish boasting that she had slept on dirt floors as a child, Gaudron was always aware of the privileges she and her family enjoyed as white Australians, compared with the nearby neglected poorer indigenous community. She and her siblings were well-fed, neatly attired and given the best education their parents and the Catholic church could afford.

It can be argued that Gaudron's "disadvantaged" working class environment aided her success. It gave her cause to think, to question things she observed around her. Both her family and her Catholic education encouraged that. As a child, she also had the benefit of being immersed in a sub-community that was welded together by union solidarity; something she no doubt recalled when resolving wage disputes as a deputy president of the Commonwealth Conciliation and Arbitration Commission.

A further help was that her parents were thoughtful and intelligent. As a child, Mary had thrust upon her every aspect of social injustice that her father associated with Australian society's class and racial prejudices. While her father's political values and union support were a strong influence, his tendency to violence when anger and alcohol got the better of him no doubt reinforced her later views on women's right to equality.

Her intelligence, emotional toughness, competitive spirit, and inquiring mind saw her progress with excellence through the Catholic education system to make possible a university education. At age 11, Gaudron earned a Catholic Diocesan bursary that plucked her out of her Moree world and into St Ursula's College, Armidale. The well-educated Ursuline nuns encouraged independent thinking. Ironically, while instilling some sound values, especially about the need to help the less-privileged, they also gave Gaudron the tools to question Catholic dogma. She accepted the social values and rejected much of the religious dogma.

Gaudron's achievements were not accomplished without having to overcome significant obstacles. Once at the University of Sydney, in the "everything is possible" 1960s, different influences affected her. She engaged on the fringes of the "Push"[5] and was awoken to the realities of the society she lived in: discrimination was not reserved for the indigenous population; it affected women as well. On first arriving at the Law School, then located in Phillip Street, she discovered that it was a boys' domain. Everyone in her classes, for example, was greeted by the salutation, "Gentlemen".

Her faith in the law as a tool for social change is likely to have had its roots in the University of Sydney Law School. She learned about the legislative and common law components of the law, its use of language and logic, and the divergent ways in which a body of law evolves, depending on the philosophic approach and style of reasoning of various judges.

She was exposed to competing philosophies of big intellects, like Julius Stone and his social progressive values, and Frank Hutley and his conservative regard for the existing law. She excelled and won the Sydney University Medal for Law; it was a close run thing – it was nearly taken from her in the interests of a male student who came second because, according to the Vice-Chancellor, he was more likely to obtain benefit from it, whereas Gaudron was now married and had a baby. That helped her determination to prove she was as effective as the best of the men. She did not have to wait to become a justice of the High Court before she did that.

Awakening – the "big end of town"

Gaudron confronted more prejudice upon entering Sydney's legal world. She has many anecdotes of absurd discrimination against women displayed by conservative male colleagues, and her gutsy reaction to it. Her witty and sharp retorts to offensive or nasty comments were exquisite, causing bystanders to laugh, and her victims to wince. Some called her "Mary the Merciless".

Gaudron's transition from being an impressionable young woman to an influential figure of power commenced at the Sydney Bar. She excelled as an advocate and earned the respect of her colleagues, notwithstanding her temperamental behaviour and use of "colourful" language. She identified with the political left at an opportune time. Jim Staples, later a fellow member of the Conciliation and Arbitration Commission, asked her to be his "junior" to represent Mount Isa mine worker, Pat Mackie, in a controversial case in which Clyde Cameron, MP, had an intense interest.[6] Gaudron saw Mackie as a fighter for workers' justice and was impressed by his passion.

The Labor leader, Gough Whitlam, became prime minister in December 1972. Before his cabinet was sworn in he asked Cameron to seek a reopening of the Equal Pay case then before the Conciliation and Arbitration Commission. Cameron remembered Gaudron from the Pat Mackie case. He arranged for Whitlam to give her the Equal Pay brief. It was a lucky break. She was the first woman to appear for the Commonwealth Government in a national pay case. The publicity put her on the legal map.

In 1974, aged 31, she was appointed a deputy president of the Commission itself, the youngest Federal judge and its second woman. Jim Staples followed soon after. Two cases in particular, both concerning equity for working women, were important to her: the Municipal Officers Association of Australia's successful claim that a clause be inserted into their award to prevent Queensland local governments from sacking women who married, and the national *Maternity Leave* case.[7]

She won Bob Hawke's praise in particular for the strong role she played in resolution of the Telecom dispute in 1978. Hawke was then President of the ACTU and led the union representatives in the conference of the warring parties, chaired by Gaudron. It was more good fortune that Hawke witnessed her ability in action; it was his government that later appointed Gaudron to the High Court.

In May 1980, Gaudron stormed out of the Commission over the Government's treatment of Jim Staples, who was embarrassing it and the Commission by speaking out publicly about his views on wage indexation guidelines. She did the unthinkable and resigned, forgoing her judgeship over a matter of principle, or so it seemed. As it transpired, her shock resignation proved to be a smart career move. The travel involved in the Commission's work was taking a toll of her personal life, and the job was not where she wanted to be for her foreseeable legal career. A Liberal government was now in power federally; Labor under Neville Wran was in power in New South Wales. She had reason to sense that there were better career prospects for her with the State government.

The "force of Gaudron's law"

Six months later, the Labor Premier of New South Wales, Neville Wran, appointed her Solicitor-General of NSW – the first appointment of a woman as solicitor-general in any of the States. Initially, the media seemed obsessed with her achievement as a wife and mother and used headlines such as "the law and the laundry" for stories about her, and "pregnant pause" when she appeared in the High Court just before her third child, Patrick, was born. It angered her. She wanted to be noted for her ability, not her size!

She had been attracted to the Wran Government's agenda of social reform although it was sidetracked and plagued by crime and corruption issues. This was the time when the so-called

"*Age* tapes" revealed dicey dealings of magistrates, police and politicians with crime bosses, gamblers and drug dealers. Yet analysis of her opinions confirms that she was "frank and fearless" in the advice she gave. She worked at high speed to study and absorb mountains of briefing material, honing in on the essence of a problem, and providing firm and correct opinions. Wran always followed her advice. "Gaudron's law" became a powerful force behind the scenes.

She appeared before the High Court in several significant constitutional cases. In 1982, in *Commonwealth v Hospital Contribution Fund*,[8] a case concerning arrangements within the State courts for the exercise of federal jurisdiction, she persuaded the court to overrule two previous High Court decisions on the point.[9] Other major cases in which she appeared included *Hematite Petroleum v Victoria* and *Stack v Coast Securities (No 9)* in 1983, and *Gosford Meats Pty Ltd v New South Wales* in 1985.[10] She also appeared in *Miller v TCN Channel Nine* in 1985, a case concerning the constitutional guarantee of free trade and commerce between the States (section 92).[11] Importantly, she appeared in the *Tasmanian Dam* case in 1983, a landmark in Australia's constitutional history over use of the Commonwealth's external affairs power.[12] In the course of this, she gained a high level of understanding of Australian federalism and interaction of State and Commonwealth powers, adding to the reasons why she was later recognised as a suitable appointment to the High Court.

At the same time, Gaudron attracted controversy by her personal support for Justice Lionel Murphy when he was charged with attempting to pervert the course of justice. He was acquitted, but died soon after, leaving the Hawke Government with two vacancies on the High Court to fill.

It was Murphy who, just before he died, suggested to Prime Minister Hawke that it was time for a woman (both knew he had Gaudron in mind) to be appointed to the High Court. From his ACTU days Hawke already had first-hand experience of Gaudron's sharp mind and capacity.

The High Court – a seat of influence

Gaudron was the first female to be appointed a justice of the High Court of Australia. While that was a memorable achievement, she contributed far more substantively to development of Australian law. In particular, in her decisions, she developed complex thinking around notions of discrimination and equality. Her personal experiences kept shaping her thinking on discrimination and strengthened her resolve to use the law to fix it.

Initially, Gaudron was part of the "Mason Court" that adopted a more liberal approach to interpreting and applying the law and the Constitution, causing it to be labelled "activist". She joined the majority of that court in some notable cases that interpreted the law to reflect contemporary values.

Debate about some controversial decisions in which she participated entered the living rooms of Australians. In *Mabo v Queensland (No 2)* the majority of judges rejected a common notion that had been incorporated into the law through an erroneous assumption, namely that Australia had been *terra nullius*, unoccupied, when settled by the British. Gaudron and Justice William Deane came under particular criticism for using emotional language in their joint judgment in describing the dispossession of the Aboriginal peoples of most of their traditional lands, for example, as a "national legacy of unutterable shame", and it being "the darkest aspect" of Australian history.[13]

Gaudron also contributed to a line of controversial cases that explored and developed implied rights in the Constitution. One such was the implied right to a measure of procedural fairness in exercise of the judicial power dealt with in Chapter III of the Constitution. Gaudron's decision provides an example of the way she used existing law, but in an original way, as a tool for social justice, displaying the influences on her thinking of both Hutley and Stone.

Following Mason's retirement, the Aboriginal land rights case of *Wik* was decided. It was perhaps more important in practical effect than *Mabo*. Gaudron utilised her special knowledge of equity principles as they applied to real property rights and entitlements and, in her separate majority judgment, she demonstrated an analytic textual approach while applying logic to reach what might be described as a social justice-oriented outcome.

Gaudron's use of subsection 75(v), the "genius" of the Australian Constitution, as she called it, to allow challenge to arbitrary administrative decision-making, caused both major political parties to revisit their immigration and refugee policies. The subsection gives everyone in Australia (whether a citizen or not) the right to approach the High Court directly to compel Commonwealth authorities to perform their constitutional and statutory duties, and to prevent them from acting in excess of their powers. Her legalistic reasoning helped to block statutory attempts to restrict review of certain administrative decisions. She was influential on later courts in developing reasoning to the effect that, if an administrative decision ignored principles of procedural fairness, it was not a "decision" from which a review could be prohibited under Commonwealth law.

Gaudron's jurisprudential approach to interpreting and applying the law is difficult to characterise. On the one hand, she was legalistic in adherence to precedent and to the natural meaning of the language of enactments. Yet she often saw issues from different angles and, with intricate reasoning and logic, reached many decisions that represented shifts in the law that accorded with changing societal expectations. She managed to bring basic principles that reflected her own value system to some decisions.[14]

Gaudron's analysis and development of concepts of "equal justice" and the intertwining notion of "discrimination" and her concern for fair trials and procedural fairness effected increased protection for the vulnerable. They are an important part of her legacy to Australia's legal history.

Conclusion

A study of Mary Gaudron's life, of her childhood exposure to the realities of racial discrimination and the obstacles she faced to achieve professional recognition, reveal some of the influences on her in shaping her values and, happily, shape the opportunities which came her way. Her story helps to illuminate broader aspects of society of the last century.

Gaudron's differences and brilliance were consistently appreciated at the right time and place. Both despite and because of her gender, working-class background and radical political views, she was provided with opportunities to use law as a tool for change and influence moments in Australia's political history. She embraced them and, as a consequence, was significant as both lawyer and judge, contributing to development of Australian law and the general political landscape.

Endnotes

[1] Pamela Burton, *From Moree to Mabo – the Mary Gaudron story*, UWA Publishing, Perth, 2010.

[2] *Mabo v Queensland (No 2)* (1992) 175 CLR 1.

[3] *Wik Peoples v State of Queensland* (1996) 187 CLR 1.

[4] *Patrick Stevedores Operations No. 2 Pty Ltd v Maritime Union of Australia (1998)* 195 CLR 1.

[5] On the Sydney push, see Anne Coombs, *Sex and Anarchy: The Life and Death of the Sydney Push*, Viking, Ringwood, Vic, 199.

[6] *Mackie v Australian Consolidated Press Ltd (unreported)*, Supreme Court of NSW, 1972; and on appeal, *Mackie v Australian Consolidated Press Ltd [1974]* NSWLR, 561.

[7] (1979) 218 CAR 120.

[8] (1982) 150 CLR 49.

[9] *Kotsis v Kotsis* (1970) 122 CLR 69 and *Knight v Knight* (1971) 122 CLR 114 in which it was held that in federal cases the judicial power of a State court could only be exercised by its judges, not by its administrative officers.

[10] (1983) 151 CLR 599; (1983)154 CLR 261; (1985) 155 CLR 368 respectively.

[11] (1985) CLR 556.

[12] *Commonwealth v Tasmania (1983)* 158 CLR 1.

[13] 175 CLR 1, at 104.

[14] Gaudron J's joint majority judgment with Deane J in *Australian Iron and Steel Pty Ltd v Banovic (1989)* 168 CLR 165, provides an example of a legal analysis of indirect discrimination which demonstrated that equal treatment did not equate with non-discrimination.

Part 5: Curriculum Vitae of John R. Nethercote

Date of birth:	1 March 1948, Sydney, Australia
Date of death:	3 May 2022, Canberra, Australia
Education:	Blakehurst High School

NSW Leaving Certificate, 1964. Ancient History, First Class Honours; Modern History, Second Class Honours; Passes in English, French, Economics, General Mathematics

Faculty of Arts, University of Sydney, 1965-68
Government and Public Administration: Honours, Second Class, Division 2, History major

Subsequently studied Political Science at Australian National University (1971-73); and Public Administration at London School of Economics (1977-79).

Career

1969 Teacher, Martyrs Memorial School, Popondetta, Territory of Papua New Guinea (Australian Volunteer Abroad)

1970 Joined Australian Public Service as Public Service Board Administrative Trainee (assignments: Department of Immigration; Public Service Board; Cabinet Office)

1971-74 Public Service Board, Secretary's Division
Research on public service management especially role and responsibilities of department heads; ethics and conduct matters; employment of people with disabilities; machinery of government. In this period also acted as minute secretary at weekly meetings of Public Service Board.

1974-76 Royal Commission on Australian Government Administration (Chair: Dr H. C. Coombs)
As assistant to Special Adviser (Dr Peter Wilenski, 1974; Tom FitzGerald, 1975-76), organized public hearings of the Commission and prepared briefs for Commissioners.
Prepared papers for Commission consideration on wide-range of topics concerning structure and management of public sector.
On behalf of RCAGA, attended OECD meeting on Structure and Organization of Government; and conducted enquiries in Whitehall and Ottawa.

1977-79 London School of Economics
Wide-ranging research on public service management in Britain, Canada and Australia.

1979 Public Service Commission of Canada (Ottawa)
Research and analysis concerning the reports of the Royal Commission on Financial Management and Accountability; and Special Committee on Personnel Management and the Merit Principle.

1979-80   Public Service Board, Canberra
Research on various topics concerning management of the public service.

1981   Department of Foreign Affairs
Conducted a comprehensive review of staff development and training in the department.
Subsequently prepared staff rules of Commission for Conservation of Antarctic Marine Living Resources and participated in subsequent international negotiations establishing the commission (CCAMLR).

1981-82   Defence Review Committee (chair: J. W. Utz)
Research on questions concerning respective roles and responsibilities of uniformed and civilian staff of Defence organization.

1982-84   Public Service Board, Management Improvement Division
Various projects on management improvement activities in departments and other government organisations, especially use of information technology.

1984-85   National Inquiry into Local Government Finance (chair: Professor Peter Self (LSE/ANU)
As Secretary, oversaw general business of the Inquiry, including organization of public hearings and related matters; and designed and conducted research program.
The purpose of the Inquiry was to review a Commonwealth revenue-sharing program which provided general purpose funds to local governments in Australia.

1985-87   Public Service Board, Research and Information Branch
As acting branch head, directed the Board's research program; and was personally responsible for media relations.

1987-88   Following abolition of Public Service Board in the Hawke Government's machinery of government changes of 14 July 1987, was appointed Secretary, Senate Standing Committee on Finance and Public Administration (chair: Senator John Coates). Organised an inquiry into the Efficiency Scrutiny Program conducted by David Block; and another on reporting of non-departmental bodies.

1988-89   Australian National University
Visiting Lecturer, Australian Government and Public Policy (on leave from the APS)
Whilst at ANU, John led a review of the Australian Safeguards Office, a government body in the Department of Primary Industries and Energy concerned with overseeing utilization, location and accountability of Australian-origin nuclear material (mainly uranium).

1989-90   A variety of assignments in universities, especially in the Federalism Research Centre, ANU. John's main activity consisted of seminars in Canberra, Brisbane and Wellington on central decision-making in government; papers presented at these seminars were published in books edited in collaboration with Professor Cliff Walsh and Professor Brian Galligan.

1991   Australian Senate
Arranged publication of J. R. Odgers, *Australian Senate Practice*, 6th edition. This was the last edition of an Australian classic prepared by its original author. Its publication had been delayed by resistance in the Senate owing to its approach to the events of 1974-75; and subsequently Jim Odgers' death.

1992-96 Prepared various chapters for the 7th edition of Harry Evans (ed.), *Odgers' Australian Senate Practice* (1995).

1996-97 Secretary, Senate Select Committee on Uranium Mining and Milling (chair: Senator Grant Chapman).

1997-99 Parliamentary Library

Wrote papers on the *Public Service Bill* 1997 (1997); mandate theory in Westminster governance (1999); and a study of changes in the departmental machinery of government since 1987 (1999).

Left the Public Service.

2000-01 Liberal Party of Australia (Federal Secretariat)/ Menzies Research Centre
Planned, organized and oversaw publication of J. R. Nethercote (ed.), *Liberalism and the Australian Federation*, The Federation Press, 2001. This volume was the Liberal Party's contribution to the Centenary of the Federation. It contained essays by Chandran Kukathas; Greg Melleuish; Winsome Roberts; Greg Craven; Ian Marsh; Margaret FitzHerbert; Clem Lloyd; Michael Keenan; Graeme Starr; Ian Hancock; Charles Richardson; Andrew Norton; J. J. Pincus; John Roskam; Campbell Sharman; and Carl Bridge.

2000-09 During these years John held various visiting appointments at Griffith University and the Australian National University and was mainly working on public service matters. He did extensive work, including contributing a number of entries to Brian Galligan and Winsome Roberts (eds), *The Oxford Companion to Australian Politics*, 2007.

Since 2009 Australian Catholic University

Adjunct Professor, Canberra Campus

John was mainly involved in publishing work on books listed below. Until 2016, he also wrote a couple of times a month for the *Canberra Times* on governmental, political and public service matters, often of a historical nature and from time to time on newly published books.

In 2013-14 John was engaged as fact-checker on John Howard's, *The Menzies Era* (2014). In 2017-18 he performed similar work for John Edwards in *John Curtin's War*, Penguin, 2017. These were major assignments. John's role in both instances is acknowledged in the book, p 655 in *The Menzies Era* and p 495 in *John Curtin's War*.

Appointments as editor

1974-75 Editor, Newsletter, Institute of Public Administration Australia (ACT Division).

1980-00 Re-named *Canberra Bulletin of Public Administration* in 1983. Edited approximately 60 issues.

2001-2003   Editor, *Australasian Parliamentary Review*
(Published by the Australian Study of Parliament Group)

2000-09   Consulting Editor, *Australian Journal of Public Administration*
(Published by Institute of Public Administration Australia)

Since 2010 edited the conference papers of The Samuel Griffith Society, *Upholding the Australian Constitution*, vols 22-27.

Since 2008 Editorial Fellow, *Australian Dictionary of Biography*, and author of six entries.

Books edited

The books John has edited, jointly or alone fall into several categories:

Parliament

> *Parliament and Bureaucracy*, Hale & Iremonger, 1982
>
> *The House on Capital Hill*, The Federation Press, 1996 (with Julian Disney)
>
> *Restraining Elective Dictatorship*, University of Western Australia Press, 2008 (with Scott Prasser and Nicholas Aroney)

Public Administration

> *Reforming Australian Government: the Coombs Commission and Beyond*, ANU Press/IPAA, 1977 (with Cameron Hazlehurst)
>
> *Australian Commonwealth Administration 1983: Essays in Review*, Canberra College of Advanced Education/IPAA, 1984 (with Alexander Kouzmin and Roger Wettenhall)
>
> *Australian Commonwealth Administration 1984: Essays in Review*, CCAE/IPAA, 1986 (with Alexander Kouzmin and Roger Wettenhall)
>
> *Hawke's Second Government*, CCAE/IPAA, 1988 (with Roger Wettenhall)

Administrative History

> *From Colony to Coloniser*, Hale & Iremonger/IPAA, 1986 (with J. J. Eddy)
>
> *Towards National Administration*, Hale & Iremonger/ IPAA, 19 (with J. J. Eddy)

Liberalism

> *The Menzies Era*, Hale & Iremonger, 1995 (with Scott Prasser and John Warhurst) (not to be confused with book of same name by John Howard)
>
> *Liberalism and the Australian Federation*, The Federation Press/Liberal Party of Australia, 2001
>
> *Menzies: The Shaping of Modern Australia*, Connor Court/Menzies Research Centre, 2016

In addition to the above books, John also oversaw, in a detailed way, the following books:

> Peter Wilenski, *Public Power and Public Administration*, Hale & Iremonger/IPAA, 1986

Mark Thomas, *Australia in Mind*, Hale & Iremonger/IPAA, 1989 (collection of portraits of leading Australians previously published in *Canberra Bulletin of Public Administration*)

Roger Wettenhall, *Public Enterprise and National Development*, IPAA (ACT Division), 1987

J. R. Odgers, *Australian Senate Practice*, 6th ed., Institute of Public Administration Australia (ACT Division), 1991

A. W. Martin, *The 'Whig' View of Australian History*, Melbourne University Press, 2007

Editorial assistance/ extensive discussion/copy-editing/proof reading (books containing an acknowledgement)

Geoffrey Bolton, *Paul Hasluck: A life*, University of Western Australia Press, 2014

Pamela Burton, *From Moree to Mabo: the Mary Gaudron Story*, University of Western Australia Press, 2010

David Clune, *Inside the Wran Era: the Ron Mullock Memoirs*, Connor Court, 2015

John Edwards, *Keating: The Inside Story*, Penguin, 1996

John Edwards, *John Curtin's War*, vol 1, Penguin, 2017

John Edwards, *John Curtin's War*, vol 2, Penguin, 2018

Peter Edwards, *Arthur Tange: Last of the Mandarins*, Allen & Unwin, 2006

Tom Frame, *The Life and Death of Harold Holt*, Allen & Unwin, 2005

Brian Galligan, *Utah and Queensland Coal*, UQP, 1989

Brian Galligan, *A Federal Republic*, Cambridge University Press, 1995

Ian Hancock, *John Gorton: He Did It His Way*, 2002

Ian Hancock, *The V.I.P. Affair, 1966-67*, Australasian Study of Parliament Group, 2004 [also published as *Australasian Parliamentary Review*, vol 18 (2), Spring 2003]

Ian Hancock, *Nick Greiner*, Connor Court, 2013

Ian Hancock, *Tom Hughes QC: A Cab on the Rank*, The Federation Press, 2016

Jeremy Hearder, *Jim Plim: Ambassador Extraordinary*, Connor Court, 2015

John Howard, *The Menzies Era*, HarperCollins, 2014

Peter Kurti, *The Tyranny of Tolerance*, Connor Court, 2017

David Lee, *Stanley Melbourne Bruce: Australian Internationalist*, Continuum, 2010

A.W. Martin, *Robert Menzies*, vol 1, Melbourne University Press, 1993

A. W. Martin, *Robert Menzies*, vol 2, Melbourne University Press, 1999

David E. Moore, *The Curse of Mungana*, Boolarong Press, 2017

G. S. Reid & Martyn Forrest, *Australia's Commonwealth Parliament*, Melbourne University Press, 1989

Michael Sexton, *On the Edges of History*, Connor Court, 2015

Sir David Smith, *Head of State*, Macleay Press, 2005

R. N. Spann, *Government Administration in Australia*, Allen & Unwin, 1978

Graeme Starr, *Carrick – Principles, Politics and Policy*, Connor Court, 2012

John Wanna et al., *Managing Public Expenditure in Australia*, Allen & Unwin, 2000

Patrick Weller, *Cabinet Government in Australia, 1901-2006*, UNSW Press, 2007

Part 6: Authors' Biographies

After arriving from the UK in 1969, **Jill Adams** became a librarian at the University of Queensland. Moving to Canberra, in 1974 she established a library and research service for the new Department of the Special Minister of State, including the Priorities Review Staff, and the Royal Commission on Ausstralian Government Administration where she first met John Nethercote.

From 1980 until 2003, Jill worked at the Public Service Board and its successors. For part of that time John, then Head of Research, was her direct 'supervisor'. In the 1990s she began a column in CBPA entitled *International Trends in Public Administration*, and project managed *Profiles of Government Administration in Asia*, jointly with University of Canberra (1995), and then *The Australian Experience of Public Reform* (2003), for the Commonwealth Secretariat. In 2000 she initiated and coordinated *Serving the Nation: 100 Years of Public Service* (2001). Her final research paper as a public servant was *Parliament: Master of its Own Household?* (2003).

From 2003 to 2005 Jill worked part-time as a research assistant to Professor John Halligan, jointly writing several articles in AJPA and drafting material for his book *The Centrelink Experiment: Innovation in Service Delivery* (2008). She is now enjoying her retirement.

Gary Banks is a Professorial Fellow at the Melbourne Institute and a Senior Fellow at the Centre for Independent Studies. He was Chairman of Australia's Productivity Commission from its inception in 1998 to 2012. He subsequently spent four years as Dean of the Australia and New Zealand School of Government. Other roles have included chairing the OECD's Regulatory Policy Committee and the Australian Statistics Advisory Council, and he has been a non-executive director of the Macquarie Group. In earlier years he was on the research staff of the GATT/WTO and a visiting researcher at the Trade Policy Research Centre in London. Gary is a Fellow of the

Academy of Social Sciences and a National Fellow of the Institute for Public Administration Australia, for whom he delivered the 2013 Garran Oration. He was awarded the Order of Australia in 2007, and in 2014 received the Economic Society's inaugural Distinguished Public Policy Fellow Award.

Pamela Burton, BA; LLM, is a Canberra lawyer and writer. She founded her own law firm in 1976 and later practiced as a barrister at the Canberra Bar. She is a former Senior Member of the Commonwealth Administrative Appeals Tribunal, and has served as legal counsel for the federal Australian Medical Association and is currently a part-time independent mediator for the ACT Magistrates Court.

She is the author of *From Moree to Mabo: the Mary Gaudron Story* (UWAP, 2010), long-listed for the National Biography Award 2012, *The Waterlow Killings: Portrait of a Family Tragedy* (MUP, 2012), winner of the 'Sisters in Crime' Davitt Award for Best True Crime, 2013, *A Foreign Affair* (Ginninderra Press, 2016) and she is the prime author of *Persons of Interest: An intimate account of Cecily and John Burton* (ANU Press, 2022).

Dr David Clune OAM was for many years the Manager of the NSW Parliament's Research Service and the Parliament's Historian. He is currently an Honorary Associate in the Department of Government and International Relations at the University of Sydney and Consultant Historian to the NSW Legislative Council History Project. Dr Clune has written extensively about NSW politics and history. He is the author (with Gareth Griffith) of *Decision and Deliberation: the Parliament of NSW, 1856-2003.*

William Coleman is an Adjunct Professor at the University of Notre Dame, Australia, and has written extensively on the history of economic thought, Australia's political economy, and the contested position of economics in society. He has recently completed a puncturing history of '1901': *Their Fiery Cross of Union: A Retelling of the Creation of the Australian Federation, 1889-1914* (Connor Court 2021).

Professor Glyn Davis AC is Secretary of the Department of Prime Minister and Cabinet. He delighted in engagements with John Nethercote over many decades as academic, public servant and occasional administrative review panel member.

Dr John Edwards is a Senior Fellow in the Lowy Institute, and an Adjunct Professor at the John Curtin Institute of Public Policy at Curtin University. He is a director of Cbus and Frontier, and has been a board member of the Reserve Bank of Australia, CEDA, and the Australian Workplace and Productivity Agency, amongst others. He was a member of reviews of Australian international trade and investment policies, and of the *Fair Work Act*.

From 1997 to 2009 John was Chief Economist for Australia and New Zealand for HSBC. From 1991 to 1994 John was principal economic adviser to Treasurer and then Prime Minister, Paul Keating.

Before returning to Australia, John was the Washington correspondent for *The Sydney Morning Herald*. Earlier, John was a journalist for the *Australian Financial Review*, *The Australian*, *The National Times*, *Bulletin* magazine and *The Sydney Morning Herald*.

He has published six non-fiction books and numerous monographs. The first volume of his biography of John Curtin, *Curtin's War* (Penguin/Viking 2017 and 2018) won the 2018 Prime Minister's Literary Prize in the history section.

John's most recent publication was the 2021 Lowy Institute Paper/ Penguin Special, *Reconstruction: Australia after COVID*.

John holds PhD and M Phil degrees in economics from George Washington University and a BA from Sydney University. His doctoral dissertation was in the field of monetary economics.

Meredith Edwards AM has had a career as a professor, researcher, and senior policy analyst. She is best known for her role in developing social and labour market policies for the Australian government and was a Deputy Secretary in the Department of Prime Minister and Cabinet, 1993-97. Meredith was also a member of the Wran Committee on Higher Education Funding (1988-1989). She was appointed Deputy Vice-Chancellor of the University of Canberra in

August 1997 and was then Director of the National Institute for Governance at the University of Canberra until 2004. Meredith trained as an economist, is a Fellow of the Institute of Public Administration Australia, Fellow of ANZSOG, Fellow of the Academy of Social Science Australia and was a member of the Committee of Experts on Public Administration, United Nations 2010-2017. Meredith's recent book (written with her sister, Pamela Burton) is about their parents: Persons of Interest (ANU Press). Meredith is currently Emeritus Professor at the University of Canberra.

Peter Edwards AM FAIIA is an independent historian and biographer who has honorary professorships at the Australian National University and Deakin University. He is the author of *Law, Politics and Intelligence: A Life of Robert Hope* (2020) and *Arthur Tange: Last of the Mandarins* (2006). As the Official Historian of Australia's involvement in Southeast Asian conflicts 1948-75, he was general editor of the nine-volume series and author of the volumes dealing with strategy and diplomacy, *Crises and Commitments* (1992) and *A Nation at War* (1997). He is also the author of *Australia and the Vietnam War* (2014) and the author, co-author, editor or co-editor of a number of other works, mostly relating to Australia's foreign policy, defence policy and intelligence agencies. The Tange biography won the Queensland Premier's Literary Award for History and the WA Premier's Book Award for Non-fiction, and was short-listed for the National Biography Award.

Henry Ergas AO is a columnist for *The Australian*. From 1978 to 1993, Henry was an economist at the OECD in Paris, where amongst other roles he headed the Secretary-General's Task Force on Structural Adjustment and was Counsellor for Structural Policy in the Economics Department. After that he worked as a consultant economist at NECG, CRA International, Concept Economics and Deloitte. Henry has held a number of academic appointments, and contributed widely to academic publishing in Australia, serving on the editorial boards of *Agenda* and *The Review of Network Economics* and contributing chapters to *Religious Freedom's History and Future* (Connor Court, 2020), *Only in Australia: The History, Politics, and Economics* *of Australian Exceptionalism* (OUP, 2016), and *Menzies, the Shaping of Modern Australia* (Connor Court, 2016) amongst others. He has served on numerous official reviews, including chair of the Intellectual Property and Competition Policy Review Committee. In 2016 he was made an Officer in the Order of Australia for distinguished service to infrastructure economics, higher education, public policy development and review, and as a supporter of emerging artists.

Professor Tom Frame AM is Director of the Public Leadership Research Group at UNSW Canberra. He was a naval officer from 1979-1993, Anglican Bishop to the Australian Defence Force (2001-2007) and then Director of St Mark's National Theological Centre (2007-2014). Frame was the Inaugural Director of the John Howard Prime Ministerial Library at Old Parliament House (2017-20). He is the author or editor of 50 books including *Where Fate Calls: The HMAS Voyager Tragedy* (1992), *The Life and Death of Harold Holt* (2005) and a four volume retrospective series on the Howard Government published by UNSW Press.

Richard French has a B.Sc. from the University of British Columbia and a D.Phil. from Oxford. He is retired from the Graduate School of Public and International Affairs of the University of Ottawa. He spent roughly a quarter of his career in each of academia, the public service, politics, and business. In the last ten years, he has been writing about the experience of public life and its implications for theories of public policymaking. He is active in privately held businesses which apply technology to the energy efficiency and safety of road transportation. Richard French is a Member of the Order of Canada.

Jeremy Hearder is the author of *Jim Plim, Ambassador Extraordinary: A biography of Sir James Plimsoll* (Connor Court, 2015). He works as a part-time historian in DFAT, and has contributed to other books about the history of Australian diplomacy. In his earlier career with DFAT his service included nine overseas postings, including being High Commissioner to Zimbabwe (1980-84) and to Fiji (1984-86).

The Hon John Winston Howard OM AC, born 26 July 1939, served as Australia's 25th Prime Minister between March 1996 and November 2007. He is the nation's second longest serving Prime Minister, was a Member of Parliament for 33 years, and was Treasurer in an earlier government.

Under his leadership Australia enjoyed continued economic growth averaging 3.6% per annum. His government delivered major economic reform in the areas of taxation, workplace relations, privatisation and welfare. $96 billion of government debt was repaid during the time in office of the Howard Government. When it left office in November 2007 the Government of the Commonwealth of Australia had no net debt, and its budget was in surplus. This strong fiscal position was a major reason why Australia suffered relatively few consequences from the global financial crisis.

Shortly after Mr Howard came to power, he responded to the massacre of 35 people by a lone gunman at Port Arthur in Tasmania with the implementation of national gun control laws, which included a general prohibition on the ownership or possession of automatic or semi-automatic weapons.

The Howard Government strongly supported the United States and other nations in the fight against terrorism. Australia contributed military forces to operations in both Iraq and Afghanistan. Australia also led the United Nations sanctioned INTERFET force following East Timor's vote for independence. The Howard Government strengthened bilateral ties between Australia and many nations in Asia. During Mr Howard's time as Prime Minister China became Australia's largest export destination.

Mr Howard is a Companion of the Order of Australia and was awarded the Presidential Medal of Freedom, the highest civilian award in the United States by President George W. Bush. In January 2012 Queen Elizabeth II appointed Mr Howard to the Order of Merit. In 2013 he received the Japanese Award, the Grand Cordon of the Order of the Rising Sun.

Don Hunn joined the New Zealand Public Service in 1952 as a clerical cadet in the Public Trust Office. From 1954 to 1956 he trained as a primary school teacher. In 1957 he entered the Department of External Affairs and during his 24 years there served in 8 overseas posts, the last two as New Zealand's first resident High Commissioner in Tonga and then as Deputy High Commissioner in Canberra. He returned to Wellington in 1981 becoming one of the then 4-member State Services Commission. In 1987 he succeeded Sir Roderick Deane as Chairman of the SSC and Head of the New Zealand Public Service. Following an amendment to the *State Sector Act* in 1989 he became sole Commissioner, a position he held until his retirement in 1997. For the next 20 years he provided advice as a consultant on public sector management both within New Zealand and in 9 other countries, including Australia.

Paul Kelly is Editor-at-Large on *The Australian*. He was previously Editor-in-Chief of the paper. He writes on Australian politics and history, public policy and international affairs. Paul has covered Australian governments from Gough Whitlam to Scott Morrison and is a regular television commentator. He is the author of ten books on national politics and history including *The End of Certainty* on the politics of the 1980s, *The March of Patriots* offering a re-interpretation of the Keating and Howard prime ministerships and *Triumph and Demise* on the Rudd-Gillard era.

Paul holds a Doctor of Letters from the University of Melbourne and in 2010 was a Vice Chancellor's Fellow at the university. He has been a visiting Fellow at Kings College, London, a Fellow at the Kennedy School of Government at Harvard University and a Fellow at the Lowy Institute in Sydney.

Peter Kurti is Director of the Culture, Prosperity & Civil Society program at the Centre for Independent Studies, and also Adjunct Associate Professor of Law at the University of Notre Dame Australia.

David Lee is Associate Professor in History, School of Humanities and Social Sciences, University of New South Wales, Canberra. He is the author, *inter alia*, of *Stanley Melbourne Bruce: Australian*

Internationalist, Bloomsbury, London and New York, 2010, and *John Curtin*, forthcoming, Connor Court, 2022, and Chair of the Commonwealth Working Party of the *Australian Dictionary of Biography*.

Loren Lomasky is Cory Professor of Political Philosophy, Policy & Law at the University of Virginia. He previously taught at Bowling Green State University and the University of Minnesota, Duluth and has held visiting positions at Virginia Polytechnic Institute, Australian National University, the Australian Defence Force Academy and National University of Singapore. Lomasky is the author of *Persons, Rights and the Moral Community* (Oxford, 1987) for which he was awarded the 1990 Matchette Prize (best philosophy book published during the preceding two years by an author under age 40). He published *Rights Angles* with Oxford in 2016 and *Justice at a Distance*, coauthor Fernando Teson, with Cambridge, also in 2016. He coauthored with Geoffrey Brennan *Democracy and Decision: The Pure Theory of Electoral Preference* (Cambridge, 1993), and he edited with Brennan *Politics and Process: New Essays in Democratic Theory* (Cambridge, 1989). His essay "Is There a Duty to Vote?," also co-authored with Brennan was awarded the 2003 Kavka/UCI Prize by the American Philosophical Association. Lomasky never enjoyed the pleasure of coauthoring a piece with John Nethercote but was inspired by him to write an op-ed "Clinton and Cricket" for *The Canberra Times*.

Luke Malpass is political editor at *Stuff*, a New Zealand news website and the country's largest newspaper publishing group including *The Dominion Post*, *The Press* and *The Sunday Star Times*. Prior to this he was an editorial writer, Opinion and Editorial Page editor and Features Editor at *The Australian Financial Review* in Sydney. His writing has also appeared in *The Sydney Morning Herald*, *The Australian* and *The Wall Street Journal*. Prior to journalism he worked in think tanks and in primary sector manufacturing.

Between 1953 and 1987, **John Martin** was a public servant in the Department of Island Territories, followed by the Treasury, where he was seconded to the Ministry of Foreign Affairs to London and

Geneva, 1961-1965 and London, 1972-1975. He was then Assistant Secretary to Treasury (1975-1980). Between 1981 and 1988 John was Deputy Director-General of Health (Administrative). Other appointments included Director of the New Zealand Planning Council, 1980, and serving on the State Sector Standards Board.

From 1989 to 2008, John was Senior Lecturer in Public Policy in the School of Government, Victoria University of Wellington. John's publications include the books, *Devolution and Accountability* (co-edited, 1988), *A Profession of Statecraft?* (1988), *Public Service and the Public Servant. Essays by John Martin* (1991), *Reshaping the State: New Zealand's Bureaucratic Revolution* (co-edited, 1991), *Public Management: the New Zealand Model* (co-edited, 1996), as well as "Changing Governance: The State Services in the Holyoake Years", in *Sir Keith Holyoake: Towards a Political Biography*, "Spirit of Service: a History of the Institute of Public Administration 1936-2006", New Zealand Institute of Public Administration, Wellington (2006), and "Governance in New Zealand 1940-1951", in *The Seven Dwarfs and the Age of the Mandarins* (2015).

Elizabeth McLeay is Emeritus Professor, School of History, Philosophy, Political Science and International Relations, Victoria University of Wellington – Te Herenga Waka, where she taught comparative politics and government. She has published on cabinet government, political representation, constitutional politics, women and politics, and comparative public policy. Recent works include: *In Search of Consensus: New Zealand's Electoral Act 1956 and its Constitutional Legacy* (Victoria University Press, Wellington, 2018), with Claudia Geiringer and Polly Higbee, *What's the Hurry? Urgency in the New Zealand Legislative Process 1987-2010* (Wellington, Victoria University Press, 2011), and with Keith Dowding, "The Firing Line", in Paul 't Hart and John Uhr, eds., *Rites of Passage: Studies in Leadership Succession* (Palgrave Macmillan, Houndmills, Basingstoke, 2011). At present she is working on a collection of her essays on democracy in Aotearoa New Zealand.

Patrick Mullins is a Canberra-based writer. His books include *Tiberius with a Telephone* (2018), *The Trials of Portnoy* (2020), and

Who needs the ABC? (2022). *Tiberius with a Telephone* won the 2020 NSW Premier's Non-Fiction Award and the 2020 National Biography Award.

Jonathan Pincus is Visiting Professor of Economics at the University of Adelaide and an economic consultant. After schooling and university in Brisbane, he took his PhD at Stanford. He was Principal Advisor Research at the Productivity Commission, having been Gollin Professor at Adelaide and Professor of Economic History at Flinders. His academic publications include *Pressure Groups and Politics in Antebellum Tariffs* and *Government and Capitalism* as well as over 60 articles and chapters. He is a Distinguished Fellow in Public Policy of the Economic Society and an EOG Shann Award holder of the Economic History Society of ANZ; and he attended many test matches with John Nethercote.

Anthony Seldon is Vice-Chancellor of the University of Buckingham and author of 40 books, including inside biographies of the last four Prime Ministers of the United Kingdom.

Index